Gaming, Governance and Public Policy in Macao

Gaming, Governance and Public Policy in Macao

Edited by

Newman M. K. Lam and Ian Scott

香港大學出版社
HONG KONG UNIVERSITY PRESS

UNIVERSIDADE DE MACAU
UNIVERSITY OF MACAU

Hong Kong University Press
14/F Hing Wai Centre
7 Tin Wan Praya Road
Aberdeen
Hong Kong
www.hkupress.org

ISBN 978-988-8083-28-2 (*Hardback*)
ISBN 978-988-8083-29-9 (*Paperback*)

University of Macau
Av. Padre Tomás Pereira, Taipa
Macau, China
www.umac.mo

British Library Cataloguing-in-Publication Data
A catalogue record for this book is available from the British Library.

10   9   8   7   6   5   4   3   2   1

Printed and bound by Liang Yu Printing Factory Ltd. in Hong Kong, China

Contents

Part I   The Gaming Industry and Its Critics

Part II   Governance

List of Figures, Plates and Tables

Figures

Plates

Tables

Preface

Since the liberalisation of its gaming industry in 2002, when a monopoly provider was replaced by six competing concessions, Macao has experienced remarkable economic growth. A score of new casinos have been built, millions of gamblers and tourists have flooded in from across the border, per capita income has more than doubled in five years, government coffers have swelled and the gaming operators have outstripped their Las Vegas counterparts both in revenue and in profits. It would be surprising if concentrated, casino-driven foreign investment on this scale and at that speed in a very small place did not result in some social dislocation and instability. Rapid economic growth has been accompanied by a range of social, economic and political problems. Labour shortages have resulted in an increase of migrant workers from China. The lack of a professional middle class has created the need to employ skilled personnel from elsewhere. Increases in per capita income have not been evenly spread and sharply rising inflation has cut into the standard of living of many citizens. Housing supply has proved to be inadequate and increasingly expensive and there are tensions between the gaming industry, government and the public over the use of scarce land resources. Educational capacity has not been able to meet the demands of the economy. Social welfare has been insufficient to compensate for the persistent structural unemployment of those who are not qualified to work in the casino industry.

Other problems relate to the capacity of the government. There are continuing difficulties with regulatory control over the gaming industry, with corruption, and with a public sector that has yet to be fully reformed to deal with new economic and social challenges. There has also been a shift in power with traditional social organizations losing their pre-eminent position within the Legislative Assembly and gaming interests assuming greater importance. New political groups are emerging with demands that cannot easily be resolved within the existing political arrangements. The rapidity of the economic change has meant that there has been some institutional lag, particularly within the administrative system, to respond to these recent developments.

Our research is focused on the juncture at which foreign investment, government, public policy and the people intersect. We ask: What has been the impact of this surge of foreign investment on Macao? Do the people perceive that it has changed their lives? How has it affected the political system? What administrative reforms have been put in place to enhance the efficiency and responsiveness of the government? Have public policies been developed to address emerging problems? What other measures have been adopted to resolve social dislocations and economic hardship? And with what success?

This project was organized around three workshops which were held at the City University of Hong Kong in May 2009, at the University of Macau in December 2009, and at the Asia Research Centre at Murdoch University in June 2010. This format helped us to benefit from each other's research, to refine our findings over time and to develop common themes that are pursued throughout the book. We would like to thank Hon Chan, Head of the Department of Public and Social Administration at the City University of Hong Kong, for funding support for the project which enabled us to employ a full-time research assistant, Matt Wong Ka Ho. Matt was not only diligent and resourceful and a great aid to the researchers but also started the timeline which forms the appendix to this book. We are also especially grateful to Joan Y. H. Leung, who besides writing the chapter on education, organized the first workshop at City University and assisted in compiling the bibliography and timeline. Mark Hayllar also made valuable contributions to the workshops, presenting papers and adding greatly to the quality of the discussion. In the latter stages of the research, Carol Chan Hin Pui, K. T. Cheung, Chik Ka Shek, Hang Chow and Kanas Lau provided very helpful support services.

In Macao, we would like to thank the University of Macau and the Macao Foundation for providing funding for research support and for a workshop. In particular, Alex Choi and Eva Hung wish to acknowledge the support of the University of Macau Research Committee for their research on croupiers (RG010/06-07S/CHK/FSH). We also thank other faculty members who contributed ideas or chapters to this book and the many research assistants who helped in fact-finding, in conducting a survey, in organizing a workshop and in arranging meetings with government officials. Wong Man, who checked the manuscript for inconsistencies and errors, deserves our special thanks. We would like also to express our appreciation to the government officials who accepted our requests for interviews and provided us with valuable information. Brian Brewer, who has written a chapter on the civil service which is published in this book, Michael DeGolyer and Garry Rodan presented keynote addresses at the second workshop at the University of Macau that focused on large and important questions that face governments in Asia and elsewhere. Each of them contributed to the success of the workshop by chairing sessions and providing insightful comments. Both Michael Duckworth, publisher of Hong Kong University Press, and Colin Day, the former publisher, attended the workshop and provided encouragement and useful advice on publication.

At Murdoch University, the research project was generously supported by the then Director of the Asia Research Centre, Garry Rodan, and by his successor, Caroline Hughes. We are grateful to Tamara Dent for organizing the final workshop.

In the course of our research, we have also incurred numerous debts from people who have helped us in all sorts of different ways. We would like to acknowledge the assistance provided by Au Kam San, Oscar Chan, Maria Francesch-Huidobro, Ho Sio Kam, Lau Sin Peng, Beatrice Leung, Terry Lui, who proofread the manuscript, Ng Kuok Cheong, Father Luis M. F. Sequeira, Maria Edith Da Silva, Tong Chi Kin, Vong Sou Kuan and Eric Yeung. We would like to thank particularly senior officials in the Macao government for sharing their vision of the future with us. We wish them every success in their efforts to write a new chapter in the fascinating history of a special place.

Newman M. K. Lam
Ian Scott
July 2011

Abbreviations and Acronyms

BOM	Boletim Oficial de Macau (Macao's Official Gazette)
CA	Commission of Audit
CCAC	Commission Against Corruption
CEA	Chinese Educators' Association of Macau
CEEDS	Research Centre for Sustainable Development Strategies
CPPCC	Chinese People's Political Consultative Conference
FDI	Foreign Direct Investment
GDP	Gross Domestic Product
Legco	Legislative Assembly
LIP	Labour Importation Programme
MICE	Meetings, Incentives, Conventions and Exhibitions
MOP	Macao pataca
MSAR	Macao Special Administrative Region
NAPE	New reclaimed areas in Outer Harbour and Nam Wan Bay
NGOs	Non-governmental Organizations
NPC	National People's Congress
OMUCP	An Outline for Macau Urban Concept Plan
SARS	Severe Acute Respiratory Syndrome
SJM	Sociedade de Jogos de Macao (Macao Gaming Company Limited)
SSF	Social Security Fund
STDM	Sociedade de Turismo e Diversões de Macau (Macau Travel and Amusement Company Limited)
SWA	STDM Workers Association
UCS	Union of Catholic Schools of Macau

A Note on the Place Name and the Currency

The official name for Macao is Macao and generally we follow that usage in this book. However, some organizations and institutions, such as, for example, the University of Macau, use the alternative spelling and we follow their practice where appropriate.

The Macao currency is the pataca (MOP) which is divided into 100 avos. It is linked to the Hong Kong dollar (HK$) at HK$1 = MOP 1.032. There are approximately MOP 8 to US$1.

List of Contributors

Brian BREWER is Associate Professor in the Department of Public and Social Administration at the City University of Hong Kong.

CHAN Kam Wah is Associate Professor in the Department of Applied Social Sciences at the Hong Kong Polytechnic University.

Alex H. CHOI is Assistant Professor in the Department of Government and Public Administration at the University of Macau.

Eva P. W. HUNG is Assistant Professor in the Department of Sociology at the University of Macau.

Newman M. K. LAM is Associate Professor in the Department of Government and Public Administration at the University of Macau.

Annie LEE Shuk Ping is with the Macao Productivity and Technology Transfer Center.

Grace O. M. LEE is Associate Professor in the Department of Public and Social Administration at the City University of Hong Kong.

James LEE is Professor in the Department of Applied Social Sciences at the Hong Kong Polytechnic University.

Joan Y. H. LEUNG is Associate Professor in the Department of Public and Social Administration at the City University of Hong Kong.

Francisco V. PINHEIRO is an Adjunct Professor at the Macao Inter-University Institute (University of Saint Joseph), part-time lecturer at the Institute for Tourism Studies and a Senior Advisor in the Municipal Affairs Bureau.

Ian SCOTT is Emeritus Professor of Government and Politics at Murdoch University and a Visiting Professor at the City University of Hong Kong.

Jeannette TAYLOR is Associate Professor in the Department of Political Science at the University of Western Australia.

Penny Y. K. WAN is Assistant Professor in the Gaming and Hospitality Management Program, Faculty of Business Administration, University of Macau.

Eilo YU Wing Yat is Assistant Professor in the Department of Government and Public Administration at the University of Macau.

1

Social Stability and Economic Growth

Ian Scott

Since the 1967 demonstrations, when a spillover from the Cultural Revolution in China undermined the colonial administration, the Macao government has been fundamentally concerned with the search for social stability and the need to find sources of sustainable economic growth. All governments, of course, have to pay attention to the stability of their societies and the means by which they seek to promote economic development. But in Macao those issues have been central to the way in which the polity functions. They found expression, during the colonial era, in the construction of a corporatist political order which was designed to promote stability and they have continued to dominate the government's policy agenda since the resumption of Chinese sovereignty in 1999. For example, in November 2009, when the outgoing Chief Executive, Edmund Ho Hau Wah, was asked about the achievements of his decade-long administration, he listed improvements in 'social stability, public order, economic development and better quality of life for residents' as his principal accomplishments (Macao SAR Government, 2009). Moreover, the government has seen stability — implicitly defined as the presence of social harmony, citizen satisfaction with the quality of life, and the absence of political disturbances — as directly linked to economic success. The assumption is that rapid economic growth will generate more gainful employment and better quality public goods and services which, in turn, will result in greater stability.

On this count, the liberalisation of the gaming industry in 2002 at first appeared to resolve any problems of social instability by fuelling a surge in foreign investment which resulted in remarkable economic growth, increased employment and higher incomes. Macao government officials believe, and surveys confirm, that a majority of citizens are happy with the overall results of foreign investment (see Chapter 3; Tong, 2009; *Macau News*, November 20, 2009). While the benefits have indeed been considerable, it would be surprising if foreign investment in a very small place on this scale — some MOP88.43 billion (about US$11 billion) in inward foreign direct investment between 2001 and 2008 (Statistics and Census Service, 2008)

— and concentrated on a single industry did not cause some social dislocation and instability. New issues emerge and old ones, such as persistent structural unemployment, which long predates the liberalisation of the gaming industry, do not necessarily disappear. Large-scale foreign investment creates inflationary pressures, an increasing gap between the rich and the poor, and a mismatch between the demand and supply for labour and social services. Cleavages may occur between those who are employed or who benefit from the gaming industry and those who do not. Change and differentiation within the society may occur so quickly that the government has insufficient time to respond with palliative measures or new policies.

Accompanying these economic and social changes are concomitant pressures on the political order. Macao's political system, both before and immediately after the formal resumption of Chinese sovereignty, was constructed in such a way that it maximised the stabilising benefits of corporatism (see Chapter 5; Lee, 2006). Business, labour and civil society were brought together under an umbrella of traditional associations with connections through their leadership to the Macao and Chinese governments. The political stability which this previously assured is threatened by newly emerging groups outside the umbrella who are irate at structural unemployment, rising prices, inadequate housing supply and other deficiencies in the provision of public goods and services. Residual corporatist structures, which are designed to maintain the status quo, may impede the government's attempts to find solutions to these problems. Gaming interests — foreign investors and their domestic supporters — have become much more powerful within the political system and are unlikely to believe that their demands can be met quickly enough through the slow-moving committees and advisory bodies that characterise the corporatist order. Government itself needs to respond more rapidly to the challenges posed by casino capitalism. Whether the traditional system can change and accommodate these increasing pressures or whether some new *modus vivendi*, which would achieve social stability and economic growth, should be sought remains a moot question. But there is evidence of growing direct government intervention in policy areas such as labour and education, which had previously been managed within the framework of a corporatist consensus, which permitted few changes to long-established policies and practices.

The Macao government has a number of strategic policy options which could be adopted to help to achieve its principal objectives. It is seeking to diversify the economy and to establish closer links with the Pearl River Delta and Guangdong. It has already taken measures to redistribute income and to increase benefits for the poor. It has devised plans, many of which are yet to be fully implemented, in some major policy areas. It has a public sector reform programme which is designed to increase the responsiveness of the government. But its efforts are also constrained by a lack of administrative and policy capacity to deal with the problems it is facing.

The ability to make and implement policy with its available manpower resources is in doubt. With limited capacity, a host of policy issues suddenly on the agenda, and the need perhaps to make strategic choices between them, which policies should have priority? Is social policymaking, which would increase the size and scope of government, necessarily the only answer? What vision does the government hold for the future?

To help to identify the factors which have triggered changes in Macao, we can employ a matrix which reflects the concern with social stability and economic growth and should enable us to describe the characteristics of Macao's present polity and the desired future state which it may wish to achieve. Figure 1.1 provides a simple classification of different types of political system that might emerge using the variables of stable and unstable social conditions and rapid or slow economic growth. Clearly, both government and citizens would prefer a situation of rapid economic growth and high social stability (Quadrant B) and would seek to avoid situations of low economic growth and low social stability (Quadrant C).

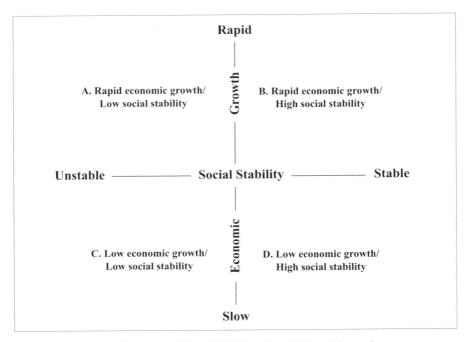

Figure 1.1: Economic Growth and Social Stability: Four Different Scenarios

Source: Ringland (2002).

Figure 1.2 is an attempt to describe the characteristics of the different types of political system in more detail. There is a rich social science literature dealing with economic growth and political and social stability and instability (see, among many examples, Olsen, 1963: 529–552; Huntington, 1968; Eisner, 1992: 70–98; Migdal, 2001; Lewis and Litai, 2004). In the following sections, I shall suggest that Figure 1.2 provides a useful framework to understand the changing nature of the Macao polity.

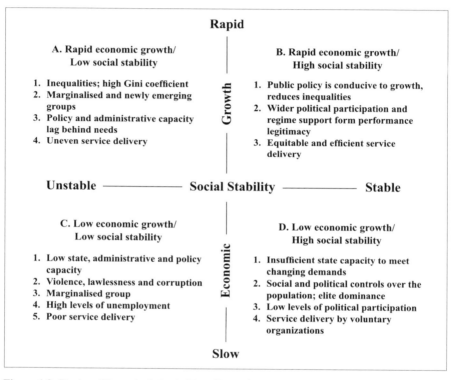

Figure 1.2: Regime Characteristics in Four Scenarios

Source: This figure is derived from Ringland (2002); Olsen (1963); Huntington (1968); Migdal (2001); Lewis and Litai (2004).

We can roughly categorise the Macao experience as falling into each of the quadrants over different historical periods:

- 1967–1992 — Stable economic growth/relatively high social stability (Quadrant D);
- 1992–2001 — Relatively low economic growth/low social stability (Quadrant C);

- 2001–2009 — High economic growth/pockets of social instability; social dislocation (Quadrant A);
- A desired future state with high levels of economic growth coupled with higher levels of social stability (Quadrant B).

We consider each of the historical periods and the projected future scenarios for Macao in turn.

Economic Growth with Social Stability 1967–1992

At first glance, Macao over the period 1967–1992 does not appear to fit into the conditions described in Quadrant D. It did experience real economic growth beginning with the granting of a gambling monopoly to the *Sociedade de Turismo e Diversões de Macau* (STDM) in 1962 which continued with an upsurge in investment in manufacturing in the 1970s and 1980s. Manufacturing made up some 40 percent of GDP for much of the period and 90 percent of all exports (Chan, 2000: 6–7). Between 1982 and 1992, the economy as a whole grew in real terms by an average of 3 percent per year (Kwan, 1992: 146). But, although this growth rate was statistically impressive, its impact on society was not as significant as might have been expected. Workers were underpaid, especially in the manufacturing industry; there were enormous disparities in wealth; and the government did very little to redistribute income through its social policies.

Economic growth, in this instance, served to promote social stability because it provided employment but it did not promote rapid change, higher incomes or better living conditions for the majority of the population. In the 1970s, manufacturing industries began to be squeezed out of Hong Kong by a combination of high costs and competition from cheaper producers elsewhere. Investment in Macao tended to be from factory owners, who sought to replicate conditions that had existed in Hong Kong in the 1960s and early 1970s. These were sweat-shops in which the labour force was unskilled and expected to work long hours for little reward. Income for workers in the manufacturing sector was (and remains) well below the mean income for all workers (Fung, 1992: 149). In short, this kind of investment did not spread wealth around the community and did not improve the productivity of workers. Unlike its counterpart in Hong Kong, which in the 1970s engaged in massive development in housing, education, health and social welfare services, the Macao government remained a truly *laissez-faire* government which had little interest in taking on a more proactive role. Social policy was not used to redistribute income and, in consequence, inequalities in income were startling. By 1988, for example, the poorer half of Macao residents earned 20 percent of the income while the other half received 80 percent; the richest 15.5 percent received half of the income (Fung, 1992: 147).

Social stability was maintained by the construction of a political order which incorporated organisations and individuals loyal to China into the fabric of the Portuguese colonial system. Following the 1967 demonstrations, the Chinese government became the *de facto* power in Macao (Sousa, 2009: 104). Portugal volunteered to return the colony to China but the Chinese government declined to accept it, probably because of the anticipated impact on the Hong Kong economy, and did so again in 1974 when a new Portuguese government embarked on a policy of decolonisation (Lo, 2008: 3; Sousa, 2009: 106). The interests of both the Chinese and Portuguese governments were in maintaining stability in Macao rather than in encouraging economic growth or diversification away from the economic mainstays of gambling and manufacturing. The major stabilising political forces were the traditional and voluntary organisations which were used to maintain social control and to provide a minimal level of services which the government had neither the capacity nor the inclination to dispense (Lee, 2006; see Chapter 5). The system incorporated business organisations, trade unions, and neighbourhood and women's associations and was intended to articulate demands to the colonial administration and, if necessary, to the Chinese government through the leaders of the associations (Sousa, 2009: 115–119). The significance of these arrangements is that formally they still remain in place. With the dynamic social and political changes that have occurred since the liberalisation of the casino industry, however, their relevance to the maintenance of social stability, the articulation of demands and the provision of services have been called into question.

The Declining Economy and Social Instability 1992–2001

The nature of the investment in manufacturing, the failure of the government to diversify or to provide adequate social policies, problems in the gaming industry and unfavourable regional and international economic conditions eventually came together in a period of stagnation and decline characterised by increasing social unrest (Quadrant C). By the early 1990s, Macao was no longer an attractive location for manufacturing industry. China offered cheaper land and labour; Western trade preferences had been reduced; and the industry had not kept pace with either quality or technological advances (Chan, 2000: 7). The decline in employment in manufacturing was sharp and has continued to fall since 1990 (see Figure 1.3). The political consequences of the decline have been considerable. Because the workers in the manufacturing industry were generally poorly educated and because the economy was so dependent on manufacturing and gambling, there were few opportunities for workers to find employment in other sectors. This created substantial structural unemployment which remained a problem even after large-scale foreign investment in the gaming industry.

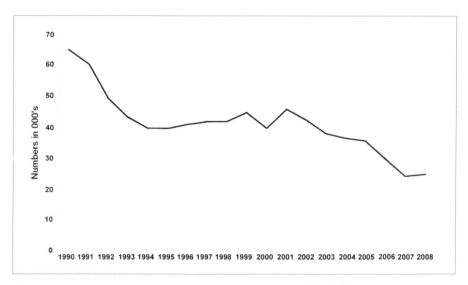

Figure 1.3: The Decline in Employment in Manufacturing, 1990–2008

Source: Statistics and Census Service (1990–2008) *Yearbook of Statistics.* Macao: Statistics and Census Service.

There were also problems in the gaming industry. STDM began to sub-contract its operations in the late 1980s which led to triad infiltration of the casino industry. The violence that ensued was sometimes attributed to competition between triads as they fought for control of operations and sometimes attributed to the actions of the dominant triad, the 14K, which appeared to try to eliminate anyone or anything that stood in its way (Lo, 2008: 84–85; *MacauCloser*, 2008). Whatever the cause, the number of homicides and crimes against the person increased substantially to the point where Macao had a homicide rate, shortly before the retrocession to China, of over seven times that of Hong Kong (see Figure 1.4).

There were kidnappings, bomb attacks, an attempted assassination of the senior government official responsible for controlling the gaming industry, and an AK47 attack on the main door of a newly-opened hotel (Lo, 2008: 85; *MacauCloser*, 2008; BBC, 1998). The Chinese government was clearly concerned about the level of crime and implied that it would take more vigorous action against lawlessness than the outgoing administration (Lewis and Lee, 1996; Lo, 2008: 86–88). In the event, the leader of the 14K, Wan Kuok Koi, was sentenced to 15 years in prison for various illegal activities in November 1999. When the formal handover occurred a month later, the triad problem, if not resolved, was at least less immediately and violently visible (Bruning, 1999).

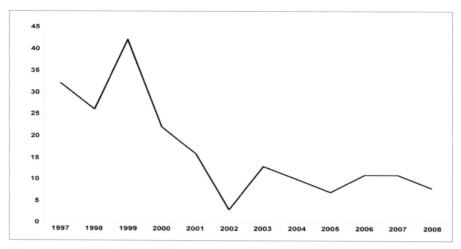

Figure 1.4: Homicides, 1997–2008

Source: Statistics and Census Service (1997–2008) *Yearbook of Statistics*. Macao: Statistics and Census Service.

Apart from the problems that Macao faced from disruptions to traditional economic activities, the international and regional situation also took a turn for the worse. As Figure 1.5 shows, the Asian financial crisis and subsequent downturns in Western markets had a significantly adverse effect on Macao with GDP contracting over the four years prior to the retrocession. Although the Portuguese colonial administration was in its final throes, it was, perhaps surprisingly, rather more active than it had been during the previous two decades. As the 1999 handover date approached, there were new infrastructural developments and attempts to improve the provision of tertiary education which had long lagged behind Macao's needs. In other social policy areas much still needed to be done and there were increasing complaints from the population. A survey, which was conducted in 1991 and 1999, for example, showed that, while only 19 percent of the respondents had been willing to complain about government actions in 1991, that number had increased to 59.7 percent by 1999 (Yu, 2002). The population was becoming more participative and more demanding. The formal political system, however, remained much as it had been over the past two decades with power concentrated in the executive. The legislature was weak, and only partially elected, and demands were still expected to be expressed through the leaders of the traditional associations. The resumption of Chinese sovereignty saw no immediate change in the political system, which remained centralised and undemocratic. Evidently, however, the Chinese government had given some thought to the question of how Macao's economy could be rejuvenated. The issue of the liberalisation of the casino industry, which had been raised in the 1990s, was once more on the agenda.

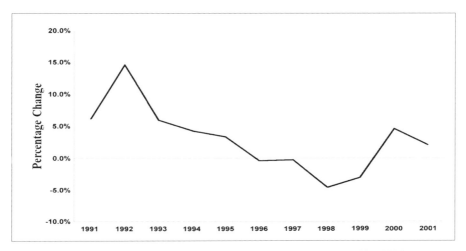

Figure 1.5: Rate of Growth of Gross Domestic Product in Real Terms, 1991–2001

Source: Statistics and Census Service (1990–2001) *Yearbook of Statistics*. Macao: Statistics and Census Service.
Note: 1. 1996 = 100.

Foreign Investment and the De-concentration of the Gaming Industry 2001–2009

According to *The New Yorker*, Sheldon Adelson, the Chairman and Chief Executive of the Las Vegas Sands company, met with Qian Qichen, a Chinese Vice-Premier, in the Purple Light Pavilion in Zhongnanhai in July 2001 to discuss the question of developing the hotel business in Macao (Bruck, 2008). Adelson had been advised not to raise the question of the gaming industry, or of STDM's continuing monopoly of it, because it was thought that this might be offensive to a stalwart of a Communist Party which had roundly condemned and banned gambling on the mainland. Instead, Qian himself raised the subject of the casinos and asked how many hotel rooms Adelson could build (Bruck, 2008). That depended, of course, on the number of visitors that would come from China; if Qian could guarantee a steady flow of visitors and clients for the casinos, as he promised to do, the prospects were set for enormous investments and profits from Macao's gaming industry. It has been suggested that the Chinese government's decision to break STDM's monopoly of the gaming industry stemmed from its concern over the actions and statements of its principal stakeholder, Stanley Ho. Ho was held to be responsible for the growth of triad influence in the industry and had also lost favour with the Chinese government for his apparent disinvestment in Macao during the transitional period and for his critical views on the arrangements for the handover in Hong Kong. These factors may have been important but it was probably also seen to be necessary to bolster Macao's economy after the resumption of sovereignty to increase the legitimacy of the new regime and to enhance social stability. The decision to liberalise the gaming industry greatly, if temporarily, increased the popularity of the Chief Executive, Edmund Ho Hau Wah, who, in contrast to his counterpart in Hong Kong, was highly praised by Chinese leaders (Lo and Yee, 2005).

In October 2001, following the expiry of STDM's monopoly, the Macao government opened the tendering process for concessions to operate casinos. Eventually, three concessions were granted to SJM (a subsidiary of STDM) and to Galaxy and Wynn (Gaming Inspection and Coordination Bureau Commission, 2009; see Chapter 2). The concessionaires then granted three further franchises to Venetian Macao, MGM Grand Paradise and Melco. As a consequence, foreign investment increased dramatically, transforming both the economy and the local landscape (see Figure 1.6). In 2004, Adelson's Sands Hotel, with construction costs of US$265 million, was the first of the new casinos to open its doors; the initial investment was recovered within the year (Bruck, 2008). The visitors that Qian had promised began to arrive, with mainland Chinese visitors making up about half of the total number of visitors, which rose from 11.8 million in 2003 to nearly 21.75 million in 2009 (Statistics and Census Service, 2009). By 2009, Macao had 33 casinos and had overtaken Las Vegas as the gaming capital of the world (Gaming Inspection and Coordination Bureau, 2009). Although gaming revenue did drop by some 12.4 percent in the first six months of 2009, by September, it had recovered to the point where monthly revenue at US$1.4 billion was the highest ever recorded, triple that of Las Vegas (Gough, 2009a; Statistics and Census Service, 2009: 48; SJM, 2009). The total number of visitors dropped in the first part of 2009 but began to increase again towards the end of the year and in 2010 (Statistics and Census Service, 2010).

The outlook, however, was not entirely untroubled. The gaming companies were badly exposed in the credit crunch resulting from the global financial crisis and began to lay off staff and delay construction (Gough, 2009b). All major companies had large outstanding loans on which they had to pay higher interest rates. Galaxy, for example, had a US$3.3 billion loan which it had to refinance by raising capital (Kwok, 2009). At the same time, gaming revenue and profits for the first half of 2009 dropped substantially (Ng, 2009; Melco Crown Entertainment, 2009). SJM, which has the largest number of casinos, saw its profits drop by 40 percent compared with the previous year (SJM, 2009). There were also fears that there would be an oversupply of hotel rooms with stocks expected to rise by 42 percent between 2009 and 2011 (Gough, 2009c). Adding to these concerns, the Chinese government appeared to be having second thoughts about allowing its citizens free access to Macao, placing restrictions on the number of travel applications that civil servants and Guangdong residents could make to visit Macao (Hu, 2009a; Gough and Zhai,

2009). As Figure 1.7 shows, GDP in Macao has risen sharply since the liberalisation of the gaming industry. By June 2010, unemployment was down to 2.8 percent and the underemployment rate to 1 percent with the unemployment of local residents slightly higher at 3.4 percent (Statistics and Census Service, 2010).

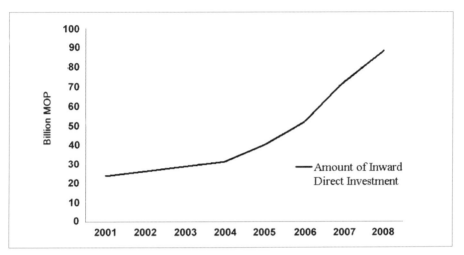

Figure 1.6: Growth in Foreign Investment, 2001–2008

Source: Statistics and Census Service (2008) *Direct Investment Statistics*. Available from: http://www.dsec. gov.mo/Statistic/Other.aspx#KeyIndicators.

Note: 1. The amount of direct investment refers to the accumulated value of direct investment.

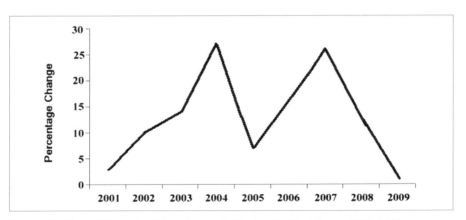

Figure 1.7: Rate of Growth of Gross Domestic Product in Real Terms, 2001–2009

Source: Statistics and Census Service (1990–2009) *Yearbook of Statistics*. Macau: Statistics and Census Service.

Note: 1. 2002 = 100.

Growth comes at the price of a volatile economy at the mercy of global economic forces and of the effects of such massive foreign investment on the high rate of inflation, income inequalities, and uneven quality in service delivery. Inflation ranged between 6.7 percent and 8.3 percent between January and December 2008, dropping to 5.5 percent in the first quarter of 2009 (Vong, 2009: Table 1). The Gini coefficient also increased between 2003 and 2007 to 0.52 but then fell sharply in 2008 to 0.37, possibly as a result of various government subsidies after the demonstrations that took place in May 2007 (see Chapter 12). Research suggests that there have been some slight income benefits to the least well-off since 2005 and that there is no extreme poverty in Macao, but income differentials between rich and poor remain substantial (Fung, 2009). These economic problems may be viewed as typical of Quadrant A type situations where rapid economic growth creates disparities in wealth.

There is also a major political dimension in the tension between economic growth and social stability. Macao government officials believe that the population is willing to accept the disjunctions of rapid economic growth provided they see longer-term benefits in their living standards and quality of life. Various surveys on the quality of life in Macao and on citizens' reaction to foreign investment industry support that view (see Chapter 3; Tong, 2009). In November 2009, for example, a survey reported satisfaction with all the major economic and social indicators with the exception of control over corruption (*Macau News*, November 20, 2009). Nonetheless, there is a proportion of the population that has seen no significant benefits from rapid economic growth and is dissatisfied with higher rates of inflation, property prices and persistent structural unemployment (Fung, 2009). Li and Tsui note an increasing number of bankruptcies among local firms and relative declines in real terms in the wage levels of civil servants and manufacturing workers (Li and Tsui, 2009b). There have also been violent clashes over social conditions between demonstrators and the police in May Day demonstrations in 2006, 2007 and 2010 (*South China Morning Post*, May 2, 2007; May 2, 2010). Significantly, protests in Macao seem to be supported by the less prosperous; in Hong Kong, by comparison, demonstrations against the government often seem to be a middle-class preoccupation. Surveys which show satisfaction with the economic situation also reveal that the lowest levels of satisfaction with life are among the 46–55 age group which correlates with the age group of the largest number of structurally unemployed (Tong, 2009; see Chapter 8).

Macao's government prides itself on a *laissez-faire* approach and an open economy. But since the liberalisation of the gaming industry pressures have been building on it to become more interventionist. Even in an open economy, there is some need for government 'to hold the ring' in terms of the factors of production: capital, land and labour (see Chapters 2 and 8). Each of the factors of production poses potentially considerable problems for a *laissez-faire* government under conditions of rapid economic growth. If foreign investment is unchecked, it can be exceptionally destabilising. In Vietnam, for example, large amounts of foreign investment over a short period of time had near-catastrophic effects, overheating the economy before the government was able to introduce stabilising measures (Pincus and Vu Thanh Tu Anh, 2008). The global financial crisis has drawn attention to the volatility of the Macao economy, its dependence on a single industry, and the possibility that capital inflows can dry up very quickly. At the local level, the government has sought to impose controls on the number of gaming tables and slot machines and to locate them away from residential areas (Gough and Zhai, 2009). But there have been problems implementing the measures. Land, which is in short supply, has also been a contentious issue. The casinos require space but there has been resentment over their allocation of scarce reclaimed land (see Chapter 2). Labour, too, represents a multiplicity of problems for government (see Chapter 8). It has required government intervention to ensure employment of locals in the casinos and to exert some controls over large numbers of imported workers. There is also the need to address the relative absence of a local professional middle class and the problem of the cost of bringing in temporary foreign workers to fill the gap.

Other problems concern the relationship between the government and the people. The arrest in December 2006 of the Secretary for Transport and Works, Ao Man Long, shook confidence in the government. Ao was found to have assets worth over MOP800 million and was eventually convicted on 57 counts involving bribery, money-laundering, abuse of power and unsubstantiated wealth. He was sentenced to 27 years' imprisonment and was convicted on a further 24 counts in April 2009 (for details of the case, see Chapter 6 and Godinho, 2010). The question of how such a high-ranking official could engage in such activities cast doubt on the integrity of the government and its decision-making processes. Ao had been able to use his power to decide who would be awarded contracts and how land would be allocated and used. The opaqueness of the process led to calls for greater openness, more attention to following procedures and regulations and increased public participation and consultation on land-use matters (see Chapter 2).

Social policies, such as education, health, housing and social welfare, also remain problematic with pockets of acceptable provision of goods and services in some areas coupled with others which remain substandard (see Chapters 10–12). For some policies, the pay-offs in terms of greater government investment may be many years in the future, while the political problems that they raise need to be addressed in the short run.

A Future Scenario: High Economic Growth and Social Stability?

In the following chapters, we examine some interrelated questions that are at the heart of any attempt to move from the rapid growth and relative instability of Quadrant A situations to the calmer waters of rapid growth with greater social stability in Quadrant B situations. We ask: what has caused the economic, social and political problems which Macao faces? To what extent have these problems resulted from the gaming industry and foreign investment? To what extent are they an unresolved legacy of the colonial period? To what extent can they be attributed to structural problems within the Macao government, to inadequate administrative and policymaking capacity? What political constraints face policymakers seeking solutions to these problems? Is the political system congruent with the objective of attaining greater social harmony and stability? Have the measures that the government has taken so far helped to alleviate the problems about which people complain? What other measures or policies might be adopted? What opportunities exist that might serve to smooth the uneven pace of economic growth and promote greater social stability?

The book is divided into three substantive parts with a concluding chapter. In Part 1, we consider the impact of the gaming industry on Macao and the response of its citizens to the changes that it has brought about in their lives. Penny Wan and Francisco Pinheiro describe the history of the gaming industry and the effects of the decision to end the monopoly held by STDM and to grant concessions to foreign companies to operate in Macao. They look, in particular, at the competition between the casinos and the public for scarce land and the ways in which designated public land has been alienated for the building of casino hotels. Newman Lam reports the results of a survey on public opinion on the gaming industry and foreign investment, notes the major problems identified by his respondents, and asks whether they attribute blame for those problems to the gaming industry or to the government.

In Part II, we focus on governance and the political system. Eilo Yu analyses the way in which executive-legislative relationships have developed in response to changing political and social circumstances and examines the reasons for the increasing importance of the legislature in articulating demands and sanctioning public policy. In Chapter 5, Annie Lee reflects on the decline of traditional associations, the success of representatives of gaming interests in recent Legislative Assembly elections and the emergence of other new groups in the political arena. Under conditions in which rapid growth is causing social problems and with a casino-driven economy which has specific needs, the ability of the Macao government to deliver goods and services effectively and efficiently has become an issue of major concern. In Chapter 6, Brian Brewer looks at how the government has viewed the challenges it faces and how it has tried to reform the public service to keep pace with increased demands and the needs of the economy. In Chapter 7, Jeannette Taylor analyses the specific question of whether the Macao government pays efficiency wages to its public servants and how this impacts on productivity.

In Part III, we consider the measures that the government has taken to deal with social problems and whether this is likely to lead to reduced levels of discontent. Implicit in this part of the book is the question of whether the government has the capacity to make long-term public policy or whether it is restricted to providing stop-gap measures, such as subsidies, when it perceives there to be pressing social problems. One area where the government has recently sought to make more broad-based policy is that of labour. In Chapter 8, Grace Lee assesses the provisions of the new Labour Law and considers whether retraining programmes can resolve the current mismatch between labour demand and supply. In Chapter 9, Alex Choi and Eva Hung present a study of croupiers, analysing the significance of the government's decision to reserve this position for local residents. Education is another area in which the government appears to be interested in pursuing a longer-term strategy. Joan Leung considers the constraints on the government's attempts to introduce a more unified curriculum and analyses the implications for the economy. In the chapters on housing and social welfare, James Lee and Chan Kam-wah analyse two social policy areas where the government appears to have retreated, with little evidence of a commitment to the provision of public housing and a social welfare approach which has changed from a previous, more institutionalised form to a system which is considered to be more 'flexible' but which relies more heavily on subsidies.

In the concluding chapter, Ian Scott and Newman Lam look at the government's overall strategy in dealing with economic and social problems and examine the constraints and opportunities which will influence whether or not Macao can achieve a situation in which it not only maintains its impressive recent economic growth record but also resolves the problems that currently afflict it.

Part I

The Gaming Industry and Its Critics

The Development of the Gaming Industry and Its Impact on Land Use

Penny Wan and Francisco V. Pinheiro

Over the past few years, the gaming industry has changed the face of Macao and the lives of its citizens. The liberalisation of casino licensing in 2002 and the implementation of the Chinese government's new visa regulations in 2003, which permitted many mainland Chinese to travel to Hong Kong and Macao on an individual basis, triggered an economic boom. Foreign investment increased dramatically as international companies began to build casinos and hotels. By 2006, gaming revenues had reached a record annual high of US$10.33 billion, far exceeding the US$6.6 billion made on the Las Vegas strip (Gaming Inspection and Coordination Bureau, 2008). Tourist numbers more than doubled from 11 million in 2002 to 21.7 million in 2009 (Statistics and Census Service, 2009a). Rapid economic growth has come at a price, however. There have been many social dislocations and challenges for public policy that can be attributed to the expansion of the gaming industry. A particular issue is land, a fundamental factor of production and an essential component of the gaming industry's success but in short supply in Macao. The tension between casino requirements for land and public needs spills over into debates on matters as diverse as building height restrictions, heritage protection, green space, the opaqueness of government decisions and its lack of consultative mechanisms.

In this chapter, we examine the growth of casino gaming and the problems that it has raised over land use. The chapter is organised into five sections. Following this introductory section, a brief history of the gaming industry is provided. The third and fourth sections discuss the economic impact of the gaming industry and the tension between the casinos' requirements and public land needs. The final section presents the main conclusions and proposes a number of practical solutions to improve the current policymaking framework on urban land use for more sustainable gaming development in Macao.

The History of Macao's Gaming Industry

A permanent Portuguese settlement was founded in Macao in 1557 when representatives of the Chinese Emperor agreed that it could be used as a base for commerce (Ping and Zhiliang, 2007). Local Portuguese paid an annual rent for the land but suzerainty remained with China. Macao's semi-autonomous status was recognised by China in 1582 and by Portugal in 1586. Local governance centred on the Senate, which had a strong representation of traders who made up the bulk of the first residents. Macao benefited from its strategic position on the sea routes between Europe and Asia, particularly in the early years when it had a monopoly of trade with Japan. When that ended in 1638, the city managed to survive as a trading port and an entrepot for China. By the 1720s, opium generated most of the income for local merchants and mandarins and attracted pirates and gamblers.

While migrants at first arrived in the city in only small numbers, they eventually became sufficiently numerous to form the majority of the population (Custodio and Teixeira, 2000). Some of those arriving by sea continued to live in boats or found illegal lodging on land and were linked with pirates and triad societies (Guimarães, 2000). Chinese were initially forbidden to live in or own property and were discouraged from mixing with foreigners (Choi, 1991). Although the mandarins formally excluded Chinese from living in Macao, in practice they were permitted to remain because they provided necessary supplies and services to the non-Chinese community. The city was geographically and administratively divided into two areas, known respectively as Chinese and Christian (Vale, 1997). As late as 1867, a police report stated that 'twenty years ago Macau constituted two separate quarters which were like two different cities; Chinese ... and Christian ... both (were) without police, completely separated with unequal rights and without reciprocity of interests' (Macao Government, 1867: 225, author's translation).

Gaming activities have been a feature of Macao for many centuries. In 1683 and 1713, for example, the Senate reported that male immigrants were gambling, drinking and provoking robberies and fights. To solve the problem was apparently sufficiently difficult that the Senate proposed to demolish the houses and shops of troublemaking immigrants (Boxer, 1988: 168). The problems worsened as time went by. A letter to the Portuguese monarch dated January 15, 1805 reported that gaming had become endemic among '[n]ot only the mandarins, but also the population because of the many vagabonds who had come to Macao for refuge, at every step making timber huts for playing games and other vices, giving us no alternative but to close some, tolerating (the existence of) others due to the lack of a (military and police) force' (Guimarães, 2000: 124, author's translation). Although piracy, opium and gaming created many social disorders in the city, it also attracted numerous Western adventurers and Chinese merchants, all seeking quick fortunes. In 1867, Comte Ludovic de Beauvoir described Macao as 'the Monaco of the

Celestial Empire (China)' and 'the rich Chinese of Hainan, Guangdong and Fujien provinces go there to lose their money' (Amaro, 1998: 229). Jules Itier went further and considered satanic influences to be involved in the fanatical attitudes of the gamblers he observed in Macao during his 1840s visit (Jorge and Coelho, 1997: 91). The licensing of fan tan gaming (番攤) houses was granted in April 1849 following a petition from Chinese entrepreneurs (Kan, 2007).

To establish order in a chaotic city and to implement a new system, a hardline navy hero, Captain Ferreira do Amaral (1846–49), was appointed as Governor by Portugal's Queen Maria II. Before Amaral, colonial rule was ineffective and Macao had been administered in practice by the outcomes of continuous negotiations between the mandarins and the Senate officials. Amaral wanted to stimulate the economy to compete with Hong Kong and the host of new ports (Canton, Nanjing, Xiamen, Fuzhou, Ningbo and Shanghai) that opened up after the Treaty of Nanjing was signed in 1842. Competition from these new ports represented the biggest challenge to Macao's survival. Economic difficulties were further aggravated in 1844 after the Portuguese government gave Macao administrative independence from Goa, and made Macao the head of the Province of Macao, Timor and Solor. As a result, Macao assumed responsibility for two territories in the Indonesian archipelago, including their administration and economic and military support.

Amaral intended to clean up economic malpractices and vice by taxing every Chinese found gambling outdoors, demolishing illegal timber houses, cleaning unhealthy areas, ordering burials in cemeteries, introducing night lighting and imposing modern urban methods in land management, such as naming streets and taxing individual home owners (Silva, 1995). He centralised taxation, abolished gifts and the land-renting system and removed the Chinese and Senate customs offices. Amaral's efforts to modernise Macao's administrative and social systems brought about the wrath of the mandarins in Canton and threatened the dual authority system under which Macao had been governed since the first settlement. A price was put on his head. He was murdered on August 22, 1849 and his head was taken to Canton. Following his death, the new governor, Gonçalves Cardoso, took steps towards reinforcing the economy by establishing a monopoly over the sale of opium, a monopoly that lasted until 1946. He forced all Chinese to pay taxes and legalised prostitution.

The legalisation of fan tan in 1849 also allowed for greater control over gambling activities (Lamas, 1998). Fan tan owners became more co-operative and the number of public disturbances caused by illegal gambling and drinking was reduced. The Macao government also benefited from legalisation. Governor Isidoro Francisco Guimarães (1852–1863) claimed that government revenue had increased from a MOP48,309 deficit in 1852 to a surplus of MOP104, 633 in 1862. By 1886, 16 gaming rooms were in operation, mostly located in the Inner Harbour Chinatown, and called the fan tan houses (Pons, 1999). By the 1920s, their number had increased to 200. As the growing number of houses made the collection of taxes from individual owners increasingly difficult, the facilities continued to spread. By 1931, the opium trade and gambling had become such powerful social forces that civilian and military personnel were forbidden to enter fan tan houses except on duty (Macao Government, 1931). Lotteries and horse races were operated separately from gaming and benefited different institutions in them. Among them was the Santa Casa da Misericordia (Holy House of Mercy) which was no longer managed by the Church but by some members of the Macanese elite.

The first monopoly licence for gambling, mainly fan tan and cussec (dices), which were the most popular Chinese games, started in February 1931 (the same year gaming was legalised in Nevada) and was run by Fok Chi Ting, the managers of Hou Heng Company (Gaming Inspection and Coordination Bureau, 2010a). Fok Chi Ting was authorised to open gambling facilities wherever they wanted, from the border gates to Barra (the Ama Temple), but they chose to concentrate their operations at the President Hotel (later named the Central Hotel) and the Cinema Victoria (later replaced by the Tai Fung Bank). The first gambling strip was established on San Ma Lou Avenue where jewellery shops, banks, restaurants and pawnshops soon followed. Even after the prohibition of gambling in China in 1949, the strip continued to prosper.

The gaming concession changed hands in 1937 when it was given to the Tai Heng Company (大繁榮, Great Prosperity) (Macao Government, 1937: 308). The Company had an investment capital of MOP1 million which was shared in different proportions by five businessmen, three from Hong Kong, one from Canton and one from Macao. They took over the management of the Central Hotel which became Tai Heng headquarters. In 1942, more floors were added to increase the casino's capacity and in 1955 the Company expanded operations with the opening of the Kan Pek Casino (Hoje Macau, 2010). According to Moisés (2006), the commercial oligarchy was also represented by Pedro Lobo, Ho Yin and Y. C. Liang, who already had a monopoly of the gold trade and controlled many of the other companies that generated larger profits than gambling. On July 4, 1961, 15 games were authorised in addition to fan tan and cussec (Macao Government, 1961). Even so, gaming revenue of MOP2,220,000 represented only 8 percent of government income, which it considered to be too small (Moisés, 2006). In 1961, Governor Silvério Marques gave the monopoly concession for casino gaming, horse racing and other lotteries to Stanley Ho, who had the backing of several Hong Kong businessmen. The government's aim was to raise income from gaming to 13 percent. In exchange for the concession, Ho agreed to invest in new hotels and guaranteed some improvements to the city, sharing the costs with the government on construction and urban development projects, such as the drainage of the inner and outer harbour for improved navigation, the introduction of faster means of transport and communications with Hong Kong (hydrofoils in 1964, jetfoils in 1975 and helicopters in 1990) and other social projects.

In the early hours of January 1962, Ho opened his casino in Hotel Estoril. However, due to strong lobbying against the new concession by the previous owners, the signing of the contract was delayed until March 30, 1962. On May 18 of the same year, the Sociedade de Turismo e Diversões de Macau (STDM, the Macau Travel and Amusement Company Limited) was formed and, on May 26, it signed a monopoly contract with the government. This process involved intense lobbying of the Portuguese local and central authorities and required the backing of a number of powerful Hong Kong stakeholders (Moisés, 2006), including Henry Fok (30 percent), Teddy Yip (27 percent), Yip Hong (16 percent), Stanley Ho (16 percent) and six other Hong Kong investors (10 percent). On January 13, 1966, the floating casino 'Macau Palace' arrived at the Inner Harbour. STDM survived the political and social storm generated by the Cultural Revolution in Macao (1966–1967) and on June 11, 1970 the company's flagship casino, the Hotel Lisboa, was inaugurated. In 2002, STDM continued its gaming operations under the name of SJM (Sociedade de Jogos de Macao, Macao Gaming Company Limited), owning 17 venues by January 2010 (SJM Holdings, 2010). Prior to casino deregulation, the gaming industry generated over 60 percent of Macao's GDP (Gaming Inspection and Coordination Bureau, 2010b).

On September 24, 2001, Decree Law No. 16/2001 was introduced, establishing the legal framework which liberalised the casino industry. The Macao government had the following objectives in mind: 'to inject new dynamics into the gaming industry and to lay a strong foundation for further future development in gaming, reinforcing the policy direction set by the Macao SAR', with 'tourism, gaming, conventions and exhibitions as the "head", and the service industry as the "body", driving the overall development of other industries' (Gaming Inspection and Coordination Bureau, 2010b). The specific goals of liberalisation were to increase competition among casino operators, to enhance service quality, to provide additional employment opportunities for Macao residents and the associated benefits of enhanced economic development and social stability, and to position Macao as the regional centre of casino gaming, with an improved reputation in the industry for fairness, honesty, and freedom from criminal influence (Commission for the First Public Tender to Grant Concessions to Operate Casino Games of Chance of the Macao SAR, 2001). In November 2001, public tendering for the licences began and closed in the following month. The Macao government received 21 tenders and finally awarded casino concessions to three syndicates, namely: SJM, Wynn Resorts SA and Galaxy Casino SA. Although only three concessions were initially awarded, an additional three sub-concessions were created in 2006. The three sub-concessions of SJM, Wynn Resorts and Galaxy Casino SA were MGM Grand

Paradise (a venture between Stanley Ho's daughter Pansy Ho and MGM Grand), Melco-PBL (a partnership managed by Stanley Ho's son Lawrence Ho and the Australian, James Packer), and Las Vegas Sands (run by Sheldon Adelson). These six companies are now completely independent from each other and have built separate and competing casino properties. Plate 2.1 shows the flagship casinos of the three casino concessions and the three sub-concessions.

Casino operations are now regulated by Decree Law 16/2001 (Macao SAR Government, 2001), limiting the concessions period to no more than 20 years as defined in individual contracts between the government and each company signed in 2002. It gives 18 years to SJM and 20 years each to Galaxy and Wynn, with the concessions expiring on March 31, 2020 (Gaming Inspection and Coordination Bureau, 2010c). Article 27 of Decree Law 16/2001 established a government tax of 35 percent on casino profits, which was later changed in the individual company contracts. Each casino company is now not only required to pay an annual premium of MOP30 million to the government during the licence term, but is also required to pay a variable premium that is calculated on the number of the gaming tables and the electric or mechanical gaming machines it operates (Gaming Inspection and Coordination Bureau, 2010c). In addition, each concessionaire has to pay a special monthly gaming tax at a rate of one-twelfth of its gross gaming revenue to the government. Another 2.4 percent of its gross revenue has to be contributed to urban development, tourism promotion and social security and a further 1.6 percent is to be spent on promoting, developing or studying culture, society, economy, education and science and engaging in academic and charitable activities (Macao SAR Government, 2002). Decree 16/2001 also requires a contribution to the Macao Foundation which has a mission to promote the development and study of cultural, social, economic, scientific, academic and philanthropic activities.

The Growth of the Gaming Industry and Its Contribution to the Local Economy

The liberalisation of gaming concessions has resulted in the expansion of the number of casinos from 11 in 2002 to 33 in the second quarter of 2009, and a rise in table numbers from 424 to 4,610 between 2003 and 2009 (Table 2.1).

Casino liberalisation has brought enormous economic benefits to Macao. Not only has it led to a sharp rise in GDP (see Chapter 1), but it has also resulted in a significant contribution to government revenue. After the opening of Sands Casino in 2004, gaming revenue contributed over 60 percent of government income, with the figure rising to 77 percent in 2008 after other giant casinos like Wynn (2006) and Venetian (2007) were opened (Figure 2.1). Overall, casino gaming contributes more

Table 2.1: Number of Casinos and Tables, 2002–2009

Concessionaires	2002	2003	2004	2005	2006	2007	2008	2009
SJM	11	11	13	15	17	18	19	20
Galaxy	–	–	1	1	5	5	5	5
Las Vegas Sands	–	–	1	1	1	2	3	3
Wynn Resorts	–	–	–	–	1	1	1	1
Melco-PBL	–	–	–	–	–	1	2	3
MGM Grand			–	–	–	1	1	1
Total	11	11	15	17	24	28	31	33
No. of tables	–	424	1092	1388	2762	4375	4017	4770

Source: Gaming Inspection and Coordination Bureau (2009a).

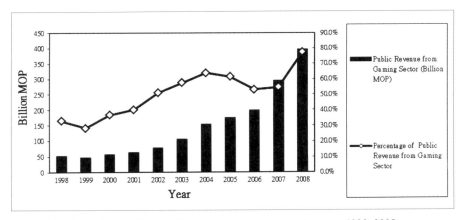

Figure 2.1: Percentage of Gaming Revenues to Government Income, 1998–2008

Source: Statistics and Census Service (2008).

than 99 percent of the gross gaming revenue. Its tax contribution alone has risen from MOP22 billion in 2002 and to MOP108 billion in 2008, a nearly 500 percent growth rate (Table 2.2).

The concession holders are also obligated to fulfil their projected investment plans. For instance, SJM has an investment plan of MOP4.74 billion for Macao Fisherman's Wharf, a joint venture with a local businessman, Ponte 16, and the East-West Cultural Village as well as extensions, renovations, and upgrades to its various casino properties. Wynn Resorts has an investment plan of around MOP4 billion that includes a hotel and casino.

Table 2.2: Growth Pattern of Revenue from Different Gaming Activities, 2002–2008 (in millions MOP)

Items	2002	2003	2004	2005	2006	2007	2008
Casinos	22,180	28,672	41,378	46,047	56,623	83,022	108,772
Horse racing	539	1,004	1,566	636	437	403	501
Sports Lottery-Football	641	510	442	333	327	273	304
Greyhound racing	76	74	84	67	67	98	186
Sports Lottery-Basketball	56	52	36	44	60	44	57
Chinese Lottery	4	3	5	7	7	6	6
Instant Lottery	0.83	0.07	0.03	0.03	0.03	0.02	0.003
Total	23,496	30,315	43,511	47,134	57,521	83,847	109,826

Source: Gaming Inspection and Coordination Bureau (2009b).

As a result of the rapid development of casinos, tourism and infrastructure, there has been a sharp rise in employment opportunities. As shown in Table 2.3, the unemployment rate dropped significantly from 6 percent in 2002 to 3.5 percent in the second quarter of 2009. The total employed population also rose from 202,000 to 321,000 in the same period. Growth in employment was particularly rapid in gaming-related sectors. The percentage of people employed in the hotel, entertainment and gaming industries rose from 25.3 percent in 2004 to over 35 percent in 2008. People working in the gaming sector alone doubled from 21,264 in 2004 to 43,975 in the second quarter of 2009 (Table 2.4).

The growth of the casino industry and the Chinese government's relaxed visa requirements, which permitted mainlanders to travel to Macao as individuals rather than in groups, led to a boom in tourism. Numbers doubled between 2002 and 2009, from only 11.53 million to nearly 21.75 million. Mainland visitors constituted

Table 2.3: Changes in the Unemployment Rate, the Total Employed Population and the Employed Population in the Gaming Sector, 2002–2009

	2002	2003	2004	2005	2006	2007	2008	2009 (to second quarter)
Unemployment Rate (percent)	6.0	5.5	4.1	4.0	3.2	2.9	3.6	3.5
Total employment	202,200	205,385	219,143	237,451	265,054	300,300	323,000	321,100
Employment in gaming (percent of total employment in brackets)	–	–	21,264 (9.7)	26,118 (11.0)	36,412 (13.7)	44,743 (14.9)	43,835 (13.6)	43,975 (13.7)

Source: Statistics and Census Service (2009b, 2009c).

Table 2.4: Comparison of Employment in the Gaming Industry with Other Major Employment Sectors, 2004–2008 (in percentages)

Year	Manufacturing	Construction	Wholesale and retail	Hotels and restaurants	Entertainment gaming and other services	Gaming (alone)	Public administration and social security
2004	16.50	8.30	16.10	11.00	14.30	9.7	7.91
2005	14.90	9.60	14.90	10.50	17.20	11.0	7.49
2006	11.10	11.70	13.70	11.30	19.80	13.7	7.18
2007	8.00	12.80	12.80	11.60	23.00	14.9	7.02
2008	6.99	12.70	12.07	12.51	22.90	13.6	6.88

Source: Statistics and Census Service (2009d).

over 50 percent of tourist arrivals in 2009 and more than half of those (56 percent) travelled to Macao as individuals. Visitors from Hong Kong and Taiwan were the second and third major sources of tourist arrivals, respectively (Table 2.5). To cope with the influx of tourists, the supply of hotel rooms was increased from 8,869 in 2002 to 34,800 in 2009. Another 21,737 rooms are planned although many of the proposed projects have no specific completion date (Loi, 2008).

Table 2.5: Visitor Arrivals by Top Three Places of Origin, 2002–2009 (percentages in brackets)

Nationality	Mainland China	Hong Kong	Taiwan	Total tourist numbers
2002	4,240,446 (36.8)	5,101,437 (44.2)	1,532,929 (13.3)	11,530,841
2003	5,742,036 (48.3)	4,623,162 (38.9)	1,022,830 (8.6)	11,887,876
2004	9,529,739 (57)	5,051,059 (30.3)	1,286,949 (7.7)	16,672,556
2005	10,462,787 (55.9)	5,611,131 (30)	1,482,287 (7.9)	18.711,187
2006	11,985,655 (54.5)	6,935,554 (31.5)	1,437,752 (6.5)	21,998,122
2007	14,866,391 (55.1)	8,174,064 (30.3)	1,444,082 (5.3)	26,992,995
2008	11,613.200 (50.6)	7,016,500 (30.6)	1,315,900 (5.7)	22,933,200
2009	10,989,533 (50.5%)	6,727,822 (30.9%)	1,292,551 (5.9%)	21,752,751

Source: Statistics and Census Service (2009a).

The Tension between Casino Requirements and Public Land Needs

Despite the gaming industry's enormous contribution to the economy of Macao, it has put great pressure on the available land supply. The gaming companies require a good deal of space for their new casino-hotels and if their needs are to be met, other important interests have to be sacrificed. Tension and conflict between the government, the casino operators and civil society often result.

Great swathes of prime public land have been eaten up by real estate and gaming interests. A critical example was the carefully drafted and detailed laws (running to 175 pages) issued on April 18, 1991 for the NAPE area (new reclaimed areas in Outer Harbour and Nam Wan Bay) (Macao Government, 1991). This legislation aimed to overcome the weaknesses of previous partial plans and to regulate high-density development comprehensively in similar ways to Hong Kong (Lima, 2009). The entire area was subject to detailed planning for mixed residential-commercial use and community facilities with green spaces (kindergartens, primary and high schools, a swimming pool, an urban park, sport fields, a municipal market, a health centre, a sports centre, a community centre, a post office and a large police station). Most of these facilities were not built and their land use was changed. There were, for example, 43 planned residential towers, but only 21 were built. After gaming liberalisation, many of the residential lots and formerly designated public spaces were occupied by hotels and casinos. The NAPE plan was finally repealed by the Chief Executive on August 16, 2007. The government justified its decision by arguing that it was necessary to build new casinos and to take their needs into account. It claimed, moreover, that the plan was outdated and difficult to follow (Macao SAR Government, 2006).

The initial NAPE guidelines restricted the building height to 80 metres for office building and 50 metres for residential units. Parts of the NAPE green public facilities and residential areas are now occupied by hotels such as StarWorld, the L'Arc Macau, Sands, Wynn and MGM, leaving only a few remaining green spaces. The building restrictions in the NAPE plan were also removed after the opening of the Sands in 2004 and Galaxy's StarWorld Casino in 2006. Many other high-rise casinos soon followed creating a 'wall effect' that resulted in a negative visual impact and poor urban ventilation (*Macau Post Daily*, December 2, 2009). The public was not properly consulted about these changes. Although some neighbourhood residents of the StarWorld site decided to take the government to court and oppose the project on the grounds that it did not follow the original urban plan for the area, they lost the battle in the end (Azevedo, 2006). Jon Prescott, architect and designer of the original NAPE plan, concluded in a magazine interview that in Macao '[w]hen something is "gazetted" it does not mean that it is going to necessarily be adhered to' (Architects Association of Macau, 1992).

Plate 2.1: The Flagship Casinos of the Macao Casino Industry

(a) Galaxy (Mystical Oasis)

(b) SJM (Grand Lisboa)

(d) MGM Grand – the sub-concessionaire of SJM

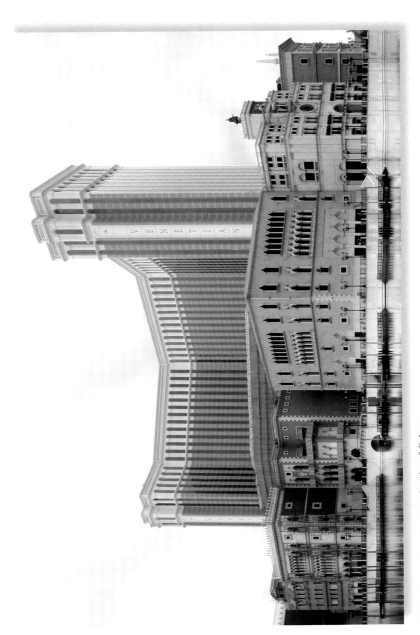

(e) Venetian — the sub-concessionaire of Galaxy

(f) Melco/ PBL (The City of Dreams) – the sub-concessionaire of Wynn

Plate 2.2 Height Restrictions near Guia Hill

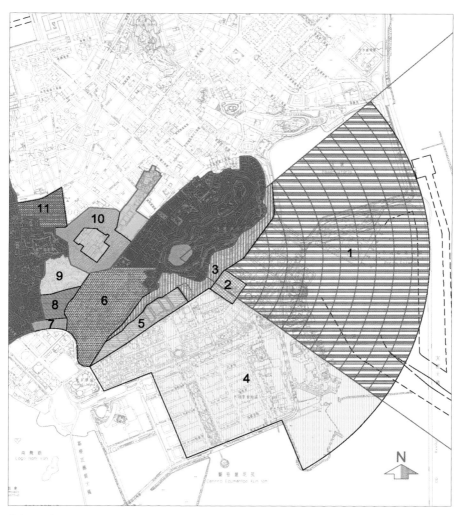

Colour code:

Blue: Light House visual corridors area.

Red; World heritage site.

Yellow: local urban law.

Building heights for the 11 zones:

Zone 1 – 5 to 52.5 metres	Zone 2 – 14 metres	Zone 3 – 52.5 metres
Zone 4 – 90 metres	Zone 5 – 60-90 metres	Zone 6 – 52.5 metres
Zone 7 – 75 metres	Zone 8 – 20.5 metres	Zone 9 – 47 metres
Zone 10 – 47 metres	Zone 11 – 47 metres	

Plate 2.3 The Oceanus Casino

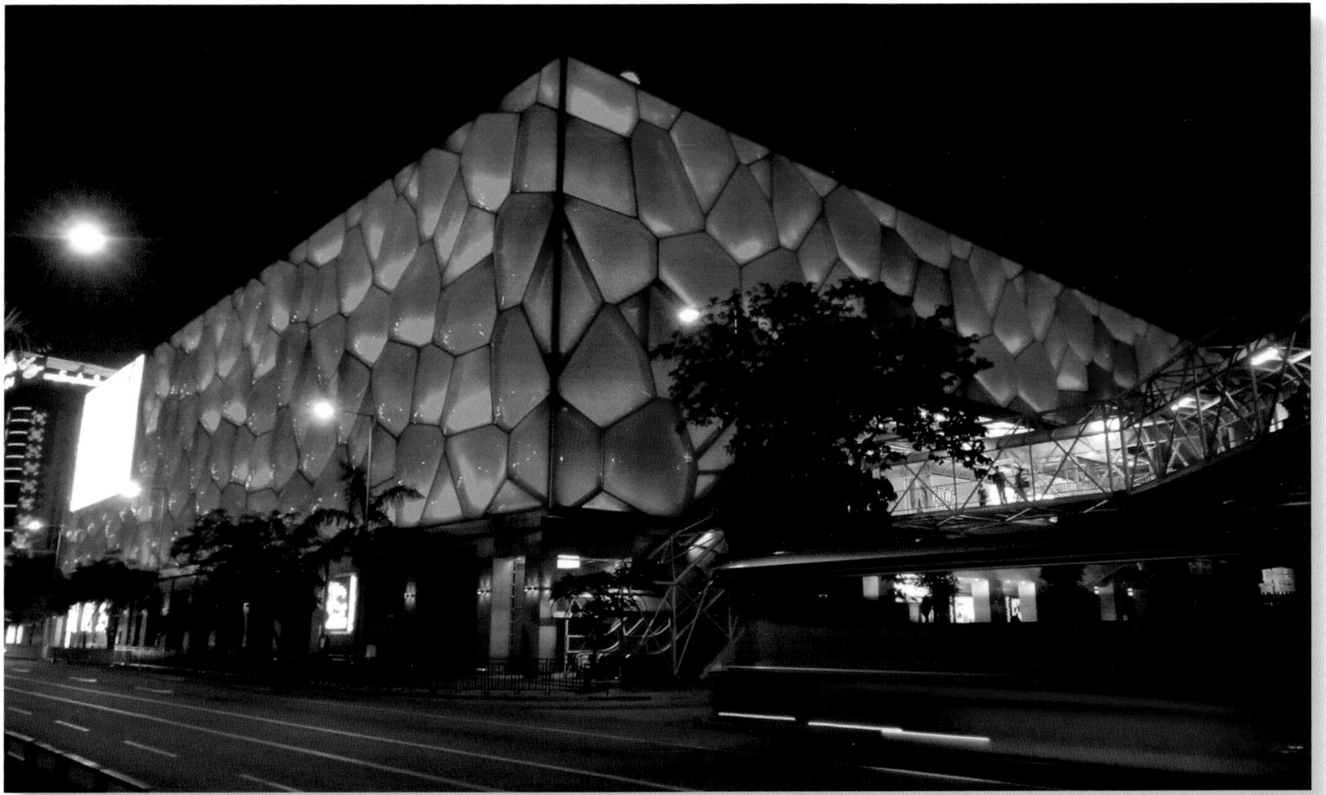

Source: Photograph taken by the authors

Another example of sudden changes to planning is the Cotai area (the reclaimed land between Coloane and Taipa Islands), which was designed during the last years of the Portuguese administration to support a total of 180,000 residents and 40,000 convention visitors and hotel guests. After the liberalisation of the gaming industry, private and public spaces such as schools, fire stations, markets, and residential areas were all 'eaten up' and have now been converted into the Cotai Strip which is mostly occupied by casino and hotel projects, including the Venetian, Studio City, Galaxy Entertainment and the City of Dreams. Some of these casino-hotel projects (for example, the City of Dreams) were started and nearly completed before the land use right was formally gazetted (*South China Morning Post*, June 13, 2008). Only the race-carting track and a small golf course remain untouched because they were built on land reclaimed from a garbage dump.

Casino and hotel developers have even bought 110,000 square metres of space in the Cotai Strip which the government had exclusively designated for educational purposes and which had previously been reserved for the extension of the Macau University of Science and Technology. After paying around MOP10 billion for the land, the developers began construction on the site before formal rezoning procedures had been completed and two years before it was officially gazetted (*Bega District News*, 2008). In the Legislative Assembly, one of the members criticised the government for its failure to enforce the provisions of the original plan, noting that the purpose of land use had been changed without any announcement or public consultation. He also asked why the construction of the casino project had already started when the negotiations with the University were still in progress (Legislative Assembly, 2008). In yet another incident, a local Portuguese school, previously classified as a heritage building, was planned for demolition to make way for expansion of the Lisboa Casino. Parents and students were not involved in the process and were kept in the dark until the negotiations had been concluded (*Jornal Tribuna de Macau*, June 2, 2008).

The priority given to the land requirements of the casinos over other public needs has resulted in the per capita green/leisure zones areas being reduced from 13.5 square metres in 2002 to 12.0 square metres in 2008 (Land, Public Works and Transport Bureau, 2008). New casino and entertainment towers are now being built to greater heights than nearby buildings, seriously affecting the visual integrity of the city landscape. High-class entertainment towers are randomly built in century-old narrow streets, standing out like toothpicks in the middle of a spaghetti mess of roads and overpasses (see the cover of this book), contributing to pollution, endemic traffic jams, an urban screen 'wall effect', and creating an unattractive environment for locals and tourists alike (du Cros, 2009; Wan and Pinheiro, 2009; Yu, 2008).

Unbalanced Power Relations as the Cause of Gaming-led Land Development

Bias towards casino interests is legitimised by the unbalanced power relations that have resulted from the government's long history of reliance on the gaming sector, a reliance that enables the casinos to assume the strongest bargaining position. While economic success in the past has overridden much community dissatisfaction, arbitrary executive decisions on land use have also been used to safeguard business interests. Most land sales in Macao are by private negotiation, not public tendering. Although Macao's Land Law requires government land sales to be carried out by public bidding, the Chief Executive has the power to grant special permission. Since the 1999 handover, only three sites out of more than 400 sold by the government have gone through the public bidding process (*South China Morning Post*, June 13, 2008). In January 2008, after the Ao Man Long corruption case, the government did use public tendering to sell a piece of land in Fai Chi Kei. Some Legislative Councillors and community members therefore have been working hard to urge the government to ensure that all land applications are transparent (*South China Morning Post*, September 19, 2008; see also Chapter 4).

Urban land use planning in Macao is top-down with very little room for public involvement. Reclamation projects, represent a territorial expansion and require the approval of the Central Government. Jurisdiction over district planning is vested in the Chief Executive and the Secretary for Land, Public Works and Transport (Land, Public Works and Transport Bureau, 2008). There is no town planning ordinance stipulating planning procedures, establishing who has the power to view and consider development proposals, or how the general public can become involved in the process. There is no independent body to oversee the way in which rights to land use are granted.

Furthermore, unlike neighbouring cities such as Hong Kong (Hong Kong SAR Government, 2006) and Zhuhai (Zhuhai Government, 2006), Macao does not have any strategic development plan that clearly stipulates its future goals and objectives. Planners and developers have long relied on private consultancy studies such as 'The 21st Century City Planning Guidelines Study 1999–2020 (21CCPGS)' as a reference (Lam and Sam, 1999). The study, which is informal and has no statutory effect, states that the city has been positioned as a tourism destination led by the gaming industry. It affirms that Macao should be 'an international tourist leisure resort whose dominating mainstay should be modern entertainment and tourist services led by the gambling industry'.

Macao has no official city master plan and the government consequently has considerable flexibility in urban land use policymaking. A senior government official in the Land, Public Works and Transport Bureau once explained the reasons why there is no plan. He said that Macao's priority was economic development and that, in turn, was driven by the prompt provision of answers to meet the needs of the gaming industry. There was a general plan, he said, inside the minds of the secretaries and senior public servants. But Macao did not need a concrete master plan because sectoral plans supported by laws and guidelines issued on a case-by-case basis were sufficient since they were more flexible and created fewer controversies (*Jornal Tribuna de Macau*, November 10, 2006). Unfortunately, the sectoral plans are not available for public scrutiny. In common with many developing countries, corruption and clientelism have therefore become common. Ao Man Long, the former Secretary for Transport and Public Works, was arrested in December 2006 for his alleged involvement in a massive public works corruption scandal (*Macau Daily Times*, January 31, 2008). He was one of the few within the government who had the power to approve or disapprove land use and casino projects, and to change building rules and land use purposes if he thought that was appropriate.

Increasing Community Challenges to Gambling-led Development

This executive-led pro-growth planning mode was not challenged to any significant extent until the Guia Hill debate broke out in 2006 (Wan, Pinheiro and Korenaga, 2007). The debate started when the media announced plans to construct an office, residential, and hotel complex with several towers over 99.91 metres in height within a 300-metre-long slot at the foot of the historic Guia Hill. Local residents believed that these developments would completely block the views of the 90-metre-high lighthouse on Guia Hill, a lighthouse that contains a 17th-century chapel and was built in 1865, making it the first modern lighthouse in China (Tso, 2006). This site had been carefully protected by the colonial administration which, in the 1990s, enforced a maximum development height of 20.5 metres (*Ponto Final*, June 14, 2007). Those guidelines were revoked without any announcement or proper consultation. The government, through the Lands, Public Works and Transport Bureau, explained that the changes stemmed from the need 'to modernise the legislation, already 15 years old and completely outdated, out of touch with the gambling sector development and the increasing need for building sites' (cited in Tso, 2006: 19).

Because of the absence of a proper channel to communicate with the Macao government, in mid-August 2007, two community groups led by architects, town planners, tourism and historical experts decided to report the case to the United Nations Educational, Scientific and Cultural Organization. This resulted in a warning letter which was sent to the Cultural Bureau of the Chinese government in September 2007. A copy of the letter reached the Macao government in November 2007 (Guia Lighthouse Protection Concern Group, 2007). This pressured the Macao government to take action. In April 2008, it lowered the maximum development height of 11 areas surrounding the Guia Hill district (Plate 2.2; Macao SAR Government,

2008a). The Vice-Secretary of the government's Cultural Institute Bureau, Stephen Chan, considered that this new height restriction was necessary to balance the community interests between heritage preservation and urban development. The Secretary for Transport and Public Works, Lau Sio Io, in a public meeting, admitted that there had been shortcomings in the urban planning approach and said that the government would put greater effort into listening to public opinion and incorporate more suggestions for protecting the environment, the urban landscape and heritage in future land use policymaking (*Macao Daily News*, 2008).

On April 19, 2010, in a seminar on urban development and protection of the cultural heritage, Guo Zhan, the Vice-President of ICOMOS (International Council on Monuments and Sites) mentioned that Macao's heritage was not only China's history but also a world legacy that should be protected for future generations. He believed that it was irrational to have no master plan in a city with so many historical sites, a view that was reiterated by Zhu Rongyuan from the China Academy of Urban Planning and Design. Gou Zhan also pointed out that the construction of massive tall buildings had created a 'wall effect', adulterated the traditional image and historical setting of Macao as a maritime trade centre, and led to the deterioration of the citizens' quality of life (*Jornal Tribuna de Macau*, April 20, 2010). In fact, many buildings are now empty and a large part of the population live in the neighbouring region of Zhuhai, which offers cheaper and larger housing. The comments and criticisms of the ICOMOS representatives mean that the Land, Public Works and Transport Bureau and the Cultural Institute Bureau will have to present a development and protection plan on February 1, 2011 before the next committee meeting.

New building limits are now in effect and have had consequences for some casino projects. The recently built Oceanus casino project, for example, has been required to reduce its size from what was to have been the biggest casino in Asia at 47,000 square metres ground implementation area to 6,000 square metres and its height from 135 metres to 25 metres (Plate 2.3; Andreu, 2010).

Having learned its lesson from the Guia Hill debate, the government put in place mechanisms for public consultation on major government policies. In 2008, five major public consultations were conducted. Two of these related to land use planning. Public consultation on a long-term strategic plan for Macao — *An Outline for Macao Urban Concept Plan* (OMUCP) — was first conducted by the Research Centre for Sustainable Development Strategies (CEEDS) (2008a). The Centre (initially called the Center for the Studies of Quality of Life) was established in 2005 by the Chief Executive, with the main task of studying 'in detail factors concerning the improvement of the quality of life of the population; and based on these studies and advanced experiences from abroad, to formulate strategies that conform with the context of Macao supported by ample scientific evidence' (CEEDS, 2008b). The form of public participation used in the production of OMUCP was criticised by some academics and professionals. Their criticisms included the compressed nature of the two-month consultation period, considering that it was the first formal large-scale urban planning consultation exercise in Macao and that the population had no idea about what urban and tourism planning involved. In addition, important definitions of terms, such as 'outline concept plan' and 'sustainable development', and the logic behind the various development options chosen were not explained (Hong Kong Institute of Planners, 2008; Macao Urban Planning Institute (IPUM), 2008; Yeung 2008). Most government consultation booklets are issued in only Portuguese and Chinese, making it difficult for international scholars to offer comments. A consultation on future urban planning strategies was also conducted in November 2008 with the publication of the 148 page *Report on Macao's Urban Planning System* (Land, Public Works and Transport Bureau, 2008). This document was more detailed and technical than the Urban Concept Plan but the consultation period was shorter at only one month. It can be concluded that regardless of the scope, degree, and intensity of public involvement, the efforts made in this direction are too limited to be classified as real participation.

The lack of community power can also be attributed to the limited public knowledge of urban planning and land use. Unlike gaming and tourism, no local training courses or university degrees are offered in the fields of urban planning, geography, resource management or sustainable development. It was not until September 2009 that a private university began to offer an architecture degree programme. The majority of local architects and urban planners receive their training in North America, Portugal, Taiwan or China. The urgent need to increase both the quantity and quality of land and planning experts was highlighted in the *Report on Macao's Urban Planning System* (Land, Public Works and Transport Bureau, 2008).

Conclusion

This chapter has examined the growth of the gaming industry and its subsequent effects, especially on urban land use. The liberalisation of casino licensing in 2002, subsequent foreign investment and the rapid increase in the number of mainland visitors have established Macao's reputation as an international gaming destination. But the gaming industry has also disproportionately consumed scarce local resources, such as land and labour, which has brought it into conflict with other users and the public. Political debates on social issues, such as the lack of green space and efforts to protect cultural heritage, show that the traditional top-down and growth-driven urban policymaking approach has been insensitive or unresponsive to fast-changing social circumstances. While this approach could be appropriately applied to the development of small hotels and resorts in the pre-mass tourism era that ended in 2002, subsequent attempts made to develop mass tourism without a comprehensive and participatory planning approach have resulted in environmental, social, and economic problems. In a fast-growing city with many development pressures and an increasingly politicised community, the ability to govern in the future will depend on a more balanced concern for diverse community interests in the policymaking process. The government has acknowledged the need to change its attitude. In the 2007 Policy Address, the Chief Executive noted that 'as Macao is entering a new phase of development, the principle of sustainability must be implemented more effectively in all areas of public administration' (Macao SAR Government, 2007: 8).

A more balanced land use policymaking approach requires, first, diversifying the economy away from the casino industry to avoid one particular sector holding too much bargaining power. The government's attempt to move towards a more even-handed approach was clearly highlighted in the Chief Executive's policy addresses between 2007 and 2009 (Macao SAR Government, 2007, 2008b, 2009). For example, the 2007 Policy Address (Macao SAR Government, 2007:11) states:

> As we [the government] implement adequate diversification of the economy, it is important to determine how to review and manage the gaming industry's development. The Government's basic premise is that the gaming industry is an integral part of Macao tourism, and Macao is not developing as a mere gaming destination, and increasing gaming tax is certainly not the Government's only goal. The recent fervent development of the gaming industry is a transient phenomenon, during the early stage of an economic boom. When other sectors of our integrated tourism in turn mature, the paces of development of various industries will gradually synchronize. The Government will take even more effective and appropriate guiding and supporting measures to promote the joint development of gaming and other industries through favourable interactions.

The recent government decision to inject more resources into the meetings, incentive, convention, and exhibition (MICE) sector and the cession of Chinese land to Macao from neighbouring Hengqing Island to build a new university campus reflect the intention of both the Macao and Chinese governments to shift away from a gambling-centred economy and to strive for a more balanced approach to meet the social, economic and environmental interests of the society.

Second, sustainable balanced land use policymaking also requires planning and land rules that are clear and fair to all parties, avoiding the case-by-case planning approach of the past. A more transparent land sale system has to replace the private negotiation method. More political space needs to be given to the public to participate in the policymaking process because this will help enhance community acceptance and support for government plans and make it easier to achieve policy consensus. Genuine public consultations should give due consideration to the scope and representation of participants, the period allowed for public discussion, and the languages and techniques used in the process. Trilingual consultation documents in Chinese, English, and Portuguese would certainly help to encourage more research and discussion within the local community. The availability of university degree programmes and training courses in urban planning, geography, sustainable development, and resource and land management would produce more professionals and would help to build local skills and capacity. Drafting a statutory town planning ordinance which stipulates the planning procedures and when and how the public is to be involved in consultation would also improve the transparency of the policymaking process.

3

The Impact of Gaming Liberalisation on Public Opinion and Political Culture

Newman M. K. Lam

Before its reunification with China, Macao had a political culture[1] which emphasised social harmony and tolerance. Its population was characterised as politically inactive and was believed to be mostly either hostile or apathetic towards politics (Lin, 1998). Community views were expressed through traditional associations and direct criticism of the government was rare. As the evidence presented in this chapter shows, this political culture has been eroding, particularly after the social impact of the liberalisation of the gaming industry began to be felt. People's attitudes towards the government have changed and their belief in the benevolence of its actions has declined. The value of social harmony has been put to the test. Organised protests have become a more frequent occurrence. There has been more criticism of both the government and the gaming industry. Macao people have become less tolerant of the circumstances in which they find themselves and more willing to become involved in politics. A number of factors might have contributed to this change in political culture, including the resumption of Chinese sovereignty under the slogan 'Macao people governing Macao', a high-profile corruption case resulting in the conviction of the Secretary for Transport and Works, changes in the electoral system and the legislature and phenomenal economic growth in the wake of gaming liberalisation. This chapter focuses mainly on the effects of gaming liberalisation on the changing political culture. It consists of two parts. The first examines the effects of the gaming liberalisation on political culture through a review of the relevant literature and news reports. The second reports the results of a public opinion survey of people's beliefs, values, attitudes and sentiment.

A Changing Political Culture

Economic development in Macao has to be strategic because it is a small economy with limited resources (Ieong and Siu, 1997: 12–13) and lacks an adequate domestic market for consumption of products or sufficiency in resources to compete in many different sectors against rival economies. Macao's strategy has been to use the gaming industry as the bait to attract investment to other sectors (Lam, 2002). Gaming liberalisation was the most significant government intervention in the industry in the last few decades and it led to almost immediate and exceptionally rapid economic growth (see Chapter 2). This growth provided job opportunities and greatly increased tax revenue for the government. However, it also led to a substantial income gap, high inflation rates, and unaffordable property prices for average income-earners, as well as many other social problems (Cheng, 2009: 87–93; Lam, 2009). Growth also changed the face of the city, although not necessarily for the better (see Chapter 2). In the last few years, public protests, something unusual previously, have become a regular feature of the political scene and a means of expressing a wide range of grievances, from labour issues, to the rising cost of living, to corruption in government, to a lack of parking spaces (see Chapter 4 and Chapter 8). On May 1, 2007, a large-scale protest resulted in confrontation between police and protestors, ending with 21 police officers injured and damage to the equipment of 91 officers. Lo argues that these protests might be a sign of a legitimacy crisis (Lo, 2008: 65–73).

Macao people were once characterised as politically inactive. A substantial number of them[2] considered politics to be either dirty or dangerous (Lo, 1995: 55–58; Lin, 1998; Yee, 1998). Yee and Lo (2000) attribute these attitudes to the absence of a high-quality civil society and insufficient communication between the previous Portuguese colonial government and the people. Lam (2009) considers the government's over-emphasis on social harmony, especially placing the responsibility of maintaining social harmony on the people rather than on the government, as an important factor causing political apathy. Yee's research (1998) offers similar findings with statistics showing that more than half of the people believed in tolerating whatever they could and in obeying the government because they thought everything done by the government was for the good of the people. The increasing political activities of the public in the last few years, especially the protests, signify that this apathetic and trusting political culture is in the process of changing.

Positive public attitudes towards the government reached their peak shortly after the gaming liberalisation, with the Chief Executive receiving an average rating of 81.6 out of 100 in a popularity survey. By 2007, the rating had tumbled to 69.3. Similar declines were also observed in the satisfaction ratings on government performance, law enforcement, the democratic process and confidence in 'one country, two systems' (Lo, 2008: 75–81). What has caused the negative changes? Lo (2008: 93–104) shows that the liberalisation of the gaming industry had a great impact on the economy, the society and the political system in Macao. But economic growth, however desirable, does not necessarily go hand-in-hand with social stability and may create tensions instead (see Chapter 1). Indeed, after the gaming liberalisation, Macao had a widening income gap and economic interests were increasingly pitted against social concerns. Those who gained from the gaming liberalisation might have a better life but others might have the opposite experience. Li and Tsui (2009a) have observed that China has begun to side with the disadvantaged and started to limit the number of mainland tourists visiting Macao in 2007. They cautioned the government to take sustainability into consideration after examining the social, environmental and political side-effects of gaming liberalisation (Li and Tsui, 2009b).

In 2002 and 2003, the period when the gaming industry was being liberalised, public opinion, as shown in news reports, was generally favourable and optimistic with the financial sector expecting increasing foreign investment, the construction sector foreseeing revival, the retail sector preparing for an influx of tourists, and legislators praising the government for its initiative.[3] A survey conducted in 2004 by the *New Generation Magazine* indicated that about 70 percent of young people supported gaming liberalisation and only 15 percent were opposed, citing worries about social disorder, moral regression, a negative city image and over-dependence on one industry.[4] Despite the optimism for the future, there were obvious concerns about the potential rise in corruption and adverse effects on the younger generation.[5] The opposition of local gaming operators to foreign investment also began to surface with Stanley Ho attacking Wynn.[6]

As the side-effects of gaming liberalisation became apparent, optimism about the beneficial effects of foreign investment began to decline. The global financial crisis caused concern over whether foreign operators would withdraw their investments.[7] As some casinos began to lay off workers, the worries turned to unemployment and whether imported workers would be retained at the expense of local ones.[8] Criticisms of the gaming industry began to intensify with some influential local figures and local gaming operators blaming foreign investment for the economic difficulties and accusing the government of bringing in foreign investors without consulting local operators; claiming that the government did not monitor or restrain foreign operators sufficiently; alleging that foreign capitalists had used tricks to reduce workers' earnings; asserting that foreign investment had triggered adverse competition in the gaming industry; and arguing that foreign investment had altered Macao's political dynamics.[9] Concern was even expressed that foreign investors came to Macao not only for business but also with an agenda to interfere in local and mainland politics (Cheng, 2009: 164–172). There were repeated calls for responsible gaming management with the implication that foreign operators should be held more accountable for the social costs of their operations.[10]

What Do the Public Think?

A survey conducted by the University of Macau was used to collect data on public opinion in order to examine attitudes and beliefs towards the gaming industry, gaming liberalisation, the economic boom and foreign investment. The survey questionnaire also asked whether the respondents blamed the government or the gaming industry for Macao's recent problems. The following issues were covered: (1) did the public agree with gaming liberalisation? (2) what were the perceived effects of gaming liberalisation? (3) what was the perceived impact of the gaming industry? (4) what were the most important concerns of the respondents? (5) what was public opinion on foreign investment, especially that in the gaming industry? (6) who was considered responsible for Macao's recent problems? and (7) what were the perceived changes needed for the future? The questionnaire also collected demographic data from the respondents.

Methodology

The survey contained mostly close-ended questions. It was administered by telephone between April 17 and April 24, 2009. The target population were Chinese-speaking Macao residents aged 18 or above. The questions were asked only in the Chinese language (both Cantonese and Putonghua) due to resource limitations. Because of this limitation, English and Portuguese-speaking Macao residents were excluded and the sample may not be totally representative of the whole Macao population. In the case of households with more than one member, only the one with his or her birth date closest to the time of the survey was selected. There were 907 respondents. The survey results are accurate within 3.25 percent, 95 out of 100 times.

In the statistical analysis, only valid data (that is, excluding non-responses and responses such as "don't know", "can't say" and "no opinion") were used. Only results meeting the criteria of $p \leq 0.05$ were considered significant and reported. The statistical analysis was based on frequency distribution and tests of association. For tests of association between nominal variables, Cramer's V (denoted by V) indicates the strength of association. For tests of association between ordinal variables, the Gamma value (denoted by G) was used.

Opinions on Gaming Liberalisation

Among the 907 respondents, 760 answered a question on whether they agreed with the policy of liberalising the gaming industry. The statistics show that 83.2 percent of these respondents agreed with gaming liberalisation, while 16.8 percent disagreed.

Demographic Factors

The statistical analysis found a large number of significant associations involving these variables: gender, age, education and household income. These variables, together with the opinions on gaming liberalisation, are referred to as key variables in this study.

Gender

As shown in Table 3.1, more men agreed with liberalising the gaming industry than women.

Table 3.1: Association between Gender and Opinion of Gaming Liberalisation (in percentage)

Gender	Male	Female
Agree	87.9	77.3
Disagree	10.3	22.7

Source: Survey of Public Opinion (2009).
Note: 1. Cramer's V=.165; p<.001.

There are a number of ways to interpret this finding. First, the gender differences reflected in the opinions expressed can be attributed to economic factors, such as income. Among the survey respondents, women had lower income than men (V=.214; p<.001). For example, 63.9 percent of the women made MOP10,000 or less a month and 20.8 percent of them made MOP5,000 or less, compared with 48.8 percent and 8.9 percent respectively for men. In addition, more of the female respondents were clerks or workers, while more men were managers or professionals (Table 3.2).

Table 3.2: Association between Gender and Job Type (in percentage)

Gender	Male	Female
Self-employed	8.5	3.7
Managers/professionals	31.1	21.8
Clerks/workers	60.4	74.5

Source: Survey of Public Opinion (2009).
Note: 1. Cramer's V=.158; p<.001.

Second, the differences can be attributed to different social concerns. In comparison to the male respondents, more of the female respondents were in the age category of 36 to 50 years (V=.112; p=.024). Presumably, these women were more likely to be married and might be more concerned about the social costs of the gaming industry, such as the negative effects on the living environment and the wellbeing of their children. In regard to birthplace, slightly more of the female respondents were from the mainland than the men (female 56.1 percent, male 47.1 percent; V=.091; p=.023) and their length of residency in Macao was also shorter (Table 3.3). It is logical to assume that the longer people have lived with a situation, the more they will accept it.

Table 3.3: Association between Gender and Residency (in percentage)

Gender	Male	Female
1 to 5 Years	5.0	10.3
6 to 10 years	6.9	13.0
11 to 20 years	13.8	25.2
Over 20 Years	74.3	51.3

Source: Survey of Public Opinion (2009).
Note: 1. Cramer's V=.231; p<.001.

Furthermore, the female respondents knew less about gaming liberalisation than the men (Table 3.4). The survey questionnaire had three questions about gaming liberalisation which were intended to test the respondents' knowledge of the industry. Those questions asked: (1) when did gaming liberalisation occur? (2) how many gaming licences were issued initially? and (3) how many licences existed at the time of the survey?

Table 3.4: Association between Gender and Knowledge of Gaming Liberalisation (in percentage)

Gender	Male	Female
Got none right	27.6	46.3
Got one answer right	23.7	27.4
Got two answers right	32.9	20.7
Got all answers right	15.9	5.6

Source: Survey of Public Opinion (2009).
Note: 1. Cramer's V=.252; p<.001.

Although education level had a positive ordinal association with knowledge of gaming liberalisation (G=.185; p<.001), there was no significant association between gender and education. The female respondents were not less educated than the men. Their relative lack of knowledge about gaming liberalisation can be attributed to the fact that 23.3 percent of the female respondents moved to Macao only in the last ten years (Table 3.3) and many would not have been in Macao when gaming liberalisation began.

Household Income

There was no significant association between personal income and opinion of gaming liberalisation. However, a weak but significant association was observed when family income was used for analysis (Table 3.5).

Table 3.5: Association between Family Income and Opinion of Gaming Liberalisation (in percentage)

Monthly Income (MOP)	5000 or Under	5001–10000	10001–15000	15001–20000	20001–30000	Over 30000
Disagree	23.9	17.8	14.4	16.0	14.1	7.1
Agree	76.1	82.2	85.6	84.0	85.9	92.9

Source: Survey of Public Opinion (2009).
Note: 1. Gamma=.197; p<.01

The result indicates that members of poor families were more likely to disagree with gaming liberalisation. It also shows that family income may be a better indication of financial wellbeing than personal income since Macao still has many traditional families in which people live with their parents and share their financial burdens collectively.

Personal income and occupation are obviously related and indeed a moderate association was observed between them (V=.305; p<.001). However, there was no observed significant association between types of occupation (for example, managers and clerks) and support for gaming liberalisation. This suggests that it was family financial condition rather than occupation that shaped people's opinions on gaming liberalisation.

Education

Education has always been considered the way out of poverty in Macao. There are strong associations between education and family income ($G=.491$; $p<.001$) as well as personal income ($G=.502$; $p<.001$). College graduates were also more likely (59 percent) to be managers or professionals ($V=.306$; $p<.001$). The educated were younger ($G=-.510$; $p<.001$), probably because Macao's efforts to improve higher education only began in the 1990s. The educated were also more often Macao-born ($V=.147$; $p<.001$) and more of them agreed with gaming liberalisation (Table 3.6). It is not unusual to see those doing well in a society advocating the maintenance of the status quo.

Table 3.6: Association between Education and Opinion of Gaming Liberalisation (in percentage)

Education	None	Elementary	Secondary	Junior Secondary	Senior College
Disagree	22.2	26.3	19.0	13.6	10.9
Agree	77.8	73.7	81.0	86.4	89.1

Source: Survey of Public Opinion (2009).
Note: 1. Cramer's $V=.131$, $p=.012$; Gamma=.249, p=.001

Age

Initially, the older generation appeared to support gaming liberalisation more than the younger generation. However, upon closer examination, this finding was due mainly to the substantial level of opposition to the gaming industry from those under 21 years of age.[11] After excluding this group (that is, counting only those above 20), a significant negative ordinal association was observed ($G=-.183$; $p=.036$). If all those above 35 years of age were grouped together, a stronger association was found ($G=-.249$; $p=.018$). As indicated in Table 3.7, those between 21 and 30 years of age were more often supporters of gaming liberalisation. This is consistent with the previous findings that the younger generation is better educated and that the educated are more supportive of gaming liberalisation. Indeed, strong negative ordinal associations were observed between age and education ($G=-.510$; $p<.001$), personal income ($G=-.265$; $p<.001$) as well as family income ($G=-.356$; $p<.001$). Furthermore, a disproportionally high number of managers and professionals in the sample (40.2 percent) were between the ages of 21 and 35 ($V=.230$; $p<.001$). Hence, younger people are more likely to be professionals and higher income-earners. However, gaming liberalisation had the weakest support from those aged 20 or under, creating an unclear ordinal association as a whole.

Table 3.7: Association between Age and Opinion of Gaming Liberalisation (in percentage)

Age	18–20	21–25	26–30	31–35	Over 35
Disagree	25.2	9.3	11.8	14.6	17.2
Agree	74.8	90.7	88.2	85.4	82.8

Source: Survey of Public Opinion (2009).
Note: 1. Cramer's V=.123, p=.021

Perceived Effects of Gaming Liberalisation

Differences in opinion can be caused by the different perceived effects of gaming liberalisation. As shown in Table 3.8, 73.7 percent of the respondents said that Macao society was overall better off after gaming liberalisation (59.6 percent slightly better; 14.1 percent much better) while 18.6 percent disagreed (13.5 percent slightly worse; 5.1 percent much worse). A small number (7.8 percent) said that the situation was the same as before.

The positive effects appear to be in economic conditions (83.6 percent), the quality of life (72.7 percent) and, less so, the living environment (59.8 percent). On the negative side, the natural environment (70.3 percent) and social harmony (56.9 percent) were considered to have deteriorated. Government performance was considered to have improved (69.3 percent). Cultural protection was also, surprisingly, considered to have been enhanced (71 percent). This contradicts a generally held belief that the new casino skyscrapers and hotels have severely damaged Macao's small town image and blocked the views to heritage sites. A plausible explanation of the contradiction is that lucrative tax revenue from the gaming industry has allowed the government to spend more on cultural activities and on advertising Macao's cultural heritage. The perceived improvement in cultural protection might be attributed to government efforts rather than a consequence of the gaming industry.

Table 3.8: Perceived Conditions after Gaming Liberalisation (in percentage)

	Much Worse	Worse	Better	Much Better	Valid Number
Economic Conditions	4.3	12.2	53.9	29.7	839
Living Environment	9.9	30.2	52.6	7.2	473
Natural Environment	20.9	49.4	26.6	3.2	719
Social Harmony	9.6	47.3	37.5	5.6	736
Quality of Life	3.7	23.6	65.6	7.1	649
Cultural Protection	5.3	23.7	60.7	10.3	692
Government Performance	8.2	22.5	61.7	7.6	681
Overall Social Condition	5.1	13.5	59.6	14.1	846

Source: Survey of Public Opinion (2009).

Table 3.9 shows the associations between a set of key variables (support gaming liberalisation or not; family income; education; age and gender) and the variables on economic and social conditions. As indicated by the reported Gamma values under 'Support Liberalisation', there are strong ordinal associations between support for gaming liberalisation and perceived improvements in economic conditions, living environment, social harmony, quality of life, government performance, and overall social conditions. However, those with lower family income were more likely to consider social harmony, natural environment, cultural heritage and government performance to have deteriorated, although they believed that economic conditions and the quality of life had improved. Those with higher education were more likely to consider social harmony, natural environment, cultural heritage protection, and government performance to have become worse although they also believed that economic conditions had become better. Older people and the male gender were more likely to consider socio-economic conditions improved after gaming liberalisation. Women were more likely to consider cultural heritage protection to have improved.

Table 3.9: Association between Perceived Conditions and Key Variables

	Support Liberalisation	Family Income	Education	Age	Gender
Economic Conditions	.563**	.176**	.182**	–	.153(M)**
Living Environment	.472**	–	–	–	.141(M)*
Social Harmony	.388**	-.096*	-.207**	.246**	–
Quality of Life	.518**	.142*	–	–	.113(M)*
Natural Environment	–	-.267**	-.342**	.367**	–
Heritage Protection	–	-.117*	-.227**	.220**	.109(F)*
Government Performance	.398**	-.153**	-.187**	.234**	–
Overall Social Conditions	.553**	–	–	.094*	.111(M)*

Source: Survey of Public Opinion (2009).
Notes: 1. Gamma value is used for all cases, except for gender, in which case Cramer's V is used.
    2. (M) denotes more male respondents considering the condition better
      (F) denotes more female respondents considering the condition better.
    3. * denotes $.05 \geq p > .01$; ** denotes $.01 \geq p$.

These findings show that those with higher family income and higher education had more concerns after gaming liberalisation. However, as earlier analysis has shown, those with a high level of family income or a high level of education were supporters of gaming liberalisation. The findings, therefore, are contradictory. Perhaps, the economic benefits of gaming liberalisation overrode social concerns. In order to gain a better understanding of this issue, people's views on the gaming industry were further examined.

Table 3.10 shows that the majority of the survey respondents believed that Macao's development should rely on the gaming industry but that gambling should not be encouraged. This is a clear indication of a psychological dilemma between moral ends and economic survival. Although most believed the gaming industry had provided high-paid jobs, they did not consider those jobs ideal. A majority attributed social problems to the gaming industry and did not believe the benefits from the industry exceeded the social costs. The results suggest that the gaming industry is seen as a mixed blessing and it is therefore not surprising that an overwhelming majority of the respondents (93.7 percent) would like Macao to diversify into other industries and rely less on the gaming industry.

Table 3.10: Views on the Gaming Industry (in percentage)

	Strongly Disagree	Disagree	Agree	Strongly Agree	Valid Number
Development always relies on gaming	1.9	16.8	67.3	14.0	856
Gambling shouldn't be encouraged	0.9	5.7	55.9	37.4	876
Gaming is a major source of social problems	0.1	18.4	70.7	10.7	841
Gaming offers high-paid jobs	0.5	19.8	74.4	5.4	835
Gaming jobs are not ideal	1.1	18.7	65.8	11.7	812
Gaming benefits exceed social costs	5.6	51.8	41.2	1.4	770
Diversify, rely less on gaming	0.5	5.9	64.7	29.0	863

Source: Survey of Public Opinion (2009).

It is evident that there are differences in opinion on the effects and desirability of the gaming industry when such variables as support for liberalisation, income, education, age and gender are taken into account (Table 3.11). Those supporting gaming liberalisation held the strong belief that Macao had to rely on the gaming industry and that the benefits from the industry exceeded the costs, although they also recognised that the jobs offered by the industry, despite the higher pay, were not ideal. Those with higher education or higher family income were more likely to consider the benefits insufficient to justify the costs. They were also more likely to support diversifying the economy and relying less on the gaming industry. Women were also more likely to favour economic diversification. Older respondents seemed to be the most positive about the gaming industry.

The findings from Table 3.11, although supporting the view that Macao people generally see large and essential benefits from the gaming industry, hence tolerating its costs, do not support the argument that the educated and the high income-earners (most of whom were professionals) also held this view. The educated did not consider the benefits from the gaming industry enough to compensate the costs. However,

Table 3.11: Association between Views on Gaming Industry and Key Variables

Views on Gaming Industry	Support Liberalisation	Family Income	Education	Age	Gender
Always relied on	.338**	.127*	–	.135**	.103(M)*
Not to be encouraged	–	–	–	–	–
Caused social problems	–	–	-.111*	–	–
High-paid jobs	.392**	–	–	.121*	–
Jobs are not ideal	-.201*	–	–	–	–
Benefits exceed costs	.372**	-.123*	-.319**	.460**	.125(M)**
Diversify, rely less on gaming	–	.125**	.203**	-.168**	.107(F)*

Source: Survey of Public Opinion (2009).
Notes: 1. Gamma value is used for all cases, except for gender, in which case Cramer's V is used.
   2. (M) denotes more male respondents considering the condition better
   (F) denotes more female respondents considering the condition better.
   3. * denotes $.05 \geq p > .01$; ** denotes $.01 \geq p$.

later statistical evidence (Table 3.15) shows that the better educated were less likely to blame foreign investment, an important element in the gaming liberalisation, for harming Macao's traditional culture, relaxing lifestyle or social harmony. Perhaps their concerns with the gaming industry were historically determined in the sense that they had concerns about the gaming industry even before liberalisation. They might even have considered gaming liberalisation a move in the right direction to solve some of the problems which the industry had experienced in the past. For example, Table 3.15 shows that the educated considered foreign investment to have brought in a better business culture.

Views on the Gaming Boom

Gaming liberalisation has led to an unprecedented boom for the industry. As shown in Table 3.12, Macao people seem to believe that their lives have become better as a result of it (74.4 percent). However, when the question was phrased in the opposite way, more of the respondents (45.6 percent) said that life had become harder for Macao people. This is perhaps an indication of the psychological tendency of answering positively rather than negatively. Nevertheless, the results do provide further evidence showing that Macao people see the gaming industry as a mixed blessing. The majority of the respondents indicated that rapid economic growth had created unaffordable property prices (88.7 percent), made it harder for small and medium enterprises (SMEs) to survive (69.6 percent), made corruption more serious (70.4 percent), complicated Macao's political situation (71.5 percent), harmed Macao's relaxing lifestyle and traditional culture (59.8 percent) and adversely affected social harmony (54.5 percent).

Table 3.12: Views on the Effects of the Booming Gaming Industry (in percentage)

	Strongly Disagree	Disagree	Agree	Strongly Agree	Valid Number
Makes life better	1.3	24.2	67.8	6.6	821
Makes life harder	2.1	52.3	40.1	5.5	805
Creates unaffordable property prices	0.7	10.6	56.0	32.7	877
Harder for SMEs to survive	1.0	29.3	56.6	13.0	805
Harms the relaxing lifestyle and tradition	1.7	38.5	48.7	11.1	826
Harms social harmony	1.0	44.6	47.8	6.7	823
Makes corruption more serious	0.9	28.7	51.3	19.1	755
Complicates the political situation	1.4	27.1	61.5	10.0	787

Source: Survey of Public Opinion (2009).

Those supporting gaming liberalisation, as shown in Table 3.13, more often saw only benefits and no problems with rapid development. Those with high family income were more likely to blame the gaming boom for high property prices. The less educated, the younger generation and low-income families were more likely to link corruption to the gaming industry. The findings show that the educated and high-income families did not blame the gaming industry for socio-economic problems any more than other people. One group, the women, appear to blame the gaming boom for all kinds of problems but, surprisingly, not for high property prices.

Table 3.13: Association between Views on the Gaming Boom and Key Variables

Effect of Gaming Boom	Support Liberalisation	Family Income	Education	Age	Gender
Makes life better	.561**	–	–	–	.126(M)*
Makes life harder	-.442**	–	–	–	.106(F)*
Unaffordable property prices	–	.117*	–	–	–
Harder for SMEs	–	–	–	–	.122(F)**
Harms the relaxing lifestyle	-.378**	–	–	–	.114(F)*
Harms social harmony	-.537**	–	–	–	.126(F)**
Makes corruption more serious	-.261**	-.123*	-.108*	-.125**	.109(F)*
Complicates the political situation	-.373**	–	–	-.195**	.105(F)*

Source: Survey of Public Opinion (2009).

Notes: 1. Gamma value is used for all cases, except for gender, in which case Cramer's V is used.

2. (M) denotes more male respondents considering the condition better

   (F) denotes more female respondents considering the condition better.

3. * denotes $.05 \geq p > .01$; ** denotes $.01 \geq p$.

Views on Foreign Investment

An important aspect of gaming liberalisation is that it brought in foreign investment. As shown in Table 3.14, the majority of the respondents considered foreign investment a major source of Macao's economic problems (59.3 percent) but also considered foreign investment to have helped the diversification of the economy (85 percent). A majority of the respondents disagreed with the notion that foreign investment had harmed Macao's traditional culture (58.3 percent) or its relaxing lifestyle (53 percent). However, Table 3.12 shows that the majority did blame the gaming boom for harming Macao's relaxing lifestyle and tradition. If they were not blaming the foreign operators, then they might have held local operators or the government responsible. The major gaming establishments built by foreign investors have classical European designs (for example, the Venetian and MGM) and are consistent with Macao's European heritage. Furthermore, these establishments cater to high-end customers and emphasise luxurious and relaxing tourism. It is therefore not surprising that blame in this regard was not attributed to foreign investors.

Furthermore, 63.7 percent of 814 respondents did not consider foreign investment to have harmed Macao's social harmony. However, an overwhelming majority (97.8 percent) indicated that foreign investors should contribute more to Macao society by becoming more involved in social affairs and providing more social services. On the positive side, a majority also credited foreign investment with making Macao a more colourful city and for improving Macao's business management culture. A noteworthy finding is that 56.2 percent of 739 respondents indicated that foreign investment had been used as a scapegoat of Macao's social problems. In addition, 41.8 percent of 787 respondents believed that foreign investors should have their own advocates in Macao's Legislative Assembly (Legco).

Table 3.14: Views on Foreign Investment (in percentage)

	Strongly Disagree	Disagree	Agree	Strongly Agree	Valid Number
A major source of economic problems	1.4	39.3	54.2	5.1	782
Helped to diversify Macao economy	1.0	13.9	77.9	7.1	868
Harmed traditional culture	0.7	57.6	38.1	3.5	805
Harmed relaxing lifestyle	1.0	52.0	42.0	5.1	831
Harmed social harmony	2.3	61.4	33.3	2.9	814
Should contribute more to society	0.2	2.0	72.7	25.1	871
Improved business management culture	0.5	14.7	78.6	6.2	794
Made Macao a colourful city	0.2	11.5	77.8	10.5	863
Used as a scapegoat for social problems	1.8	42.1	53.6	2.6	739
Should have advocates in Legco		58.2	41.8		787

Source: Survey of Public Opinion (2009).

As shown in Table 3.15, those supporting gaming liberalisation saw only benefits from it and had no problems with foreign investment. This is consistent with the previous findings on opinions about rapid development. However, they were not inclined to support foreign investors having their own advocates in the Legislative Assembly. It seems that those supporting gaming liberalisation valued only the financial benefits of foreign investment and did not want to see gaming interests involved in politics. However, the older generation was more likely to hold the opposite view. The educated were also less inclined to see problems with foreign investment. Poor families and males were more inclined to expect foreign investors to contribute more to the society. Those who blamed foreign investment for Macao's problems were more likely to be young, less educated and from low-income families.

Table 3.15: Association between Views on Foreign Investment and Key Variables

Views on Foreign Investment	Support Liberalisation	Family Income	Education	Age	Gender
Source of economic problems	–	–	-.208**	–	–
Helped diversification	-.454**	–	–	–	–
Harmed traditional culture	-.388**	-.135**	-.243**	–	–
Harmed relaxing lifestyle	-.481**	–	-.117*	–	.101(F)*
Harmed social harmony	-.541**	–	-.251**	.107*	.113(F)*
Should give more to society	–	-.129*	–	–	.134(M)*
Better business culture	–	.193**	.214**	-.155*	.109(M)*
Made Macao colourful	.399**	–	–	–	–
Used as a scapegoat	.299*	–	–	–	–
Should allow Legco advocates	-.240*	–	–	.138**	–

Source: Survey of Public Opinion (2009).
Notes: 1. Gamma value is used for all cases, except for gender, in which case Cramer's V is used.
    2. (M) denotes more male respondents considering the condition better
      (F) denotes more female respondents considering the condition better.
    3. * denotes $.05 \geq p > .01$; ** denotes $.01 \geq p$.

Who Is to Blame?

This analysis suggests that a certain level of blame for Macao's various problems has been attributed to the gaming industry, gaming liberalisation, the gaming boom, and foreign investment. Who else was blamed? As shown in Table 3.16, the Macao government was considered by the majority as the most responsible for Macao's social problems (64.6 percent), followed by foreign investment (13.4 percent), local gaming operators (6.8 percent) and then mainland tourists (4.3 percent).

Table 3.16: Responsibility for Social Problems (in percentage)

	Valid Responses
Macao government	64.6
Foreign investment	13.4
Local gaming operators	6.8
Mainland tourists	4.3
None of the above	10.8

Source: Survey of Public Opinion (2009).
Note: 1. Valid number = 760.

Regarding Macao's high property prices, the respondents considered that the government was to blame (39.6 percent) although an equally large number of respondents (38.4 percent) blamed high prices on mainland and Hong Kong investors. Foreign gaming investment (9.1 percent) and local investors (8.2 percent) were blamed to a much lesser extent.

Table 3.17: Responsibility for High Property Prices (in percentage)

Responsible for High Property Prices	Valid Responses
Government housing policy	39.6
Mainland and Hong Kong investors	38.4
Foreign gaming investment	9.1
Macao's own investment	8.2
None of the above	4.8

Source: Survey of Public Opinion (2009).
Note: 1. Valid number = 821

These results indicate that Macao people are not putting the greatest blame on foreign investment for their problems. It is, therefore, not surprising that reducing foreign gaming investment was supported by only 7.8 percent. A large majority (73.4 percent) preferred to maintain the status quo but to increase control and monitor foreign investment. About 10 percent preferred a higher level of foreign investment with 8.4 percent finding no problem with the present level of foreign investment and concluding therefore that no change was needed.

Table 3.18: Policy Preference for Foreign Gaming Investment (in percentage)

	Valid Responses
Maintain status quo, more control and monitoring	73.4
Attract more foreign gaming investment	10.5
No problem, don't change	8.4
Reduce foreign gaming investment	7.8

Source: Survey of Public Opinion (2009).
Note: 1. Valid number = 837.

Conclusion

The research findings presented in this chapter show that the political culture in Macao has been changing since the liberalisation of the gaming industry. The social effects of gaming liberalisation have been identified as one of the causes for the change. The survey results show that Macao people see the gaming industry and foreign investment as a mixed blessing. Slightly more than half of the respondents did not consider the benefits from the industry sufficient to outweigh the social costs. However, a large majority supported gaming liberalisation. Therefore, people's concerns about the gaming industry may precede gaming liberalisation rather than be caused by it. This is particularly the case for the better educated and the high-income families, who are most likely to be managers and professionals. These groups tend to see foreign investment as very positive.

Those who supported gaming liberalisation tended to see only the good sides of foreign investment and the industry. Women, young people, and those from poorer families tended to attribute more blame to the gaming industry and foreign investment for Macao's recent problems. However, the government was consistently identified by the respondents as the major source of their problems. Blame attributed to foreign investment tended to be more directly linked to economic problems. In spite of the attacks in the media on foreign investment, the majority of the respondents did not believe that it had harmed Macao's culture, social harmony or relaxing lifestyle. Those who supported gaming liberalisation tended to believe that foreign investment had been used as a scapegoat for Macao's problems. Although 41.8 percent of the respondents supported foreign investors having their advocates in the legislature, these respondents were surprisingly less likely to be those supporting gaming liberalisation. Reducing foreign investment was not an option preferred by most of the respondents. Some wanted to increase foreign investment but an overwhelming majority supported maintaining the status quo with increased control and monitoring of foreign investment.

Overall, the evidence suggests that public support for gaming liberalisation has not waned in spite of the impact that it has had on Macao society. Most people do not blame foreign investment for Macao's problems. The government is the focus of their grievances. Its lack of success in dealing with social problems, which may have their source in the gaming industry, seems to have caused discontent. There has been a change in Macao's political culture as a consequence. People have become more demanding, more participative and less willing to accept that the government is always right. If Macao's new Chief Executive does not adequately handle these problems in the near future, a legitimacy crisis may be imminent.

Part II

Governance

Executive-Legislative Relationships and the Development of Public Policy

Eilo Yu Wing Yat

The political system of the Macao Special Administrative Region retains the colonial practice of executive domination over other governmental institutions. This role is formally recognised in the Basic Law, which concentrates administrative and legislative power in the hands of the Chief Executive, and reflects the assumption of its drafters that the government will be 'executive-led' (Luo, 2005: 883). As the head of the Special Administrative Region, the Chief Executive has, among many other powers, wide-ranging and largely unconstrained authority to decide government policies, to issue administrative regulations, to nominate Principal Officials, to appoint and remove judges and some members of the Legislative Assembly, to approve motions on revenue and expenditure, to return bills to the Legislative Assembly for further consideration, to order officials to testify or to give evidence before the Legislative Assembly, to confer medals and honours, to pardon persons convicted of criminal offences, and to handle petitions and complaints (Basic Law: Article 50). Although the legislature has the responsibility for passing bills, the Chief Executive remains dominant in the law-making process because almost all bills are proposed by the administration and because legislators are restricted by the conditions under which they can introduce private members' bills. If it so wished, the Macao government could use its powers to govern with only minimal involvement of the legislature. The Chief Executive could employ his considerable powers to make law by decree and to appoint legislators, thereby reducing the legislature to little more than a rubber stamp. Constitutionally, the Legislative Assembly is a 'minimal legislature' (Olson and Mezey, 1991: 1–2; also see Mezey, 1985) that has little influence on the government and plays only a nominal role in policymaking. It has very limited powers to hold the executive branch accountable and its members are marginal players in the decision-making process.

Despite its formidable powers, the executive has found itself challenged in an increasingly difficult political situation that has affected its ability to exercise its full constitutional rights. Changing socio-economic circumstances have generated many social problems and the government has not always coped effectively with growing public demands for resolution of those problems. There is increasing pressure for greater accountability of the government to the people. Legislators have demanded that officials be answerable and responsible for policy failures and have aimed to expand their influence on policy formulation. Economic development has triggered political dynamics that have led to a reconfiguration of the relationships between the executive and legislative branches.

This chapter focuses on the ways in which legislators have tried to increase executive accountability while extending their own policymaking powers. It is divided into three parts, covering the evolution of the legislature, the present powers and authority of the Legislative Assembly, and the dynamics of the transformation of executive-legislative relationships in their socio-economic context. A case study on the development of labour policy is presented to illustrate the nature of the transformation.

The Evolution of the Legislative Assembly

The Legislative Assembly was established in 1976 when the Portuguese government promulgated the Organic Statute of Macao.[1] Its membership was (and still is) composed of directly and indirectly elected members and the appointees of the Governor and, after 1999, the Chief Executive. Portuguese and Macanese elites dominated the first legislature and local Chinese were in the minority. Chinese residents were only permitted to participate in elections if they could claim five years of residency in Macao (Lo, 1996: 32); there was no such restriction on Portuguese and Macanese living in Macao or Hong Kong. To balance the representation of ethnic groups in the Assembly, successive Governors appointed four leaders of the local Chinese community to the legislature.

Macanese elites dominated the legislature in the early 1980s, eventually clashing with the Governor over the powers of the Assembly. The chairman of the legislature, Carlos d'Assumpção, and three Macanese members put forward a proposal to amend the Organic Statute to enlarge the authority of the legislature and to allow it to pass votes of no confidence in the government (Lo, 1996: 32). This proposal was rejected by Governor Egidio as well as by the Portuguese and the Chinese governments because it was seen as jeopardising the principle of executive-led government. A new Governor, Costa, decided to dissolve the legislature and, at the same time, bring in electoral reforms that would enlarge the franchise by allowing Chinese with three years of residence to register to vote. Costa's aim was to dilute the power of the Macanese in the Legislative Assembly by expanding the participation of local Chinese through direct and indirect elections and he was successful in meeting this objective. After the 1984 elections, the Macanese were no longer the dominant group in the legislature.

The extension of Chinese participation led to an increase in the size of the legislature. Victor Ng Wing Lok and Alexandre Ho Si Him, who entered the Assembly after the 1984 elections, petitioned for changes and were able to secure the agreement of the Portuguese government to enlarge the membership to help achieve the goal of 'Macao people ruling Macao' after 1999 (Lo, 1996: 34; see also Yee, 1999: 29–30). In 1990, the Portuguese government amended the Organic Statute of Macao and increased the number of Legislative Assembly members from 17 to 23, with two members added for both the directly and indirectly elected seats and two more appointments made by the Governor (see Table 4.1).

Table 4.1: Composition of the Legislative Assembly

	Directly Elected Seats	Indirectly Elected Seats	Appointed Members	Total
1976–1991	6	6	5	17
1991–2001	8	8	7	23
2001–2005	10	10	7	27
2005 onwards	12	10	7	29

Sources: Yee (1996: 30) and the MSAR government's 2005 Legislative Assembly election website. Available from: http://www.e2005.gov.mo/cn/default.asp [Accessed October 17, 2005].

The Basic Law which was promulgated in 1993 provided for the democratisation of the Legislative Assembly by gradually increasing the number of elected members after the handover. There were to be two extra seats in each of the direct and indirect elections in 2001 and another two additional directly elected seats in 2005, which would bring the total membership of the legislature to 29. However, the Basic Law does not stipulate any further democratisation of the legislature after 2005. Neither does it confirm that the Assembly's size will increase further or that the eventual goal is to elect the legislature by universal suffrage.

Constitutional Constraints on the Powers of the Legislature

According to the Basic Law, the Legislative Assembly is responsible for passing legislation, examining and approving the government budget, holding discussions on matters of public interest, and impeaching a Chief Executive who breaches the laws and is derelict in his duty (Basic Law: Article 71). Although the Assembly is authorised to pass legislation, its discretionary power is limited. It can pass bills proposed by the government but legislators are not permitted to propose private bills relating to elections to the legislature, public finance, the operations of the government, or the political structure of the Special Administrative Region (Basic Law: Article 75). Article 75 of the Basic Law does permit legislators to propose private bills that do not relate to these matters but such bills require the written consent of the Chief Executive for their introduction in the legislature. The Legislative Assembly's standing orders further reinforce this provision by preventing members from submitting private bills on the matters prohibited in Article 75 (Standing Orders: Article 103). There must be absolute majority support in the legislature for approval of private bills whereas only a simple majority is required for the passage of a government bill. Legislators do have the power to propose amendments to government bills but, for the most part, they simply discuss and pass legislation proposed by the executive branch; members do not play a proactive role in proposing new legislation.

The Legislative Assembly has been marginalised in the legislative process because of the 'bi-rail' system of legislation, which allows both the executive and legislative branches to make laws. During the colonial era, the Governor could issue a decree in any area in which the Legislative Assembly did not pass legislation. Constitutionally, decree law was equivalent to any law passed by the legislature. As a result, most legislation was made by the Governor rather than the Assembly. After the handover, the government continued the practice in which the Chief Executive issued administrative regulations in the form of decree law. This avoided the inconvenience of submitting bills to the Assembly, reducing it to a forum for debate.

Table 4.2: Number of Laws and Decree Laws, 2000–2009

Year	Number of laws passed by the Legislative Assembly	Number of decree laws issued by the Chief Executive
2000	13	41
2001	18	35
2002	10	36
2003	13	41
2004	14	42
2005	9	25
2006	10	19
2007	7	22
2008	16	26
2009	24	37

Source: Government Printing Bureau, Macao Special Administrative Region Government. Available from: http://en.io.gov.mo/Search/default.aspx [Accessed June 15, 2010].

The marginalisation of the Legislative Assembly can be illustrated in the critical case of the issuing of gaming concessions. The legislature passed a gaming law for the regulation of casino operations in 2001, specifying that three gaming concessions would be granted by the government (Law 16/2001: Article 7). However, the government then issued administrative regulations that allowed each concessionaire to sub-contract the right to operate casinos to another group. The reason lay in internal disagreements between the Galaxy Group and the Ka Wah Group, which had been jointly awarded one of the concessions. After winning the concession, the Galaxy Group, which itself was in collaboration with the Venetian Group, and the Ka Wah Group disagreed over the business strategy that they should adopt in Macao. In order to accelerate the Galaxy Group's casino project, the government allowed the divorce of the Venetian and the Ka Wah Group and approved a sub-concession to the Venetian, which was permitted to manage its gaming business independently (Fok, 2004). Similarly, the other two concessionaires, Wynn Macau and Sociedade de Jogos de Macau (SJM), demanded that the government allow them to sub-contract their concession rights to other groups. Their intention was to 'sell' the right to operate casinos in order to finance their own projects (Wang, 2009: 9–10). To avoid what promised to be a lengthy dispute, the government allowed both of the other concessionaires to sub-contract the right to operate casinos. As a consequence, six companies were authorised to operate casinos.

The legislature did not hold a formal session to discuss the gaming franchise extension and did not vote on it. Susanna Chou, who served as the President of the Legislative Assembly in the decade after the handover, was critical of the government's unwillingness to bring the issue before the legislature (*Jornal Cheng Pou*, November 23, 2007). Other legislators pointed out that the government would not benefit from the gaming franchise extension because the new concessionaires did not have to pay for their right to operate casinos. The Secretary for Economy and Finance, Francis Tam Pak Yuen, argued to the contrary that the process of granting the sub-concessions not only corresponded to existing laws and procedures but that government income from the gaming tax would not decrease because of the franchise extension (*Jornal Cheng Pou*, November 23, 2007). There was nonetheless still considerable dissatisfaction among legislators. Kou Hoi In, for example, noted that this was an important change in gaming policy but that the government had not explained it to the legislature and had failed to address public concerns (*Jornal Cheng Pou*, November 23, 2007). The executive branch, in effect, dealt with the concessionaires unilaterally, issuing decree laws to regulate casino operation and allowing the sub-contracting of the gaming concessions without involving the legislature. For example, the Chief Executive signed a decree law to allow casinos to introduce a system for junket operators which enabled casinos to recruit agencies to promote high-roller gambling in their betting rooms (Decree Law No. 06/2002). The executive branch's principal aim was to bring the casinos on-stream as quickly as possible and its perception was that the legislature could potentially delay that process.

Nevertheless, the executive branch did submit a bill to the legislature to allow casinos to give loans to gamblers, a measure which had been requested by the casino operators. The government was required to go to the legislature because, under the criminal law, gaming credit offered by casinos was regarded as usury and casinos could not legally collect debt from gamblers (*Macao Daily News*, July 10, 2003). The government, therefore, proposed a law regulating credits to gaming in casinos to the Legislative Assembly which was approved in 2004 (Law No. 5/2004). In this case, the government recognised the convention that decree law could not be used to amend or to replace laws which had been approved by the Legislative Assembly; amendments to legislation had to be passed by the legislature.

The constitutional status of decree law has been challenged in court. In 2005, an expatriate disputed the legality of decree law 17/2004, 'Regulation of Debarment from Illegal Work'. The immigration office had attempted to deport the expatriate because he did not have a valid work visa in accordance with the decree law. The complainant argued that the office did not have the authority to prevent him from working in the territory because the decree law issued by the Chief Executive was unconstitutional (*Jornal Va Kio*, May 13, 2006). First, it was argued, the Legislative Assembly was responsible for legislation and no other body in the territory could make law without its approval. Second, although the Chief Executive could issue administrative regulations according to the Basic Law (Article 50), these were not equivalent to the decree laws issued by the Governor during the colonial era. In the lower courts, the Courts of First Instance and Second Instance agreed with the complainant and ruled that decree law was not equivalent to laws made in the legislature. However, the Court of Final Appeal overrode the decisions of the lower courts when the Macao government appealed the decision. The Court concluded that the Chief Executive could share legislative power with the Legislative Assembly because the Basic Law placed no restriction on the use of administrative regulations by the Chief Executive and because the Chief Executive could veto bills passed by the Legislative Assembly and therefore did not need the approval of the Assembly to issue administrative regulations (*Macao Daily News*, July 19, 2007; also see Cheang, 2006). The Court of Final Appeal noted that in countries such as Portugal and France, the constitution allows the head of government to issue administrative regulations in areas for which the legislature is not specifically responsible. In mainland China, the State Council can also issue administrative regulations, which are regarded as the equivalent of law and can legally restrain individual behaviour.

The Court of Final Appeal's judgment did not end the dispute. Wang Yu, a law professor at the Macau University of Science and Technology, argued that the Basic Law clearly defined the Legislative Assembly as a unique body for legislation and that administrative regulation did not enjoy the same legal status as decree law during the colonial period (Wang, 2006a: C12). In addition, he argued that administrative regulation by the State Council was a supplement to law in mainland China. The aim of administrative regulation, he asserted, was the implementation of law, the enforcement of the constitution, and the fulfilment of duties delegated by the National People's Congress. Xu Chong De, who was a member of the Macao Basic Law Drafting Committee and was regarded as an authority on Basic Law, acknowledged the legal issues arising from administrative regulations and observed that the legal status of administrative regulation had been overlooked during the drafting of the Basic Law (*Macao Daily News*, December 20, 2006). His view was that a remedy might be to enact legislation further defining the Chief Executive's power to use administrative regulations.

The government eventually agreed to narrow the scope of administrative regulation through legislation. In November 2008, it submitted a bill to the Legislative Assembly that defined 19 types of legislation to be approved by the legislature. The Chief Executive was restricted to issuing decree law for the implementation of government policy and the management of government administration (Law 13/2009, 'Legal Framework for Legislation'). The bill, which consolidates the legislative authority of the Assembly and, to some extent, strengthens its role in policymaking, was passed on July 14, 2009. Since the legal dispute regarding decree law in 2005, the proportion of legislation made by the legislature has increased from 25 to 40 percent (see Table 4.2).

Budgetary approval is potentially one of the major ways in which the legislature could influence public policy but the process that has been adopted actually curbs its ability to influence the government. The Legislative Assembly could, constitutionally, change policy when scrutinising specific allocations for projects and plans, and it could vote down expenditure on any item that would prevent a project from proceeding. In practice, however, the Assembly is not able to challenge the government over the budget because the government has adopted the procedure of requesting the legislature to approve the total amount of expenditure for the fiscal year in a block vote. In consequence, the Assembly does not scrutinise and approve line-by-line budgetary items but simply gives the budget blanket approval. Its options are either to approve or to reject the budget *in toto*. It has relinquished its potential bargaining power with the executive on specific issues.

Furthermore, the government reserves money for special projects and policies that it does not specify among the projects and policies for which it seeks approval. It treats this special reserve as pocket money that it can spend on whatever it desires during the year. The budget is drafted in such a way that the government will prescribe operational expenditure for departments and agencies. Any surplus will then be allocated to the special reserve account so that the government can spend all of its revenue during the fiscal year. This follows a ruling by Susanna Chou, the former President of Legislative Assembly, that government can freely adjust spending on individual projects and that it is not necessary to seek further approval for spending from the legislature unless overall government expenditure exceeds the originally approved budget (*Jornal Cheng Pou*, May 31, 2008). The practice gives the government wide discretion on expenditure on new items unless it spends all the money in its special reserve account. In 2007 and 2008, for example, the government used the special reserve account to cope with rising public discontent, introducing various social welfare measures, such as a cash subsidy scheme, a bus fare subsidy, and a household electricity subsidy scheme, without the approval of the legislature.

Table 4.3: The Budget of the Macao Government, 2000–2009 (in billions MOP)

Fiscal Year	Revenue	Expenditure	Reserve for Special Projects
2000	12.9	9.6	3.3
2001	13.5	9.6	3.9
2002	12.4	10.1	2.3
2003	14.1	11.5	2.6
2004	15.8	13.3	2.5
2005	21.6	18.9	2.7
2006	25.3	21.7	3.6
2007	30.9	28.4	2.5
2008	41.0	32.5	8.5
2009	44.7	44.0	0.7

Source: Website of Macao government. Available from: http://www.gov.mo/egi/Portal/rkw/public/view/area. jsp?id=21 [Accessed November 30, 2009].

In summary, the Legislative Assembly exerts little influence on government policy. First, under the constitution, most bills must be submitted by the executive branch. Second, the executive branch can issue decree law to shape policy implementation although the definition and scope of administrative regulation has been narrowed as a result of a recent dispute. Third, budgetary process practices have removed the teeth of the Legislative Assembly, limiting its ability to check the executive branch. Under these circumstances, the Legislative Assembly has been operating principally as a 'policy-questioning' forum (Choy and Lau, 1996: 239–241; also see Curtis, 1978) in which legislators can discuss, debate, and criticise government policy while the executive branch enjoys a high degree of autonomy in policy design.

Executive-Legislative Dynamics and the Policy Process

Executive-legislative harmony was emphasised when the Special Administrative Region was established in 1999. Most legislators were pro-government and sought to maintain harmonious relationships with the executive branch in the interest, as they saw it, of maintaining political stability. The first Legislative Assembly consisted of eight directly and indirectly elected representatives from the traditional pro-Beijing groups, including the Federation of Trade Unions, General Union of Neighbourhood Associations of Macao (kaifongs), Women's General Association of Macau and the Macao Chamber of Commerce, who were supportive of the government (see Chapter 5). In addition to the seven politically appointed positions in the Assembly, pro-government forces occupied two-thirds of the elected seats in the Assembly and tended to be co-operative and supportive of the executive branch.

The two pro-democracy legislators, Antonio Ng Kuok Cheong and Au Kam San, were the sole opposition forces checking the government in the legislature. Ng, a prominent pro-democracy leader since the late 1980s, has been very critical of the authorities. He has held a directly elected seat since 1992; his teammate, Au Kam San, was also elected to the Legislative Assembly in the 2001 elections. They have fully utilised their constitutional rights to issue written questions on government policy and performance. In the first and second Legislative Assemblies, over 60 percent of the written questions for the executive branch were raised by Ng and Au (see Table 4.4).

Ng and Au have focused particularly on the government's land policy (personal interview, Ng Kuok Cheong, October 14, 2004). They have questioned the criteria used in granting rights to developers and individuals and have sought greater transparency. Macao has neither a tendering system nor open bidding for land-use rights and government officials have monopolised the process of granting such rights. The New Macao Association, which Ng and Au lead, has identified six land-grant transactions that might involve business-government collusion (New Macao Association, 2008: 15–16). They have also asked the government to explain why it has permitted land owners to change the agreed purpose of land grants. For example, the government granted land to a bus company, Transmac, to build a bus station and a factory for the repair of buses. However, Transmac not only built a factory on the land but also, with government approval, granted a developer the right to build apartments on it (*Macao Daily News*, November 17, 2005). The then Chief Executive, Edmund Ho Hau Wah, explained that the existing laws allowed Transmac to use the land in this manner but he did not explain why the government agreed to transfer the right to build housing on the land. Ng Kuok Cheong argued that this case reflected business-government collusion (personal interview, July 26, 2005). Au Kam San also published documents questioning the criteria by which the government granted three parcels of land, asking why it had allowed a change of purpose in two of those cases (document numbers: 119/III/2006; 157/III/2006; 172/III/2006).[2] As a reform measure, the legislators suggested that the government install a tendering or open bidding system for granting land. However, the Chief Executive had already argued that an open bidding system would probably result in an increase in land prices, which would ultimately lead to an increase in property prices (*Macao Daily News*, November 17, 2005). Although the two pro-democracy legislators have worked hard in their efforts to check and monitor government performance, they have not been able to generate sufficient political pressure to change government policy and they have not had much support from their fellow legislators, who tended to stay silent during the first and second Legislative Assemblies. Executive-legislative harmony was maintained during that period through the domination of the pro-government elite.

Table 4.4: Number of Written Enquiries Submitted by Legislators

Year	Number of Written Questions by Legislators	Number of Written Questions from Antonio Ng and Au Kam Sam*
1999–2000	39	34 (87.2%)
2000–2001	90	64 (71.1%)
2001–2002	168	121 (72.0%)
2002–2003	126	90 (71.4%)
2003–2004	130	82 (63.1%)
2004–2005	112	68 (60.7%)
2005–2006	274	81 (29.6%)
2006–2007	353	91 (25.8%)
2007–2008	394	98 (24.9%)
2008–2009	421	94 (22.3%)

Source: Website of the Legislative Assembly. Available from: http://www.al.gov.mo/interpelacao/2009/list2009.htm [Accessed November 30, 2009].
Note: 1. * The figure in the parenthesis is the portion of written questions by Ng and Au.

With increasing economic prosperity and a larger government revenue base after the liberalisation of the gaming industry, Macao residents had greater expectations that the government would intervene to solve the various social problems that had resulted from rapid growth. There was also some feeling that the legislature should exert more pressure on the government to be accountable to the public. Although many residents enjoyed increased job opportunities and better salaries after the liberalisation of the gaming industry, their quality of life did not necessarily improve (Cheng and Wong, 2007). Workers, in particular, complained about unemployment and the government policy on imported labour (see Chapter 9). Housing became another major issue. Although many residents had seen considerable increases in their incomes, they remained unable to afford to buy their own apartments (see Chapter 11).

The government has been blamed for its failure to solve the social problems that have been created and aggravated by rapid economic development (see Chapter 3). Although there has been escalating political pressure for it to take stronger initiatives to solve social problems, confidence in the government has also been shaken by scandals in the administration and the belief that business-government collusion has undermined the public interest. The Ao Man Long case reinforced adverse perceptions of the corruption of government officials at both the grassroots and senior levels. Ao, the former Secretary of Transport and Public Works, was arrested for taking bribes, estimated at MOP800 million, from land developers and government project contractors (*Macao Daily News*, December 8, 2006). During his trial, officials responsible for land projects and government tender projects testified that their superiors, instructed by Ao, had required them to adjust the grading of particular bidders arbitrarily so that they could win contracts for government projects (*Macao Daily News*, November 14, 2007). Ao's case sheds light on the extent of bureaucratic discretion and the lack of proper institutional control mechanisms for checks and balances within the government.

In another example, the Commission of Audit investigated the financial accounts and management of the Organizing Commission of the East Asian Games, which was fully funded by the government. The Commission of Audit discovered various instances of malpractice that could be traced to the Organizing Commission and that had resulted in serious over-budgeting problems (Commission of Audit, 2006). According to the Audit Commission's report, the overall expenditure for the Games was MOP4.4 billion — 50.6 percent over the budget — which constituted a waste of government resources. Many facilities had to be reconstructed because of the poor quality of the original designs, providing an opportunity, some suspected, for contractors to make extra money (Commission of Audit, 2006). Some political activists believed that the elite was using government institutions for their own benefit while the rest of the population suffered from social problems that were not receiving proper attention.[3] Discontent has served to highlight the need for fair and equal mechanisms for distributing public resources and has increased participation in the political process.

Changing socio-economic conditions and the social problems that have resulted have led to the greater empowerment of the legislature in the policy process. There is now also an increasingly strong belief that legislators should check and monitor the administration in the public interest. There is less tolerance of the silence of legislators in the Assembly and a growing inclination to use the ballot box to sanction directly elected legislators whose performance has not lived up to expectations. In the 2005 elections, the two pro-Beijing candidate lists,[4] United Forces and Development Union, found themselves in a difficult situation (Yu, 2007). In the past, both the United Forces, which was linked to the General Union of Neighbourhood Associations of Macao (kaifongs) and the Women's

General Association of Macau, and the Development Union, which was associated with the Macao Federation of Trade Unions, enjoyed relatively strong support in elections, each receiving two directly elected seats. However, in the 2005 elections, they lost support and, for a time, it appeared that they might only capture one seat instead of two. Although each ultimately captured two seats, they encountered fierce competition from other candidates who had a better track record in public affairs and were more vocal in criticising the government. In the 2009 elections, the United Forces and Development Union only won one directly elected seat (*Macao Daily News*, September 28, 2009; see also Chapter 5). The problem for the pro-Beijing groups was that, because they had traditionally been pro-government, they were seen to be ineffective in holding the executive branch accountable.

In addition, there has been an increasing number of casino businesspeople running for, and winning, seats in the Legislative Assembly (see Chapter 5). Their intent is clearly to promote the interests of their casinos. For example, Legislator Angela Leong On Kei, who serves on the board of directors of Sociedade de Jogos de Macau (SJM), has constantly criticised the MSAR government for its favouritism toward foreign gaming concessionaires and its unfair treatment of casinos operated by local businessmen. She noted that the Venetian Group had failed to appoint a permanent Macao resident to its Board of Directors in accordance with the gaming laws and that the government had not investigated the case and had not sanctioned the company (*Macao Daily News*, June 5, 2008). Leong also complained that the Venetian Group had failed to keep its promise to build a casino project during the 2008 global financial crisis. She called on the government to investigate the Venetian Group and to better protect local interests (*Macao Daily News*, November 20, 2008). Another legislator, casino businessman Chan Meng Kam, wanted the government to cap the commission to junket operators in order to reduce casinos' operational costs and to reduce competition among casinos which were using higher commission rates to motivate agents to attract high-roller gamblers to their betting rooms (*Macao Daily News*, July 12, 2008). He also requested the government to protect the interests of casino businessmen by establishing a debtor list archive in order to lower their risk when they gave loans to gamblers (*Macao Daily News*, April 27, 2009). It would appear that casino operators are increasingly intent on participating in the legislature and pressuring the government to protect and promote their interests.

Executive-legislative harmony was of less importance to legislators after the 2005 elections. In response to public demands, they increasingly began to question administrative action. In each session of the first and second Legislative Assembly, the number of written enquiries was fewer than 200 (see Table 4.4). Those figures rose to 274 in the 2005–2006 session and continued to rise thereafter, reaching over 400 in the 2008–2009 session. Although the two pro-democracy legislators, Antonio Ng Kuok Cheung and Au Kam San, raised about 90 written questions in each session, new members from directly elected seats, such as Chan Meng Kam, Ung Choi Kun, and José Maria Pereira Coutinho, were also outspoken and questioned the administration on a range of issues. Legislators from pro-Beijing groups, too, became more active and vocal in the Assembly after their experience in the 2005 elections.

Legislators tend to be critical when questioning government policy and expect officials to answer their questions clearly. For example, José Maria Pereira Coutinho raised a question about the low morale in the civil service and argued that the government was doing nothing to resolve the problem. In response, José Chu, the Director of the Public Administration and Civil Services Bureau, only talked about the reform of the pension scheme. Coutinho was highly critical: 'Your reply,' he said, 'does not answer my question and cannot answer it. You are wasting my time' (*Jornal Cheng Pou*, February 21, 2008). In another example, some legislators questioned the Secretary for Administration and Justice, Florinda da Rosa Silva Chan, about the accountability of senior officials for policy failures. Chan read out the rules and procedures but did not explain how the government could improve the accountability of officials. The President of the Legislative Assembly, Susanna Chou, noted that:

> The Secretary did not answer the questions ... You are expected to talk about the sanctions applied to senior officials when they make mistakes on policy; otherwise, the dialogue is meaningless. If a legislator questions you on an event and you talk about another, there will be no dialogue at all *(Jornal Cheng Pou*, April 24, 2008).

Legislators have been trying to exert pressure on officials at question time and officials are beginning to find that they have less room for evasion than was previously the case.

The Legislative Assembly has improved its ways of conducting business and investigating the administration by forming *ad hoc* committees. After the Ao Man Long case in 2007, the Assembly created two such committees to study procedures for land grants and to examine the public finance system. This was the first time that the legislature had set up committees to investigate the administration. The *ad hoc* committee on public finance made ten recommendations to improve the transparency of public finances and suggested that the Legislative Assembly take more initiative in monitoring the use of public money by government departments. It recommended, for example, that the executive branch consult with the legislature on government expenditure on projects and programmes (*Jornal Va Kio*, August 7, 2009). The executive branch, according to the committee, should also inform the Assembly when a department overspent on a project that exceeded the original budget by 25 percent. The *ad hoc* committee on land grants suggested that the government revise the Land Law and grant land through an open bidding and tendering system (*Macao Daily News*, April 23, 2009). These developments provide some evidence that legislators have been seeking to respond to demands for greater accountability and transparency in the critical areas of land and public finance.

Legislators have also sought to extend their role and participation in the policy process with the aim of improving government performance. Towards the end of her term as President, Susanna Chou became a strong advocate of strengthening the role of the Assembly in making policy (*Macao Daily News*, August 14, 2009). She argued that the government could not make good policy without the input of legislators and that policy had to be written in the form of law; otherwise, the administration, she said, would face difficulties in implementation. She criticised the executive branch for lacking a legislative plan and for expecting the Assembly to make law in a very short time, as was evident in the process for the Legal Framework on Gambling and Casino Operation in 2001 and the Chief Executive Election Law in 2004 (*Macao Daily News*, August 14, 2009). As a result of this pressure, she claimed, the quality of legislation had suffered. Chou's remarks reflected the perception that the executive branch had undermined the legislature's efforts to become more involved in the making of public policy.

Case Study: The Making of Labour Policy

The formulation of labour policy demonstrates the Legislative Assembly's growing influence in the policy process. Labour issues have been among the major causes of social instability in Macao. There were violent clashes between the police and protesters at the May Day demonstrations in 2000, 2006, 2007 and 2010. As a response to these events, the government has begun to reform its labour policy while recognising that its lack of capacity to implement policy means that it will need support from various social and political groups and organisations, including the legislature. Therefore, the development of labour policy over time shows the way in which the government's relationship to the legislature has changed.

Before the establishment of the Legislative Assembly, the colonial government issued decree laws to regulate labour processes as well as to protect the interests of the working class. For instance, in the 1960s, the Macao Governor issued various decree laws covering working hours and holidays embodying the principles of the International Labour Organization. When the Legislative Assembly was inaugurated in 1976, the Macao government continued to rely on decree law in making policy on matters such as workplace hygiene and the protection of labour. Disregarding opposition from the trade unions, the government issued two important decree laws in the 1980s on the importation of labour which were designed to reduce labour costs to maintain the competitiveness of the manufacturing sector (Choi, 2005). In 1995, the government did submit a bill on employment and labour rights to the legislature which defined general principles on the protection of labour interests. However, the law focused mainly on general principles and did not provide details on implementation. The government was able to issue decrees freely to shape policy with little check from other political forces.

Since the handover, the government has been under pressure to adjust its policies to provide more protection of working class interests. Hundreds of unemployed people demonstrated on the streets during April and May 2000, many complaining that the imported labour policy had resulted in their unemployment (personal interview, Jeremy Lei Man Chow, June 18, 2005).[5] The demonstration turned violent and the police used tear gas to disperse the protesters. The labour issue had begun to threaten political stability and the government decided to review the decree laws regarding the importation of labour in October 2000 (*Jornal Va Kio*, October 10, 2000). Additionally, it planned to issue decree laws to regulate the labour process and the indemnification rules on industrial accidents. The government recognised that it could not determine the policy unilaterally but had to find a consensus among the various interested parties. The proposals were discussed in the Standing Committee for the Coordination of Social Affairs, a consultative body for labour issues composed of representatives from trade unions and business groups. However, the representatives could not reach a consensus on such issues as quotas, minimum wages and the industrial sectors for which imported labour could be recruited, and so forth (*Jornal Va Kio*, December 25, 2001; *Macao Daily News*, January 21, 2002). The government consequently halted the consultation process in 2002 although it did go ahead with a decree law that empowered the administration to deal with the black market for labour (*Jornal Va Kio*, June 25, 2002). It might be argued that the government did not show much initiative in guiding the discussion and leading labour and business interests towards a consensus; it tended to be reactive both to the demonstrations and to the failure of the Society Coordination Committee to reach an accord.

Meanwhile, trade unionists were trying to promote labour interests in the Assembly. In 2005, Kwan Tsui Hang, David Chow Kam Fai, Cheang Hong Lok, Leong Iok Wa, and Jorge Manuel Fäo submitted a private bill regarding labour union law that was designed to enhance the bargaining power of workers and to provide greater protection of their interests (*Macao Daily News*, July 5, 2007). José Maria Pereira Coutinho also proposed a labour union bill in the legislature in 2007. Although a simple majority of legislators voted in favour of these bills, they were not approved because private bills must have absolute majority support in order to be passed. Legislators have also brought pressure to bear on the government to review the imported labour policy and to provide better protection for local residents seeking job opportunities. Although the government rejected a proposal to end the imported labour policy and to set a quota for migrant workers, it did agree in 2005 to make the scheme more transparent by making public the quota for migrant workers for individual enterprises (*Macao Daily News*, October 5, 2005). While the Legislative Assembly as an institution was shut out of the policymaking process at this stage, individual legislators did manage to exert political pressure which helped to influence the form that policy took.

The reform debate on labour policy was reopened in the Standing Committee for the Coordination of Social Affairs in 2005 when the number of labour disputes rose sharply in conjunction with the rapidly growing economy (*Macao Daily News*, December 12, 2005). In the light of the constitutional argument over the status of decree law, the government agreed in 2006 that new labour policy would be made in the form of law rather than by decree, but it sought a labour-business consensus before submitting a bill to the Assembly (*Macao Daily News*, March 15, 2006). It extended consultation on the imported labour law to the newly formed Human Resources Development Committee, an advisory body on the sustainable development of the labour force (*Macao Daily News*, March 15, 2006). However, the clashes between police and demonstrators during the 2006 and 2007 Labour Day demonstrations made the matter more urgent. The government decided to accelerate the legislative process and submitted two proposals, the 'Labour Relations Law' and the 'Law of the Recruitment of Migrant Workers', to the Legislative Assembly in 2007 (*Macao Daily News*, April 4, 2007). Government officials attended the meetings of the Assembly's Third Standing Committee,[6] which functions in the manner of a Bills Committee scrutinising legislation, and answered questions from legislators in an effort to secure their support. Before the Committee could recommend the bill to the Assembly for approval, the government resubmitted two revised versions of the proposal. In the past, government officials had seldom attended meetings of standing committees on legislation and tried to avoid submitting revised versions of bills to meet the demands of the standing committees. As this example shows, the attitude of officials toward the legislature has changed; they have become somewhat more responsive and answerable to legislators.

However, the labour-business gridlock over labour policy had not yet been resolved by the legislature itself. Pro-business legislators, believing the labour bills to be biased in favour of the working class and detrimental to the interests of business, expressed strong opposition to the legislation (*Macao Daily News*, December 7, 2007). To narrow the business-labour gap and concentrate the discussion on a single bill, the legislature decided to scrutinise the new Labour Relations Law first and to postpone discussing the imported labour law (*Macao Daily News*, April 10, 2008). The pro-business legislators nonetheless remained adamantly opposed to the legislation. To persuade them to change their minds, the Chief Executive held a special dinner with pro-business legislators and representatives of business groups before the legislature voted on the Labour Relations Law (*Macao Daily News*, August 4, 2008). After the meeting, the representatives of business interests changed their position and supported the bill. The Labour Relations Law was passed by the Legislative Assembly and went into force on January 1, 2009. The legislature continued to scrutinise the imported labour law which was eventually passed in October 2009 (*Macao Daily News*, October 27, 2009).

The making of labour policy demonstrates that the policy environment in which policy is being made has become more complex and that there has been a decline in the government's capacity to balance the interests of various forces. There has been an intensification of class conflict in the wake of economic growth and, while the government seeks to mediate that conflict by introducing balanced policies, it still receives the blame for its apparent bias in favour of particular groups. The legislature has a role to play in ameliorating this process because it can serve as a means of legitimising government action. Its own credibility, however, is dependent on the way in which it continues to act to hold the government to account. Should it fail to do so, it will become, paradoxically, less useful to the executive because its own legitimacy as the mouthpiece of affected groups will have been compromised. Should the Assembly continue to evolve as a 'policy-questioning' body, changing socio-economic circumstances and political pressure from legislators may incline the executive branch towards greater power-sharing with its members.

Conclusion

During the colonial era, the Macao legislature was little more than an approval mechanism that served to 'rubber stamp' already-decided executive actions. The 'bi-rail' system of legislation and the budgetary process undermined the Assembly's ability to hold the executive accountable, to scrutinise expenditure, and, in the broadest sense, to play a role in policymaking. However, the changing socio-economic circumstances of Macao and the emergence of new groups after the handover have strengthened its position. Rapid economic growth has triggered tensions and conflicts to the extent that the government has felt that it can no longer make policy unilaterally and that it needs allies and endorsements to ensure that its decisions are accepted as authoritative. Furthermore, the power of the Chief Executive to make decree law has been successfully disputed and constrained. Conventions are beginning to emerge which draw the line between what is properly the domain of the executive and what should be the functions of the legislature. The area that seems to be expanding most rapidly is the means by which the executive is called to account through questioning and investigative committees. As these procedures become more institutionalised, so the legislature itself will be become more a focus for political forces in the society who wish to express their grievances and demands.

Constitutionally, the executive branch remains the dominant force in policymaking. However, economic growth and the problems that it has brought with it have generated momentum from the grassroots for the transformation of executive-led government. Increasingly, there is a feeling that the government should be more accountable and that the legislature has obtained something of a public mandate to check the executive branch and to participate in the policy process. The political pendulum is swinging from executive domination toward a greater role for the legislature in the governance of Macao.

5

Challenges and Threats to Traditional Associations

Annie Lee Shuk Ping

Associations, comprising groups of like-minded citizens sanctioned, recognised and funded by the government, have long occupied a unique position within Macao's polity. The traditional associations — the Macao Chamber of Commerce, the Macao Federation of Trade Unions, the General Union of Neighbourhood Associations (kaifongs) and the Women's General Association of Macau — were established to serve as bastions of political and social stability and to act as a bridge between the government and citizens. They have specific characteristics which relate to that role. First, they are peak associations in the sense that they control, organise and represent many subsidiary organisations in their particular sectoral fields. They have a high-density of membership which meant that, until recently, they had a virtual monopoly over the ways in which economic and social interests could be expressed. Second, they are conservative pro-Beijing associations which continue to be embedded and important in the post-1999 political order although not to the same extent as they had been under the colonial system. The appointment of their leaders is carefully monitored by the Central Government Liaison Office (Macao SAR) and the Chief Executive's Office. Third, they have considerable political power, social influence and a role in providing community services which has in the past enabled them to obtain strong grassroots support. Historically, they mediated disputes between Portuguese political elites and the Chinese community and were an important voice in the Legislative Assembly with many of their leaders elected for the functional seats where they controlled the vote. The traditional associations have distinct policy positions and they make their views known in the legislature, on the more than 30 government functional advisory committees on which they are represented, and in the media. Their social influence is also considerable because they still provide a significant proportion of Macao's welfare services (see Chapter 12).

The formal role of the associations suggests that they are a critical component of a corporatist conception of interest representation in which, in Schmitter's terms, the constituent units are organised into 'a limited number of singular, compulsory, non-competitive, hierarchically ordered and functionally differentiated categories, recognised or licensed by the state and granted a deliberate representational monopoly within their respective categories in exchange for observing certain controls on their selection of leaders and articulation of demands and supports' (Schmitter, 1979: 13). A major objective of such systems is to ensure political stability for the existing social order (Williamson, 1989: 12). The 'licensed' organisation acts as an intermediary between the government, economic and social decision-makers, and society.

Despite their important corporatist role within the political system, the influence of the traditional associations in Macao seems to be declining. Although the total number of associations has increased substantially in the last few years, membership in the traditional associations has been dropping. They are under threat from a society which may be looking to express its views through other channels and from organised gaming interests which are seeking greater political influence. This chapter examines the changing position of the traditional associations in the face of those threats and the implications of those changes for Macao's political system and mode of governance.

The Size, Form and Functions of the Associations

The Macao Special Administrative Region, with a population of only 544,200 in 2009 (including imported workers) (Census and Statistics Department, 2009), has over 4,000 associations (see Table 5.1). The major groups may be classified into five clusters: business organisations, labour unions, neighbourhood (kaifong) groups, sports groups and new professional (middle-class) groups. Traditional associations, particularly the peak associations, have longstanding connections with the community. Under Portuguese rule, they acted on behalf of the government to deliver social services but also served the Chinese government by transmitting its policies to the colony. They were consequently critical to political stability in assisting and consolidating Portuguese rule and in minimising discontent. Since Portuguese was widely used inside the civil service, creating a language barrier between the ruling class and the predominantly Chinese society, the government needed the associations both as conduits to society and as a means by which it could balance the relationship between the contending forces of business and labour.

The associations continued to play an important formal role within the system after 1999. The objective remained to provide an umbrella which would cover all interests in society and within which leaders could maintain social control, represent the views of their members and provide some social services. The peak associations have been designed to incorporate similar types of subsidiary associations over which they can exert control. In 2009, for example, the Macao Chamber of

Table 5.1: Number of Registered Associations

Year	Number of new registered associations	Cumulative number of associations
1997	92	1482
1998	98	1580
1999	150	1732
2000	117	1849
2001	149	1998
2002	196	2192
2003	146	2340
2004	201	2541
2005	232	2773
2006	682	3455
2007	274	3729
2008	290	4019
2009 (January–April)	89	4108

Source: Personal interview with officials of the Identification Services Bureau, Macao SAR, May 6, 2009.

Commerce claimed a membership of over 90 business organisation members, 1,500 company members, and 1,000 individual members, all drawn from the most affluent strata of the society. The Macao Federation of Trade Unions and the General Union of Neighbourhood Associations of Macao (kaifongs)[1] both seek to represent the working class. In 2009, the Macao Federation of Trade Unions had 56 member unions, including the unions from different industries such as construction, gaming and manufacturing. The General Union of Neighbourhood Associations of Macao (kaifongs) comprises 26 neighbourhood groups based in working class communities. It consists of 30 subsidiary service centres (including elderly care centres), six students' study corners, three primary schools, three clinics and two kindergartens. The Women's General Association of Macau was established in 1950 and seeks to represent women's interests in the society. It is comprised of 38 subsidiary associations, four service centres, one primary school and six kindergartens.

What functions do the associations serve in post-1999 Macao? First, we may note that groups with a high density of membership can claim a strong degree of legitimacy because of their representativeness (Richardson, 1993: 86). Traditional associations, in accordance with their prime objectives, have sought to build extensive grassroots support and influence. In 2009, for example, the formal membership of the associations, which claimed to come under the rubric of the three peak associations, was estimated to be: General Union of Neighbourhood Associations of Macao (kaifongs), 31,115 members; Macao Federation of Trade Unions, 80,000 members; and Women's General Association of Macau, 16,441 members.[2] In addition to their support in the community, the associations have also enjoyed strong support from the Chinese central government. Association leaders, especially from the peak associations, are elected only after a consensus is reached between group members, the Central Government's Liaison Office in Macao and the Macao government. Representatives of the associations are nominated in similar ways to the Legislative Assembly, both for directly and indirectly elected seats, the Executive Council and every government functional advisory committee (*Macao Daily News*, February 6, 2006). The Chief Executive, some of the Secretaries (the highest policymaking position within the government) and senior civil servants are second-generation pro-Beijing leaders. Many have also been former leaders or members of the traditional associations and have patron-client networks. It would appear that a strong relationship between the government and traditional associations is the Chinese government's preferred governance model for Macao. It is clear, too, that most Macao people believe that the traditional associations play a critical role in the system.

A second function of traditional associations has been the provision of social and community services. The Macao Chamber of Commerce, for example, representing the interests of the trade and commerce sector, acts as an intermediary to resolve disputes between the government and business. It organises regular meetings with its associate members to collect their views and then puts their proposals to the government. The General Union of Neighbourhood Associations of Macao (kaifongs) has numerous service centres, elderly care centres, schools, clinics and kindergartens, which provide extensive community services. The Macao Federation of Trade Unions, which claims to represent the working class, mediates in disputes between business and labour, and even fights for workers' rights. The Union established 'labour clinics' as early as 1951 which continue to provide inexpensive or free services for members. The Worker's Children High School in Macao, the Vocational Training School and the Continuous Training School (evening school) offer education for the families of poorer workers. Other organisations, professional bodies, and cultural or sports groups may also sometimes articulate the views of their members and the community and may provide services which prove difficult for a government with limited administrative capacity to monitor or support directly (Langton, 1978: 7). The associations may, however, apply for sponsorship or subsidies from the government-controlled Macao Foundation to support their activities and to assist in funding the construction of new buildings and facilities. The government entrusts and encourages the associations because they play a role in the community which it would be difficult for the government itself to fulfil.

A third function of traditional associations is that they mediate between groups with different interests, serving the aggregation function of political parties in other countries. There is a considerable diversity among the 4,000 associations in Macao and many have been formed with the intention of influencing the government on group or policy issues. A unique relationship can emerge from co-operation between these interest groups which, according to Lijphart, might not necessarily result in increased segmental cleavages but could lead to the explicit recognition of the segments as constructive elements with interests that might be accommodated in larger groupings (Lijphart, 1977: 42). Leaders of peak associations, tycoons and senior business people in Macao are usually invited to be chairpersons or honorary chairpersons of different interest groups. These leaders can then act as intermediaries and coordinate and share information within the interest group system. This kind of open communication provides transparency among associations, government and citizens. Interest group activity does not always set segmental or particular interests against common interests but may assist in overcoming differences and conflicting individual interests. The specific issue for Macao, however, is whether newly emerging groups can be incorporated within this traditional framework. The evidence from recent elections and the formation of groups, which are not easily accommodated or do not wish to be accommodated under the umbrella of the peak associations, suggests that the latter's monopoly over interest groups has been supplanted by a more diverse and pluralistic system.

A fourth function of the traditional associations is that they help ease the process of formulating and implementing policy. Since Macao associations claim strong representativeness and influence with the public and the legislature, the government tends to work with the associations to ensure the smooth progress of its policy measures through the Legislative Assembly and their acceptance by the community. Coalitions of associations may be able to clarify and articulate the needs and wants of citizens and provide important information which provides justification for government decisions. The integration of groups in highly centralised clusters enables them to become a part of the decision-making process.

A fifth function of the associations is that they may encourage the development of new political leaders. According to a survey conducted by the Macao Strategic Research Center on the quality of life of Macao residents, two age groups, 16–24 and 45–54, have the highest frequency of active participation in interest groups among the five different age sectors (Macao Strategic Research Center, 2005: 202). Moreover, the respondents with higher education and higher income have a greater tendency to participate in associations, whether or not they are traditional. There is a career path in the traditional associations from leadership roles to appointment to government positions which might attract politically ambitious young recruits. Leaders of peak associations and business groups are keenly aware of their ability to extend their influence by putting the next generation of leaders into key positions in the different associations.

The Changing Role of Traditional Associations

The changing role and influence of traditional associations and their relationship to the government and society are critical factors in explaining the evolution of Macao's post-1999 political landscape. In what ways have these associations changed? To what extent have their longstanding political functions continued to have relevance in the new Macao? Have they been able to maintain their political power and influence? Do they continue to serve as important mediators between government and society as they did under Portuguese rule?

Prior to the handover of sovereignty to China, Macao had been under Portuguese colonial rule for more than 400 years. Portuguese and Macanese (descendants of Portuguese and Chinese marriages) dominated the political process, but members of the traditional associations were co-opted into the colonial legislature. The associations played a critical role in maintaining political stability, especially after the 1967 riots which saw leftist forces loyal to Beijing exert considerable pressure on the Portuguese administration. Subsequently, pro-Beijing labour unions and neighbourhood associations (kaifongs) facilitated the publication and explanation of government policy to the public. Most residents did not participate in politics or in debating policy issues. The lack of consultation with citizens, an inefficient civil service, and serious corruption were underlying factors which led in turn to the formation of other interest groups. The weak colonial administration strengthened the power and importance of the associations because it gave them functional, and sometimes specialised, roles to play within the political system.

During the Portuguese administration, the traditional, pro-Beijing associations were part of mainstream institutions mediating between the Portuguese government and the Chinese community. To maintain Macao's political stability and orderly social changes, a secret agreement was made between China and Portugal in 1979 (*Macao Daily News*, 1987: 68; *Sing Tao Daily*, 1987: 9). Portugal agreed to continue administering Macao but to transfer sovereignty to China. Traditional associations acted as agents for the Beijing government, built up patriotic alliances deep into the community, leaving only a veneer of colonial administration. As a consequence, it was relatively easy to legitimise and consolidate Chinese rule in Macao after 1999. The peak associations simply assumed a more visible role than prior to the handover. Their influence made the resumption of Chinese sovereignty much easier than the parallel process in Hong Kong where the leftist associations were less dominant (Lo, 1995: 68). To ensure a stable transition and to reward their patriotism, the traditional associations were assured of seats either in the legislature or on the functional advisory committees.

Table 5.2, however, shows the relative, but slow, decline of traditional associations in the legislature in comparison with gaming interests. After the 2001 elections, the traditional associations held 11 seats compared with the four held by gaming interests. In 2005, the gap was closed, with ten seats going to traditional associations and eight to gaming interests. In 2009, traditional associations and gaming interests each won nine seats, with one legislator representing both sets of interests, while the democrats won three. For the first time, pro-Beijing groups won only three seats in direct elections. The traditional power base of the pro-Beijing groups in the northern district and the older districts of Macao has been strongly eroded by the Union Citizens' Association (Fujian group) and the Love Macao General Union. Apart from receiving the highest vote in the 2009 Legislative Assembly direct elections, the leader of the Fujian group, Chan Meng Kam, was also appointed for the first time to the Executive Council in December 2009. When comparing the membership of the traditional associations with the votes they received in the elections, it appears that many voters have multiple affiliations and do not necessarily cast their votes for candidates of the traditional associations. With a choice of candidates, voters may determine their choice on the basis of the material benefits provided by other groups. The conservative and 'watchdog' style of the traditional associations has not been able to retain their supporters and many middle-class citizens probably voted for the newly emerging groups. There is some evidence that the attitudes, perspectives and demands of the public have gradually changed.

There was an unusual increase in the number of associations registered after the 2005 Legislative Assembly elections. More than 600 new associations were registered in 2006 and many more new groups participated in the 2009 elections. These groups are comprised, at least in part, of new participants in the policymaking arena who have recognised that they have a stake in a process which has long been dominated by groups which do not necessarily represent their interests. The further development of the economy and the government's intention to push for economic diversification will probably result in increasing political and social differentiation in Macao along these lines.

The traditional associations have a particular interest in winning the ten indirectly elected seats to the Legislative Assembly that are filled by business/monetary groups (four seats), labour groups (two seats), professional groups (two seats) and community service/cultural/education/sports groups (two seats). Similar to the appointment of new leaders of peak associations, a consensus is reached between the Central Government's Liaison Office in Macao and the Macao government and a list of candidates for the indirect elections will be put up for each sector. To strengthen the connections with China, most of the indirectly elected members from the peak associations are appointed to positions on the National Committee of the Chinese People's Political Consultative Conference (CPCC) or the National People's Congress (NPC) (see Table 5.3). To further extend this united front, professionals, businessmen and second-generation pro-Beijing group leaders have also been appointed as members of the CPPCC of different provinces.

Table 5.2: Results of Legislative Assembly Elections, 2001, 2005 and 2009

	Interest groups	2001	Elected Candidate	2005	Elected Candidate	2009	Elected Candidate
Direct Election	New Macao Society (APMD, ANMD)	2	Ng Kuok Cheong Au Kam San	2	Ng Kuok Cheong Au Kam San	3	Ng Kuok Cheong Au Kam San Chan Wai Chi
	Association for Promoting Prosperity (CODEM)	1	Chow Kam Fai*	1	Chow Kam Fai*	1	Chan Mei Yi*
	Neighbourhood Associations and Women's Association (UPP)	2	Leong Heng Teng Iong Weng Ian	2	Leong Heng Teng Iong Weng Ian	1	Ho Ion Sang
	Macao Federation of Trade Unions (UPD)	2	Kwan Tsui Hang Leong Iok Wa	2	Kwan Tsui Hang Leong Iok Wa	2	Kwan Tsui Hang Lee Chong Cheng
	Federation of Labor Union - casino employees (AEA)	1	Joao Bosco Cheang	–	–		
	Association for Economic Reform (ARSEM) *Representing business interests*	1	Cheung Lup Kwan*	–	–		–
	United Citizens' Association (ACUM) *Representing the grassroots, mainly the Fujian citizens interests*	–	–	2	Chan Meng Kam* Ung Choi Kun*	2	Chan Meng Kam* Ung Choi Kun*
	Macao Development Alliance (NUDM) *Representing the gaming industry interests*	–	–	1	Leong On Kei*	1	Leong On Kei*
	New Expectation (NE) *Representing the civil servants and middle-class interests*	–	–	1	Jose Maria Pereira Coutinho	1	Jose Maria Pereira Coutinho

	Love Macao General Union (UMG) *Representing business interests*	–	–	1	Fong Chi Keong*	1	Mak Soi Kun*
Indirect Election	**Commission for the interest of employers (OMKC)**	4	Susana Chou Hoi Sai Iun Kou Hoi In Cheang Chi Keong	4	Susana Chou Kou Hoi In Cheong Chi Keong Ho Teng Iat	4	Ho Iat Seng Kou Hoi In Cheong Chi Keong Fung Chi Keong*
	Commission for the interest of labour (CCCAE)	2	Lau Cheok Va Tong Chi Kin	2	Lau Cheok Va Lee Chong Cheong	2	Lau Cheok Va Lam Heong Sang
	Commission for the interest of Professionals (OMCY)	2	Chui Sai Cheong Leonel Alberto Alves	2	Chui Sai Cheong* Leonel Alberto Alves	2	Chui Sai Cheong* Leonel Alberto Alves
	Commission for the interest of philanthropic/ social, cultural, education and sports (DCAR)	2	Chan Chak Mo* Fong Chi Keong*	2	Chan Chak Mo* Cheung Lup Kwan* (UE)	2	Chan Chak Mo* Cheung Lup Kwan* (UE)
	Total number of seats	19		22		22	
	Pro-Beijing seats	11		10		9	
	Gaming seats	4		8		9	

Source: 2001 Legislative Assembly Election, available from http://www.el2001.gov.mo/; 2005 Legislative Assembly Election, available from: http://www.el2005.gov.mo/; and 2009 Legislative Assembly Election. Available from: http://www.eal.gov.mo/election/public/eal/html.jsf?article=finalResult.

Notes: 1. Gaming industry or gaming-related industry representatives are marked with an asterisk.
2. Traditional associations are marked in bold.

While the core of the Macao system is the relationship between the traditional associations and the Macao and Chinese governments, the government has also encouraged the growth of other associations which, provided they meet its requirements, are formally registered and often funded. This form of licensing ensures that all associations fall under the government's regulatory powers while promises of funding provide incentives to create such associations. The government's aim to encourage the formation of new associations would appear to be principally related to its concern with political and social stability. However, the development of new or expanded areas of public policy in fields such as education and transport, for example, may itself create formal or informal groups which have specific ideas and demands. The government seeks to regulate and control these newly emerging groups through its funding powers and perhaps also through attempts to bring them within the framework of a broader corporatist consensus.

Table 5.3: Appointments of Legislative Assembly Members to Chinese Consultative Committees, 2005, 2009

	Legislative Assembly members in 2005	Affiliation	Legislative Assembly members in 2009	Affiliation
Direct Election	Chow Kam Fai	–	Chan Mei Yi	Zhuhai CPPCC
	Leong Heng Teng* Iong Weng Ian	National CPPCC –	Ho Ion San	Hebei Province CPPCC
	Chan Meng Kam Ung Choi Kun	National CPPCC Fujian Province CPPCC	Chan Meng Kam* Ung Choi Kun	National CPPCC Fujian Province CPPCC
	Leong On Kei	Jianxi Province CPPCC Zhuhai CPPCC	Leong On Kei	Jianxi Province CPPCC Zhuhai CPPCC
	Fong Chi Keong	Guangzhou CPPCC	Mak Soi Kun	Jiangmen CPPCC
Indirect Election	Susanna Chou Kou Hoi In Cheong Chi Keong* Ho Teng Iat*	National CPPCC NPC – NPC	Fung Chi Keong Kou Hoi In Cheong Chi Keong* Ho Iat Seng	National CPPCC NPC Tianjin CPPCC NPC
	Lau Cheok Va Lee Chong Cheong	NPC –	Lau Cheok Va Lam Heong Sang	NPC –
	Chui Sai Cheong Leonel Alves*	National CPPCC National CPPCC	Chui Sai Cheong Leonel Alves*	National CPPCC National CPPCC
	Chan Chak Mo Cheung Lup Kwan	Shanghai CPPCC –	Chan Chak Mo Cheung Lup Kwan	Shanghai CPPCC –
Chief Executive Appointed	Lei Pui Lam Jackson Tsui Jose Chui Philip Xavier Ieong Tou Hong Lao Pun Lap Sam Chan Io	National CPPCC Chongqin CPPCC NPC – Guangdong CPPCC Heibei Province CPPCC	Ho Sio Kam Jackson Tsui Jose Chui Tong Io Cheng Sio Chi Wai Lau Veng Seng Vong Hin Fai	Guangdong CPPCC Chongqin CPPCC NPC – Tianjin Province CPPCC Hubei Province CPPCC Tianjin Province CPPCC

Source: The Central Government Liaison Office (Macao SAR). Available from: www.el2005.gov.mo, http://www.eal.gov.mo/election/public/eal/html.jsf?article=finalResult.

Note: 1. * Executive Council member.

If a corporatist system were fully in place in Macao, certain political relationships should be apparent. Wilson argues that in such situations there will be *inter alia* relatively few centralised groups representing major economic interests; that compromise between group leaders and government officials will be the usual pattern of interaction; that there will be a widespread acceptance of functional representation; and that interests can be represented legitimately by associations (Wilson, 1990: 149). From this, it follows that practices in such systems often involve authoritative bargains between economic interests and the government. In addition, the power enjoyed by associations implies a reduction in the influence of elected politicians, who are likely to find themselves excluded from the exchanges and deals done between government and the interest groups (Wilson, 1990: 149). From the standpoint of the state, this represents an important way of reducing and managing the pressures of potentially divisive interests.

Does this describe Macao? How will the traditional associations fare if they are faced with new interests that might have status within a broader corporatist consensus? Does the government by-pass elected politicians and deal directly with the leaders of associations? Have the newly emerging associations been successfully integrated into the system? While there is some evidence that the government would prefer to retain and work within a corporatist system, there are clearly also pressures for change which are leading the political system and the traditional associations, in particular, in a different direction. We consider those pressures for change and their effects on the traditional associations in the following section.

The Diminishing Influence of the Traditional Associations

Traditional associations appear to have undergone a critical change of influence after 1999 rather less because the government sought to diminish their influence than because new practices and the emergence of a liberalised casino industry undermined their former ways of doing business and politics. Following the handover, communication between government and the people was more direct and less likely to be mediated by traditional associations. Although the support of the associations was still seen to be critical for the government, it began to launch programmes in many fields which led to the creation of new agencies and the direct provision of services. This reduced the importance of the traditional associations as service-providers. Leaders of those associations continued, however, to remain influential in policy-making circles and with the Chinese government.

The political change that had the greatest impact on the political system was the liberalisation of the casino industry. It is conceivable that gaming interests could be accommodated well within a corporatist system; in principle, they might well prefer direct exchanges with the government rather than an overly attentive legislature and they do tend to act in that way when seeking particular concessions, such as land grants, from the Macao government. However, the social impact of the gaming industry on Macao extends far beyond the control of the government and the industry. It generates tax revenue for the government — some MOP37.3 billion in June 2008 (Statistics and Census Service, 2008) — which, in turn, creates pressure for expenditure on social policy. As government spends, education levels rise and citizens begin to make demands for an even better quality of life.

The impact of the gaming industry on the economic wellbeing of Macao citizens can be illustrated at the macro-level by the dramatic growth in GDP per capita income from MOP113,739 in 2000 to MOP331,091 in 2008, the second highest after Japan in Asia (*Macao Daily News*, March 29, 2009). Although this new-found wealth is not distributed evenly and considerable income disparities between groups exist, the gaming industry has also created employment which results in a reduced dependence on the social welfare function of the traditional associations. Increases in income have resulted in a high level of individual self-reliance rather than a dependence on the community. Families have become less cohesive and more likely to look to the government directly for social assistance than to rely on the traditional associations. Over the past decade, for example, private enterprises have established 706 healthcare centres in the community while the government has set up a further 15 (Statistics and Census Service, 2008). Social services are now provided to a greater degree by the government and other new groups rather than by the traditional associations and they are becoming more standardised and more attuned to the changing environment.

Emerging new groups are gradually changing the pattern of interest representation. For example, the Union Citizens' Association (Fujian group) and the Love Macao General Union have been offering scholarships and various subsidies to their members. The Fujian group has established service centres and offices in different locations, especially in the northern district of Macao. Both the traditional and new associations are in competition for the large number of teenagers who will become eligible to vote at the next election. There are also some signs that young professionals are beginning to organise. Civic Power was established in 2008 and had a candidate in the 2009 Legislative Assembly direct elections who polled a respectable 5,396 votes. In the Macao tradition, the government uses subsidies to interest groups as a means of maintaining social and political control. However, the gaming-related groups are financially strong and do not need to depend on government subsidies. Some gaming tycoons even establish and fund their own interest groups. The groups under the control of gaming interests could also represent a new challenge to the government and the traditional associations.

With an improving standard of living and higher levels of education, there is more independent political thinking, more criticism of the government, and, above all, more demand for effective and efficient service delivery. As people become more educated, articulate and wealthy, and as knowledge and information become more widespread, people come to recognise where their interests lie and to press for policy changes. The new generation in Macao has reduced the vitality of traditional associations. There is less volunteering, less philanthropy, less trust, and less shared responsibility for community life. A survey conducted in 2005, for example, revealed that of 1,244 respondents, 814 said they did not participate in any associations (Macao Strategic Research Center, 2005: 198). While the number of participants may have increased in recent years with the rapid rise of new associations, most of these associations only have a few members and some have overlapping membership (Lou, 2005: 1015–1028).

The way in which traditional associations are run has not attracted professionals or educated young people. Those who feel that there is no longer a necessity to depend on traditional associations to oversee community services or to liaise with government have found that they have an alternative source of funding in the Macao Foundation if they want to form new associations. With contributions from gaming taxes, the Foundation was created to promote, develop and research cultural, social, economic, educational, scientific, academic and philanthropic activities and activities that serve Macao. Many different types of associations can apply for subsidies for organising activities. As shown in Table 5.4, there were enormous increases in the subsidies paid out to associations between 2003 and 2008. In addition to subsidies from the Macao Foundation, interest groups can also receive subsidies from relevant government bureaus or the Secretary's office. This has encouraged the growth of all kinds of groups and associations. There are now many different activities and services easily available to the community which are provided by newly created associations or by the government itself. Since the provision of services used to be one of the principal purposes of the traditional associations, this change in the service provision system tends to reduce the influence of the traditional associations. With a more stable economic and political environment and a larger revenue base, the government need not rely as heavily on the traditional associations to provide community services. The loss of monopoly over service provision has had an effect on perceptions of the representativeness of the traditional associations. They are seen to act only as a government 'watchdog' and are unable to reflect public opinion effectively.

The increase in the number of organisations, the heightened level of social contradictions, the obsolete style of traditional groups, and the emergence of alternative political forces have all resulted in challenges for the government and traditional associations. The Macao government and the Central Government's Liaison Office have to re-engineer the traditional associations to make them more relevant if they wish to continue to base their legitimacy on the patriotic support of the associations. Whether tangible or intangible subsidies and the nomination of group leaders to the legislature can sustain legitimacy in the future is an important

Table 5.4: Subsidies Granted by the Macao Foundation

Year	Total amount of subsidy granted (in MOP)
2003	82,148,131
2004	95,147,664
2005	407,297,012
2006	449,203,843
2007	709,344,843
2008	1,108,201,165
2009 (till 3rd quarter)	878,953,261

Source: *Annual Report of the Macao Foundation*. Available from: http://www.fmac.org.mo/Chin/index.html.

factor of consideration for the government. Maintaining social stability and a smooth policymaking process has become more complex as a consequence of the widening mobilisation of interests in society. Changing economic, social and political conditions inevitably result in the formation and development of organised interests. In the Macao case, this has been accelerated by rapid economic growth which has led to greater social differentiation over a short period of time. There has been a dramatic increase in the number of associations and people tend to participate more in increasingly diverse activities. Whether this heralds a new political order and a new basis for the legitimation of authority or whether the traditional associations can find a fresh rationale for their activities and their previously pre-eminent political position is not yet clear. But the rate of their present decline suggests that only a reinvention of their role and government intervention to halt their decline can save the traditional associations from a loss of status in the political system and in society.

6

Civil Service Reform:
Building Basic Administrative Capacity

Brian Brewer

Introduction

In a situation of high economic growth and low social stability, even if in the short term rapid economic development has a stabilising effect, longer term structural destabilisation is a likely result. A preferred scenario is, obviously, therefore to have rapid economic growth combined with high social stability (Eisner, 1992). The government's administrative capacity would then serve to reinforce regime legitimacy through well-developed policies and an equitable and efficient delivery of public services. Since the Macao gaming industry's 2002 liberalisation and expansion, the situation can be characterised broadly as one of high economic growth and low social stability. Responses to the demands of this fast-changing socio-economic environment, including problems arising from marginalised groups and substantial social inequalities, have suffered because of civil service shortcomings in formulating relevant public policies and delivering needed community services. It has been argued that this weak administrative capacity compares particularly badly with the strong leadership of the Macao Special Administrative Region (SAR)'s first chief executive (Lo, 2008) despite the fact that the Ho administration focused consistently on civil service reform during both of its two five-year terms of office.

In this chapter, the nature of Macao's civil service reforms is discussed. It begins with a brief outline describing the pre-1999 Macao civil service. An account of current administrative structures and a discussion of the major characteristics of the current civil service establishment follow. Next, the roles of the two watchdog agencies, the Commission of Audit (CA) and the Commission Against Corruption (CCAC) are reviewed. The vulnerability of their independence is discussed in relation to the change of leadership imposed on both the CA and the CCAC by the new Fernando Chui administration as well as the serious challenges arising from the gaming industry's explosive development. This is illustrated by the Ao Man Long case, which involved extensive high-level corruption in the civil service. An analysis of the Chief Executive's annual policy addresses is presented next to determine what civil service development and reform issues dominated the Ho administration's policy agenda during its ten years in office. Corruption control and civil service integrity management have been serious concerns as has the need to build effective administrative structures and policies. The weak public service infrastructure in place at the time the Macao SAR was established has also seen the need for greatly increased inter-departmental co-operation. The attempt to reinvigorate the reform process with the 2007–2009 *Road Map for Public Administration Reform* is discussed in the penultimate section of this chapter, which then ends with a concluding section.

Background

From December 1999 to December 2009, public sector reforms were recurrent items on the Ho administration's policy agenda but these reform initiatives represented a fundamental construction of administrative capacity rather than improvements to an already well-established civil service system. Macao's public administration infrastructure was relatively underdeveloped prior to 1999 and certainly inadequate to meet the challenges posed by the socio-economic changes unleashed by the rapid expansion of the gaming and tourism sectors after 2002.

Under the colonial administration, legal documents and government policies were usually written in Portuguese and the ability to read, write and speak Portuguese was a defining skill, determining who was qualified to work in the civil service. Importing public administrators from Portugal was an established practice. However, because front-line services were delivered mostly by Cantonese-speaking civil servants, the Macanese (those of Portuguese and Chinese lineage) were uniquely placed to act as intermediaries between the government and the people (Chiu and Kong, 2006). Employment in Macao's colonial civil service was consequently perceived to be a privilege available only to the Portuguese or those with a Portuguese background; career-building depended on making good personal connections and avoiding serious mistakes; and civil service employment was seen to be an attractive option for those of lesser competence.

Even after the 1987 Joint Declaration, which designated December 20, 1999 as the end of the Portuguese administration, officials from Portugal continued to occupy many higher-level positions in the Macao civil service. These numbers even increased in the late 1980s when the size of the civil service expanded. Although the numbers did begin to decline in the early 1990s, as indicated in Table 6.1, they were only reduced substantially between 1996 and 1999 when many Portuguese working for the Macao government were integrated into Portugal's civil service (Baptista, 2006). This lack of succession planning prior to 1999 meant that the new Macao SAR government had to fill substantial numbers of senior civil service posts with relatively younger and less experienced administrators.

Table 6.1: Macao Civil Servants Born in Portugal

Year	Number of People	Percentage Change	Percentage of Macao Civil Service	Percentage Change
1987	1076	–	10.69	–
1990	1811	+68.31	12.35	+15.53
1993	1617	–10.71	10.31	–16.52
1996	1517	–6.18	8.93	–13.39
1999	431	–71.59	2.72	–69.54
2008	201	–53.36	1.05	–61.40

Source: Liu Tai Gang (2000) *Localization Policy of the Macao Civil Service*. Hong Kong: City University of Hong Kong Press (in Chinese); Macao SAR Government (Departamento de Recursos Humanos do SAFP) (2009a) *Recursos Humanos da Administracao Publica da RAEM 2008: Dados Relativos a 31 de Dezembro de 2008*. Macao: Macao Government, 161.

In the pre-1999 Macao civil service, there was no policy-based system of recruitment, appraisal, career development, promotion or retirement and no standardisation of practices across different government units. Little attention was paid to training local people because the required technical or managerial expertise could be imported from Portugal (Chiu and Kong, 2006). The support services needed to facilitate public policy decision-making were underdeveloped. A statistics and census system in line with international standards was only established in the late 1990s (Li and Tsui, 2009). Therefore, the newly established Macao SAR civil service had only a weak administrative capacity and was not well positioned to meet the challenges posed by rapid economic development. In terms of administrative capacity, it was in no way equivalent to the public services in developed countries which have undertaken various types of reform over the past twenty years.

The Macao Civil Service

The post-1999 structure of the Macao SAR government is presented in the following organization chart (Figure 6.1) and in Table 6.2. The five policy secretaries (Administration and Justice, Economy and Finance, Security, Social Affairs and Culture, Transport and Public Works) report directly to the Chief Executive. So, too, do the Unitary Police Service, which is responsible for the Public Security Police Force, and the Judiciary Police, although the latter falls under the jurisdiction of the Secretary for Security. The same arrangement applies to the Macao Customs Services. Other organisations under the Chief Executive's supervision are the Government Information Bureau, the Macao Foundation and trade and liaison offices in Beijing, the European Union, Lisbon, and the World Trade Organization. The Commission Against Corruption and the Commission of Audit are independent watchdog agencies whose commissioners are accountable only to the Chief Executive.

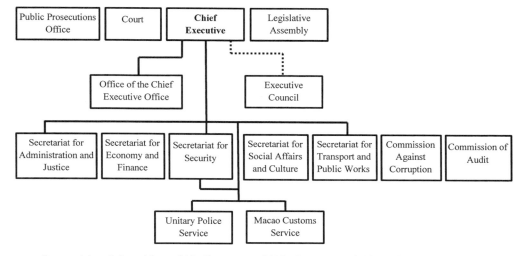

Source: Adapted from Macao SAR Government (2011) *Organizational Chart of the Macao Special Administrative Region.* Available from: http://portal.gov.mo/web/guest/org-chart [Accessed April 7, 2011]

Figure 6.1: Organization Chart of the Macao Government

Table 6.2: The Macao Civil Service: Secretariats and Bureaus

Secretariats	Bureaus
Chief Executive	Government Information Bureau; Gabinete para a Protecção de Dados Pessoais; Gabinete do Porta-voz do Governo; Gabinete de Estudo das Políticas do Governo da Região Administrativa Especial de Macau; Gabinete Preparatório do Parque Científico e Industrial de Medicina Tradicional Chinesa; Macao Foundation; Science and Technology Development Fund; Macao Economic and Trade Office to the European Union; Macao Economic and Trade Office in Lisbon; Office of the Macao Special Administrative Region in Beijing; Macao Economic and Trade Office to the World Trade Organization
Secretariat for Administration and Justice	Office of the Secretary for Administration and Justice; Public Administration and Civil Service Bureau; Legal Affairs Bureau; Identification Bureau; Printing Bureau; Law Reform and International Law Bureau; Civic and Municipal Affairs Bureau; Legal and Judicial Training Centre; Pension Fund
Secretariat for Economy and Finance	Office of the Secretary for Economy and Finance; Macao Economic Services; Financial Services Bureau; Statistics and Census Bureau; Labour Affairs Bureau; Gaming Inspection and Coordination Bureau; Consumer Council; Human Resources Office; Financial Intelligence Office; Supporting Office to the Secretariat of China and Portuguese-speaking Countries Economic Cooperation Forum (Macao); Macao Trade and Investment Promotion Institute; Macao Monetary Authority
Secretariat for Security	Office of the Secretary for Security; Public Security Forces Affairs Bureau; Public Security Police Force; Judiciary Police; Macao Prison; Fire Services Bureau; Academy of Public Security Forces

Secretariat for Social Affairs and Culture	Office of the Secretary for Social Affairs and Culture; Health Bureau; Education and Youth Affairs Bureau; Cultural Affairs Bureau; Macau Government Tourist Office; Social Welfare Bureau; Macao Sport Development Board; Tertiary Education Services Office; Institute for Tourism Studies; Social Security Fund; Macau Grand Prix Committee; Tourism Crisis Management Office; Macao Tourism Promotion and Information Centre in Portugal; University of Macau; Macao Polytechnic Institute
Secretariat for Transport and Public Works	Office of the Secretary for Transport and Public Works; Land, Public Works and Transport Bureau; Cartography and Cadastre Bureau; Maritime Administration; Macao Post; Meteorological and Geophysical Bureau; Housing Bureau; Bureau of Telecommunications Regulation; Transport Bureau; Environmental Protection Bureau; Infrastructure Development Office; Energy Sector Development; Gabinete para as Infra-estruturas de Transportes; Civil Aviation Authority

Source: Adapted from Macao SAR Government (2011) *Organizational Chart of the Macao Special Administrative Region*. Available from: http://portal.gov.mo/web/guest/org-chart [Accessed April 7, 2011]

Note: The table does not cover all the entities under the supervision and tutelage of the Government of the Macao Special Administration Region.

Posts are classified as belonging to the Administrative System or to the Security System. The latter consists of personnel managed by the Secretary for Security who, as indicated in Table 6.3, constitute nearly 40 percent of the civil service. The statistics provide direct evidence of the Macao government's strong executive-led nature. In 2008, the Chief Executive's office employed 414 individuals, whereas the Legislative Assembly Secretariat, with only 65 posts, was provided with less than 16 percent of that number of support staff. In addition, 2008 data drawn from the same source as Table 6.2 indicate that the Chief Executive's office had supplementary staffing of an additional 55 individuals compared with a paltry seven for the Legislative Secretariat.

Data on the growth of the Macao civil service over the past 28 years are presented in Table 6.4. To serve a population estimated to be about 488,000 in 2005, the size of the public sector appears to be relatively modest. Substantial expansion took place between 1980 and 1999, prior to the establishment of the Macao SAR, with numbers growing from 4,602 to 17,239, representing a 275 percent increase in 20 years. The 3,241 staff added between 2000, when there were 17,412 civil servants, and 2008, when the numbers increased to 20,653, signify only an 18.6 percent expansion. Despite a huge increase in government spending, from MOP8,764.9 million in 2000 to MOP40,977.5 million in 2008, increases in staff clearly did not match the additional expenditure. The trend has been for a slowing expansion of the civil service. This suggests that, despite heavier responsibilities and improved financial

Table 6.3: Macao Civil Service Establishment by Department, 2008

Government Department	Staff Numbers	Percent of Total
Chief Executive	414	2.0
Secretariat for Administration and Justice	2808	13.6
Secretariat for Economy and Finance	2034	9.8
Secretariat for Security	7840	38.0
Secretariat for Social Affairs and Culture	4878	23.6
Secretariat for Transport and Public Works	1876	9.1
Commission Against Corruption	135	0.7
Commission of Audit	78	0.4
Legislative Assembly Secretariat	65	0.3
Public Prosecutions Office	212	1.0
Court	313	1.5
Total	20653	100.0

Source: Macao SAR Government (Departamento de Recursos Humanos do SAFP) (2009a) *Recursos Humanos da Administracao Publica da RAEM 2008: Dados Relativos a 31 de Dezembro de 2008.* Macao: Macao Government, 100.

resources from substantially increased gaming revenues, the Macao government has tended to use strategies to build administrative capacity which have relied to only a modest extent on expanding civil service numbers.

In 2008, the Macao civil service numbered 20,653, supplemented with 2,030 non-permanent contract posts. The gender distribution of 61.2 percent male and 38.8 percent female represented a 5 percent increase in female post-holders since 1999. Female participation was substantially the same as in the Hong Kong civil service (65.8 percent male and 34.2 percent female), while according to an OECD 2006 survey on national-level public sector workforces, it was higher than countries such as Switzerland and Japan, where less than 30 percent of civil servants were women, though less than the over 50 percent female participation rates of countries like Ireland, Portugal, and New Zealand (Civil Service Bureau 2009; Macao Government 2009a: 6, 156; OECD 2009). Women were employed in 40.4 percent of the 705 positions classified as 'management', though sectoral differences were substantial, with women occupying 43.4 percent of the management posts in the administrative system compared with only 24.3 percent in the security system (Macao Government 2009a: 10).

An examination of the age profile and seniority of the Macao civil service confirmed that the system was staffed primarily by younger, less-experienced individuals, particularly at the senior levels. Over 80 percent of the civil service including contractual employees had less than 20 years' seniority. Even in the managerial grades less than one-third (31.6 percent) had more than 20 years of

Table 6.4: Macao Civil Service, 1980–2008

Date	Total Number of Civil Servants	Percentage Change
1980	4602	–
1981	5603	21.75
1982	5685	1.46
1983	6285	10.55
1984	7039	12.00
1985	8433	19.80
1986	9027	7.04
1987	10064	11.49
1988	11499	14.26
1989	13125	14.14
1990	14664	11.73
1991	15371	4.82
1992	15111	-1.69
1993	15679	3.76
1994	16415	4.69
1995	16574	0.97
1996	16992	2.52
1997	17589	3.51
1998	17037	-3.14
1999	17239	1.19
2000	17412	1.00
2001	17533	0.69
2002	17368	-0.94
2003	17496	0.74
2004	17778	1.61
2005	18250	2.65
2006	18958	3.88
2007	19629	3.54
2008	20653	5.22

Sources: Liu Tai Gang (2000) *Localization Policy of the Macao Civil Service*. Hong Kong: City University of Hong Kong Press (in Chinese); Macao SAR Government (Departamento de Recursos Humanos do SAFP) (2009a) *Recursos Humanos da Administracao Publica da RAEM 2008: Dados Relativos a 31 de Dezembro de 2008*. Macao: Macao Government, 161.

experience upon which to draw, while close to 85 percent were under 50 years of age and those less than 40 made up nearly a quarter of the total (Macao Government, 2009a: 12, 20, 25).

Integrity Agencies

Established in 1999 as required by Macao's Basic Law (Articles 59 and 60), the Audit Commission (AC) and the Commission Against Corruption (CCAC) are independent watchdog agencies accountable to the Chief Executive. The AC endeavours to supervise and improve financial operations and the management of public departments by means of financial, performance, and special audits, while the CCAC has dual functions as an anti-corruption body and as an ombudsman concerned with issues of redress. The CCAC's predecessor was the semi-autonomous High Commission Against Corruption and Administrative Illegality. The 1992 Organizational Law which established it was passed as a belated response to agitation by Macao citizens for a corruption-fighting agency similar to Hong Kong's successful Independent Commission Against Corruption (ICAC) which had been set up in 1974. Prior to 1999, the Macao civil service did not have an audit department.

Commission of Audit

In establishing the new Audit Commission (AC), the first Commissioner of Audit, Fátima Choi Mei Lei, was faced with a shortage of auditors and accountants and an unenthusiastic response from within the civil service as 'no department would like to be evaluated' (*Macau Daily Times*, December 4, 2009). Despite having completed 37 audit reports during its first ten years and receiving a generally positive assessment of its work from Macao citizens, defensive attitudes within the civil service have persisted. In December 2009, the CA published a performance audit on building and renovation work carried out by the Education and Youth Affairs Bureau at its 16 education and youth activities centres. The report revealed that no written rules existed for project company selection, written quotes had not been obtained and over-priced items, such as 28 toilet-paper holders costing MOP3,150 each, had been purchased. Rather than committing to an examination of possible remedial measures, the Education and Youth Affairs Bureau responded by criticising the CA's report as not 'appropriate' and not corresponding to 'the truth' (*Macau Daily News*, December 17, 2009). It claimed that the firm that won the contract was actually one of the cheapest although it was willing to concede, in private, that it did need to be more diligent.

In mid-November 2009, as speculation grew about the identity of the Principal Officials whom Chief Executive-designate Fernando Chui Sai On would choose for his new administration, Fátima Choi told the media she was available to serve with the next executive: '... I'm available, I'm still young. It's not time to retire yet', though she did acknowledge that 'it depends on the new Chief Executive's will' (*Macau Daily News*, November 19, 2009). The Audit Commissioner was subsequently dropped as one of the ten Principal Officials in the third-term government. In the widespread speculation that followed, Fátima Choi's non-reappointment was linked directly to the AC audit reports released between 2007 and 2008. These reports focused attention on the 70 percent or MOP1 billion budget overrun for the 2005 East Asian Games. The Chief Executive-designate had the Games within his portfolio when he was Secretary for Social Affairs and Culture. As might be expected, Chui denied any connection between the audit reports and the Audit Commissioner's replacement, referring to such changes in government posts during a transition as 'normal'. For her part, Fátima Choi told the media she was 'not surprised' that she was required to leave her post (*Macau Daily Times*, November 25, 2009). Subsequently, Choi was given a two-year appointment as advisor to the Secretary for Economy and Finance, Francis Tam.

Commission Against Corruption

Established as part of the Macao SAR's post-reunification public administration infrastructure, the Commission Against Corruption (CCAC) is independent of the civil service. Its Commissioner, appointed by the central government, is nominated by and accountable to the Chief Executive. Between 1992 and 1999, anti-corruption matters were the responsibility of the High Commission Against Corruption and Administrative Illegality (ACCCIA) headed initially by Mr. Justice Jorge Alberto Aragao Seia from Portugal and then, from 1995, by Luis Manuel Guerreiro de Mendonça Freitas, the former director of the Judicial Police. During the Ho administration, from 1999 to 2008, Cheong U was the CCAC Commissioner.

While the CCAC represents a new entity within Macao's public sector, corrupt practices have been a longstanding concern. As far back as 1975 the Governor, José Eduardo Garcia Leandro, had suggested that a corruption-fighting body should be created. The gaming industry's greatly accelerated growth has given rise to additional lucrative corruption opportunities and increased the challenges faced by the CCAC. According to Transparency International's Corruption Perception Index (CPI), which measures the perceived level of public sector corruption in 180 countries and territories around the world, Macao's international ranking has slipped steadily downwards from 26 in 2006, to 34 in 2007 and to 43 in both 2008 and 2009 (Transparency International, 2010). The 2009 ranking placed Macao seventh in Asia after Singapore, Hong Kong, Japan, Taiwan, Brunei Darussalam, and South Korea. While still ahead of China at thirteenth place in the regional rankings, these data indicate a decidedly negative trend. Comparative figures in Table 6.5 on the control of corruption as an aspect of good governance provide further confirmation, with Macao's performance substantially less satisfactory than that of Hong Kong. It has, however, been suggested that even when Macao's data are relatively more positive there is a failure to account for hidden forms of corruption. For example, election campaigns provide opportunities for voters to be swayed through the distribution of various kinds of benefits.

Table 6.5: Control of Corruption: Hong Kong/Macao Comparison

Political Jurisdiction	Sources	Year	Percentile Rank (0–100)*	Governance Score (-2.5 to +2.5)**	Standard Error
Hong Kong	11	2008	94.2	+1.88	0.15
	9	2003	91.3	+1.45	0.15
	5	1998	85.9	+1.16	0.17
Macao	2	2008	58.0	-0.03	0.28
	1	2003	77.7	+0.82	0.36
	1	1998	68.0	+0.48	0.38

Source: World Bank (2009). Available from: http://info.worldbank.org/governance/wgi/mc_chart.asp [Accessed February 3, 2010].

Notes: 1. *Indicates rank among all countries in the world. 0 corresponds to the lowest rank and 100 corresponds to the highest rank.

2. **Estimate of governance measured on a scale from approximately -2.5 to + 2.5. Higher values correspond to better governance.

Collusion between business people and government officials, money-laundering and corruption have been longstanding problems in Macao, but the perception that only 'relatively low' levels of corruption existed in the civil service was dealt a major blow when the CCAC exposed the Ao Man Long case in early December 2006. The Macao SAR's first Secretary for Transport and Public Works, Ao Man Long, along with another eight men and three women, were arrested on suspicion of graft while, at the same time, the Central Government acted on the Chief Executive's recommendation to dismiss Ao from his post. Investigations undertaken by the CCAC and Hong Kong's ICAC (Independent Commission Against Corruption) had found that Ao and his wife, Chan Meng Leng, were in possession of assets worth over MOP800 million, which was equivalent to 57 times the total earnings of their official posts between 2000 and 2006. Searches uncovered money in savings accounts and bonds in Macao, Hong Kong and the United Kingdom, watches, jewellery, cigars and 300 bottles of wine, a few of which were valued at MOP400,000. Money had been deposited in 39 Hong Kong bank accounts in Ao's name and over 90 overseas bank accounts opened in the names of close relatives (Basel Institute on Governance: ICAR, Asset Recovery Knowledge Centre, 2010).

In June 2007, when the cases were transferred to the Public Prosecutions Office, which laid charges in the Court of Final Appeal, they had expanded to involve three companies and 30 people. Subsequently, in January 2008, Ao Man Long was found guilty of 40 counts of accepting bribes, 13 counts of money-laundering, two counts of abuse of power, one count of false income declaration and one count of unsubstantiated wealth. Ao was sentenced to 27 years' imprisonment and a fine of MOP240,000, with assets and properties worth MOP850 million confiscated by the government. In further judgments handed down by the Collegial Bench of the Court of First Instance on June 4, 2008, Ao Man Long's wife, brother, Ao Man Fu, sister-in-law, Ao Chan Wa Choi and father, Ao Veng Kong were found guilty of money-laundering, while three businessmen, Ho Meng Fai, Chan Tong Sang and Frederico Marques Nolasco da Silva were convicted of money-laundering and, in Ho Meng Fai's case, 18 counts of giving bribes for the performance of illegal acts. Chan Tong Sang and Ho Meng Fai both fled from Macao, as did Chan Meng Teng, a civil servant found guilty of money-laundering and possession of unjustified wealth. In April 2009, a second corruption case against Ao Man Long was concluded with additional convictions on 24 charges including bribe-taking, money-laundering and abuse of power and a sentence of 28-and-a-half years in prison (CCAC, 2009). Had Macao SAR law not provided for a maximum sentence of 30 years Ao's combined convictions could theoretically have put him in jail for a total of 368 years and nine months.

The Ao Man Long case, which involved the highest-ranking official arrested on corruption charges in the history of Macao, revealed high-level and extensive corruption and has been a major setback in the efforts to develop clean and effective governance. It is also an indication of how lucrative corruption has become as a result of the rapid development of the gaming industry and of how extensive are the challenges that the CCAC faces. Although the CCAC's work has been regarded relatively favourably to date, the agency's future leadership is a concern. In his new line-up of senior civil servants, Fernando Chui removed the experienced Cheong U from his CCAC commissioner's post in favour of an appointment as Secretary for Social Affairs and Culture, which Chui had held until he decided to make a bid for the Chief Executive's job in May 2009. The appointment of Vasco Fong Man Chong, a judge of the Court of Second Instance, as the new Commissioner Against Corruption has engendered considerable controversy. Fong's younger sister, Fong Mei Lin, was a former legal consultant in Ao Man Long's ministerial office and appeared as a witness at his corruption trial in November 2007 when she testified that she had received Tiffany diamond rings and other jewellery worth US$37,000 in total as birthday gifts from Ao (*Asia Times/China Business*, December 1, 2009).

Despite having the highest per capital expenditure on corruption control in Asia (Quah, 2010), tackling corruption and developing a 'clean government' image are major challenges for the Macao administration as it endeavors to enhance the administrative capacity of the civil service. The importance of these tasks was highlighted in mid-December 2009, just before Fernando Chui's term as Chief Executive was about to begin, when an 'urgent procedure' mechanism was invoked in the Legislative Assembly to pass a government-drafted bill on 'restrictions imposed on the holders of the post of chief executive and other principal government positions after leaving their posts' (*Macau News*, December 15, 2009). The bill bars the Chief Executive, policy secretaries, commissioners and directors-general from engaging in any private business activities for one year after leaving office and requires the ex–Chief Executive to obtain permission from the incumbent Chief Executive to engage in private business activities in the following two years, while other Principal Officials require this authorisation only for one more year.

The Civil Service Policy Agenda: Building a Modern Public Sector Infrastructure

Ever since the 1999 change of sovereignty, 'one country, two systems' and 'Macao governed by its people with a high degree of autonomy' have been the government's oft-stated principles of public administration. However, behind this rhetoric and pronouncements of commitment to civil service reform, there has been an increasingly urgent need to build, on relatively weak foundations, a modern civil service system capable of coping with an ever-expanding array of public governance challenges. The priorities and structural and procedural strategies to develop the civil service during the Edmund Ho administration can be discerned from the Chief Executive's annual policy addresses to the Legislative Assembly. The first address, which was styled a policy plan, took place in March 2000. From 2000 onwards, the policy address has been delivered annually in November and includes a summary of the government's work in the past year and plans for the year ahead.

While overall challenges concerning economic recovery, improvements in security, and renewing and drafting laws were acknowledged, the Government Policy Plan of March 2000 had the upbeat tone generally associated with the launch of a new enterprise. Public administration was to benefit from the rise to positions of responsibility of 'a group of qualified, energetic civil servants' motivated by a deep sense of responsibility towards citizens and a desire to improve the efficiency of the public services. At the same time, public administration was to be modernised. New institutions were to include a Primary Court, a Court of Second Instance, a Court of Final Appeal, and a Customs Department. Legislative amendments and increased human and financial resources were to bolster the work of the Commissioner Against Corruption, while the activities remit of the new Audit Commission was outlined.

In the early years of the Ho administration considerable attention was given to developing better quality interactions between government officials and the public. The 2001 Policy Address committed the government to front-line service improvements such as the provision of quick responses and solutions to public complaints, simplified administrative procedures and more easily obtained service information. At the same time, it was candidly admitted that the concept of 'service to the public' was not well-established, even at the highest levels of the administration. A recurring theme in the three policy addresses from 2001 to 2004 was the need to reform public administration for improved efficiency, to foster a spirit of public service and to develop a stronger culture of service quality. Ho created the Public Administration Observatory, headed by the Chief Secretary for Administration and Justice, a consultation think tank for public sector reform, to consider ways to achieve these goals. The think tank eventually produced *The Road Map for Public Sector Reform*, the programme that was introduced and implemented between 2007 and 2009.

During the Ho administration's second term the original emphasis on front-line service improvements was replaced by concerns focusing on strengthening internal work processes and external community networks to provide ideas and feedback on policy initiatives. The 2005 Policy Address indicated that the government's intention was to improve the 'holistic quality of life' with greater attention given to understanding the ideas of community groups and more open dealings with the media. The Public Administration Observatory was disbanded in 2007 and replaced by the Council for Public Administration Reform Consultation, chaired by the Chief Executive himself. The Council is divided into two sub-committees, one on policy study and assessment, the other on policy consultation and interaction, which has responsibility for considering relations between the government and the public. External links were emphasised again in 2008 when a commitment was made to establish a consultative committee to facilitate communication between community representatives and district service centre staff. A proactive stance with respect to building civil society was signalled with the announcement that '. . . [the government] will establish an organization in the government structure to undertake the tasks of cultivating and developing civil society' (Policy Address 2008: 32). Beyond these general themes of strengthened administrative capacity and stronger links with the community, a number of key issues have been consistently at the forefront of civil service development and reform. These are discussed in the following sections.

Tackling Corruption and Promoting Integrity

From its earliest days the Ho administration acknowledged the importance of dealing with corrupt practices and ensuring a 'clean' civil service. The 2006 Policy Address reiterated the critical role of anti-corruption and audit functions in monitoring the operations of government departments, particularly at the middle and upper levels.

Accountability was to be a major priority that would include the passing of laws limiting the post-service business relationships of senior officials who retired or resigned from the civil service. Then, as a consequence of the Ao Man Long case, corruption also became a much more high-profile and urgent issue for the government. In 2007, the Commission Against Corruption (CCAC) tightened its monitoring of civil service ethics and the Commission of Audit was reorganised. It was noted that the anti-corruption agency had been too inclined to interpret the letter of the law rather than its spirit and that it needed to address political issues related to corruption.

Efforts to tackle corruption and financial impropriety were given particular prominence in the 2008 Policy Address:

> The Government will further improve the anti-graft and auditing mechanisms as part of our efforts to enhance public financial management. We will upgrade anti-corruption activity that may arise in the wake of rapid economic development, and strengthen anti-corruption and auditing monitoring of departments or administrative procedures that are more prone to corruption (Policy Address, 2008: 29).

The statutory powers of the Commission Against Corruption were to be extended to include the private sector. The 2009 Policy Address announced, as a part of *The Road Map for Public Administration Reform*, the development of revised rules and standards for enhanced accountability requirements among mid-to-high-ranking civil servants. Better financial supervision of public departments was to be realised through more effective account auditing, special auditing and value-for-money auditing.

Civil Service Structure

Strategies for building the structures, processes and attitudes required and expected in a modern civil service have been another consistent feature of the reforms. The 2001 Policy Address highlighted the need to review obsolete laws and to enhance civil servants' ability to strike a balance between rule-enforcement and flexible understanding of people's circumstances. In 2002, government departments were directed to prepare restructuring plans to deal with overstaffing, overlapping functions and inadequate staff selection procedures. Attention was to be given to human resources management issues concerning salary scales and the employment and promotion of career civil servants. Specific internal initiatives identified for 2005 included a new appraisal system for civil servants and stepped-up vigilance against corruption. The 2008 Policy Address presented plans to revise labour laws in support of a new government department dealing with human resources issues.

Other initiatives announced were the establishment of a Traffic Affairs Bureau, improvements in the release of government information, and a strengthening of accountability by removing enforcement decisions from the jurisdiction of senior officers and extending coverage to include retired or former civil servants. Tasks announced for 2009 included the completion of work on a revised rank and grade system for civil servants and a special grade system for relevant professionals.

Inter-departmental Co-operation

Major barriers to improved capacity in the civil service came from its legacy of fragmented administration and low levels of inter-departmental coordination. This was identified as an area for improvement in the 2001 Policy Address along with personal integrity deficiencies and neglect of performance quality. In 2003, the establishment of an inter-departmental, across-the-board task force to handle public complaints was announced. A year later, the emphasis was on the need to promote cross-departmentally those reforms that had proven their effectiveness at the departmental level, while recognising that problems had arisen because the reforms had been implemented hastily and unevenly. Cross-departmental co-operation was the main thrust of public administration reforms in 2005 and the 2006 Policy Address promised service consolidation based on one-stop integrated multi-departmental service centres. The 2009 Policy Address identified future developments related to the continued evolution of service reforms from a single departmental base to involve more inter-departmental co-operation. Specific mention was made of district service centres, a comprehensive government services building, and a Public Information Centre.

Re-invigorating Civil Service Reform

Despite its stated intention to deal effectively with corruption, establish sound administrative structures and develop a 'customer-oriented', integrated public service culture, Edmund Ho admitted quite candidly, early in his second term, that the government was experiencing many difficulties in its attempts to build a modern civil service. Reflecting on progress in 2005, the Chief Executive stated rather pessimistically: 'Following several years of hard work in the early period after reunification, the enthusiasm and fighting spirit of some Government officials and departments have begun to wane' (Policy Address, 2006: 5). Mention was made of passivity and signs of inertia and confusion. In starkly honest terms, it was concluded that: 'The MSAR Government will remain a young and inexperienced government for a fairly long time' (Policy Address, 2006: 6).

In outlining his plans for 2006, the Chief Executive once again gave a critical evaluation of public reform efforts:

> Since the establishment of the MSAR Government, the overall quality of our administrative reform has been relatively low. From now on, we must raise the degree of sophistication and level of quality of our reforms.... We must also eliminate common mistakes that occur in the reform process, such as focusing on improving service attitudes rather than the effectiveness of services, improving particular parts of a service rather than the overall service flow, or improving the forms of services rather than their efficiency (Policy Address, 2006: 9).

The need to reinvigorate the process of capacity-building was highlighted in the 2007 Policy Address, which announced the government's commitment to drafting a road map and timetable for public sector reform in the first half of 2007. Internal priorities included the continued development of a one-stop service strategy supported by digital delivery, the launch of an accountability system for civil servants, and extra attention to anti-graft and auditing work in government departments connected with market activities and major projects involving public expenditure. Externally-oriented work was directed towards building on the 2006 initiative to reform the mechanism for public consultation on government policies by comprehensively expanding advisory bodies through the addition of new members. Consequently, *The Road Map for Public Administration Reform, 2007–2009* was launched with a stated commitment to the further development of 'people-oriented' governance as a core value.

The 2007–2009 Road Map for Public Administration Reform

The Macao government acknowledged directly that there was an urgent need to respond to accelerated socio-economic development in the gaming and tourism sectors by speeding up public sector reform plans when its *Road Map for Public Administration Reform* was introduced. The *Road Map*'s reform vision was not only ideologically oriented towards improvements in internal public administration but also expressed a social commitment to addressing the 'pressing problems of society'. The *Road Map*'s starting point was the construction of a high-level central organisational structure for public reform that was responsible for improvements in three distinct yet overlapping areas. Systemic capacity was to be improved through reforms to the legal system; policy capacity was to be enhanced through reforms in policy processes; while internal management reforms were to enhance organisational capacity. Internal administrative improvements were directed towards the management of civil service structures, functions and resources. Externally, the emphasis was on creating high-level mechanisms to coordinate the reforms centrally which were to be linked to consultation and evaluation mechanisms geared to providing multi-level input on social issues.

The *Road Map* had four internal management priorities. One concern was with the need to ensure the institutionalisation of integrity through improved mechanisms of control and supervision over public resources and the punishment of corrupt acts. Another concern had to do with the development of a stronger public service ethos based on an administrative culture committed to 'better serving the people'. Aspects of this were to include the proper exercise of discretion, accountability and the need for high levels of efficiency. The third issue focused on infrastructural reforms related to legal and human resources management in the civil service, such as recruitment, terms and conditions of service, and professional development. Fourthly, there was a commitment to study the broad political structures including macro and micro-level administrative structures, distribution of powers and responsibilities, and strengthening of inter-service coordination.

The *Road Map* focused externally on developing mechanisms for policy coordination, consultation and evaluation within a sequential framework of problem identification, solution development and decision, implementation and evaluation. Responsibility for consultation, policy decision-making and policy enforcement was to be extended beyond elites to include a stronger input from citizens and associations and a more centralised coordination of decision implementation. The stated goal was to improve governance quality by 'merging the wisdom of the masses' or, in other words, to collect public opinion during the policymaking process to ensure better need-identification and, ultimately, greater public support for government policies.

The government's self-evaluation on the *Road Map*'s effectiveness in achieving a renewal of the reform process and providing a sound basis for additional capacity development concluded that the two-year programme exceeded its predefined objectives. In the administrative area, 34 projects were planned, of which 33 were identified as completed and the remaining one started. Of the 38 projects planned for the justice area, 25 had been completed while the other 13 had been started (Macao SAR Government, 2009b).

Conclusion

The Macao government was not heir to a well-developed governance capacity. Administrative infrastructure was weak and only elite participation could be accommodated in policymaking. The capacity-building challenges have been extensive and, as the process has unfolded, the priorities and strategies have changed. In the early years of the Edmund Ho administration, public sector reforms focusing on service improvement were given priority with efforts directed at improving quality and efficiency and enhancing the degree of public satisfaction with services. Initiatives included the introduction of performance pledges, support for the one-stop model of service delivery, and the collection of public opinion to assess service satisfaction. Given the civil service's weak administrative capacity due to outdated laws, limited organisational infrastructure, underdeveloped human resources systems, and minimal inter-departmental co-operation, the focus on front-line service improvements was premature. The government admitted as much in 2006 when it announced that the original reform strategy directed at front-line services was to be adjusted in favour of reforming internal work processes.

Following the shock of the Ao Man Long corruption case and recognition that the reform processes were losing momentum, there was a renewed emphasis on administrative and legal reforms with the introduction of *The Road Map for Public Administration Reform 2007–2009*, which included reforms in public consultation systems, encouraging public participation and cultivating civil society. The 2009 policy agenda framed the government's approach to public services as a commitment to fulfilling government duties and multiplying the effects of reform. Within the past two to three years, the government has emphasised to a much greater extent than previously the upgrading of policy consultation by strengthening input from advisory bodies and reform of public consultation mechanisms to better inform government policymaking. Greater attention to the external aspects of public sector reform appears to be a priority initiative moving forward.

Several reform issues stand out as having been consistently important over the past ten years. Certainly, fighting corruption and bolstering integrity with respect to conduct and use of resources have been major concerns. The establishment of a principled system of human resources management with a defined career structure that integrates recruitment, selection, development, assessment and retirement elements, and which ensures high levels of cross-departmental communication and coordination has also been critical to capacity-building. In the long run, however, the construction of a strong civil service will depend upon the extent to which the Macao government can improve administrative structures and processes that can function independently of short-term political considerations and develop greater public trust in government through such integrity agencies as the Commission of Audit and the Commission Against Corruption.

7

Improving Productivity through Efficiency Wages: The Case of the Civil Service

Jeannette Taylor

This chapter analyses the efficacy of the Macao government's attempt to improve the motivation and productivity of its civil service by achieving higher effort levels through a wage increase. Wages are probably the most popular motivational tool used by employers to raise the effort levels of employees (Deckop, 1995) and it is a strategy which enjoys theoretical support. The efficiency wage model, for example, argues that organisations which pay their employees a high relative wage or a wage that is above the wage paid by other organisations for comparable labour are able to improve employee performance and productivity (Shapiro and Stiglitz, 1984; Solow, 1979). On the basis of this theory, one would expect a rise in the wages of Macao civil servants to be related to higher employee effort and productivity. Alternatively, however, there is a possibility that a strategy of using financial incentives to raise the productivity of the Macao civil service could produce disappointing results. Although the promise of higher pay with a higher salary point could be motivating for most Macao civil servants, Lo (2008) has argued that small differences in the salary points between any two levels may simply lead some civil servants to choose to remain in their existing positions, rather than to seek promotion by becoming more productive, because a small pay increase is perceived to be insufficient to justify heavier responsibilities and work pressures. From a behavioural point of view, people react to both external and internal environments. In other words, it is possible that higher wages will not motivate Macao civil servants to exert higher effort levels because of conditions in the external environment, such as insufficient opportunities to move to equivalent middle-class positions in the private sector, and the internal civil service environment, such as poor market competition within that sector.

This chapter is divided into six sections. In the first section, the barriers to the Macao government's strategy of motivating its civil service to higher productivity through wages are discussed. In the second section, the Macao government's revived civil service financial incentive system advocated in the recent administrative reform programme is briefly covered. In the third section, the theoretical support for the government's strategy of motivating staff to raise productivity through wages in the form of efficiency wage theory is reviewed. In the fourth section, the methodology is described. Next, the results are presented. Government statistics on labour and public finance from 1998 to 2009 have been used in order to present a trend analysis of the following variables: the wage ratio between the public sector and the private sector; the annual change in wages in the public sector and the private sector; and the elasticity of effort with respect to wages and the total factor productivity of the Macao public sector. The wage-effort link is compared between the public sector and the private sector in Macao and between the Macao civil service and the civil service in a selection of countries, including Portugal. These comparisons provide an insight into the efficacy of wages as a strategy to increase the effort and productivity of the Macao civil servants under the government reform programme. The final section will present the main conclusions and discuss practical issues relating to this reform measure.

Motivating the Civil Service through Wages: Barriers in Macao

The Macao government's strategy of using wages to motivate its civil servants to higher productivity may produce disappointing results because of conditions in the external environment and within the civil service. In terms of the external environment, one constraint is the absence of a sufficiently large professional middle class in Macao. Macao's civil servants make up most of the country's professional middle class. The private sector does not provide sufficient professional jobs to provide possible alternatives. In a survey of 1,351 Macao citizens' self-perceived social class and occupations, Wong et al (2007) reported that 75 percent of the respondents considered themselves to be middle class. Of this 75 percent, however, only 28 percent reported that they were managers, administrators or professionals. Of the whole survey, therefore, only 21 percent of the respondents regarded themselves to be members of the professional middle class. According to Wong et al (2007), many respondents categorised themselves as middle class largely based on increases in their income. Those working in the casino industry, for example, found themselves earning an income much higher than those working in other service sectors, such as restaurants, but the casino jobs nonetheless provide only limited opportunities for upward mobility. Wong et al (2007) found that only 0.3 percent of Macao citizens considered themselves as upper class and 4.7 percent as upper middle class. This suggests that the few middle-class professionals find difficulty advancing to the executive level, probably because the economy is heavily dependent on a single service-oriented industry consisting of mainly low and semi-skilled jobs. Thus, the absence of a sufficiently large number of positions for middle-class professionals may discourage civil servants from seeking career advancement in the private sector by raising their effort levels to make themselves more marketable.

Another external constraint on higher productivity is the low unemployment rate in Macao. If workers fear that they might lose their jobs as a result of shirking and this motivates them to raise their effort levels (Shapiro and Stiglitz, 1984), then there is a possibility that their effort levels will drop if that fear is removed when the unemployment rate is low. Under such circumstances, they may perceive that they can easily get similar jobs elsewhere. In 2000, Macao's unemployment rate was 6.78 percent but this figure continued to drop until it fell below 3 percent in 2010 (Statistics and Census Service, 2010b).

A third external constraint is that the labour market environment created by the gaming industry could serve as a disincentive for workers to raise their effort levels. If workers' effort level is primarily driven by high relative wage levels, the fact that workers in low-level jobs would find difficulty in moving into a higher position or a position that pays significantly higher than their current position may explain their low motivation to raise effort levels. In 2009, professionals earned a median monthly wage of MOP22,500; technicians and associate professionals earned MOP14,858; clerks earned MOP12,000; and craftsmen and similar workers earned MOP9,375. By comparison, the wage levels were MOP7,000 for services and sales workers; MOP6,375 for plant and machine operators, drivers and assemblers; and MOP4,500 for unskilled workers (Statistics and Census Service, 2010c). With the exception of the civil service, there are only a small number of professionals. The wages of lower job levels do not differ significantly. Although workers at these levels can easily find another poorly paid job because of the low unemployment rate, they are unlikely to be able to secure a position that pays significantly higher wages. In short, the conditions in the public and private sectors may contribute to low productivity and effort levels.

Conditions within the civil service itself might also be a factor in low productivity levels. The civil service is the highest paid employment sector in Macao. On average, in 2009, civil servants earned more than twice that of the general labour force. Based on Frey's (2008) argument, they could be experiencing the diminishing utility of money. Frey states that, although higher income can make people happy, the higher utility derived from material goods will wear off as people adapt to the higher income level. He reasons that satisfaction comes from change and disappears with continued consumption. If money has higher utility for poorer rather than wealthier people, then the fact that Macao civil servants have continued to receive high relative wages over the period from 1998 to 2009 suggests that they may be experiencing the diminishing utility of money.

A second factor concerns the lack of perfect competition within the Macao civil service. Although it could be argued that there is market competition to get into the civil service, with demand exceeding supply,[1] once civil servants are employed and tenured, it is difficult to remove them for substandard performance. In his review of the Macao civil service, Lam (2009) concludes that, prior to the recent administrative reforms, there was little emphasis on meritocracy. Traditionally, the Macao civil service suffered from inefficiency and distance from ordinary citizens; low educational qualifications; a lack of training; corruption; frequent restructuring that inflated the size of the bureaucracy; and a power struggle among the departments (Lo, 1995). According to Chou (2004), the government has yet to escape from the spoils system inherited from the colonial administration. Until the reform programme was introduced, many features of the civil service seemed more characteristic of the nineteenth than the twenty-first century. Competitive recruitment examinations were not mandatory. Recruitment procedures were confusing and lacking in transparency and open recruitment exercises were often symbolic. There was a legacy of nepotism and patronage that dated back to colonial times with many civil servants, usually friends and relatives of existing civil servants, recruited through the 'back door' (Lam, 2009). Favouritism was also common in promotion exercises. Some employees had job security similar to a tenure arrangement and an attractive civil service pension plan while others had no employment protection and were ineligible for the civil service pension plan. The inequitable treatment of employees contributed to low staff morale (Lam, 2009).

Furthermore, the performance appraisal system was not rigorous or effective in providing feedback on performance or in motivating civil servants. Most civil servants were rated either excellent or good. In 1999, for example, 5,746 of 9,269 civil servants received an excellent grade, and 3,496 were rated good (Chou, 2004). The remaining 27 were rated average and none received poor grades. Even mediocre civil servants presumably received some sort of performance-based reward. This practice of awarding a high performance rating to employees in spite of poor performance undermined morale in the civil service. In 2005, the staff performance assessment system was modified. Although the new process was similar to the United Kingdom's performance contract and strongly emphasised meritocracy, the fact that managers and executives were not included in the new scheme contributed to staff dissatisfaction because of perceptions of discriminatory treatment (Lam, 2009). It is clearly a challenge to motivate civil servants when they are convinced that they are being discriminated against by their government (Lam, 2007).

The third constraint to higher civil service productivity levels lies in its culture and practices. Although administrative reforms have led to some service improvements, the pace at which they have occurred has been reported to be unsatisfactory because of a conservative culture and fundamental problems that still need to be addressed (Lam, 2006a). The promotion system, for example, is rigid and places great emphasis on seniority. There is no guarantee that civil servants who work harder will be promoted faster than those with lower productivity levels. The problems arising from the difficulty of terminating the employment of civil servants for substandard performance is compounded by the fact that high-performing civil servants are not always promoted quickly. As far back as 2001, the Chief Executive noted the counter-productive activities of some officials such as paying lip-service to government-advocated reforms and putting the blame on others for failures or substandard performance (Ho, 2001). Yet despite the concerns of the Chief Executive these undesirable practices continued to persist (Lam, 2009 and see Chapter 6).

Financial Incentives in the Macao Civil Service

Civil service pay is based on a salary index, ranging from 100 to 1,100 points. The salary points of the civil servants, which are hierarchical and complex, are shown in Table 7.1. The value for each point is altered from time to time with salary adjustments proposed by the government and then endorsed by the Legislative Assembly.

The use of money to shape actions and to send a message is a function at every level of public budgeting. According to Lam (2006b: 1), budgeting is more than a revenue and expenditure plan; it is a tool for socio-economic management, for meeting the demands of stakeholders, for reflecting the ideals of a government, and for holding the government accountable to its people. Its relevance can be observed in the Macao situation in the way in which the Chief Executive described the government's policy on wages for its public servants. Stating that the government 'will spare no effort in setting a good example' in 'ensuring employees receive reasonable remuneration', which 'is a major feature of an advanced and harmonious society', the Chief Executive proposed the establishment of a minimum wage scheme in 2007, starting with those employed by contractors as cleaners and security guards in the public sector (Ho, 2006). Administrative procedures that were to be revamped included recruitment, pay and benefits. In his Policy Address in 2008, Ho said that the government had decided to raise each point on the public service salary scale from MOP55 to MOP59 and proposed a scheme which would increase allowances for civil servants.

Table 7.1: Salary Points of Macao Civil Servants, 2009

Rank	Level	Grade	Designation	Salary point (increment)										Main tasks	Qualifications
				Step 1	2	3	4	5	6	7	8	9	10		
Director			Director	1015	1100										University education
			Deputy director	905	960										
Chief			Department head	850											Professional experience or special qualifications
			Divisional head	770											
			Sector head	735											
			Section head	495											
Superior Technician	6	5	Assessor Principal	660	685	710	735							Policy analysis and advice	University education
		4	Assessor	600	625	650									
		3	Principal	540	565	590									
		2	I	485	510	535									
		1	II	430	455	480									
Technician	5	5	Specialist Principal	560	580	600	620							Planning policy implementation	College education
		4	Specialist	505	525	545									
		3	Principal	450	470	490									
		2	I	400	420	440									
		1	II	350	370	390									
Technician Administration Assistant	4	5	Specialist Principal	450	465	480	495							Policy implementation	Post-secondary education
		4	Specialist	400	415	430									
		3	Principal	350	365	380									
		2	I	305	320	335									
		1	II	260	275	290									

														Job type	Education
3		5	Specialist Principal	345	355	370	385								
		4	Specialist	305	315	330									
		3	Principal	265	275	290									
		2	I	230	240	255									
		1	II	195	205	220									
	Skilled Labour	2		150	160	170	180	200	220	240	260	280	300	Administrative and clerical support	Secondary school education
														Mechanical operation	Primary school education and professional training or work experience
	Labor/ Assistant	1		110	120	130	140	150	160	180	200	220	240	Manual labour	Primary school education

Source: Lam (2010), forthcoming.

In 2009, the Macao government submitted a bill to the Legislative Assembly titled the 'Civil Service Ranking and Establishment System', which sought to make a number of changes in order to improve administrative capacity. The bill, which applied to all civil servants on permanent and contract employment, aimed to improve recruitment in several ways. One provision created an internal mechanism through which any civil servant would be eligible to apply for any government-advertised position and external arrangements through which all permanent residents would be eligible to apply for the advertised posts. Another measure involved a shift from the longstanding tradition of decentralisation towards centralisation of the recruitment and promotion system. The bill was also intended to streamline the civil service system by merging some ranks while eliminating others. For some ranks, the reforms consisted of changes to the entry educational requirements and starting salaries. According to Lo (2009), the delineation of clear educational requirements was expected to improve the professional image of the civil service.

Notable among the reform measures were the new financial incentives which were introduced to encourage high performance among civil servants. One of these involved integrating on-the-job training of civil servants into the promotion criteria. Another reform modified the rankings of different grades to motivate improved performance. Based on the assumption that a civil servant who reached the top rank of his or her grade would lack the incentive to work harder because s/he was primarily motivated by money, one vertical rank and three to five horizontal ranks were added to some grades. Civil servants who reached the top rank of their grade and whose performance was deemed to be 'satisfactory' would be able to proceed into the newly created rank. How effective are these financial measures, particularly the revised wage system, for motivating high performance? Specifically, to what extent is the level of effort and productivity of Macao civil servants influenced by the level of wages that they receive? Where did the notion that higher wages would lead to higher productivity come from?

The Relationship between High Wages and Efficiency

Efficiency wage theory proposes that employees will increase their productivity in response to increases in wages, or, more specifically, high relative wages (Alexopoulos, 2004; Raft and Summers, 1987). Goldsmith et al (2000) state that paying employees wages that are above the prevailing market rate or a wage premium will raise employees' productivity by encouraging them to put in more effort (Shapiro and Stiglitz, 1984); by boosting employee morale (Solow, 1979); by attracting higher quality employees (Stiglitz, 1976; Weiss, 1980); by encouraging greater commitment to the firm's goals (Akerlof, 1982); by reducing resignations and the disruption caused by turnover (Stiglitz, 1974); and even by improving nutrition (Leibenstein, 1957).[2]

Various models have been put forward to explain the linkage between high relative wages and high productivity. The 'shirking model' of efficiency wages claims that employees who are paid higher than the prevailing market rate will be less likely to shirk for fear of losing their job. By paying employees a wage premium, employers are making alternative jobs less financially attractive and are increasing the costs of shirking to employees (Shapiro and Stiglitz, 1984). The labour-turnover model asserts that high wages may reduce employee turnover by making the high-paying job more financially attractive to employees than alternative employment opportunities (Stiglitz, 1985). The adverse selection model assumes that wage rates are positively correlated with employee ability. Employers who offer low wages will mainly attract low-ability employees and those who increase wages are more likely to attract higher-ability employees (Weiss, 1980). Finally, the 'gift-exchange model' proposes that paying employees high relative wages can elicit feelings of gratitude from them and consequently higher effort levels (Akerlof, 1982).

The relationship between wages and effort can be summarised as follows:

$$E_i = W_n/W_m \tag{1}$$

According to Solow (1979), effort (E) per employee (i) is a function of the employee's wage inside the organisation (W_n) relative to the expected prevailing wage outside the organisation (W_m). By dividing W_n with W_m, we get a ratio that can be interpreted as an index for effort. Based on equation (1), we would expect employees to put in higher levels of effort if they are convinced that they are being treated relatively well, that is, that they are receiving a higher relative wage (Akerlof, 1982; Akerlof and Yellen, 1990; Shapiro and Stiglitz, 1984). Relative wage or wage premium may be captured by the level of wages inside an organisation relative to that of an external organisation. For our purposes, the internal wage is represented by the wage paid to civil servants while the external wage is the private sector wage. Efficiency theory assumes that effort level follows closely that of wage premium.[3] All things being equal, the larger the wage premium, the greater the effort exerted. This assumption is based on the presence of a competitive market where employees are indifferent to their jobs because there are identical and similar paying jobs available in the labour market. As a result of this indifference to jobs, employees are less likely to exert high effort but are more likely to shirk. And the worst case scenario that they are fired from their jobs for substandard performance or shirking activities will have a minimum impact on them because they can always find another job. Based on equation (1), it is possible to work out the optimum wages paid to workers in order to secure maximum effort. This is done by calculating the elasticity of effort with respect to wages, e (Solow, 1979), as shown below:

$$e = W_n/E_i = 1 \tag{2}$$

This equation does not insist that employers have to strive to achieve the equilibrium point where $e = 1$. What the equation suggests is that it would be more desirable for employers to show an e value closer to unity than an e value above unity. It thus functions as an indicator for employers to analyse the relationship between wages and effort.

The assumption of a relationship between relative wages and productivity is supported by empirical evidence. Cappelli and Chauvin (1991) reported an inverse relationship between relative wages and employee layoffs in a large, multi-plant firm. An increase in wages relative to local wages was found to decrease the annual rate of disciplinary lay-offs. They attributed the lower number of lay-offs to lower incentives to shirk. Using a sample of 219 British manufacturing companies, Wadhwani and Wall (1991) found that increasing firm wages relative to wages in the industry had a positive impact on firm sales. Levine (1992) utilised a sample of business units of large American manufacturing corporations and found that increasing a firm's wages relative to the wages of the firm's nearest three competitors raised output. Wiseman and Chatterjee (2003) found a significant relationship between the wages that sports teams received and their on-the-field performance (in terms of average number of games won). But perhaps the most commonly cited textbook evidence of efficiency wage theory is the Ford Motor Company's high-wage policy introduced in 1914 when Henry Ford doubled the daily wage rate of auto workers to five dollars (Raff and Summers, 1987). Turnover at Ford factories fell from 370 percent to 16 percent; productivity increased between 40 and 70 percent; and profits rose 20 percent within a year of the announcement of the wage increase. Regardless of his real motive for raising wages (Taylor, 2003), Ford's high wage rate is believed to have had a positive impact on worker productivity. In sum, the efficiency wage literature suggests that paying employees a wage premium — a wage rate that is higher than others in comparable jobs — should generally lead to a rise in the levels of effort and productivity of employees.

Data

This study utilises data from 2000 to 2008 from the Macao government's *Yearbook of Statistics*. More recent data was obtained from the Statistics and Census Service website, notably its *Table of Frequently Used Indicators*. The public sector is represented in these tables by the public administration, defence and compulsory social security industries. The private sector consists of all other categories of industry with the exception of the following: education, health and social welfare, other community, social and personal services and households with employed persons. A mean wage is determined for the public sector and another for the private sector. The mean wages permit the estimation of the efficiency wage ratio between the public sector and the private sector, and the elasticity of effort with respect to wages (*e*) for the public sector workforce. While the efficiency wage ratio indicates the wage disparity between the public sector and the private sector, the *e* value shows the relationship between wages and effort among civil servants.

The determination of a wage ratio in each of the private industries is calculated by dividing the wage within the private industry concerned with that of the private industry as a whole. The total factor productivity (TFP) of the Macao workforce is calculated using the Solow (1957) methodology which includes output, capital and labour. Comparison with civil servants from other countries, notably those from Portugal, is possible through the 2005 *International Social Survey Programme (ISSP): Work Orientations* data set. This data set is derived from a survey conducted across a selection of countries including the United States, the United Kingdom, Europe and Australasia. The data set provides the income of each respondent by sector and country, which permits a mean wage to be calculated by sector for each country. Consequently, the efficiency wage ratio and elasticity values can be established.

Findings

Efficiency Wage Ratio and the Relationship between Wages and Effort

In this section, the findings on the wage ratio and *e* value are presented for the Macao civil service. A comparison is then made between the public sector and the private sector and also between the Macao civil service and the civil services in a selection of countries.

Table 7.2 shows the efficiency wage ratio and the *e* value of the Macao civil service for the period from 1998 to 2009. On average over this time period, Macao public servants received more than twice the amount of wages received by their private sector counterparts (ratio = 2.3:1), indicating that civil servants were far better paid than workers in the private sector.

The second column in Table 7.2 shows the results of the relationship between wages and effort. The average *e* value of 0.26 suggests that a 0.26 percent change in the wages received by Macao civil servants is associated with a 1 percent change in their effort levels. A rise in their wages by 0.26 percent appears to be related to a 1 percent rise in their effort level while a drop in wages by a similar amount is related to a reduction in effort level of 1 percent.

Table 7.2 also shows that despite some variance in the wage differential between the public sector and the private sector between 1998 and 2009, the *e* value of the civil service has more or less remained constant. This trend is shown diagrammatically in Figure 7.1. Figure 7.1 indicates that in 2001, when the wage differential was at its peak of 2.59, the *e* value was 0.27. Yet when the wage ratio

Table 7.2: Efficiency Wage Ratio and Elasticity of Effort of the Macao Civil Service, 1998–2009

Year	Efficiency wage ratio	Elasticity of effort with respect to wages (e)
1998	2.24	0.27
1999	2.39	0.27
2000	2.45	0.27
2001	2.59	0.27
2002	2.41	0.27
2003	2.49	0.27
2004	2.41	0.27
2005	2.29	0.26
2006	2.15	0.26
2007	1.95	0.26
2008	2.14	0.25
2009	2.29	0.25
Average	2.32	0.26

Source: Statistics and Census Service, 2001–2008a; Statistics and Census Service, 2010a.

dropped to its lowest in 2007 at 1.95, the *e* value did not change much but remained at 0.26. Although wages are usually a driving force in any sector, including the public sector, it seems that one could narrow the wage ratio to at least 1.95 and expect little change in the effort level of the Macao civil service. But is this trend applicable to other industries in Macao? The next step is to extend the analysis to private industries.

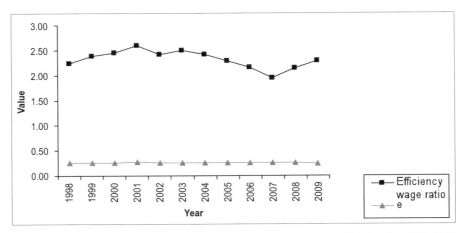

Figure 7.1: Efficiency Wage Ratio and Elasticity of Effort of the Macao Civil Service, 1998–2009

Source: Statistics and Census Service, 2001–2008a; Statistics and Census Service, 2010a.

Figure 7.2 shows the efficiency wage ratio and *e* value by industry in Macao. The values are mean values for the period between 1998 and 2009. Despite the large wage discrepancy between the public and private sectors and between the industries within the private sector, the *e* value did not vary much by industry. For example, the mean ratio of the civil service relative to that of the private sector between 1998 and 2009 was 2.30. In contrast, the mean ratio of the industry covering hotels, restaurants and similar activities relative to that of the whole private sector was 0.73 whereas that for the manufacturing industry relative to that of the whole private sector was 0.51. Yet the mean *e* value for all these three industries was 0.26. The findings imply that regardless of the wages received within an industry relative to that of the private sector as a whole, the workers in that industry appeared to exert levels of effort similar to that of workers in another industry in the private sector. These findings will be discussed later.

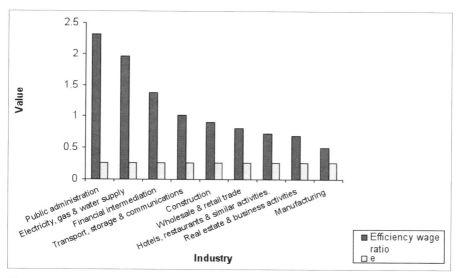

Figure 7.2: Efficiency Wage Ratio and Elasticity of Effort of the Macao Workforce by Industry (average values for 1998–2009)

Source: Statistics and Census Service, 2001–2008a; Statistics and Census Service, 2010a.

When the efficiency wage ratio and *e* value of the Macao civil service are compared with those of the civil service in a selection of countries, the results in Table 7.3 show three prominent features. First, most countries in the group were similar to Macao in that the civil servants appeared to be better paid than their national private sector counterparts. Although there were a few countries, such as the United States and France, in which wages were lower in the public sector than in the private sector, many countries, such as Portugal and Japan, showed an efficiency wage ratio above one. Second, the high wage differential enjoyed by Macao civil servants as opposed to their private sector counterparts was greater than that of any country in the group. In 2005, the efficiency wage ratio was 2.29 for the Macao civil service compared with 1.32 for the Portuguese civil service. Macao appeared to be the only country in the group in which the civil servants received wages that were more than double those of their private sector counterparts.

Table 7.3: Efficiency Wage Ratio and Elasticity of Effort of the Civil Service in Selected Countries, 2005

Country	Efficiency wage ratio	*e*
Macao	**2.29**	**0.26**
Portugal	1.32	0.26
Cyprus	1.17	0.25
Spain	1.22	0.24
Germany	1.20	0.23
France	0.88	0.23
Bulgaria	0.85	0.28
Latvia	0.83	0.30
Taiwan	1.17	0.18
South Korea	1.11	0.22
Japan	1.26	0.15
Philippines	1.46	0.20
Australia	1.08	0.21
Canada	1.07	0.21
United States of America	0.62	0.20
Great Britain	1.09	0.23

Source: Statistics and Census Service, (2006) *2005 International Social Survey Programme (ISSP): Work Orientations* data set.

Third, the *e* value in Macao, which was higher than most countries in the table, suggests a greater reliance on high wages in driving the effort levels of the Macao civil service. The Macao and Portuguese civil services show a similar *e* value of 0.26 despite the larger public sector-private sector wage differential in Macao. Only two countries in the group had a higher *e* value than Macao and Portugal: Bulgaria at 0.28 and Latvia at 0.30. The high *e* values in these two countries can be partly explained by their low wage efficiency ratio. In both countries, the civil service received wages that were less than their national private sector counterparts. This comparative exercise suggests the relative importance of wages in explaining the effort levels of the Macao civil service; more wages were required to bring about a change in effort level by 1 percent in Macao and Portugal than in countries like Taiwan and South Korea. It appears that the use of wages as a motivator to improve the effort levels of the Macao civil service is less cost-effective than in other countries with a lower *e* value.

Although the results suggest that the Macao civil servants require an increase in wages as large as their Portuguese counterparts, and more than many other countries, to bring about a rise in effort level, the earlier results show that changes in their effort levels between 1998 and 2009 did not closely follow changes in the wage ratio. If Macao civil servants require a large increase in wages to raise effort, then surely the trend in their expended effort will be similar to the trend of their received wages. Perhaps the lack of effort change in the Macao civil service can be better explained by tracing the annual wage growth over time. It is possible that, despite the large wage differential between the public and private sectors, the wages in the public sector did not change much between 1998 and 2009, particularly when inflation figures are taken into account

Annual Change in Wages, Unemployment Rates and Total Factor Productivity Growth

Figure 7.3 traces the annual percentage change in nominal wages in the public sector and the private sector from 1998 to 2009. It also shows the annual change in inflation rates over this period. The figure shows two prominent features. First, the annual percentage growth in public sector (nominal) wages appeared to be lower than that of private sector (nominal) wages. Second, the annual change in inflation rate exceeded the annual change in nominal public sector wages over most of the period studied. It was only after 2007 that the annual change in nominal wages in the Macao civil service became larger than the annual change in inflation. However, nominal public sector wages dropped in 2009. These two reasons, particularly the fact that inflation exceeded wage increases for most of this period, may explain why effort levels did not improve significantly in the Macao civil service.

The annual total factor productivity (TFP) growth of the general workforce and public sector workforce (see Table 7.4) was calculated from data in the Macao government's *Yearbook of Statistics*, using the Solow (1957) methodology, which includes output, capital and labour. The average annual nominal GDP growth of Macao between 1998 and 2008 was estimated to be 13.8 percent, of which 12.4 percent of capital, 2.6 percent of labour and -6.8 percent of TFP contributed to this value. For the public sector, the annual nominal GDP growth between 1998 and 2009 averaged 7.4 percent, of which 6.9 percent of capital, 1.2 percent of labour and -0.8 percent of TFP contributed to this value. As is evident in Table 7.4, the annual nominal TFP growth of the Macao public sector over the past decade appears to reflect the annual nominal TFP growth of the economy to some extent in that both show negative values.

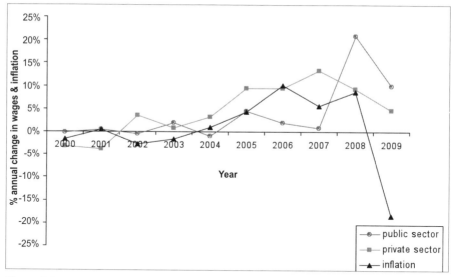

Figure 7.3: Annual Percentage Change in Public Sector Wages and Private Sector Wages and Inflation in Macao, 1998–2009

Source: Statistics and Census Service (2001–2008a); Statistics and Census (2010a).

Table 7.4: Total Factor Productivity of the Macao Workforce and Public Sector Workforce, 1998–2008

Workforce	Annual GDP change (%)	Annual capital change (%)	Annual labour change (%)	Annual TFP change (%)
All Macao	13.81	12.39	2.55	-6.87
Public sector	7.38	6.96	1.2	-0.77

Source: Statistics and Census Service (2001–2008a).

Discussion and Conclusion

In its recent reform programme, the Macao government has indicated its intention to increase administrative capacity, partly through a revised wage system. The Macao government appears to be convinced of the motivational powers of wages as indicated by the high salary it pays the civil service in comparison with the average private sector wage level. Cross-country comparisons also show that the Macao civil service is better paid than its counterparts from other countries in terms of the wage ratio between public sector wage and private sector wage levels; Macao appears to be the only country in the group in which civil servants receive wages that are more than double those of their private sector counterparts. Despite their favourable position, Macao civil servants require a larger increase in wages than civil servants from other countries to increase their effort output by an equal amount. They share some similarities with their Portuguese counterparts as far as the elasticity of effort with respect to wages is concerned. The extent to which their change in effort is explained by a change in their wages is similar to that of the Portuguese civil servants. Cross-sectoral comparisons in Macao also suggest a similar trend. Despite being better paid than their national private sector counterparts, Macao civil servants require a rise in wages similar to that of private sector workers in order to raise their effort level. If it takes more wage increases to bring about a specific effort increase, then the Macao government's utilisation of wages as a motivational tool in the civil service needs to be questioned. The findings suggest that wages do not appear to be a cost-effective strategy for raising the effort and productivity levels of the Macao civil service.

Although wages may be the most popular motivational tool used by employers to shape employee actions (Deckop, 1995), one should not always assume that their common application is a testament to their effectiveness as a mechanism for achieving higher worker productivity. This appears to be true of the Macao civil service. Although Macao civil servants may give high priority to wages, in that they require a large increase in wages to bring about a 1 percent increase in effort level, the fact that their effort and productivity (as captured by the low TFP findings) have failed to change in line with changes in their wages suggests that there has been a culture of inefficiency within the public service. Civil servants appear to be a privileged and protected group of workers and seem to have little motivation to raise their productivity. Chui Sai On, when declaring his intention to run for the Chief Executive position, promised that he would transform the government into a 'truly clean and highly efficient one' (*People's Daily Online*, 2009). However, if the Macao government believes in the philosophy of high wages as a driver of high effort and productivity, then it should pay heed to the efficiency wage theory assumption of a competitive labour market. High wages will only have an impact in a competitive labour market which is not present in Macao. In addition, the fact that annual inflation growth exceeded annual civil service wage rise implies that the real wages of the Macao civil service dropped over most of the period studied. The lack of a sufficiently large job market for middle-class professionals may also have discouraged civil servants to seek career advancement through a rise in their effort levels. In short, the civil service culture and the external environment both militate against higher productivity.

An obvious question is: what should be done about the current public sector wage system? Despite being paid more than double their private sector counterparts, the wage disparity between the public and private sectors has not been associated with a proportionate gap in the effort level between the public and the private sectors. The better paid civil servants in Macao required a similar change in wages as their private sector counterparts and Portuguese civil servants to bring about a change in effort of 1 percent. In fact, when compared to the civil service from other countries in Table 7.3, the Macao civil service showed the largest wage gap with the private sector but also one of the highest elasticities of effort value. If it takes a large increase in relative wages to bring about the same effort improvement, obviously wage cuts would not be too damaging for the effort levels of the Macao civil service. However, given that wages are a hygiene factor (Herzberg, 1966), substantial wage cuts are likely to have a negative effect on effort and productivity levels in spite of the high *e* value and are likely to reduce motivation. On this basis, it would not be appropriate to reduce the current wage levels of the civil service significantly.

On the other hand, if government wages rise considerably in the near future, then it is likely that the wage gap between the public and the private sectors will widen even further. Although government jobs have always been attractive to Macao residents, the rising wages paid by casinos may put pressure on the civil service to increase its wages in order to attract young talent.[4] At the moment, there are barriers preventing the labour force from being more mobile across different industries in Macao (see, for example, Chapter 9). The identical *e* value across all industries in Macao suggests that workers have not moved much from one industry to another over the past decade. About 12.1 percent of the employed population was reported to have changed their jobs in 2008 (Statistics and Census Service, 2008b). Analysis by industry found that most of this labour mobility has been confined to the service industry. A majority of the workers who changed their jobs had been working in three service industries: recreational, cultural, gaming and other services; hotels, restaurants and similar activities; and the wholesale and retail trade. Workers who changed their jobs tended to move to another service industry. For example, the industry that registered the highest movement in 2008 was recreational, cultural, gaming and other services; 26.5 percent who changed their jobs had previously worked in this industry, and 41.4 percent who changed their jobs had decided to join this industry. Perhaps this is an institutional problem. Further research should examine the barriers and facilitators of cross-industry labour mobility, particularly between the private and the public sectors. If the workforce is largely immobile in Macao, then a democratisation of the labour market could address this issue and exert the necessary pressure on civil servants to raise their productivity. As more citizens become better educated under an improved school and higher education system, the removal of labour access barriers in different industries means that more local citizens will be able to secure highly sought-after government positions. The large influx of workers into the public sector at the expense of other local industries would imply that other industries would encounter labour supply issues. An obvious solution is to import foreign labour. But imported labour also puts a strain on local society, particularly its infrastructure. In other words, the government's plan to revive its wage and incentive system could have a negative spillover effect on other industries in the private sector.

A more prudent approach is to avoid making substantial changes to public sector wage levels and allow the wage discrepancy between the public and private sectors to progressively narrow with time. It should be kept in mind that this recommendation may be more or less applicable to some occupational groups than to others. Drawn from aggregate data of the various industries in Macao, this study focuses on the aggregate findings which cannot be generalised or disaggregated to apply to every occupational group and worker.

Ultimately, the government's plan to improve administrative productivity will be more effective if it addresses the obvious institutional shortcomings, such as an inefficient wage and incentive system (notably, high wages without effective performance assessment), as much as the less visible but more challenging and longstanding barriers present in the civil service, such as a poor public service culture (Lam, 2009). This research suggests that, although the Macao civil servants require a large rise in wages to bring about a rise in their effort levels, wages alone are insufficient to raise productivity. Clearly, well-integrated measures are required to improve administrative productivity, especially those targeted at eliminating inefficient practices and a dysfunctional civil service culture. In its reform programme, the government has introduced other measures, such as training courses for civil servants, which it hopes will improve productivity. In particular, it has laid down the need to '[c]hange the ideology of civil servants' in terms of creating a 'culture that advocates better serving the people…' (Macao SAR, 2007). Courses that educate civil servants on the significance of pursuing the common good, and the significance of their job for the well-being of the wider community, could be a step in the right direction.

This research has demonstrated the ineffectiveness of using wages as a motivational tool for improving the effort levels of the civil service. Rather, it suggests that the Macao government should consider other strategies to raise the effort and productivity of its civil service. Non-monetary incentives, such as individual and team awards for outstanding performance, may be one of them. This in turn highlights the importance of a performance appraisal system in the public sector which is able to discriminate between levels of performance outcomes and which civil servants can trust. There is obviously no place for favouritism and tokenism if the civil service is to be reformed effectively. With a better incentive system, notably one that incorporates non-monetary incentives and is integrated with other systems in the civil service, particularly supportive organisational practices and culture, perhaps then the Macao government will have a better chance of 'build[ing] a committed, capable, upright, pragmatic and innovative civil service' (Ho, 2006).

Part III

Public Policy

Labour Policy:
Resolving the Mismatch between
Demand and Supply

Grace O. M. Lee

Macao suffers from the dual problems that the local labour supply is insufficient to meet the demands of a sophisticated economy but that it has nonetheless persistent structural unemployment concentrated mainly among the less educated and the older age groups. Although the gaming and construction industries have sought to resolve their manpower problems by importing labour, in the longer term, the government has an important role to play in creating a domestic labour market through appropriate government-sponsored, market-oriented training programmes. This chapter examines the characteristics of the labour market, analyses the Macao government's labour and training policies, and assesses the likelihood that those policies will help to resolve the mismatch between supply and demand.

The Macao Labour Market

In 2009, Macao had a population of about 557,400 with a labour force of around 333,000 of whom 321,000 were employed (Statistics and Census Service, 2009). Of those employed about 24 percent were migrant workers. Analysed by industry (see Table 8.1), the majority of the employed were engaged in community, social and personal services (23.2 percent) and hotels, restaurants and related activities (14.12 percent). Since the handover to China in 1999, the employed population has grown by more than 50 percent.

The only industry that has experienced a decline in employment is manufacturing. Many factories have either moved across the border to relocate their production in mainland China or have simply shut down (Sousa, 2009). Over the last decade, most of the other industries, including construction, hotels, restaurants and real estate, renting and business activities, have more than doubled the number of people that they employ (see Table 8.1). The community, social and personal services category has tripled the numbers employed since 1999. In terms

Table 8.1: Employed Population by Industry in 1999 and 2009

	1999 (000)	2009 (000)
Manufacturing	42.7	16.1
Construction	16.2	30.5
Wholesale and retail trade; repair of motor vehicles, motorcycles and personal and household goods	30.4	41.2
Hotels, restaurants and similar activities	21.0	44.6
Transport, storage and communications	14.5	17.2
Financial intermediation	5.8	6.9
Real estate, renting and business activities	9.3	26.3
Education	8.7	12.6
Health and social welfare	5.0	7.3
Other community, social and personal services	19.3	73.4
Others	23.1	39.6
Total	196.1	315.8

Source: Macao Labour Affairs Bureau (2009). Available from: http://www.dsal.gov.mo/english/otherstat.htm, http://www.dsal.gov.mo/pdf/work/eng/2_EmpCAM_q(Eng).pdf.

of occupation, employment has traditionally been dominated by the positions of clerks and service and sales workers (see Table 8.2). Clerks include positions such as casino dealers, hard and soft count clerks,[1] cage cashiers, pit bosses,[2] casino floor persons, dealers and betting service operators. Service and sales workers include casino and slot machine attendants/hosts, security guards and surveillance room operators. These occupations accounted for around 30 percent and 23.1 percent of the total workforce in 2009. Table 8.3 shows the rapid increase in the number employed in the gaming industry, starting from a modest 4,360 in 2003, peaking at 38,008 in 2007, and declining to 26,938 by the third quarter of 2009.

Macao has been heavily reliant on two categories of imported workers: highly skilled professionals and managers at one end and low-paid workers in the construction, manufacturing, and service industries, which include domestic helpers, at the other end. In 1988, when the manufacturing sector contributed 37.8 percent of Macao's GDP and provided about 45 percent of local employment (Sit, 1991: 9), Macao's manufacturing industry was already heavily dependent on 'free floating work groups' from elsewhere. 'The problem for employers is that they cannot be sure of getting the labour they need when they want it most, and they cannot afford to retain a high head-count during troughs in the business cycle' (Sit, 1991: 205).

Such labour flexibility was institutionalised in 1988 when the Labour Importation Programme (LIP) was officially introduced, legalising the importation of unskilled and skilled workers. Migrant workers are a flexible and disposable labour force because 'they are employed under short-term contracts with minimal job security, and thus can be hired and fired with minimal costs' (Choi, 2006). Table 8.4 shows a similar pattern to Table 8.3 of a rapid rise in imported workers from 25,925 in 2001, peaking at 92,161 in 2008, and dropping to 77,239 in the third quarter of 2009.

Table 8.2: Employed Population by Occupation in 1999 and 2009

Occupation	1999 (000)	Median monthly earnings in 1999 (MOP)	2009 (000)	Median monthly earnings in 2008 (MOP)
Clerks	35.5	6,247	80.7	12,000
Service and sales workers	39.2	4,862	74.7	7,000
Unskilled workers	32	3,367	58.0	4,500
Craftsmen and similar workers	24.5	4,574	30.5	9,000
Technicians and associate professionals	17.2	9,797	29.3	15,000
Plant and machine operators, drivers and assemblers	28.8	2,933	18.7	6,500
Legislators, senior officials of government and associations, directors and managers of companies	11.9	12,512	15.0	20,000
Professionals	5.9	18,741	11.6	23,000
Skilled workers in agriculture and fisheries	1.2	6,458	1.6	5,000
Total / Overall median	196.1	4,920	323.0	8,500

Source: Macao Labour Affairs Bureau (2009). Available from: http://www.dsal.gov.mo/english/otherstat.htm, http://www.dsal.gov.mo/pdf/work/eng/2_EmpProf_q(Eng).pdf.

Table 8.3: The Number of People Employed in the Gaming Industry, 2003–2009

Year	2003	2004	2005	2006	2007	2008	2009
Total	4.360	5,636	10,975	28,353	38,008	32,775	26,938

Source: Macao Labour Affairs Bureau (2009). Available from: http://www.dsal.gov.mo.
Note: 1. The numbers include people working in hotel and catering industry as well as the recreation, gaming and other service industries.

Table 8.4: The Number of Imported Workers, 2001– 2009

Year	2001	2002	2003	2004	2005	2006	2007	2008	2009
Total	25,925	23,460	24,970	27,736	39,411	64,673	85,207	92,161	77,239

Source: Macao Labour Affairs Bureau (2009). Available from: http://www.dsal.gov.mo.

The vast majority of the imported workers are from mainland China followed by other Asian countries. Most of the mainland Chinese imported workers have been employed in the low-skilled manufacturing and service sectors; they are paid a third to half of the wages earned by their local counterparts (Choi, 2006). The LIP has certainly exerted downward pressure on the equilibrium wage rate which employers have been willing to offer. From the standpoint of government and business, however, the low wages of workers have made a major contribution to attracting foreign investment and to enabling Macao to develop its infrastructure rapidly. Paradoxically, the government argues that the major reason for continuing with the LIP is that 'locals shun the low-paid jobs' (*Macau Daily*, October 19, 2009).

The only job that is protected from labour importation is that of casino croupiers (see Chapter 9). The rapidly rising number of gambling tables has meant that young people with relatively little training have been able to start earning good salaries very quickly. The average earnings of full-time paid clerks and service and sales workers in the gaming industry in 2009 were MOP15,100 and MOP9,800 respectively; much higher than the overall median salary of MOP8,500 (see Table 8.2). Many Macao residents appear to share the view of 63-year-old Sit Chi Shin that 'young people don't want to study any more. They think they can take a shortcut to getting rich by working for the casinos' (*Global Issues*, 2009). Supporting his observation is the fact that the university enrolment rate dropped to about 34 percent in 2008, down from 39 percent prior to 2004. As employment soared, the unemployment rate in 2008 fell to its lowest level since the handover. The economic downturn caused the unemployment rate to climb to 3.7 percent by the third quarter of 2009 (see Table 8.5) but by mid-2010 it had dropped again to under 3 percent.

Table 8.5: Unemployment Rate, 1999–2009

Year	1999	2000	2001	2002	2003	2004	2005	2006	2007	2008	2009
Unemployment rate (in percent)	6.3	6.8	6.4	6.3	6.0	4.9	4.1	3.8	3.1	3.0	3.7

Source: Macao Labour Affairs Bureau (2009). Available from: http://www.dsal.gov.mo/english/otherstat.htm.

Structural Unemployment and Volatility in the Labour Market

The stability of Macao's labour market has been affected by the long-term problem of structural unemployment dating from the decline of manufacturing in the 1990s (see Chapter 1), by short-term changes to Chinese government visa regulations, and by the impact of the global recession on the local economy. We examine the effects of each of these factors in the following section.

Structural Unemployment and Political Protests

Labour discontent over the unemployment situation and government policy on imported labour and job creation was a feature of the last years of colonial rule. After the handover, a confrontation between workers and the government occurred in May 2000 when 500 unemployed workers held a demonstration. In June and July of the same year, a further 2,000 unemployed workers and 5,000 protesters demonstrated against the government's failure to take measures to improve the unemployment situation. On July 2, the police used tear gas to disperse workers protesting against unemployment. In 2006, some 3,000 workers joined a May Day rally and clashed with police as they tried to reach the government headquarters to express their demands for more effective control of illegal workers and a limitation on imported workers. Eight labour organisations[3] participated in the May Day march although the pro-Beijing Macao Federation of Trade Unions chose not to attend the event (ITUC-CSI-IGB, 2007). On May 1, 2007, an estimated 10,000 demonstrators, including 2,000 civil servants, took to the streets. Their protest 'provided a rallying point for all sorts of demands to be raised by groups including workers, civil servants, and parents of mainland children. It was a cross-class protest despite the fact that the major protagonists were the local workers' (Lo, 2008: 70). Immediately after the 2007 protests, pro-government and pro-Beijing groups denounced the protestors, supporting the LIP which had essentially served to keep wages low. From the standpoint of government and business, low wages have made a major contribution to economic development, attracting foreign investment and enabling Macao to develop its infrastructure rapidly. The problem of discontented local workers has not gone away, however. On May 1, 2010, there were further violent clashes between demonstrators and the police in which over 40 people were injured (*South China Morning Post*, May 2, 2010).

Although the liberalisation of the casino industry has improved the employment situation, it has not provided relief for those who, because of their low skills or education levels, cannot find jobs in the new economy. Even for those who have been employed in the casino industry or in related activities, such as construction, hotels and recreation, their continued employment is subject to volatile external forces over which the government has little or no control. In the first quarter of 2009, for example, Macao's GDP contracted 12.9 percent year-on-year in real terms (*Macau Daily News*, December 21, 2009). In the private sector, total investment dropped 32.4 percent. Overall construction investment fell 35.5 percent. The export of gaming services declined by 13.3 percent with the total exports of services dropping by 14.6 percent and the imported services falling by 21.6 percent. The unemployment rate for the first quarter of 2009 increased to 3.8 percent and there was a sharp decline in the number of non-resident workers (*Macao Daily News*, May

7, 2009). The main causes of the downturn, which continue to loom as uncertainties for the future, were the policies of the Chinese government and the state of the global economy.

The China Factor

The Chinese government has been somewhat ambivalent towards the growth of the casino industry. While it welcomed the immediate economic benefits that foreign investment brought, it has also been increasingly concerned about the negative effects of the gaming industry. It has, for example, placed more restrictions on mainland tourists going to Macao and has taken stronger action against the illegal transfer of money. In 2007, the *People's Daily* suggested that Macao should diversify away from the gaming economy to promote cultural and vacation tourism and conference and exhibition activities (*People's Daily Online*, December 17, 2007). This recommendation was made in the context of a string of corruption and money-laundering scandals involving Chinese Communist Party officials and managers of state firms that were reported in the Chinese official press. Editorials warned of an 'epidemic of gambling' afflicting large portions of the mainland population which had led to countless losses of family savings and public money on Macao's casino tables. An investigation by the *China Business Journal* found that 'in 2008, Zhejiang private entrepreneurs gambled away at least 1.3 billion RMB in Macau, leading to the closures of scores of factories in the province' (*Global Issues*, May 17, 2009). There were concerns that 'the survival of China's entrepreneurial culture [was] in danger' after a series of gambling-related bankruptcies hit Zhejiang, China's export powerhouse (*Global Issues*, May 17, 2009). Melco Crown Entertainment, a casino that opened in May 2007 and claimed around 15 percent of the market share, confirmed that in 2008 its main [VIP] clientele came from mainland China, with an average personal spending of up to US$125,000 per visit (*Ming Pao*, November 15, 2008).

Responding to concerns that mainlanders were losing too much money in Macao's casinos, the Guangdong Provincial Public Security Department announced that entry visas for mainlanders were tightened in 2009 from an informal one visa per month to an official one visa every two months (*Ming Pao*, October 15, 2009). There is statistical evidence of a continuous decrease in the number of visitors on package tours, down sharply by 35.7 percent year-on-year to 261,349 in July 2009 (Statistics and Census Service, 2009). During that month, visitors on package tours from mainland China decreased by 42.2 percent. In the first seven months of 2009, visitor arrivals on package tours from all countries fell by 10.1 percent year-on-year to 2,535,849 (Statistics and Census Service, 2009). If the Chinese government continues to place restrictions on visitors to Macao, there is little doubt that it will have an important impact on the whole economy. The shortfall in visitors cannot be made up from elsewhere and a detrimental impact on employment in the casino and related industries is highly likely.

The State of the Global Economy

Another threat to employment is the volatility of the global economic system. The casino companies have been quick to respond to the financial crisis by stopping construction projects and laying off workers or reducing their working hours. In 2008, for example, Stephen Weaver, Asia Region President of the Las Vegas Sands Corporation, announced the temporary suspension of the building of the Shangri-la and Sheraton hotels because the parent company had a deficit of US$32 million and debt liabilities of up to US$9 billion (*Ming Pao*, November 14, 2008). Phase Seven and Phase Eight were supposed to begin in 2008 but were also called off. As a result of the stoppage, around 10,000 imported workers, 5,000 from the mainland and 4,000 from Hong Kong, were retrenched. Hotels also sought to cope with fewer visitors by reducing the working hours of their staff from 48 to 40 per week and by asking them to take unpaid leave.

There is some short-term evidence that the frenetic pace of development in Macao and the employment opportunities that it has offered cannot be sustained in the future (see Ricardo Siu in *Macau Closer*, May 11, 2009). The number of newly established companies, property transactions and completed buildings has been dropping with a consequent impact on employment. Employed workers who lost their jobs during the crisis or who have been working reduced hours have shown their discontent in demonstrations. At the end of 2009, on the day when the Chinese President Hu Jintao visited Macao to celebrate the tenth anniversary of the return of sovereignty to the mainland, around 1,100 Macao residents participated in the 'Anti-corruption, Fight for Democracy, Maintain Livelihood' demonstration organised by pro-democracy groups (*Ming Pao*, December 21, 2009). Among the demonstrators were students who were concerned about escalating property prices and workers who were dissatisfied with the government's labour importation policy, claiming that the non-resident and illegal workers were reducing their job opportunities. Many locals, particularly the underprivileged, have become disgruntled with the huge income gaps, high inflation rate, serious traffic congestion, rising property prices that have far exceeded ordinary citizens' affordability, high flat and rent prices that have increased the cost of doing business, the consequences of young people becoming too materialistic, the greater social impact of the gaming industry with more casinos opening in residential areas and their advertisements seen in newspapers and on television, pathological gambling, and bureaucratic and political corruption, most notably, the corruption case of Ao Man Long, the former Secretary for Transport and Public Works (see Chapter 6). Labour protests in a climate of economic uncertainty and social discontent have the ability to draw support from other sections of the population who also believe that they are disadvantaged under the new order.

The Government's Reaction to Labour Unrest

The Macao government has traditionally been pro-business. Its first Chief Executive, Edmund Ho Hau Wah, came from an elitist business family. His father was a prestigious Chinese community leader who was elected as the chairman of the Macao Chamber of Commerce in 1950 and played an important liaison role between the Portuguese administration and Beijing. The second Chief Executive, Fernando Chui Sai On, who assumed office in December 2009, came from a similar background. They share a belief in the desirability of a *laissez-faire* approach and a mistrust of the high taxes and bureaucracies required by welfare states. Macao's economic policies have consequently focused on attracting foreign companies which, the government promises, will be permitted to operate with minimum interference. In the 2001 and 2004 Policy Addresses, Ho described the main focus of economic development as the 'gaming industry as the dragon's head, with balanced development of other industries' (Ho, 2009a). As it turns out, the gaming industry has become almost the sole driver of economic development and other industries have suffered from cost increases and a shortage of labour because of its rapid development.

To maintain labour stability under conditions in which government action (or inaction) strongly favours business, the government has relied upon the pro-Beijing Macao Federation of Trade Unions, which incorporates most of the private sector unions in Macao (ITUC-CSI-IGB, 2007). The Chinese government has a strong influence over the Federation and directly selects its leadership. This has undermined the independence of the trade unions, since support for central government policies, such as the minimisation of workplace disruption and a concern for stability generally, overrides the rights and interests of local members of the Federation. The absence of the Federation from the May Day march in 2006 is an illustration of the importance that it places on stability over potentially disruptive activities. The government does invite labour representatives to sit on its Standing Committee for the Coordination of Social Affairs but the Committee also has business representatives who can block proposals if they find them inimical (see Chapter 4). Usually, at least until the more recent labour demonstrations, the government took action on labour issues with relatively little or no consultation.[4] The Labour Importation Programme implemented in 1988 is a case in point. It came in the form of decree law as a government decision which was not subject to the Legislative Assembly's approval or the scrutiny of labour representatives (Sousa, 2009).

This situation has changed with rising discontent not only over specific labour issues but also about social problems. A gap has developed between government capacity and public expectations. Labour protests are part of this rising discontent but it has become increasingly evident following the protests that dealing with these and other social problems cannot be resolved solely through traditional channels.

Government Reactions

Reacting to the vehemence of the Labour Day protests, the government has become much more proactive. In April 2007, it set up a Human Resource Office to improve social protection policy, stopped accepting new applications for immigration in an attempt to stabilise rising property prices, promised to build more public housing units, and vowed to accelerate the implementation of a provident fund (Ho, 2009b). In reviewing the government's policies at the end of 2009, the outgoing Chief Executive announced that the government would fully implement a two-tier social security system. He said:

> The SAR Government will first open individual central provident fund accounts for eligible Macao permanent residents in the first quarter of 2010. Considering that the financial surplus for the 2008 financial year was MOP25.1 billion, the Government has decided to deposit 10,000 patacas to each of the eligible persons' accounts as initial capital, amounting to a total of 3.3 billion patacas (Ho, 2009b) (see also Chapter 12).

There was also an announcement of stronger measures to control illegal workers and to restrict further importation of labour. Tam Pak Yuen, the Secretary for Economy and Finance, announced that the government planned to reduce imported labour by at least 50 percent to ensure work for Macao residents (*Macao Daily News*, March 26, 2009) and increase fines of up to MOP10,000 for each employee who was found to be violating the Law on Employment of Non-Resident Workers (*Macao Daily News*, March 26, 2009). Additional penalties included revoking 'in whole or in part, the employer's permit for employment of non-resident workers and depriv[ing] the employer's right to apply for new employment permits for a period of six months to two years; and suspend[ing] the employment agency from engaging in business for a period of six months to two years' (Macao Special Administrative Region Law No. 21/2009). The law came into effect in October 2009.

A new Macao Labour Relations Law was also passed by the Legislative Assembly on August 5, 2008 and came into effect on January 1, 2009. The Macao Labour Relations Law (Decree Law No. 24/1989) which had been in place since 1989 was repealed. The Executive Council completed discussions on the bill in

April 2006 and submitted the bill to the Legislative Assembly for further study. The bill was a result of lengthy discussions within the Standing Committee for the Coordination of Social Affairs and took into account the views of employers and labour association representatives. The Committee had been considering the issue of a new labour law since 2001 but could not reach agreement. The deadlock between business and labour was finally broken by the need to take more positive action after the May Day demonstrations (see Chapter 4). The bill was intended to better protect both employers and employees and to clarify the rights and obligations for part-time, domestic and contracted workers. It provided compensation for overtime, working on public and mandatory holidays, and allowances for late-night work and shifts (Macao SAR Government Information Bureau, 2006).

The new labour law was brought into effect after 14 months' deliberation by the legislature and was finally passed in principle in June 2007 with only one abstention. The debate in the Legislative Assembly focused on whether work suspension compensation should be applied in specific situations and whether wage reduction would affect guarantees to employees (*blogmacau.info*, June 6, 2007). Legislators Lee Chong Cheng and Lao Cheok Va argued that companies falling behind in wage payments should be liable for criminal prosecution but the Director of the Labour Affairs Bureau, Shuen Ka Hung, pointed out that there were technical difficulties in existing regulations which would not enable the government to do so. He also claimed that criminalisation would involve major amendments to a series of laws including the Criminal Prosecution Code and the Labour Prosecution Code.

During the debate, Ng Kuok Cheong and Au Kam San argued in favour of retirement benefits and a provision that the retirement age should be set at 60. Provisions for long-service payment had been included in an earlier draft of the bill but they were removed from the final draft (Macao SAR Legislative Assembly, 2007). The pro-business stance of the government has traditionally been reflected in the fact that there has been minimal labour protection and the new labour law caused concern among business representatives in the legislature. Many pro-business legislators complained that 'the bill was biased in favour of the employee interest and that it violated the government policy of protecting and assisting small and medium enterprises' (Lo, 2008: 62). The President of the Legislative Assembly, Susanna Chou, also believed that the bill was tilted toward the interest of the employees. She added that 'as a representative institution of all the Macao people, the legislature should also care for the interests of employers without whom there would have been no employees' (*Macao Daily News*, June 5, 2007). In their statements on the bill, Kou Hoi In, Chui Sai Cheong and Ho Teng Iat, representing business interests, said that it tended to support the interests of workers at the expense of small and medium enterprise employers (*blogmacau.info*, June 6, 2007).

The new labour law is an improvement over the old one because it defines the responsibilities and obligations of employers and employees and provides greater, if still limited, protection for workers. Around 50 modifications have been made to the old law. The provision of maternity leave has been increased from 35 days to 56 days and the entitlement to statutory holidays has been increased from six to ten days. Domestic helpers, who were previously not covered by the old labour law, now receive some protection (Price Waterhouse Coopers, 2009). The penalty level for an employer who violates the law has been increased and employers are required to keep employee records. It had previously been common practice for workers not to have formal employment contracts with their employers. The power of employers to change unilaterally the wages and working conditions of employees or to terminate their employment was unchecked and workers were often victimised and discriminated against if they engaged in union activities (*blogmacau.info*, June 6, 2007).

Although the new labour law is an improvement over old practices, pro-democracy legislators and the pro-labour camps are not satisfied with it, mainly because the longer-term protection of labour in the form of pensions and long-service payments is still outstanding. The new law cannot in itself resolve the political tensions caused by unemployment and other social problems; large-scale protests have continued after its introduction. It does, however, serve a window-dressing function, addressing some issues but failing to give workers the comprehensive protection that they seek.

The Mismatch between Labour Demand and Supply

Macao has witnessed a structural change towards service activities because of the expansion in the gaming and tourism sectors. Chan (2003) raised the concern that 'service industries require less manual workers, but more workers with professional knowledge and formal education. It therefore represents an occupational upgrade for workers in the local labour market. At issue here is whether the local labour force can adapt to new working environments and meet new job requirements'. The high unemployment rate of 6 percent in 2003 was an indication of the extent of the supply-demand mismatch in the labour market. It was soon accompanied by vacancies in the casino industry which the local labour market could not fill (see Table 8.6).

Such a mismatch is generally attributed to a lack of skills in the local labour force, low educational attainments and low adaptability. On the basis of international experience, the best way to reduce the mismatch between labour supply and demand rests with government-sponsored, market-oriented training programmes, which aim to equip the unemployed with the practical skills required by employers (Layard et al, 1991; O'Connell and McGinnity, 1997). Most of the unemployed in Macao are the less educated with the highest numbers falling in the age brackets of 14

Table 8.6: Number of Vacancies in the Gaming Industry, 2004–2009 (by Position)

Gaming industry	2004	2005	2006	2007	2008	2009
Directors and managers of companies	18	127	51	19	14	10
Professionals	10	3	13	11	2	7
Technicians and associate professionals	118	64	63	118	14	41
Clerks	4,673	3,714	4,230	1,872	167	141
Services and sales workers	1,900	1,777	1,008	994	41	118
Skilled workers in agriculture and fishery	10	3	8	–	–	1
Craft and similar workers	–	140	110	38	3	14
Plant and machine operators, drivers and assemblers	1	2	21	3	1	3
Unskilled workers	368	337	127	25	16	26
Total	7,104	6,167	5,631	764	258	361

Source: Macao Labour Affairs Bureau (2009). Available from: http://www.dsal.gov.mo/english/otherstat.htm.

to 24 and 45 to 54 (see Table 8.7). To take a common example, women workers made redundant by the textiles and garments industries are low-skilled and middle-aged. These women cannot move to the services sector because those positions have been filled by young migrants from China, the Philippines or Thailand. Macao entrepreneurs usually prefer to 'recruit young and pretty workers [female] and not middle-aged, low-skilled ones' (Sousa, 2009).

Table 8.7: Unemployed by Age Group in 2009

Age group	2009 (000)
14–24	3.3
25–34	1.4
35–44	2.3
45–54	3.2
55–64	1.6
>65	–
Total	11.9

Source: Macao Labour Affairs Bureau, http://www.dsal.gov.mo/pdf/work/eng/3_DempSA_q(Eng).pdf.

Results of the Employment Survey released by the Statistics and Census Service (DSEC) for the second quarter of 2009 show that the unemployed population was 12,000, with 90.6 percent looking for a new employment, of whom 9.4 percent were fresh labour force entrants searching for their first job. With regard to educational attainment, 40.8 percent of the unemployed had primary education or lower, 27.9 percent had junior secondary education and 19.7 percent had senior secondary education. For the structurally unemployed who were searching for a new job, analysed by the industry in which they were previously engaged, 23.9 percent had worked in construction and 18.1 percent in recreational, cultural, gaming and other services. Analysed by their previous occupation, 29.7 percent were service and sales workers and 18.9 percent were craftsmen or in related professions (Statistics and Census Service, 2009).

Employers have not seemingly been prepared to upgrade staff through training. The unemployed are usually not financially able to invest in training and rely on government-sponsored programmes. Vocational retraining was introduced for the first time in 2002 to address the unemployment issue arising from the Asian financial crisis. The Vocational Training Department under the Labour Affairs Bureau provides the following courses for job-seekers and employees:
- Apprenticeship training courses
- Advanced training
- Professional qualification training courses
- Retraining
- Employment training for the middle-aged.

The Apprenticeship Training Programme provides two-year pre-job training for teenagers on engineering maintenance. The programme has trained around 330 technicians in the last ten years. Another two 900-hour training courses for catering were added in 2009. Only in 2006 did the Labour Affairs Bureau organise professional qualification training courses for aspiring carpenters, elementary chefs /dim sum cooks, and car mechanics. There were 98 students who completed the course in that year. Of those, less than half (46.9 percent) were successful in finding jobs.

The Labour Affairs Bureau has also launched retraining programmes in engineering, home decoration, truck driving and facial treatment, which have been offered in collaboration with organisations such as the Public Transport Association, the Macao Federation of Trade Unions and the Women's General Association of Macau. Although the retraining programmes aim to equip the unemployed and increase their competitiveness in re-entering the labour market, statistics suggest that they are ineffective. Only 37 of 124 re-trainees in 2006 (29.8 percent) were able to find jobs after finishing the programme. The main reasons for low re-employment were that the job-seekers were relatively old and with low levels of education.

Employment training for the middle-aged was launched by the Labour Affairs Bureau in 2006. Courses, which were offered in collaboration with the Macao Federation of Trade Unions, focused on training for such positions as waiters, kitchen assistants, office assistants, facial care assistants, and hotel room attendants. The effectiveness of the programme is in question since it only offers single-module courses that last for not more than two months. This training programme is also a *de facto* form of subsidy: any trainee who is over 35 years old and has achieved 70 percent attendance on the course is given a MOP10 transportation allowance per hour. Each person can apply for up to three courses.

According to government statistics, non-resident workers peaked at 103,153 in August 2008. About half of the migrant population was from mainland China with Hong Kong as the second largest source of labour importation. Of the 16,000 workers from Hong Kong, around 8,500 were engaged in gaming and other service industries. The vacancy situation in the different industries (see Table 8.8) and in the gaming industry in particular (see Table 8.6) shows that there is still a mismatch between what is needed and what is locally available.

Table 8.8: Number of Vacancies in 2008 and 2009 (by Industry)

Industry	2008	2009
Manufacturing	1,822	1,534
Electricity, gas and water supply	11	18
Hotels and restaurants	4,020	3,790
Financial intermediation	179	163
Wholesale and retail trade	1,728	1,686
Transport, storage and communications	313	295
Investigation and security activities	476	480
Public sewage & refuse disposal	18	2

Source: Macao Labour Affairs Bureau (2009). Available from: http://www.dsal.gov.mo/english/otherstat.htm.

If one compares the statistics of the employed population by educational attainment in 1999 and in 2008, there has been a dramatic increase in those with tertiary and secondary education, from 62.7 percent to 78.5 percent (see Table 8.9). The increase in educational standards can be attributed to the proliferation of degree-offering bodies, including the three universities, in Macao. However, a strategic development policy in tertiary education is needed to align it with economic restructuring. As a small economy, Macao needs coordinated human resources planning because it is limited by a lack of large consumer and labour markets. Such planning should be focused on the development of knowledge and skills in areas demanded by productive industries. The high demand for managers and professionals cannot be met by the short-term, elementary and remedial training which has been coordinated by the Labour Affairs Bureau. Its market is the structurally unemployed who have low educational levels and few skills. The prospect for this group remains poor although the problem will diminish as more of them move towards retirement age.

Table 8.9: Employed Population by Educational Attainment in 1999 and 2009

Educational attainment	1999 (000)	2009 (000)
No schooling/pre-primary education	21.4	15.7
Primary education	51.7	52.3
Secondary education	100.7	172.6
Tertiary education	22.3	75.2
Unknown	0	0
Total	196.1	315.8

Source: Macao Labour Affairs Bureau (2009). Available from: http://www.dsal.gov.mo/pdf/work/eng/3_DempSA_q(Eng).pdf.

Conclusions

The labour market environment is not conducive to resolving the mismatch between demand and supply. The gaming industry has short-term needs which may represent a strong demand for labour, but the labour market cannot meet that demand and there is therefore a need for imported labour. The importation of labour, however, has been a perennial source of unrest among the structurally unemployed and those who believe that its presence prevents upward job mobility into managerial positions. The efforts of the Macao government and traditional associations to meet demand through retraining do not yet appear to have borne fruit and are unlikely to satisfy the demand for professionals and specialists required by the gaming industry. Tertiary institutions may eventually help to meet the shortfall, but many of their graduates will return to China and others may be attracted by opportunities elsewhere in the region. Macao is an open economy and the relatively free flow of labour means that it is difficult to devise manpower plans which will resolve the demand problem. Establishing a balance between imported and local labour, investing in relevant training and retraining programmes, and enhancing labour protection are desirable goals. But they all present considerable difficulties in an economy dependent on a single industry which is highly sensitive to economic and political factors well beyond Macao's boundaries.

The global financial crisis illustrates just how volatile Macao's economy can be in the face of adverse external conditions. Workers were laid off, construction stopped and domestic political tensions increased as imported workers were seen to be taking jobs away from locals. Economic diversification is probably the best longer-term solution and one which is supported by both the Chinese and Macao governments. In his campaign for election as Chief Executive, Chui Sai On said that 'striving for the appropriate diversification of the economy is an indispensable move' in order to realise the sustainable development of Macao and to maintain its long-term prosperity and social stability (*People's Daily*, July 13, 2009). He promised to 'take an integrated approach to development and make great efforts to promote the sustainable growth of gaming-related industries, such as the tourism industry, MICE industry, cultural industry and retail business… [I]mportance shall be attached to the optimisation and diversification of the industries, cultivation of the other emerging industries, and the upgrading and transformation of the manufacturing industry and logistics industries' (*People's Daily*, July 13, 2009).

Beyond its macro-economic goal of diversification, the government has an important role to play in ameliorating the present situation. Despite the constraints with which it is faced, training programmes can be upgraded and made more relevant to fill the vacancies for managers and professionals that are much needed in the gaming industry. Practical and flexible in-service training programmes can be set up to improve the quality of staff in enterprises. The Employees Retraining Board (ERB) of Hong Kong, for example, has been very successful in offering a tailor-made programme for employers with a placement rate of 91 percent in 2007–2008. It offers 'a one-stop recruitment, pre-employment training and post-employment follow-up service to employers at no cost' (ERB, 2009). The ERB assists in organising recruitment days, in placing recruitment advertising as well as providing an intensive follow-up service to enhance trainees' placement and retention. The employers discuss course design with an appointed training body and participate in the selection of trainees to ensure that those enrolled will meet their requirements, provide vacancies exclusively for the ERB, offer a one-off training bonus to trainees and assist in the provision of an on-the-job training and job retention survey (ERB, 2009). The programme aims to equip jobseekers with the necessary skills for entry into jobs and helps to resolve employers' manpower needs. These training programmes can help the unemployed, especially the unemployed middle-aged and the young who drop out of schools, to gain better professional skills and secure employment. In November 2009, the government and the Macao Federation of Trade Unions launched an on-the-job training and employment scheme to promote employment of local workers by providing training allowance according to the needs of enterprises. Its provisions, however, are different from the tailor-made programmes in Hong Kong and its results are yet to be seen. Finally, the government needs to look at unemployment security which can be improved by setting up funds to protect those who lose their jobs in volatile times.

With an adequate supply of human resources, the government can lessen its reliance on imported workers and cut the costs of imported workers, both in salaries and in discontinuity of employment. This would have the political benefit of reducing public discontent against the government's labour importation policy and the social benefit of enabling local workers to secure employment and improve their living standards, leading to more sustainable development.

9

Labour Regulation in the Liberalised Casino Economy: The Case of the Croupiers

Alex H. Choi and Eva P. W. Hung

The proliferation of casinos over the past few decades has gone hand in hand with the advance of the neoliberal global economy. The governments of the developed world have resorted to casinos as a source of painless taxation to bridge shortfalls in social expenditure and their reduced ability to tax business in a world of capital mobility. Third World governments have also sought to boost their economies and their tourism industry, in particular, by encouraging the development of resort gambling. In the words of Austrin and West (2004: 145), 'new sites of urban pleasure' have been created for the mass gambling market in an era of global consumption. One of the key promises to win popular acceptance of gambling legalisation is economic development and job opportunities. With the exception of Las Vegas, however, where strong labour unions have boosted the wages and benefits of casino workers, research has generally found that casino jobs are low-skilled and poorly paid with little job security. Casino management tends to favour the employment of non-locals, ethnic minorities and women workers to fill these positions. Even croupiers, who directly handle the games, are no exception to this rule. Frey and Carns (1987: 38) note that:

> … casino work, particularly that of the dealer, is characterized by low skill requirements, few prospects of advancement, little or no reward for seniority, high turnover, low employer investment in individual worker careers, and very low job security. In a word, then, the occupations in gambling casinos are *interchangeable* (our emphasis) in the sense that units can be inserted to replace existing units with little or no consideration of human values in the process. The only primary labour market characteristically found in the casino work place is that of high wages, which has thus become the only claim the organization has on the worker, and vice-versa.

The working conditions of dealers in Macao are significantly different from those experienced elsewhere. Croupiers have grown in number since the liberalisation of the casino industry in 2002. In mid-2009, there were 18,084 croupiers, representing 5.4 percent of the total working population of 332,700. Some 57 percent of the croupiers were women. The average monthly earnings of the croupiers was MOP13,170, which was 60 percent higher than the median monthly earning of MOP8,200 of the working population as a whole. Most of the croupiers (17,979) were full-time employees. Less than 1 percent of them were part-timers (Statistics and Census Service, Macao SAR Government, 2009). None was a non-local. They enjoyed a package of fringe benefits (such as annual leave and medical coverage) which were considered to be luxurious by local standards. New recruits were said to be career-minded and prepared to work their way through the ranks into higher positions.

The traditional image portrayed in most studies of casino workers does not therefore apply in Macao. What particular conditions make Macao different? Why have the casino moguls been prepared to honour their promise of delivering decent jobs in Macao? What has made them willing to alter their employment practices to come to an accommodation with their workers? This is particularly interesting because Macao does not have a strong trade union movement and labour protection lags behind neighbouring jurisdictions (Choi, 2008: 61–64). This chapter is an attempt to resolve that puzzle and, in the process, to throw light on the politics of production and the legitimation of the state in Macao.

The Politics of Production

Michael Burawoy's (1983; 1985) 'politics of production' thesis argues that the production process involves not simply transformation of materials into productive goods by labour but also the reproduction of wider political and social processes. Burawoy maintains that the state plays a significant role in regulating the relations between labour and capital in the production process and thus shapes the contours of labour relations and capital profitability. By this means, Burawoy helps to broaden the study of labour process from the narrow confines of labour-management relationships and technological transformation into a wider process involving political intermediation. The term 'politics of production' is used to illuminate the struggles in the labour process and to highlight the role of the state in regulating these struggles.

Burawoy identifies three historical forms of labour control. One of these, which is of particular relevance here, is market despotism which was traditionally associated with a competitive form of capitalism. Workers were put under a rigorous regime of extraction under the tyranny of the market and the logic of profit. However, with the demise of competitive capitalism and the rise of monopoly capitalism, market despotism gave way to a hegemonic regime in which the consent of labour is secured through persuasion, though coercion is never entirely excluded. This is a situation fostered by state intervention. On the one hand, welfare schemes and social policies cushion workers from the onslaught of market forces so that labour is no longer solely reliant on the market to secure its reproduction. On the other hand, the state interferes with the practice of management, setting limits on their areas of autonomy such as wages, termination of contract and work hours. While this helps to reduce workers' market dependence, the hegemonic regime encounters contradictions when more costly state interventions erode capital's profitability. Capital seeks to escape from the control of the national state through a strategy of globalisation. The threat of relocation re-establishes the dominance of capital in the politics of production and re-entrenches market discipline in a regime Burawoy calls 'hegemonic despotism'.

Burawoy's hegemonic theory is useful for an understanding of the controversies surrounding Macao's croupiers, especially their aggressive demands for tips in the monopoly era and their subsequent ascent to the status of a labour elite. The reconstruction of labour consent through the elevation of the croupiers into an elite reflects partly the change in the economic order. More profoundly, however, it has to be understood as a feature of the post-transition political order in which the state attempts to claim legitimacy by cultivating a social stratum of direct beneficiaries of the liberalisation policy. We argue that the emergence of this consent took place through three successive critical events. The first event can be dated back to the late 1990s. The despotic labour control regime encountered a major crisis which found expression in its inability to motivate the casino workers to provide courteous service. In a period of serious economic recession, the necessity of bringing in competition to shake up outdated practices became a necessity. The resolution of the crisis was found in the break up of the casino monopoly and the reform of the labour process.

The second event took place during the critical years of 2001 and 2002. During this period, the institutional framework of the casino sector was revamped and two new operators were granted casino concessions. The changing casino economy led to a period of labour activism aimed at protecting wages and which was accompanied by demands for fair treatment. This brought back state regulation of labour management practices in the casinos and prepared the ground for the emergence of the hegemonic regime.

The third event covers the period after 2003 when the government decided to reserve the job of the croupiers for local people. This policy created conditions of high wages and benefits for this occupational group in a tight market environment. The croupiers were strategically created and positioned to secure the hegemonic consent of the working class in a largely market despotic sector. Their emergence reflects unique local conditions in which global casino capital has to collaborate with the local state in concocting a labour control regime that is critically important to the legitimacy of the state. It also partially reflects the despair of the organised labour sector which had been domesticated by the state and had become part of the control apparatus. Labour protests, which have sometimes been violent, have been marginalised to the periphery of state power but they have exposed the social tensions inherent, though suppressed, in the liberalised casino economy. In this political environment, the croupiers hold positions carrying fundamental contradictions. It is a strategic occupation crucial for securing the legitimacy of the casino economy but its members lack autonomy and are subject to strict disciplinary control. The croupiers have been used to capture the imagination of Macao citizens but their well-publicised position also obscures the fact that they are but a small enclave in a low-cost and low-wage economy. Casino capitalists are willing to participate in legitimacy politics so long as they see lucrative returns. However, in an Asian environment where casino gambling has rapidly proliferated, the game in Macao may eventually come to be too costly. The enhanced mobility of the casino capitalists enables them to be less reliant on the blessing of the political regime. And should they decide, or even threaten to move elsewhere, the death knell of the high-paid croupiers in Macao may be sounded.

The Monopoly Period

From 1962 until 2002, the casino monopoly in Macao was tightly held by Stanley Ho's Sociedade de Turismo e Diversões de Macau (STDM). In addition to providing Ho with handsome profits to expand his empire beyond the gaming industry into areas like hotels, banking and real estate, the casino monopoly also furnished the colonial state with a steady flow of tax revenue, which rose from 13.2 percent of total government income in 1982 to 57 percent in 1998 (Liu, 2002: 323). Two events that took place in the 1980s further enhanced the dependence of the state on casinos and consolidated a symbiotic relationship between the two, essentially turning the colonial state into a 'casino state' (Leong, 2001). First, the monopoly contract was revised in 1982 to raise substantially the gaming tax rate on gross casino revenue from 10.8 percent to 25 percent, eventually reaching 30 percent in 1991.[1] Second, STDM invented a new business strategy in 1985[2] to subcontract VIP gaming rooms to outside operators. This strategy was clearly successful because casino income has risen rapidly ever since with the share of VIP room reaching 70 percent of total casino revenue in 2001 (Eadington and Siu, 2007: 14). But the strategy also brought with it major problems because operators of the VIP rooms often had dubious underworld connections. However, eyeing increased casino and hence tax revenue, the colonial state condoned this practice despite its apparent breach of the STDM contract which explicitly prohibited subcontracting.[3] The VIP rooms became the foothold for the underworld's presence in Macao's casinos and presented an enormous threat to law and order in the late colonial state (Leonard, 2006: 162; Leong, 2001: 187; Pina-Cabral, 2002: 205–221, 2005).

The acquiescence of the colonial state in the VIP room system reveals the fundamental nature of colonial rule in Macao. Firstly, since Macao's economy had never gone through robust and sustainable growth like neighbouring Hong Kong, the casino monopoly was the most important source of government revenue. The central concern of state regulation was, and only was, to ensure the continuous flow of tax revenue from the casinos to the government coffers. Secondly, the colonial regime's will to govern was seriously compromised after the so-called '123-incident' in 1966, in essence an anti-colonial movement which compelled the colonial governor to make a public apology for police brutality. Henceforth Beijing had a veto on major policy initiatives and the co-operation of local pro-China groups had to be secured for issues affecting the livelihood of local residents. The result was that the colonial regime took a detached and passive approach, refraining from 'meddling' in local politics (see for example Dicks, 1984: 125; Liu, 2004: 126; Lo, 1995: 59; Yee, 2001: 34).

The consequences of these developments can be seen in economic and labour policies. The colonial regime never had the vision and will to diversify the economy and to deliver itself from dependence on gambling income. For instance, in face of the rising labour costs in the 1980s, instead of upgrading the labour-intensive export-oriented industries, the colonial regime succumbed instead to the pressure of pro-China business groups by opening the floodgates to the importation of migrant workers (Choi, 2006: 153). The economy therefore operated on the logic of cost-reduction by cheapening labour rather than by enhancing productivity through reinvesting in human and capital resources. In addition, the colonial regime hesitated to bring in legislation to protect labour rights. The first labour law providing pitiful protection was not enacted until 1984 (Choi, 2008: 61). Similarly, a rudimentary social insurance scheme was not put in place until 1990 and provided only minimal retirement benefits (Lai, 2008: 383).

In this context, the colonial state and the market produced a labour regime comprising both coercion and consent which found full expression in the position of the croupiers. On the coercive side, the colonial state policies of allowing an influx of migrant workers into the local market and the provision of minimal social welfare reinforced market discipline and management control. This market discipline, in turn, allowed the casino operator to exert full control over its workers since the state had withdrawn from internal industrial relations. Labour relations in the casino became a state within a state (*Jornal San Wa Ou*, August 15, 2001). This legal vacuum was a result of the lack of penetrative power of the colonial regime and of the great political influence wielded by the casino.[4] The outcome was that casino workers enjoyed no benefits, no days-off, no retirement benefits, no pregnancy leave, and no protection from arbitrary dismissal (*Macao Daily News*, August 19,

2001; *Jornal Va Kio*, October 5, 2001). The rule was that casino workers got paid only if they came to work. Essentially, they were treated like casual labour and a practice of hiring and firing at will prevailed.

However, the casino operator realised that pure market coercion was not the best way to secure optimum labour output from the croupiers. In many service-oriented occupations, employers may want to persuade their workers to provide 'emotional labour' by allowing them to collect tips from customers receiving their service. The tipping system seems to motivate workers to provide good service (Azar, 2007: 257; Lynn and Withiam, 2008: 332; Ogbonna and Harris, 2002: 728). In his study of Las Vegas croupiers, Sallaz (2002, 2009) portrays the croupiers as entrepreneurs rationing out their service to the best tippers. This tipping 'game' is taken to be the core of a hegemonic regime securing worker consent in an otherwise monotonous, repetitive and tightly scripted work routine. We argue, however, that in Macao the casino also used the tipping system to transfer labour and other costs onto the players. When the casino allowed over-zealous croupiers to hustle tokes (tips), tipping was turned into extraction. But why did the casino allow the tipping system to become synonymous with bad service? What had this to do with its labour regulation practices?

In Macao, the significance of an effective labour control regime for croupiers could not be more important because table games represented more than 90 percent of casino income (Gaming Inspection and Coordination Bureau, Macao SAR Government, 2007). STDM developed an ingenious system of labour regulation that produced and maintained a compliant but self-motivated cohort of croupiers at minimal cost to itself. It managed to achieve this goal by taking advantage of its monopoly position in the market. The focal point of this incentive system was the tipping practice. Croupiers were only given a nominal daily wage (MOP15 per day as late as 2001) but were allowed free rein to hustle for tips from players. The amount of tips turned the total remuneration received by croupiers into one of the best salaries in Macao. Hustling for tips in a casino requires skills (Sallaz, 2002, 2009) but to describe card-dealers as entrepreneurs managing their business by rationing good service to the best tippers is far from the picture in Macao. Players were made to realise that tipping was the rule whether or not they liked the service rendered; they were obliged to pay tips because there was no way to escape from it. All casinos in Macao followed the same practice because they were all owned by Stanley Ho. The croupiers were required to extract tips from the players whenever they won three games. Failure to observe the company rule was considered a dereliction of duty and could be subjected to disciplinary actions (*Jornal San Wa Ou*, September 13, 2001), mainly because STDM also had a direct stake in the tip pool. A significant proportion of the tip pool was in fact expropriated by STDM to pay for its operation costs, including for example 'comps' (complimentary goods or services used to attract players to the casino), insurance expenses and salaries for senior management. Only around 60 to 70 percent of the tip was shared with the croupiers.[5] The croupiers had little autonomy in managing the way they hustled for tips. Nor did they consider it as an exchange for good service. Non-tippers were frowned upon and treated like outcasts. As one veteran dealer said, 'The players accepted that tipping was the rule here ... The management did not concern themselves about offending the customers because it was a monopoly. As long as you wanted to gamble in Macao, you had to come to our casinos. There was no escape.'[6]

The tips made a dealing job a highly coveted commodity in Macao. However, securing a job was not an easy task because, as might be expected, there was a great deal of competition and the openings were few. In August 2002, STDM claimed that about 3,500 workers were employed as croupiers (*Macao Daily News*, August 1, 2002). The high level of remuneration was intended to secure croupiers' consent to work but, paradoxically, it also increased the casino's control over workers because STDM was the sole purchaser of their labour power in Macao and the job skill itself was not transferable. In other words, the high remuneration helped to increase casino security by raising the costs of non-compliance.

In addition to the tipping system, STDM built an internal labour market based on seniority, an integral component of the labour control regime. Seniority dictated promotion, income levels and privileges, such that the longer one stayed, the more the identification with the company. Usually, a new recruit would enter the casino as a waiter or waitress. Upon satisfactory performance, a selected few would be elevated to go through dealer training in an in-house training school, the experience of which was widely regarded as exceptionally stressful. Training took place after a long day at work and trainers took an authoritarian approach with public humiliation not infrequently meted out when trainees made mistakes. Tips were shared on a graduated scale. Newly trained dealers were entitled to 50 percent of the tips a veteran dealer made. From then onwards, there was a 5 percent annual increase until the entitlement of a full share was reached after 11 years on the job.

Job promotion was scarce and required 'juice', that is, connections with influential people in the casino (see Frey and Carns, 1987: 39; Smith, Preston and Humphries, 1976: 235). But seniority was recognised through the award of a largely honorary title called 'regular position' (正位) to those with more than 15 years of service. Holders of these positions were readily recognised by fellow workers with their unique staff numbers inscribed on their badges. Other than the status and prestige associated with these positions, they were exempted from the humiliation of being temporarily 'rusticated' (下野) to the waiter or waitress positions if they made mistakes, such as a lapse in following protocols on the gaming table. In addition, these dealers could sell their position for a substantial sum if they were no longer able to work. Apparently, this served as their retirement benefit (*Macao Daily News*, August 21, 2001). Over 30 percent of STDM employees had accumulated 20 to 35 years of service with the company when the casino monopoly came to an end (*Jornal Va Kio*, August 31, 2001).

The casino company managed to keep its workers under tight control through simultaneously using these despotic and hegemonic measures. Although a labour union, the STDM Workers' Association (SWA 澳門娛樂職工聯誼會) was set up in the 1970s, its leaders were often co-opted by the management. Grievances from the workers were not effectively addressed. One set of those concerns related to the non-entitlement of labour rights laid down in the 1984 labour law. Another set of concerns related to the tipping system because the croupiers not only felt they were short-changed but were also unfairly blamed for offending players. These grievances came to a head with the drive to liberalise the casino industry. Part of the liberalisation discourse was couched in terms of improving services by abolishing tip-hustling, hence with grave implication to croupiers' income. This resulted in a period of change and of labour activism.

The Moment of Change

Soon after the handover, in July 2000, the government declared the end of the gambling monopoly and announced that three operators would be allowed to run casinos in Macao. In February 2002 the three winners were named: Stanley Ho's Sociedade de Jogos de Macau (SJM, a subsidiary of STDM), Wynn and Galaxy (in partnership with Venetian). With the opening of Venetian's Sands Casino in 2004, Stanley Ho's gambling monopoly effectively passed into history. In fact, the government's desire to liberalise the casino economy was signalled in a series of newspaper columns which made blunt and highly critical comments of STDM's management of the casinos (see, for example, *Jornal San Wa Ou*, August 10, November 11, November 16, 2000). The politically ambitious labour leader, João Bosco Cheang (鄭康樂), then chairman of SWA, also started to rally the croupiers under its banner to fight for their rights. Apparently, the croupiers wanted to make their voices heard and defend their interests in the liberalisation process. Cheang filled this role and received, at least initially, a fair share of support in his campaign from the rank and file.

The formation of the SWA impinged on state labour regulation of the liberalised casino sector. Liberalisation had been couched in terms of ridding the state's traditional dependence on the casino monopoly by constructing a better regulatory system. Emphasis was put on law and order, casino credit, and VIP rooms and junket operations. Labour issues received only scant attention and were usually focused on improving the quality of croupier service, in particular, by abolishing the practices of tip extraction. Cheang's approach sought to involve the state in the labour dispute and to ensure that its non-interventionist approach was no longer an option.

Cheang's crusade began with his electoral campaign to win a seat in the Legislative Assembly in 2001, which included a platform promise to fight for holiday compensation from STDM (*Jornal Va Kio*, October 5, 2001). The Labour Relations Law enacted in 1984 provided for compensation if employers required their employees to work on weekly holidays and paid statutory holidays, something with which STDM had failed to comply. Cheang took his case to the media explaining the logic behind his action. When the negotiations with the company produced little result, he mobilised his members to lodge a formal complaint with the Labour Affairs Bureau. A total of 4,656 workers did so (*Jornal Va Kio*, July 12, 2002). Cheang further sought retirement benefits and a more healthy work environment for the croupiers. He also maintained that they were more than happy to give up the practice of hustling for tips and opt for a fixed salary instead. He claimed that by averaging the last ten years' monthly salary, the croupiers earned MOP15,200 but that his members would take a discount by accepting a fixed monthly salary of MOP14,000 (*Jornal Va Kio*, March 23, 2002).

Cheang's approach to trade unionism was mild and non-confrontational. He urged state mediation although he also threatened to take his case to court. He made known that he did not agree with the radical approach of a strike or a demonstration because the casino was too important for the economy of Macao (*Jornal San Wa Ou*, June 28, 2002). Instead, he emphasised his connections with the government and with mainland Chinese officials. Moreover, his union was affiliated with the Macao Federation of Trade Unions (MFTU) which was part of the powerful pro-China network which, in turn, was committed to maintaining political stability for the smooth transition of Macao to China. Cheang also applied pressure at a time when the casino tender was about to open. STDM was concerned about its image as a good employer for it hoped to win the bid. Cheang's approach also meant that the state was thrust into the centre of the dispute and could no longer avoid labour issues in the casino business. A powerful enterprise such as STDM had to be scrutinised on the treatment of its workers in the same way as any other business. In November 2001, the Chief Executive acknowledged the force of the argument and said that the government would treat industrial relations in the casino sector in the same way as any other sector (*Macao Daily News*, November 22, 2001). The recognition of the relevance of state in this often considered 'special' sector enhanced the power of the state to penetrate into society. The inevitable corollary of such an intervention was that issues of equality and fairness became matters of public debate.

With the issue of holiday compensation awaiting mediation by the Labour Affairs Bureau and the tender process about to begin, STDM started to change its approach. It announced that it would tender for the casino concession through a newly set-up subsidiary company, SJM. SJM would take over from STDM all casino employees if it were awarded a casino concession. Subsequently, SJM was awarded a concession and started operation in April 2002. SJM required all STDM casino employees to sign a new contract. Although the contract recognised their seniority with STDM, it stipulated a pay structure of MOP5,000 basic salary plus around MOP2,000 holiday compensation and tips. It prohibited croupiers from hustling for tips although they could still accept tips voluntarily offered by the players. STDM maintained that voluntary tipping was essential for good service (*Jornal Do Cidadao*, July 2, 2002). Cheang rejected this contract claiming that the pay level of croupiers would be substantially reduced because their tips would dwindle to almost nothing without hustling (*Macao Daily News*, April 1, 2002). Cheang was also unhappy with some of the other provisions in the contract, such as requiring employees to pay training compensation to SJM if they resigned from their jobs but took up croupier positions in other casinos (*Jornal Va Kio*, July 8, 2002). He asked his members not to sign the contract pending further negotiations with SJM. In the meantime, he sought the opinion of the Labour Affairs Bureau to see if this contract fully complied with Macao's labour law. Not unexpectedly, the bureau found nothing objectionable in it (*Jornal Do Cidadao*, July 12, 2002).

The government began to mediate in the dispute and a memorandum of understanding was reached on July 19, 2002. Key agreements included a commitment by SJM to review the croupiers' salary periodically, the lowering of the penalty for croupiers resigning from their jobs, and the setting up of a provident fund and retirement benefits for casino employees (*Jornal San Wa Ou*, July 20, 2002). Cheang then urged his members to sign the contract. Some of his union members, however, accused him of betrayal because the memorandum did not address the key issue of income protection (*Jornal Va Kio*, July 22, 2002). They argued that SJM's agreement to periodic review did not obligate it to maintain the income level of the croupiers after the practice of hustling for tips was abolished. Although a maverick group continued on with the fight,[7] the memorandum effectively dissolved resistance. By September 2002, SJM claimed that only 123 croupiers had not signed the contract (*Jornal Va Kio*, November 21, 2002). In addition, the Labour Affairs Bureau ruled on July 8, 2003 over the dispute on holiday compensation that compensation should be paid by STDM but should be calculated on the basis of the basic salary of the casino workers and that tips should not be included. This ruling significantly reduced STDM's financial liability and also brought to a close this phase of labour unrest in the casino sector.[8]

The workers had won a hollow victory. Income level was not guaranteed and holiday compensation fell far short of expectation. However, the significance of this period of labour activism cannot be underestimated. Not only had the croupiers asserted their right to be treated as equally as any other worker, they had also asserted the important principle that no enterprise, big or small, could be exempted from state regulation of labour practices. Reproduction of labour power in the casino was no longer a purely market affair and state regulation was entrenched. This episode heralds a new chapter in state-capital relations in the joint management of labour relations in the post-colonial era. Croupiers were brought within the orbit of the state rather than subject to the sole authority of their employer. The new contract offered by SJM had to be scrutinised by the Labour Affairs Bureau and had to pass through the labour law's litmus test just as any other labour contract did. In this process, the post-colonial state effectively established itself as a useful tool in resolving labour conflicts for the casino, albeit by means of enforcing market discipline rather than workers' rights. How much the state could do to strengthen market discipline depended very much, of course, on its legitimacy. In the ensuing years, a new state-capital consensus on the management of croupiers emerged which had as its aim the reinforcement of state legitimacy.

The Politicisation of the Issue

With the liberalisation of the casino economy, billions of dollars of investment capital poured into Macao within a short period of time. The management of this capital reflects a typical developmentalist approach in which the pursuit of rapid economic growth was prioritised over all other social considerations. For instance, casino concessions were granted on the basis of the experience and size of the investment of potential operators, both of which could help Macao to diversify into convention and resort types of casino development. Moreover, the Macao government allowed the three gambling concessionaries to each sell a sub-concession,[9] the result of which was that six competitors scrambled to claim a market share by rushing to build facilities and to expand their operations. There was no government-imposed limit on the number of casinos and gaming tables for each operator (Liu 2008: 120). The influx of Chinese tourists into Macao under the Individual Tourist Scheme in the wake of the 2003 SARS outbreak further generated optimism that a fathomless market was waiting to be tapped. All this resulted in an overheated economy driving up the costs of labour and land. In the process, small businesses were cannibalised and local residents suffered from traffic congestion, the high cost of housing, and a deterioration of the living environment (see Chapter 2).[10]

The primary contradiction in this casino explosion was the problem of the importation of migrant workers, which has been a major source of conflict between workers and their employers and the government since the 1980s. The government claimed that migrant workers only supplemented the shortfall in Macao's labour supply. But local workers complained of indiscriminate importation threatening their job opportunities and depressing their wage levels. The structure of the importation programme also caused concern; there was no minimum wage, no maximum import quota, and very little occupational restriction. There was also very little accountability on how many migrant workers could be imported to which sectors and under what terms. The construction of casinos and entertainment complexes since liberalisation created an acute labour shortage that the government sought to resolve quickly by opening the floodgates for migrant workers. Yet this was done without any regulatory mechanisms to ensure local workers would be given the first opportunity to find employment. Local workers complained that they were fired at precisely the moment their employers received government approval for labour importation. The issue of the migrant workers became the lightning rod driving the working class on to the streets in many demonstrations after 2006 (see for example Choi, 2008: 69–71; Liu, 2008: 121–123; Lo, 2008: 65–73).

The stance of the post-colonial state over the issue of migrant workers to a large extent reflects its class nature. The state is dominated by a close-knit pro-Beijing network, the pinnacle of which is the pro-China business sector (Chou, 2005; Dicks, 1984: 125; Yee, 2001: 159). This network has monopolised the electoral college responsible for the selection of the Chief Executive and controls many of the indirectly elected seats in the Legislative Assembly (Yu, 2007: 420–425; see Chapter 4). Formidable business interests inside the state have made any contemplation of reform of the migrant worker system extremely difficult. However, after the Ao Man Long corruption case was exposed, the government suffered serious questions of credibility and increasingly felt an erosion of political support at the societal level. Its response was partly found in the creation of dependent and loyal croupiers who fully identified with the state development strategy. The croupiers emerged as a labour elite in the post-liberalisation configuration, embodying the aspirations of the workers for secure, well-paid jobs.

To be a croupier one must be a Macao citizen. Tradition is usually invoked to explain this: it has been that way for a long time and there is no reason why it should be changed. That leaves the unanswered question of why the tradition emerged in the first place. Earlier discussion of the tipping system has shown that prescribing a Macao-only croupier regime made ample economic and political sense. Their high salary was paid by tips, thus their labour was offered practically free to the casino. Giving these positions to the locals allowed the casino to earn political credit by claiming that it was making very tangible contribution to the local economy. With the abolition of the practice of hustling for tips, however, the casinos had to absorb the labour cost. The notion of a Macao croupier thus became much less affordable. This practice was sustained largely because of the political benefits that stemmed from a policy of disallowing the importation of migrant workers into this labour sector.

The change started with SJM in March 2002 which substantially raised the basic salary of the croupiers to MOP5,000 but made it a part of the labour contract to prohibit the practice of tip extraction. Tips voluntarily offered by players were still permitted and deemed necessary by SJM to motivate croupiers to render good service. Apparently, however, SJM never seriously enforced the new tipping system. Tip extraction went on as usual until the Sands casino came into operation in May 2004. Sands differentiated itself from SJM by advocating and providing high-quality customer service and banning the practice of hustling for tips. A wage system composed of a basic salary plus a guaranteed amount of tips pegged the croupier's monthly salary at a level of around MOP13,000 per month (*Macao Daily News*, September 25, 2004). Since the income level was fixed no matter how much in tips was collected, this wage system effectively undermined any incentive for aggressive tip-extraction behaviour. SJM's business was adversely affected and the amount of tips slid. It was soon forced to match its competitor's wage package to prevent a haemorrhaging of workers. Aggressive tip-hustling in Stanley Ho's casinos then became a thing of the past.

Eventually, a more or less uniform wage package was adopted across all the casinos. Operators chose to compete for workers by offering better benefits, holidays and working environment rather than with wage hikes. This strategy was intended to contain wage costs in a tight labour market, especially when the bulk of costs could no longer be shifted on to customers through tipping. Apart from the concern of rising labour costs, casino operators wanted to know why they were being singled out for the ban on the importation of migrant workers and why they had to pay the same workers two or three times the salary that their previous employers had been paying.

Casino operators could have insisted that they had never promised to use only local workers in their facilities. In fact, the grant of the concession was based on their ability to bring in new forms of gaming experience to revitalise a declining industry. Job opportunities and staff benefits were apparently not the key concern. Only the MFTU and João Bosco Cheang sporadically voiced demands for the protection of the interests of current employees in the liberalisation process (*Jornal Va Kio*, August 14, 2001). The importation of migrant workers was raised from time to time but Stanley Ho only promised that SJM would rehire all STDM employees (*Jornal Va Kio*, October 2, 2001). Other bidders for the casino concessions made only vague commitments about giving local residents priority in their employment opportunities. The government was similarly vague in its pronouncements. In April 2002, in response to Ng Kuok Cheong's question in the legislature on how the government could ensure that casino operators would honour their promises on job protection, the government simply said that 'it would create the right conditions' for the casino operators to do so (*Jornal Va Kio*, April 22, 2002).

When many more casinos came into operation in 2005, the high demand for workers to run the facilities became a real issue for the casino operators. In July 2005, Galaxy became the first casino to speak out openly on the shortage of Macao croupiers and wanted the government to allow it to import croupiers from Hong Kong. In response, Francis Tam, the Secretary for Economy and Finance, said that the existing practice of not importing croupiers was actually consistent with the migrant worker policy (*Jornal Cheng Pou*, July 21, 2005). Since the government felt there was no shortage of croupiers, it had no reason to lift the ban. Tam's answer was interesting for two reasons. First, it indicated that there was no special policy on croupiers. The ban was based on an assessment which was the usual process applicable to any sector. Second, his answer was self-contradictory because if the same standard was applied to any other sector, there would hardly be any sector in Macao that would qualify for labour importation. Apparently, at that time, the government had not yet formulated a clear policy of labour importation in the croupier business and thus the status quo had to be justified by reference to the law on migrant workers.

One year later, the situation had profoundly changed. The increase in the number of migrant workers as well as illegal workers coupled with the uncontrolled expansion of the casino economy had caused congestion, high land prices, and inflation, all of which stirred social discontent. Even the pro-government Macao Federation of Trade Unions found it necessary to organise a major indoor gathering condemning the government's 'unrestrained' importation of migrant workers (*Macao Daily News*, April 13, 2006). A few maverick unions planned to stage an anti-migrant workers' demonstration on Labour Day.[11] In an attempt to defuse the situation, the Chief Executive informed the Legislative Assembly on April 4, 2006 that the government had decided 'to reserve the casino industry to be an economic sphere that belonged to Macao talents'. He understood that croupiers carried 'special meaning' to Macao people because, 'after going through appropriate training, people can earn a higher income'. Hence, despite tremendous pressure from the casino industry, his government 'would not consider importing labour until the moment all proper methods including retraining and job switching have been exhausted but [the industry] still could not find the workers to fill up the vacancies' (*Macao Daily News*, April 5, 2006).

This statement could be considered to be a shrewd move. Many of the unemployed were middle-aged unskilled workers whose jobs had been taken away by the migrant workers. Croupiers were considered to be a low-skilled occupation without high educational requirements. The Chief Executive's mention of retraining may have been directed at this group of workers. Indeed, hundreds of people lined up, many for over 48 hours, for an application form for a croupier training class during this period (*Jornal Cheng Pao*, July 12, 2006). João Bosco Cheang's government-funded croupier training centre was said to be specialised in retraining low-skilled workers because it did not require potential trainees to pass English-speaking and computer-literacy tests.[12] In fact, Cheang was proud of his training centre's success in transforming the lives of thousands of people. He pointed out that more than 80 percent of his training centre graduates obtained jobs in the casinos.[13] Their income instantly doubled or tripled, lifting the entire family from poverty to the level of a middle-class income. Those were the hopes and aspirations that the Chief Executive tried to capture in his policy of constructing a Macao identity for the croupiers. The beauty of the policy was that the cost of improving the status of the croupiers was borne by the casino operators while local businessmen could continue to enjoy the benefits of an unimpeded supply of low-cost migrant workers. In addition, the policy implied that becoming a croupier could provide a way out from the migrant-dominated labour market. The infusion of young people into the job because of the high wages offered also meant that the public image of croupiers improved from the previous perception that it was an exclusive sector reserved for those with the right connections. Becoming a croupier was now a proper and well paid position that was available and attainable for ordinary people as long as they had the necessary document, that is, a Macao identification card.

With the policy of reserving the croupier positions for local residents established, casino operators were permitted to import workers for other jobs. This dashed the hopes of those demanding that all casino jobs should be reserved for local workers (*Jornal San Wa Ou*, April 15, 2006). Three months after the policy was announced, the government allowed Wynn to import migrant workers and the casinos became one of the largest employers of migrant workers in Macao.[14] An ethnic hierarchy is thus constructed: the bottom level of unskilled cleaning and waiting jobs is filled mainly by migrant workers from China, well-paid croupier jobs are reserved for locals, and higher positions in the managerial ladder are recruited from Southeast Asia and Hong Kong. The top echelon, however, is usually seconded from their respective overseas headquarters.

The Federation of Trade Unions and Cheang's SWA accepted the concession on croupiers without fighting for other casino workers, thus essentially betraying their rights. They celebrated their success in pressing the government to safeguard this last bulwark for local workers. Their chief means of defending the rights of casino workers was to urge the government to discipline the casinos whenever deviations from this policy were detected (*Jornal Va Kio*, November 7, 2006). The Federation of Trade Union's strategy relied heavily on government action. For instance, upon receiving a report that non-local game supervisors had been assigned to act as croupiers, the Federation called on the government to require all casino workers to wear a staff badge indicating their citizenship status so that migrant workers would be placed under a popular surveillance system (*Macao Daily News*, July 9, 2008).

Unquestionably, during this phase of development, the pivotal element in the construction of consent was the government's policy of not allowing migrant workers to work as croupiers. The croupiers were elevated to a privileged status enjoying high pay and good benefits in a position reserved only for the local residents. This policy was formulated with a far wider goal than simply maintaining labour consent within the confines of the workplace. The creation of the croupiers as a labour elite served to stabilise class contradictions and to maintain the legitimacy of an authoritarian political regime. Ordinary workers were implicitly asked to remain hopeful of being freed from the difficulty and despondency of competing with migrant workers. The regime has created a loyal and dependent group which identifies with the existing pattern of development. In this light, croupiers have become one of the most politicised sectors in the economy. This politicisation, however, entails from time to time disciplining the croupiers to reinforce their subordination.

Disciplining the Croupiers

The government has to ensure that croupiers do not use their privileged position to hold the casinos and the state to ransom. In other words, this labour elite has to be domesticated *and* disciplined. This has been achieved by both political and social means.

In the first place, the decision to prohibit the importation of migrant labour for croupiers was made verbally without any written policy statement. The Chief Executive claimed that this decision was based on an assessment of the existing situation in the industry. In other words, the government has reserved the right to amend this policy whenever the situation changes. The croupier's status is therefore highly dependent on the government's good will. Aggravating the uncertainty are newspaper reports occasionally claiming that casino operators have been using various tactics to test and break the government's resolve on the ban.[15]

Secondly, the government has begun to study seriously the possibility of creating a government-run centralised licensing system for croupiers. This system would not simply be established for the purpose of maintaining the skills and knowledge of the workers in the trade. It would also be set up to monitor their conduct, for example, their gambling habits. If this system is put in place, the government will be able to exert considerable influence in deciding who can enter the trade and who can become a member of the labour elite (*Jornal Do Cidadao*, September 10, 2009; *Macao Daily News*, April 7, 2009).

Thirdly, the high income of card-dealers has lured some youngsters to quit school to join the trade (*Jornal San Wa Ou*, May 23, 2007; *Jornal Va Kio*, June 23, 2004). Social commentaries have been particularly harsh on this group of young croupiers. They claim that young dealers lead a hedonistic life because they earn a large salary too easily and too early and do not have the maturity to handle their new wealth in a proper way. Many of them are said to have picked up bad habits such as drug use and problem gambling. Self-destruction is not far away if they are lured to steal gaming chips to feed their addictions (see, for example, *Jornal San Wa Ou*, June 7, 2004). The commentaries have led to pressure on the government to raise the working age of croupiers from 18 to 21 (*Macao Daily News*, April 18, 2009). It is also possible that other control measures will be put in place.

Finally, some commentators have pointed out the irrationality of the system. They claim that the policy represents a distortion of the labour market because it has led to serious difficulties for small and medium enterprises that simply cannot afford the salaries offered by casinos (*Jornal Do Cidadao*, May 5, 2004). Others claim that the policy has been poorly conceived and is counterproductive because it deprives management of the incentive to promote croupiers into higher positions. Eventually, it is the more capable croupier who will be hurt by this policy (*Jornal Do Cidadao*, July 13, 2007; *Jornal Va Kio*, September 13, 2007). Still others point to potentially gloomy social and economic outcomes: that the policy devalues educational qualifications because poorly educated youngsters can earn better salaries than university graduates (*Macao Daily News*, July 7, 2004).

The government's measures and the adverse commentaries have left the croupiers in a state of apprehension. Their income and status are not derived from their skills or their organisational strength, but from the state's political expediency in the creation of a labour elite associated with the casino sector.

Conclusion

Burawoy's concept of hegemonic consent is helpful in understanding the politics of labour regulation in Macao. Politics has never been far from the conditions of the production of casino labour. During the monopoly era, croupiers could be treated like casual labour partly because of the overwhelming power of STDM in the colonial regime and partly because of a high demand for these positions stemming from a lucrative tipping system. Liberalisation, however, has profoundly transformed the politics of croupier labour. Although high wages remain the primary instrument for maintaining consent, its basis has been shifted from the tipping system to the policy of banning migrant labour in this trade. Paradoxically, the ban on imported croupiers has been put in place to contain social instability generated by the unimpeded importation of migrant labour into other sectors of the Macao economy. Hence, the production politics inside the casinos cannot be separated from the politics of production outside the casinos in the political 'game' of maintaining regime legitimacy.

Casino capital is willing to foot the bill of this political game as long as it is making profits. But money-making itself is another political game that depends very much on the calculation of Macao's usefulness to China. If China imposes tighter controls on issuing tourist permits to Macao, casino revenue and share prices will drop. It is not unlikely that casinos have realised that croupiers provide them with a lever to put some pressure on China. When business slows down, the firing of a handful of croupiers can easily unnerve society and unleash political concerns, which will then be transmitted back to the Chinese government through the local pro-China network. Croupiers are pawns in all these games; they are political constructions and are addressed as political objects. There is no easy way out of this subjugation. The deliverance from their present status probably starts with the emergence, within the rank and file, of an autonomous force that can balance the short-term privileges of their job against the long-term weaknesses of their political position.

10

Education Governance and Reform: Bringing the State Back In

Joan Y. H. Leung

This chapter examines education policy, reform and governance in Macao over the past two decades, a story of increasing state intervention with the impetus for change coming from the Sino-Portuguese Joint Declaration of 1987 and the establishment of the Macao Special Administrative Region Government in 1999. Through a series of reforms in the decade before and after the handover in 1999, Macao's education governance has shifted from a system of self-governing private providers with minimal state intervention to a system of codependence between public and private providers under a state-regulated framework. Underlying greater state intervention in education has been the policy objective of spreading mass schooling, which has been reflected, particularly, in the expansion of secondary education in post-1990 Macao. The change of government policy has also had significant implications for education governance and the relationship between the state and societal actors which, in turn, is a key element affecting the capacity of the state in policy implementation.

The rapid economic growth after liberalisation of the gaming industry in 2002 positively strengthened the state's legitimacy by increasing its tax revenues and the financial resources available for education expansion. However, it also had some negative repercussions for schools and society, such as student drop-outs and the loss of experienced teachers who quit for higher-paid jobs in the casinos. Given the government's intention to diversify the economy to reduce reliance on uncertain global conditions, educational development has become an important means of meeting the challenges of a changing economy and of world competition.

The discussion in this chapter focuses on the education reforms in the school sector as Macao experienced the dual processes of political decolonisation and economic transformation. It reviews the expansion of mass schooling in the 1990s and 2000s and the changing nature of education governance after the reconstruction of the school sector. What was the role of the state in the post-1990 Macao education reforms? Have these reforms enhanced state capacity in education governance and reform implementation? Is the output of schooling under the post-1990 reformed education system congruent with the requirements of the government's current economic policy? The focus of the analysis is on state-directed education reforms and the capacity of the state to steer societal actors to implement the kinds of policy changes that it wants. The chapter argues that the post-1990 education reforms have only been a partial success. State intervention in education has resulted in the expansion of mass schooling which has helped provide political legitimation for the Macao government. But it has not been sufficient in itself to require the societal actors to restructure the education system to meet the functional needs of a rapidly expanding and diversified economy.

Education everywhere has been used as a political tool to construct political identities and assist in state formation (Lall and Vickers, 2009). It is an instrument of social integration and control. Apart from meeting the functional needs of economic development, school systems are designed to consolidate the authority and legitimacy of the governing regime and the ruling elite. Ramirez and Rubinson (1979), for example, believe that mass education is an instrument of 'political incorporation' for 'creating members' of a nation-state. Boli, Ramirez and Meyer (1985) also point out that through the institution of 'citizenship', the members of a polity have 'strong obligations to participate in state-directed national development':

> [E]ducation becomes the vehicle for creating citizens. It instills loyalty to the state and acceptance of the obligations to vote, go to war, pay taxes, and so on. It also equips citizens with the skills and worldview required for them to be able to contribute productively to national success. The state promotes a *mass* devotion to a common set of purposes, supports a *uniform* system to build devotion to a common set of purposes, symbols, and assumptions about proper conduct in the social arena. (Boli, Ramirez and Meyer, 1985: 159)

Education is, therefore, an important policy area to prepare the Macao community for the reintegration with China. Although Macao is not a nation-state, the government still has to build its political legitimacy and identity, especially so because its education system has been fragmented and provision has been through uncoordinated privately owned schools with no standardised structure or unifying system. Without central regulation and funding support, the qualifications of teachers and school conditions in most private schools have been well below desirable standards. Since education is an instrument of political legitimation and social integration, there has been a need to 'bring the state back in',[1] revamp the system, reform the academic structure and curriculum, upgrade teacher professionalism, and improve the quality of school services.

Education governance in Macao is shaped by its past. Consequently, the first part of the chapter examines educational developments in pre-1987 Macao which strongly affected the trajectory of changes and reforms introduced by the state. The chapter then focuses on state-directed reforms before and after the handover in 1999 and analyses the tensions in the codependent relationships that have developed between the state and autonomous societal actors. The last section discusses the limitations on state capacity and the inadequacies of Macao's existing education system — even after two decades of reforms — to meet pressing economic challenges.

Educational Development in Pre-1987 Macao

Unlike most countries whose education systems are relatively unified and systematised, there was no single system of education in Macao before 1990. Rather, there was a combination of different education systems, which coexisted without proper state guidance or supervision. Because of the non-interventionist attitude of the Portuguese administration in Macao, the school service for the majority of the population was provided by a variety of community organisations, such as church groups (Catholic and Protestant), charitable bodies, cultural or trading associations, and individuals. More than 93.5 percent of the school population attended private schools with little administrative or financial support from the government (Rosa, 1990). Only a few Portuguese or Luso-Chinese schools[2] were state-funded. Some Macao scholars depict this as a colonial discourse of the centre-periphery divide of the Portuguese administration, which provided an education service mainly for the ethnic or Macao-born Portuguese, and the interests of the Chinese community which was marginalised at the periphery (Shan and Ieong, 2008). Another scholar refers to it as pluralistic: private schools enjoyed a high degree of autonomy, flexibility and adaptability and were able to flourish without strong government control (Lau, 2007).[3] Others refer to the education system as a polycentred collection of externally dependent subsystems imported from abroad, namely Portugal, the People's Republic of China, Taiwan and Hong Kong (Rosa, 1990; Tang and Bray, 2000; Adamson and Li, 2005). Despite their different interpretations of education development in pre-1987 Macao, most scholars — including Rosa who was an advisor to the Macao Government on education policy and a convener of the Education Reform Committee in 1989 — agree that the education systems were an uncoordinated mix. There was a 'total lack of an organised and systematised structure, in the absence of which several systems of education — rather than a single encompassing one — [were] allowed to coexist and develop separately'(Rosa, 1990: 16).

The diverse school systems that coexisted can be classified into four main categories:

(1) a very small number of government-run Portuguese-medium schools which followed a 4+2+3+2+1 structure based on the model in Portugal,
(2) a few government Luso-Chinese schools which operated a 6+5+1 structure,
(3) the majority of private schools which used a Chinese medium of instruction following a 6+3+3 model borrowed from mainland China or Taiwan, and

(4) the English-medium religious schools which followed a modified Hong Kong's Anglo-Chinese model with a 6+5+1 structure (Adamson and Li, 2005: 42–43).

In addition to the public-private divide and the language-medium classifications, the categorisation of schools in Macao was further complicated by political affiliation; some Chinese schools were pro-Communist China whereas others were pro-Nationalist Taiwan (Tang, 1998; 2003).

In sum, the development of school education before the 1990s, apart from a small number of Portuguese and Luso-Chinese public schools, was societal-driven and outside the ambit of the state. The private schools which provided schooling for the majority of the population were autonomous, uncoordinated, non-standardised, and mostly under-resourced. There was a pressing need to upgrade the academic and professional qualifications of teachers and to improve the overcrowded space and substandard conditions of most of the private schools (Rosa, 1990; Lau, 2007; Yee, 1990). The inadequacies in education were so critical and so apparent that the state had an implicit mandate to revamp the sector.

Education Reforms in the 1990s and 2000s: Bringing the State Back In

Soon after the signing of the Sino-Portuguese Agreement in 1987, under the spearhead of the Education Reform Committee, the state began to take a more active role in education reform. The promulgation of the 1991 Education Law (Law No. 11/91/M) — the first comprehensive education law in which the Portuguese, Luso-Chinese and Chinese schools were all included in one system — was a milestone in Macao's education history (Sou, 1998). It marked the birth of a Macao education system and a change of government policy from non-commitment to active involvement in education matters.

The 1991 law defined the structure, organisation, and functioning of the education system and introduced administrative measures to support the restructuring of the school sector. In 1992, the Education Committee was officially established as a government advisory body and the Education and Youth Affairs Department was reorganised to take the lead to regulate and make school education more systematic. Moreover, through a series of legislative measures over the next two decades, the state reasserted its command role in education governance. As Vong (2009: 6) points out, it was 'by legislative means such as establishment of regulations, implementation of universal free education, establishment of the "public school net", construction of a localised curriculum framework and others [that enabled the state] to create different terrains of governance'. Table 10.1 outlines the major legislation through which the state intervened and restructured an uncoordinated society-centred education system into a regulated state-sponsored education system.

Table 10.1 State Construction of the Macao Education System, 1991–2009

Year	Legislation	Content
1991	Law No. 11/91M	Enactment of the first comprehensive Education Law in Macao.
1992	Decree Law No. 81/92 M	Restructuring of the Education and Youth Affairs Bureau.
1992	Decree Law No. 15/92/M	Establishment and regulations on the composition and powers of the Education Committee.
1993	Decree Law No. 38/93M	Regulations governing private educational institutions.
1993	Decree Law No. 63/93/M	Regulations concerning accounting statements of non-profit private educational institutions.
1994	Decree Law No. 38/94/M	Regulatory framework on pre-school and primary school curriculum.
1994	Decree Law No. 39/94/M	Regulatory framework for the junior secondary school curriculum.
1995	Decree Law No. 29/95/M	Provision of seven years of free education (one pre-school year + six years of primary education).
1995	Decree Law 32/95/M	Regulatory framework for the development of adult education.
1996	Decree Law No. 15/96/M	Regulations governing teaching staff in private schools that had joined the public school net.
1996	Decree Law No. 33/96/M	Regulations governing special education.
	Decree Law No. 54/96/M	Regulatory framework for technical and vocational education.
1997	Decree Law No. 26/97M	Regulations governing school inspection activities.
1997	Decree Law No. 46/97M	Regulatory framework for the senior secondary school curriculum.
1997	Decree Law No. 34/97/M	Provision of ten years of free education (one pre-school year + six years of primary + three years of junior secondary education).
1999	Decree Law No. 42/99/M	Regulations on compulsory education for children between five and fifteen.
2004		Consultative Document on the education system of Macao SAR (Draft Law).
2006	Dispatch of Chief Executive Order No. 102/2006	Establishment of the Curriculum Reform and Development Committee
2006	Law No. 9/2006	Regulations governing the non-tertiary education system of Macao (Law No. 9/2006 has replaced Law No. 11/91M). Standardisation of the school structure in Macao: three years of pre-school/kindergarten, six years of primary education and six years of secondary education.
2006		Provision of twelve years of free education (extension to include three years of pre-school education).
2007		Provision of fifteen years of free education (extension to include three years of senior secondary education).
2007	Administrative Regulation No. 16/2007	Regulations for the Education Development Fund scheme.
2007	Dispatch of Chief Executive Order No. 230/2007	Specification of the dates for the implementation of the new school structure.
2009	Administrative Regulation No. 29/2009	Subsidies for purchase of textbooks (MOP1,500 per year for every Macao resident/student attending regular school education).

Source: Compiled by the author based on the education-related legislation. Available from the Education and Youth Affairs Bureau website (original in Chinese): http://www.dsej.gov.mo/~webdsej/www/inter_dsej_page.php?con=grp_db/edulaw.htm.

An Active State in Education: Funding, Regulation and Provision/Delivery

There are three principal dimensions of state participation in Macao's post-1991 education governance: funding, regulation and provision/delivery (Dale, 1997). State funding is the most important of those dimensions because it signifies a change in past government policy and recognition that education is a key to economic development as well as a political tool to transform society. In common with most other countries, the Macao government has now taken up the responsibility of becoming the principal funder of education. As Boli, Ramirez and Meyer (1985) put it, with the provision of mass education by the state, individuals have been politically incorporated as members of the polity.

State Funding: The Development of a State-sponsored Education System

A critical problem faced by Macao in the 1980s and 1990s was an acute shortage of school places and overcrowded space in most private schools (Lau, 2007; Sou, 1998). To support the expansion of schools, the government introduced the land grant policy in 1992. Private bodies could apply for the land to build new schools. In the first phase, ten pieces of land were granted and, in 1995, a second phase was introduced to meet strong demand.[4] The land grant policy is still in force today but on a much smaller scale. After more than a decade of education expansion, there are enough school places to meet the needs of society. Rather than building new schools, the government is now focused on the enhancement of school campus and facilities.

Another important achievement was the provision of free education through the establishment of the public school net. In 1995, seven years of free education was provided and there were gradual extensions of that provision to ten years in 1997, 12 years in 2006, and 15 years in 2007.[5] Private schools which have joined the public school net receive subventions from government based on the number of classes with no more than 45 students each. In the 2008/9 school year, about 70 percent of private schools joined the public school net, providing free education for about 85 percent of the student population in Macao (Table 10.2). The subventions per class to schools which have joined the public school net are as follows: MOP51,000 for kindergarten and primary, MOP69,000 for junior secondary and MOP80,000 for senior secondary education. Students studying in the non-free education schools also receive a tuition subsidy from the government. The amount for each student is MOP10,000 for kindergarten and primary education and MOP12,000 for secondary education (Education and Youth Affairs Bureau, 2009).

In addition, the government also gives subsidies to individual teachers to top up the low salaries of teachers in private schools. In 2009, for example, a teacher with an undergraduate degree and teacher training qualifications received a government subsidy of MOP4,000 per month, while a teacher with an undergraduate degree but

Table 10.2: Number of Schools and Students within/outside the Free Education System, 2008–2009

School Types	Public Schools	Private Schools		Total
		Within the Free Education System	Outside the Free Education System	
Number of Schools	13 (15.8%)	54 (65.9%)	15 (18.3%)	82 (100%)
Number of Students	3,175 (4.16%)	61,635 (80.66%)	11,599 (15.18%)	76,409 (100%)
	64,810 (84.82%)			

Source: Macao SAR: Education and Youth Affairs Bureau (2009) 'Statistics'. Available from: http://appl.dsej. gov.mo/edustat/edu/stat_d/mainpage.jsp?lang=e [Accessed November 10, 2009].

no teacher training received MOP3,200 per month.[6] This is a large increase compared with the subvention in 1985 when teachers received only MOP400 per month.[7] The direct monthly subsidy to teachers is linked to professional qualifications. Clearly, the government realises the importance of teachers' contribution to quality education and has therefore emphasised the importance of training and professional development.

Apart from subventions to schools and teachers, the government has also disbursed scholarships, financial grants and subsidies for students. Since September 2009, for example, every student who is a Macao resident attending regular school education is provided with a book allowance of MOP1,500 per year (Administrative Regulation No.29/2009). The percentage of public expenditure on education is another good indicator of the changing role of the state. In 2008, the funding on education was 14 percent of public expenditure (Macao SAR: Statistics and Census Service, 2009), which was more than double that of the 5 to 7 percent of the late 1980s (Yee, 1990: 5). Through the provision of free and compulsory education, the state has attempted to create a common identity in the community (Ramirez and Rubinson, 1979). Various kinds of financial subsidies granted to schools, teachers and students also facilitate social consent and help enhance the political legitimacy of the state.

State Regulations: Social Control and Institutionalisation of State Authority

The role of the state in educational development involves not only the financial provision of mass schooling but also the institutionalisation of state authority through the rules which regulate the education system. The provision of funding and state regulation are, in fact, two sides of the same coin. Authority and control are expressed in decree laws, administrative regulations and executive orders governing various aspects of the system. In the decade between 1989 and 1998, 155 education laws were published in the official bulletin (Vong, 2006: 15). The major ones included the statutory requirement of compulsory enrolment of all school-age children, the regulation of school curricula and qualifications of teachers and the regulatory framework governing the administration of schools as private enterprises (see Table 10.1). Through these processes, the state has assumed the leading role in guiding education development, and has also institutionalised its political authority and social control within the system. It has, for example, attempted to construct a localised curriculum framework, promote moral and civic education, and design programmes of studies for schools. In 1994, the government published a curriculum framework for kindergarten, primary and secondary schools which could be regarded as the birth of a local school curriculum in Macao. It has been implemented in government schools which use Chinese as the medium of instruction. Though it is not compulsory in the private schools, it serves as a model for the Chinese private schools. The diverse schooling systems were unified by the enactment of Law No. 230/2007 which provided for three years of pre-school, six years of primary, three years of junior secondary and three years of senior secondary education. The schooling system is now the same as those in mainland China, Taiwan and Hong Kong.

With the enactment of the non-tertiary education system regulation (Law No. 9/2006) in 2006, the government launched a second wave of curriculum reform. The existing curriculum was to be totally revised and new guidelines were to be drafted. This process is still continuing and it is not expected that the new curricula frameworks for pre-school, primary, junior and senior secondary education will be completed until 2011 or 2012. In the new curriculum framework, instead of detailed curricula outlining the syllabi contents of respective subjects, there will be an inventory or checklist, stating explicitly the basic academic requirements of the various subjects, the abilities that students should attain and their expected levels of achievement. Teaching guidelines will also be prepared and teacher training courses will be organised. When the new curriculum framework is ready for implementation, it will be made compulsory in all schools that have joined the public school net. This is another indication that the state is trying hard to control the school curriculum which could then be used more effectively for political socialisation and legitimisation. With state intervention in curriculum design, the school curricula in Macao — in common with others elsewhere — will reflect the ideologies and values of the established political order.

Political Construction and State Capacity-Building

With the implementation of 15 years of free education in 2007, the focus of the Macao government has shifted from quantity to quality education. In addition to formal legislation, the state has also been providing direction in education policy in the form of the annual Policy Address presented by the Chief Executive. Within the broad framework of the Policy Address, there is a Social Affairs and Culture (SAC) Policy Document which elaborates on the education policy that will be followed during the year. Issues covered in the 2007 SAC Policy Document included, for example, 'promotion of students' extra-curricular activities and all-round development', 'teachers' professional development', 'enhancement of education environment and facilities (for example, laboratory, library and IT facilities)', and 'promotion of community education and life-long learning' (Macao SAR Government, 2007). In the 2008 Policy Address, the Chief Executive announced the establishment of the Education Development Fund to help schools improve campus environments and facilities (Macao SAR Government, 2008). The focus of education policy has been on the enhancement of quality education, which includes issues such as curriculum reform, improvement of school management, teachers' training and small-class teaching. The theme of 'Deepening Human Development and Raising Standards' was highlighted in the 2009 Policy Address. It stressed, in particular, the importance of the state as a regulator in the quest for quality education:

> We will continue to increase our investment in non-tertiary education, and closely *monitor the returns*. We will further *develop relevant appraisal systems to ensure education quality*. We will also enhance teachers' professional development and job security (author's emphasis) (Macao SAR Government, 2009).

Until the late 1990s, educational development in Macao was still slow because of limited financial resources. When the ten-year free education system was implemented in 1997, for example, it was referred to as 'universal and towards free education' only because government subsidies granted to private schools were still inadequate.[8] Regulations governing compulsory education for children between 5 and 15 were enacted only in 1999. Free education was extended to 12 years in 2006 and 15 in 2007 when the government was more able to afford it. The capacity of the state to revamp the education sector has been greatly enhanced by increased tax revenues after 2002. This has resulted in a relatively more logical and organised education system with the potential for greater integration and social control. The end result is an enhanced and more institutionalised state presence in society.

With increased revenue has come a shift from an emphasis on the supply of school places to a focus on the monitoring of the quality of education services. This may have the effect of increasing the authority of the state by affirming that it has now assumed a role in education within society from which it will not retreat. Education policy has helped to build up the capacity of the state and embedded it to a greater degree within society (Evans, 1995). Its capacity remains, however, relational to the strength of other societal actors in the education process (Barkey and Parikh, 1991; Chandhoke, 1995). The sections below analyse state-society interactions in Macao's educational governance system.

The Codependent Relationship between the State and Societal School Organisations

Although the state has taken up responsibility for the funding of school education, the delivery of school services is still largely provided by private bodies: the religious, charitable and community organisations. The state is the major sponsor but not the sole provider. In the 2008–9 school year, for example, there were a total of 82 schools and 76,409 students in Macao. More than 95 percent of the student population were studying in private schools (69 out of 82) and less than 5 percent were in public schools (Table 10.3 and 10.4). Obviously, the state has to rely on the co-operation of the private schools to deliver school services efficiently and effectively and trust between the state and societal school organisations is therefore important.

Table 10.3: Number of Public and Private Schools in Macao, 2008–2009

School Type	Public Schools	Private Schools	Total
Pre-primary Education	2	4	6
Pre-primary and Primary Education	5	15	20
Pre-primary, Primary and Secondary Education	0	30	30
Primary Education	1	2	3
Primary and Secondary Education	0	9	9
Secondary Education	4	6	10
Special Education	1	3	4
Total number of Schools	**13** **(15.9%)**	**69** **(84.1%)**	**82** **(100%)**

Source: Macao SAR: Education and Youth Affairs Bureau (2009) 'Statistics'. Available from: http://appl.dsej. gov.mo/edustat/edu/stat_d/mainpage.jsp?lang=e [Accessed November 10, 2009].

Table 10.4: Number of Students in Public and Private Schools, 2008–2009

Year	Public/ Official Schools	Private Schools		Total
		Within Free Education System	Outside Free Education System	
Student Number	3175	61635	11599	76409
Percentage	**4.16**	80.66	15.18	**100.00**
		95.84		

Source: Macao SAR: Education and Youth Bureau (2009) 'Statistics'. Available from: http://appl.dsej.gov. mo/edustat/edu/stat_d/mainpage.jsp?lang=e [Accessed November 10, 2009].

As partners of the state in the provision of school education, the views and consent of the private schools in the formulation of education policy and the implementation of reforms are critical for the success of the new policies. The two largest community organisations representing the private schools and teachers are the Union of Catholic Schools of Macau (UCS) and the Chinese Educators' Association of Macau (CEA). While the membership of the UCS is based only on schools/organisations, the CEA consists of both organisations (school) and individual (teacher) members. Since its establishment in 1920, the CEA has been a patriotic organisation with a good relationship with the mainland government. In 2009, it had 31 school members and more than 3,100 teacher members.[9] There are about 5,000 teachers in Macao. The CEA therefore represents a majority of the teachers in Macao. The UCS was set up by Bishop Arquiminio Rodrigues da Costa in the 1970s to coordinate all Roman Catholic schools in Macao. It is composed mainly of the principals of the Catholic schools in the territory. Since the Catholic Church runs many of the renowned schools in the community, it is an important actor in the sector. In the early 1990s, the Catholic Church alone accounted for 47 percent of the total schools in Macao with a student population of 52 percent (Rosa, 1990). After the handover in 1999, its position was overtaken by the CEA. Nevertheless, it remains one of the leading societal school organisations whose voice cannot be ignored by the government.

Since the reforms of the 1990s, the government has maintained close consultation with the two leading school bodies in Macao. The Education Committee of Macao, an advisory body set up by the state in 1992, is the institutional linkage and the main channel of communication between the state and society on education policies. It is chaired by the Secretary for Social Affairs and Culture who appoints all the members of the committee. Apart from the Chairman, the Education Committee includes five other *ex-officio* members: the Director and Deputy Director of Education and Youth Affairs, the Rector of the University of Macau, the President of Macao Polytechnic Institute, and the Director of Tertiary Education Services Office; a maximum of 14 representatives from societal school organisations and a maximum of seven outstanding community leaders (Law No. 15/92/M). Table 10.5 gives the names, backgrounds and societal groups represented by the members in November 2009. Among the organisations and individual members, the representatives of the CEA, the UCS and the Macau Management Association, Mr. Tong Chi Kin, the Supervisor of the Workers' Children High School, and Father Luis Manuel Fernandes Sequeira, S.J., Principal of Colégio Mateus Ricci, are Standing Committee members. This clearly reflects the standing and importance of the Catholic and Chinese community organisations' contribution to school education.

Table 10.5: Education Committee of Macao: Members and Their Institutional Affiliations

Membership	Members	Representation
Ex-officio members	Secretary for Social Affairs and Culture	Official Representatives of the Government
	Director of Education and Youth Affairs Bureau (Standing Committee Member & Coordinator)	
	Deputy Director of Education and Youth Affairs Bureau	
	Rector of University of Macau	Tertiary Education Sector
	President of Macao Polytechnic Institute	
	Director of Tertiary Education Services Office	
Education/ Community Organisations	The Chinese Educators' Association of Macau (Standing Committee Member)	Schools sponsored by Community Organisations
	Union of Catholic Schools of Macau (Standing Committee Member)	Schools sponsored by the Roman Catholic Church
	Macau Management Association (Standing Committee Member)	Adult Education
	Associação Promotora da Instrução dos Macaenses	Education for Macanese
	Associação de Educação de Adultos de Macau	Adult Education
	Associação Educativa da Funcao Publica de Macau	Teachers in Public Schools
	Associação dos Educadores de Macau	Teachers in Catholic Schools
	Associação Promotora da Educação de Macau	Teachers in Catholic Schools
Individuals	Pe. Luís Manuel Fernandes Sequeira, S.J. (Standing Committee Member)	Principal of Colégio Mateus Ricci
	Tong Chi Kin (Standing Committee Member)	Supervisor of the Workers' Children High School & Executive Councillor
	Leong Heng Teng	Chairman of the General Union of Neighbourhood Associations (kaifongs), Executive & Legislative Councillor
	Maria Edith da Silva	Principal of Escola Portuguesa de Macau
	Tam Chon Weng	Chief of Office, Office of the Secretary for Social Affairs and Culture, Macao SAR
	Iao Tun Ieong	Principal of Hou Kong Middle School and National Committee of the Chinese People's Political Consultative Conference, Macao Representative

Source: The name list of members was obtained from the Macao SAR: Education and Youth Affairs Bureau website [Accessed November 10, 2009]. Background information has been collected by the author from interviews.

The attempt to make Portuguese a compulsory subject for all school curricula before the handover illustrates the power of these societal actors. Portuguese is not an international language and the proposal was strongly opposed by both the CEA and the UCS. Eventually, the government dropped the proposal. As the prime representatives of the schools, which provide education to more than 95 percent of the school children in Macao, the two leading societal school organisations can be a facilitator or an obstacle to the state in education reforms. As the Director of Education and Youth Affairs Bureau, Mr. Sou Chio Fai, aptly commented in a symposium: 'Education reform is complicated. Co-operation between the government and the private schools will be a crucial factor in determining the success of Macao's education reform' (Sou, 1998: 243).

Empowerment and Limits of the State's Policy Capacity

The relationship between the state and societal school organisations is sometimes paradoxical. On the one hand, the private schools providers are dependent on the state for financial support; on the other hand, they are independent of the state because they maintain their autonomy in school management and their own diverse school curricula. They are autonomous actors in these respects but they are also dependent on the state, which may use the power of the purse to steer the societal school providers in the direction in which it wishes them to go. Under the government policy of 15 years of free education, more private schools have been forced to join the public school net as a consequence of their need for state funding. By the school year of 2008–09 — if the few international, Portuguese and evening schools are excluded from the list — less than ten private schools remained outside the public school net. Through the provision of subsidies given to both the teachers and schools, the state exercises a soft form of control in monitoring learning and teaching activities in schools.

The present Macao, however, is still shaped by its past; school diversities and autonomy remain a strong tradition in education governance. Despite a series of post-1990 state-directed reforms to strengthen its influence in the private school sector, the state is often kept at arm's length. The long and well-established Catholic diocese schools (Colégio Diocesano de São José and Colégio Diocesano de São José 5), for example, prefer to remain outside the public school net because of the fear of political control. Most of the other private schools which remain outside the public school net are elitist Christian schools, such as Pui Cheng Middle School, Colégio do Perpétuo Socorro Chan Sui Ki, Colégio de Santa Rosa de Lima and Colégio do Sagrado Coração de Jesus (English section). They have a well-established standing in society and possess the financial resources to maintain their independence from the state. Private schools — including Christian schools sponsored by church groups and non-Christian schools sponsored by traditional Chinese organisations — continue to enjoy a high degree of autonomy in both school administration and the academic curricula. Each of them retains its own traditions, education principles and values. Diversities within the school curricula still represent a problematic area for a government, which is seeking a more uniform education system.

Macao's Economic Development and the Function of Education

After the liberalisation of the gaming industry in Macao, there was a need for the government to reorient its education system to meet the goal of economic diversification and increase its competitiveness. The government has sought to move away from an over-reliance on the gaming sector and both the outgoing and incoming Chief Executives have pointed to diversification as the key to future economic stability. In his 2009 Policy Address, for example, Edmund Ho Hau Wah said that the government aimed to 'capitalise on the resources generated by the growth of the gaming industry to foster the development of leisure, holiday-making, cultural tourism and other related industries', promote the growth of service industries, such as the convention and exhibition industry, and develop high-tech and high-value-added industries (Macao SAR Government, 2009). Similarly, in his electoral policy platform, Chui Sai On noted that 'striving for economic diversification at an appropriate level is in the long-term interest of Macau, and therefore should become the focus of future governance' (Chui, 2009). In spite of the government's awareness of the need to diversify the economy, its plans have yet to be matched with appropriate education policies (see also Chapter 8).

Education is an important component of the city's global competitiveness. However, a substantial portion of Macao's labour force is not well educated and, compared with Hong Kong and Singapore, the educational attainment of the employed population in Macao is relatively low (Table 10.6). Only about 20 percent of its employed residents have received tertiary education (university and higher diploma) whereas in Hong Kong and Singapore, it is around 30 percent and 38 percent respectively. In addition, the percentage of employed residents who have attained senior secondary education is considerably lower than that of Hong Kong and Singapore. In Macao, it is 26.5 percent whereas in Hong Kong and Singapore, it is 40 percent and 37.7 percent respectively. Nearly a quarter of Macao's employed population has primary education or below, compared with only 12.5 and 13.6 percent in Hong Kong and Singapore respectively. In terms of government expenditure on education as a percentage of GDP, Macao spends about 2 percent (Macao SAR: Education and Youth Affairs Bureau, 2009: 26), lower than that of Hong Kong (3.3 percent) (Hong Kong SAR: Census and Statistics Department, 2009). The government still has to invest further in education to take

Macao forward and diversify its economy. Only with high-quality professionals, expert technicians, well-trained managers and highly skilled workers can Macao respond flexibly and strategically to changing market conditions and enhance its competitiveness in the region.

Table 10.6: Employed Population by Educational Attainment: Macao, Hong Kong and Singapore

Education Level		Macao (Q2 of 2009)	Hong Kong (Q2 of 2009)	Singapore (June, 2008)
Tertiary	Number of Employed (000s)	71.0	1161.3	707.8
	(in percent)	(22.1)	(31.3)	(38.2)
Senior Secondary	Number of Employed (000s)	85.2	1484.4	697.9
	(in percent)	(26.5)	(40.0)	(37.7)
Junior Secondary	Number of Employed (000s)	90.5	599.6	195.3
	(in percent)	(28.2)	(16.2)	(10.5)
No Schooling/	Number of Employed (000s)	74.3	463.9	251.1
Pre-Primary/ Primary	(in percent)	(23.2)	(12.5)	(13.6)
Total	**Number of Employed (000s)**	**321.0**	**3709.2**	**1852.0**
	(in percent)	**(100)**	**(100)**	**(100)**

Source: Macao SAR: Statistics and Census Service (2009) 'Employment Survey'. Available from: http://www.dsec.gov.mo/Statistic/LabourAndEmployment.aspx [Accessed November 8, 2009].

Hong Kong SAR: Census and Statistics Department (2009) 'Quarterly Report on General Household Survey'. Available from: http://www.censtatd.gov.hk/products_and_services/products/publications/statistical_report/labour/index_cd_B1050001_dt_latest.jsp [Accessed November 10, 2009].

Singapore Government: Ministry of Manpower (2009) 'Employed Residents by Highest Qualification Attained and Sex'. Available from: http://www.mom.gov.sg/publish/momportal/en/communities/others/mrsd/statistics/Employment.html [Accessed November 10, 2009].

Note: As the types of classification vary among countries, similar types of education level have been grouped to simplify the categorisation. Below is the description of the classifications used in different countries.

Hong Kong — The original categories of 'post-secondary, non-degree' and 'post-secondary, degree' are grouped under 'tertiary education'. 'Upper secondary, sixth form' is classified under 'senior secondary education'. 'Lower secondary' is classified under 'junior secondary education', and 'primary and below' is classified under 'no schooling/pre-primary/primary'.

Singapore — The original categories of 'degree' and 'polytechnic diploma' are grouped under 'tertiary education'. 'Secondary' and 'upper secondary' are grouped under 'senior secondary education'. 'Lower secondary' is classified as 'junior secondary education'. 'Primary and below' is classified into 'no schooling/pre-primary/primary'.

In addition, a relatively high attrition rate, particularly in junior secondary and the first year of senior secondary education, is a weakness of the system (Table 10.7). Good employment prospects in the gaming industry have been cited as one of the reasons for the high drop-out rate. During the peak years of the expansion of casinos between 2005 and 2007, many senior secondary students dropped out to work as croupiers in the casinos (see Table 10.7). An additional reason for student drop-outs is the desire of private schools to maintain their reputation as producers of high-achieving graduates. All private schools retain the right to expel students whose academic performance is regarded as weak or unsatisfactory. The high rate of student drop-outs may also be a result of a failure of the academic syllabus to meet the interests of some students. According to the Education and Youth Affairs Bureau, only about 66 percent of those students who are in the secondary education age group manage to complete their secondary education (Macao SAR: Education and Youth Affairs Bureau, 2009: 30). Although the percentage of secondary school leavers continuing to tertiary education is high in Macao (more than 75 percent), this has to be balanced against the substantial number of students who do not actually complete secondary school (Table 10.8).

Table 10.7: Number of Student Drop-outs, 2003–2007

	P1	P2	P3	P4	P5	P6	S1	S2	S3	S4	S5	S6	Total
2002/2003	67	57	73	91	125	119	310	316	359	258	131	80	1986
2003/2004	78	80	74	70	129	146	437	366	316	374	217	115	2402
2004/2005	64	44	45	72	88	111	513	352	371	353	220	125	2358
2005/2006	45	47	45	47	81	104	344	370	361	383	207	172	2206
2006/2007	56	39	40	75	97	118	430	388	323	401	234	187	2388

Source: Statistics and Census Service (1999–2007) *Education Survey*. Macao: Statistics and Census Service.

Table 10.8: Academic Attainment and Rate of Further Studies of Secondary Students in Macao

Education Level	Complete Rate of Secondary Education[1]	Promotion Rate of Senior Secondary Graduates[2]	Rate of Senior Secondary Graduates Entering University[3]
2003/2004	68.5	75.0	71.1
2004/2005	66.0	77.1	70.8
2005/2006	67.4	76.8	68.8
2006/2007	66.6	77.9	69.3
2007/2008	66.3	84.4	76.4

Source: Macao SAR: Education and Youth Affairs Bureau (2009) 'General Survey of Education in Figures'.
    Available from: http://www.dsej.gov.mo/~webdsej/www/statisti/2008/edu_statistics08_e.html
    [Accessed November 30, 2009].
Note: 1. School completion rate refers to the percentage of students of the various education levels successfully
    completing school at that educational level.
    2. Promotion rate of senior secondary graduates refers to the percentage of graduates of Senior 3 taking
    courses organised by tertiary institutions.
    3. University-entering rate of senior secondary graduates refers to the percentage of graduates of Senior
    3 taking higher diploma or degree courses.

Even for those students who do go on to tertiary education, only about half of them choose to continue their education in Macao. The other half prefer to pursue their studies in mainland China or Taiwan with a small percentage going overseas (Table 10.9). Tertiary education is usually tailored to meet the political, economic and social needs of the local population. If half of the students choose not to continue their education in Macao, this should be an issue of concern for the government. Students who go overseas for their university education often do not return home to work. As a result, Macao does not have sufficient local professionals and technocrats with a strong identity to the community who are committed to supporting its political, economic and social development. The government has yet to introduce strategies to address the problem of the brain drain of its school graduates.

Table 10.9: Number of Macao Students Receiving Higher Education (by Place of Study)

Place of Study	Macao (%)	Mainland China (%)	Taiwan (%)	Others[1] (%)	Total (%)
2003/2004	1810 (53.61)	900 (26.66)	415 (12.29)	251 (7.43)	3376 (100)
2004/2005	1903 (53.92)	981 (27.80)	466 (13.20)	179 (5.07)	3529 (100)
2005/2006	1944 (49.40)	1193 (30.32)	521 (13.24)	277 (7.04)	3935 (100)
2006/2007	2114 (50.20)	1013 (24.06)	753 (17.88)	331 (7.86)	4211 (100)
2007/2008	2539 (56.38)	754 (16.74)	878 (19.50)	332 (7.37)	4503 (100)

Source: Education and Youth Affairs Bureau (2008) *2007/2008 Survey of Senior Secondary Graduate: Further Studies and Employment* (Original in Chinese 2007/2008 學年澳門高中教育畢業升學與就業調查簡報告). Available from: http://www.dsej.gov.mo/~webdsej/www/inter_dsej_page.php?con=inter_dsejdoc_page.php&layout=2col.

Note: 1. Including the United States, Australia, Switzerland, Hong Kong, Portugal, United Kingdom, Canada, New Zealand, Japan, The Netherlands and France.

If Macao aims to develop as a centre for international tourism, holiday-making, conventions and exhibition, the government also has to help promote and upgrade the teaching of English language in schools. An emphasis on the teaching of English would enhance Macao's international image and competitiveness in the global environment. At the moment, only a small percentage of the students (about 10 percent) are studying in English-medium schools (Table 10.10). Yet 73 percent of employers in one survey thought that English was necessary in their work but only 6.8 percent were satisfied with employees' spoken English, 29.1 percent were dissatisfied, and 45.6 percent thought the employees' English was average (Hao, 2006). The government still has no major programme for improving standards of teaching English language in the schools.

The expansion of the gaming sector also resulted in the loss of English teachers to higher-paid jobs in the casinos.[10] Their communication and interpersonal skills were valued in the industry and many left at the height of the expansion of the gaming industry between 2005 and 2007, a time when their skills were particularly needed in the schools.

Table 10.10: Classification of Schools According to the Medium of Instruction, 2002–2008

	Chinese (%)	Portuguese (%)	English (%)	Total (%)
2002–2003	92, 247 (91.77)	977 (0.97)	7, 295 (7.26)	100,519 (100)
2003–2004	90, 854 (91.25)	926 (0.93)	7, 785 (7.82)	99,565 (100)
2004–2005	88, 130 (90.85)	845 (0.87)	8, 030 (8.28)	97,005 (100)
2005–2006	83, 409 (88.91)	785 (0.84)	9, 616 (10.25)	93,810 (100)
2006–2007	79, 206 (88.34)	742 (0.83)	9, 711 (10.83)	89,659 (100)
2007–2008	72, 128 (87.53)	607 (0.74)	9, 665 (11.73)	82,400 (100)

Source: Macao SAR: Statistics and Census Service (2008) *Education Survey*. Available from: http://www. dsec.gov.mo/Statistic/Social/EducationSurvey.aspx [Accessed October 30, 2009].

Finally, Macao does not have a territory-wide public examination system. Schools set and mark their own examinations and issue their own certificates. This creates inconvenience for employers because there is no uniform standard of assessment across schools and internal assessment by the schools lacks credibility and reliability. The validity and transparency of the assessment criteria are also of concern (Morrison and Gu, 2008). A territory-wide examination would help reduce irregularities and inconsistencies in standards, and provide a fairer and more systematic framework for employers and tertiary institutions, both locally and overseas, to assess the quality and performance of Macao school graduates. The students would also benefit if there were a single unified entrance examination to local universities and post-secondary institutions. Under the existing system, students have to sit for a number of entrance examinations separately designed by different tertiary institutions in Macao. In addition, most of the students also take the university entrance examinations of mainland China and Taiwan (for students studying in Chinese-medium schools) or the GCE (London) examination (for students studying in English-medium schools). The existing arrangements are obviously inefficient. For the benefit of the students, business and the tertiary institutions, there is a need to reform the existing examination arrangements.

Conclusion

Under the direction of the state, Macao has made significant achievements in education in the past two decades, including the provision of 15 years of free education, improvements in teachers' training and professionalism, the introduction of a local curriculum as a model for schools, and the expansion of tertiary education. There has been increasing state intervention in the provision of funding and financial support, in the regulation of school administration, and in monitoring the quality of education. There has in the process been a redefinition of the state-societal relationship in education governance.

Critically, it was the expansion of mass education that gave the state an expedient handle to assert its control in education governance. There was no major disagreement between the state and societal groups on the provision of free and universal education, which has been widely regarded as a right of citizenship. However, when the state attempted to move deeper with its reform measures, such as the school curriculum reform, its capacity for action became constrained. Basically, there is a conflict of interest between the state and societal groups on issues such as a unified school curriculum or a territorial-wide public examination system in Macao. The education system in Macao remains externally oriented. Many of the teachers are educated and trained in mainland China, Hong Kong or Taiwan, rather than locally. The majority of schools adopt their own school-based curricula modified from teaching materials imported from these places. The school curricula, in practice, are closely linked to the targeted university entrance examination requirements. As a result, nearly half of the secondary school graduates leave Macao to continue their tertiary education elsewhere. To enable the city to meet local needs and economic development, Macao's education system has to undergo further changes. However, given that the state is dependent on the co-operation of societal school organisations in the delivery of school services, the education policy has to reflect the values and interests of the private schools as well.

Because the diversities of school curricula are rooted in Macao's history, politics, and cultural backgrounds, the policy capacity of the state to implement changes is constrained. Education reforms can only be brought about through co-operation and compromise between the state and its societal partners. As it stands, it would be difficult for the state to enforce a unified curriculum for all schools because there is no consensus on the issue. Other alternatives, such as outlining the basic requirements of academic attainment of various subjects at various educational levels, have to be adopted instead as a compromise. But such an approach is ineffective in enabling Macao to move forward to meet its economic challenges and it is questionable whether the government has the manpower and expertise to assess the performance of all schools. The guidelines which seek to establish basic requirements of academic attainment are vague and it seems likely that most schools will continue with their diverse curricula and teaching materials. The private schools will retain their autonomy and the state, at least for the foreseeable future, does not seem able to effect major changes.

11

Housing Policy: A Neoliberal Agenda?

James Lee

Introduction

Concomitant with the macro-economic changes that have taken place in Macao over the last decade is the transformation of its built environment. Investors have been looking beyond the roulette and baccarat tables for better investments, particularly investors from mainland China. House prices in the residential sector have consequently been increasing steadily since the change of sovereignty in 1999. The average price of private residential units completed in the years between 1990–1999 rose 33.5 percent in 2005 and 9.7 percent in 2006 (Un, 2007). For buildings completed in 2000 and after, a quarter-to-quarter increase of 20.4 percent was recorded. At the end of 2009, average house prices rose to MOP24,154 per square metre (Statistics and Census Service, 2009: 4). The average residential price of Macao properties is now largely comparable with Hong Kong as residents commute much more frequently for work and pleasure between the two cities (Yiu, 2007). The good economic times have also seen rents rocketing with average apartment rents of MOP400 a month in 2001 rising to MOP6,000 in 2009 (Centaline, 2009), an inflation rate of 15 times. Macao residents are finding both home ownership and renting more and more unaffordable. Rapid asset appreciation has attracted property speculators who, though encountering a combination of problems associated with red tape, lack of transparency and scarcity of space, still find real estate returns to be profitable. Unwelcome consequences of this speculation are its impact on land value and the potential for corruption. The former Secretary of Transport and Public Works, Ao Man Long, who was one of the officials who decided on land allocation, was convicted in 2008 on 57 counts of bribe-taking and sentenced to 27 years in jail (Commission Against Corruption, 2008: 31).

House prices are already beyond the reach of ordinary households and there will remain a major shortage until the government comes to grips with the issue of affordable housing. Most housing stock in Macao was built by the colonial government to house the influx of people fleeing China's Cultural Revolution and subsequent government provision of public housing has been quite small. Macao's 27 square kilometre of land already provide homes for half a million people and there is little room left for residential development. What land might be available for public housing is subject to fierce competition from casino and real estate development. A 100,000 square metre reclamation earmarked to house 20 casinos and hotels in the Cotai Strip, for example, has been strictly zoned for commercial use, depriving the residential sector of the chance to build condominiums (see Chapter 2). With these problems in mind, this chapter attempts to answer two questions. First, in what ways is the Macao housing system affected by the development of the casino sector and by heightened economic growth? Second, how do we interpret these changes in the Macao housing system in the light of its socio-political development and in the wider context of neoliberal urbanisation that has been widely taking place in East Asia?

Urbanisation, Neoliberalism and a Housing System under Stress

To place Macao's housing problems in perspective, we have to begin by considering the macro socio-economic context in which they are situated. Macao is part of China and the development of Macao's housing sector is intimately linked with two separate but related processes: first, the urbanisation of Macao is a small part of a much larger urbanisation process that has taken place in all other Chinese cities over the last two decades; second, the development of the Macao property sector and housing market is closely associated with the new-found wealth of mainland Chinese people who can now afford to travel, invest and gamble in Macao. There is a symbiotic relationship between the gambling industry and the development of the speculative housing sector. The liberalisation of Macao's gambling industry has opened up new opportunities for real estate development and offers scope to satisfy the desire for asset investment of the *nouveau riche* from the mainland. On the positive side, the weight of gaming taxes in total fiscal revenue grew from 50 percent in the 1990s to over 70 percent from 2002 onward. In 2007, the gaming industry constituted 35.6 percent of GDP and 83.6 percent of all tax revenues with a revenue source amounting to MOP32.04 billion in the third quarter of 2009 (Statistics and Census Service 2009: 19; Lam, 2009). More residents are treating home ownership as an investment asset leading to quick returns. There is accordingly a noticeable discrepancy between the large number of vacant flats that have been bought for speculative purposes and the lack of affordable housing for local residents. The public side of the housing system is manifestly inadequate and under stress (see Tables 11.7 and 11.8). Housing has become much less accessible to lower and marginal middle-income residents. Since 2005 there has been rising public discontent in the form of protests and marches, at least three of which were associated with housing price inflation and the inadequacy of the policy to deal with the problem (Lai 2008: 295). Ironically, the main bulk of the public housing stock (particularly economic housing) was built during the last decade of colonial rule. New production of public housing (including both social and economic housing) has been minimal for the period since 2001 (a mere 1,689 units) (see Tables 11.7 and 11.8), hence creating further tensions for the housing system.

Before we examine Macao's housing market, we need to have an understanding of the way in which China has developed its current urban centres. Since the commencement of economic reform in 1979, China has quietly undergone one of the world's most dramatic urbanisation processes. While in 1978 only 18 percent of its population were classified as urban residents, the 2000 Census put it at 456 million — some 36 percent of China's total population. If the urbanisation rate of 1995 is maintained, China will be 64 percent urbanised by 2020 (*People's Daily* 2009). Supra rapid urbanisation is also evidenced in the increase in the number of cities. In 1978, there were only 193 cities in China. By the end of 2000, this had increased to 663, more than threefold in two decades (Wang 2004). Successive rural reforms in the 1980s meant a huge supply of surplus rural labour. Coupled with the concentration of capital and policies in the new cities or new urban centres, China has managed to create what David Harvey has described as a capital and space amalgam (Harvey 1989). Rising fixed capital formations succeeded in transforming the value of the urban landscape, enabling city land, which used to be worth almost nothing, into property now worth millions. In many ways, the development of Macao's urban sector is similar to what has happened elsewhere on the mainland, and in Hong Kong. Anna Haila's concept of a 'Global City Politics I' points to an almost homogeneous global process of real estate development as national development strategy aimed at attracting capital investment, first from developers and then from housing consumers. House price inflation quickly produces household wealth accumulation and many homeowners quickly shift from the use-value of housing to exchange-value, hence completing the first cycle of capital circulation (Haila, 1999).

This real-estate-driven urban development has its genesis in neoliberalism. Neoliberalism gained widespread prominence during the late 1970s and early 1980s as a political strategy to deal with the sustained global recession of the preceding decade. Faced with the decline of traditional industrial production, as well as Keynesian welfare policies, the old industrial West began to dismantle the basic institutional components of post-war politics and instead began to create a series of new institutional arrangements to justify the deregulation of state control over major industries. The impact of neoliberalism on the urbanisation process is apparent when major economic activities are taking place in cities. Neoliberalism has come to transcend, not simply the physical structure, but also the social relationship among people, work and place, notably the value of the 'home'. Housing inequalities widely exist and reflect a much more complex picture of deprivation of space and basic needs. The liberalisation of China's new political economy is closely intertwined with the process of socio-spatial division and reflects the central feature of its new approach to urban issues. The linchpin of China's economic reform policy is the belief that the market, properly regulated and liberated from all forms of unnecessary intervention, represents the optimal mechanism for economic development — people will satisfy their housing needs through free market forces. However, this is not the way that neoliberalism has actually worked out in the urbanisation process (Brenner and Theodore, 2002). There is an obvious disjuncture between the ideology of neoliberalism and its actual operation in capitalist cities. On the one hand, while neoliberalism aspires to create the ideal of free markets, it has in practice entailed a dramatic intensification of coercive, disciplinary forms of state intervention in order to impose market rules upon all aspects of social life. On the other hand, whereas neoliberal ideology implies that self-regulating markets generate an optimal allocation of resources, neoliberal political practice has generated massive market failures, social polarisation, housing inequalities and a dramatic intensification of uneven development in all spatial dimensions (Forrest, Murie and Williams, 1990). In short, the neoliberal shift in government policies in many Western industrial economies has subjected the majority of the population to the power of market forces while preserving protection for the strongest (Brenner and Theodore, 2002: 15–16).

A Framework for Analysis

At a more practical level, neoliberalisation affects urban development in at least three distinct ways. First, capitalist urban development is always characterised by a pattern of *uneven development*. This is a key feature of the way in which capital seeks to mobilise particular territories and places as forces of production. Each stage of capitalist development is associated with a distinctive, historically specific geographical landscape in which some places, territories, and scales are systematically privileged over and against others as sites for capital accumulation (Harvey 1982; Massey 1995).Second, since the social relations of capitalism are permeated by tensions and conflicts that undermine or destabilise the accumulation process, the state is seen as a vital institution in which successive *institutional fixes* evolve to regulate these uneven developments. Neoliberalism thus represents a complex, multi-faceted project of socio-spatial transformation by the state to maintain and restore disequilibrium arising from the system's inherent instability. It represents both a fully commodified form of social life and a concrete programme of institutional modifications through which the dominance of capitalist interests may be maintained. Third, all neoliberal urban projects involve what may be called 'the creative destruction' of existing institutional arrangements and political compromises through market-oriented reform initiatives, and the creation of a new infrastructure for market-oriented economic growth, commodification and the rule of capital (Brenner and Theodore, 2002). In Table 11.1, we can observe the likely effects of destruction and creation in three dimensions of this process: the restructuring of the housing market; the transformation of the built environment; and the restructuring of the welfare state. One consequence of the process is that low-rent social housing will be reduced, eliminated or replaced by private home ownership for every household. In the United Kingdom, for example, by 1998, most social rented housing had been turned into home ownership through deliberate neoliberal housing policies (Forrest, Murie and Williams, 1990). Concomitant with changes to the mode of housing provision is a widespread retrenchment of social welfare at both national and local levels. It can be observed from these three linked urban processes that neoliberalisation has brought instability and change to the social system through various institutional measures. The role of the market has assumed many former state responsibilities in terms of forging a new housing, social welfare and neighbourhood configuration, one which constantly emphasises competition and privatised consumption. New urban spaces with much clearer boundaries (for example, gated communities and self-enclosed housing estates) are being developed to replace extant communities. This spatial process is both inclusive and exclusive with the ultimate result that cities will become increasingly central to the reproduction, mutation, and continual reconstitution of neoliberalism itself.

In the remainder of this chapter, an adapted version of Brenner's framework of neoliberal urbanisation is used to explain how the process has evolved in Macao. Its purpose is to ascertain what is happening in three distinct domains: the housing system, the built environment, and the welfare state, all seen in the context of the dimensions of the site of regulation, destruction and the creation of institutions (see Table 11.1).

Table 11.1 illustrates the consequences of neoliberal urbanisation for existing institutions. In terms of the housing system, neoliberal market activities will result in the elimination or the reduction of low-income housing which makes available more land for private housing development. Moreover, dominant rent-seeking behaviour will extract resources from low-rent social housing because there is more profitable housing investment in the private sector. The natural consequence of neoliberal housing strategies will be to attract more and more private housing investments for the development of upmarket private renting or private home ownership. The destruction of existing low-cost housing and the accompanying creation of new private renting or home ownership lead to the exclusion of those who once found housing affordable and accessible. Likewise, the new demand for urban land provides great incentives for developers to buy out traditional neighbourhood housing to make way for large-scale housing development projects.

Table 11.1: Neoliberal Urbanisation and Its Impact on Institutional Change

Site of Regulation	Destruction of existing institutions	Creation of new institutions
Restructuring the urban housing system	Elimination of public housing and other forms of low-rent accommodation; elimination of rent control	Creation of new opportunities for speculative investment in the real estate markets; introduction of market rents and more owner-occupation housing
Transforming the built environment	Destruction of traditional working class neighbourhoods in order to make way for speculative redevelopment real estate projects	Creation of new privatised spaces of elite/ corporate consumption; reconfiguration of local land use patterns; creation of gated communities and other purified spaces of social reproduction; intensification of socio-spatial polarisation; competitive pricing for urban land
Restructuring the welfare state	Local welfare services are retrenched	Expansion of community-based sectors and private approaches to social service provision; imposition of work on welfare recipients

Source: Adapted from N. Brenner and N. Theodore (2002) *Spaces of Neoliberalism*, Oxford: Blackwell, 24–25.

Restructuring of the Housing System: Speculative Housing Investment and the Primacy of Home Ownership Policy

The Macao real estate market has been growing over the past 40 years despite its sensitivity to internal and external economic shocks. In some periods, large fluctuations in property prices have been caused by the cross-border flow of capital. Other factors have also been important in the development of the real estate market. A major influence has been the economic business cycle. While it is difficult to tell whether the performance of the real estate market has been a cause or an effect of the ups and downs of the economy, there is no doubt that the two variables have been closely related. Another factor has been population growth. Immigration has been a significant cause of population growth and has also seriously affected the demand for housing in Macao. Table 11.3 shows that population grew steadily after 1999, mainly as a result of new immigrants from Hong Kong and the mainland. The increase in foreign labour in the gaming industry certainly put more pressure on housing supply. Finally, the economic development of Macao's close economic partners, particularly China, has also had an impact on the housing market (Yiu, 2007). The economy of Macao registered positive growth between 3 and 5 percent until 1996, and fell into recession in four consecutive years between 1996 and 1999 as a result of the Asian financial crisis and China's more prudent macro-economic policy (Lam, 2002). However, GDP rebounded in the new millennium and has continued to pick up in the years since the change of sovereignty. In 2007, it reached a historical high of 31.4 percent. For the period 2000–2008, the average GDP increase was 14.2 percent, a level that reflected unprecedented growth and the rapid inflation of asset prices. Table 11.2 illustrates the degree of volatility in the housing market since the liberalisation of the gaming sector.

Table 11.2: House Price Inflation, 2002–2006

Year/ Quarter	Average Price per Square Metre		Year of Building Completion					
			2000 and after		From 1990 to 1999		1989 and before	
	MOP	Annual Change (in percent)	MOP	Annual Change (in percent)	MOP	Annual Change (in percent)	MOP	Annual Change (in percent)
2002	6,261	...	7,797	....	6,919	...	4,235	...
2003	6,377	1.9	8,444	8.3	7,095	2.5	4,077	-3.7
2004	7,984	25.2	13,654	61.7	8,162	15.0	4,525	11.0
2005	10,024	25.6	16,280	19.2	10,894	33.5	6,047	33.6
2006	10,578	5.5	16,354	0.5	11,953	9.7	7,170	18.6

Source: Statistics and Census Service (2008) 'Construction Statistics'. Available from: www.dsec.gov.mo, 45. Un, P.S. (2007) *House Price Developments in Macao*. Working Paper, Research and Statistics Department. Macao: Macao Monetary Authority, 88. Available from: http://www.amcm.gov.mo/ publication/quarterly/Apr2007/HousePrice_en.pdf

Taking house prices from 2002 to 2009 as an illustration, one can also observe a high degree of inflation and volatility. While the annual appreciation in 2003 was only 1.9 percent, it was 25.6 percent in 2005, and 27.6 percent in 2009 (Statistics and Census Service, 2009). In addition, the degree of speculative activities can also be inferred from the increasing number of non-resident buyers in the housing market, mostly coming from mainland China. In 2002, only 22.6 percent were non-resident buyers. That had increased to 35.2 percent in 2006 as the total value of all property transactions by non-residents rose to 51.3 percent, meaning that non-residents buyers were investing more in higher-value properties, a typical situation in any speculative property market that begins to build a bubble (Un, 2007). New property sales have always been sites of speculation. New condominiums built in 2000 and after had an appreciation rate of 61.7 percent while that for older buildings (those built in 1989 and before) was a mere 11 percent. Property transactions experienced a dramatic drop in 2007 and 2008 as the global financial crisis gathered momentum. Sales were down by 33.3 percent over 2007 (Statistics and Census Service, 2008: 24). In addition, Table 11.3 suggests that against a context of steadily rising gaming revenue, there was no corresponding increase in the volume of public housing (with only marginal increases since 2003) although the population increased from 0.43 million in 1999 to 0.55 million in 2008. The pressure for government intervention has been mounting. Like most other real-estate-driven economies in East Asia, housing policy in Macao has been used as an important policy instrument to pump prime a slackening economy. The most evident example is the period before and after the Asian Financial Crisis when the poor performance of the property sector deeply affected the economy. In order to salvage a sluggish property sector, the government restructured its housing policy from a tenure-favouring social rented housing to one favouring private home ownership. Such a shift marked a watershed in Macao's housing policy as the interest rate subsidy policy detailed below shows (Chiang 2005).

Table 11.3: The Macao Gaming Economy, Population and Housing

Year	a) Public revenue (million MOP)	b) Gaming tax (million MOP)	Percent b/a	Population (in millions)	Public Housing (social + economic)
1999	9,859	4,767	48.4	0.429	–
2000	8,815	5,646	49.8	0.431	–
2001	9,814	6,292	64.1	0.437	–
2002	11,084	7,765	70.1	0.440	–
2003	14,120	10,579	74.9	0.446	29,947
2004	23,864	15,237	63.8	0.462	–
2005	28,201	17,319	61.4	0.484	–
2006	37,188	20,748	55.8	0.513	30,631
2007	40,694	30,948	76.1	0.538	30,841
2008	57,632	41,896	72.7	0.549	30,445
2009	40,670	30,699	75.5	0.542	–

Source: Modified with updated housing data from Statistics and Census Service; S. Li and Y. Tsui (2009) 'Casino Booms and Local Politics: The City of Macau', *Cities*, 26, 68.

The 4 Percent Interest Rate Subsidy Policy

Prior to the 1990s, public housing in Macao remained highly residual in terms of social policy planning. The market played a dominant role in housing provision and was largely efficient. Speculative activities were rare because house prices were comparatively low and stable. Overall public housing provision was limited to two main types: social housing for rent and the Home Ownership Scheme for sale (economic housing). The public housing sector then comprised only 12,000 units, serving around 10 percent of the population (see Tables 11.7 and 11.8). However, in the late 1980s and early 1990s, 'hot money' began to flow from the mainland, especially from neighbouring cities such as Hong Kong, Guangzhou and Shenzhen, which fuelled a period of rapid expansion and house price inflation. Unfortunately, this short buoyant spell was soon overtaken by a sharp slump in the market, partly the result of over-investment in the property sector and partly the knock-on effects of escalating incidences of organised crimes, which dampened the consumption climate (Lo, 2005). In view of the negative impact of these factors on the economy, the Macao government decided to introduce an interest subsidy of 4 percent for first-time homebuyers in order to boost the housing market. The scheme, which started in August 1996 and ended in June 2002 when applications had reached 15,640, had a substantial impact on the local housing market.

In the East Asian context, this policy has particular theoretical significance. An emerging area of comparative housing policy research concerns the salience of state policy to combine the promotion of home ownership with economic policy. The production or promotion of owner-occupation housing, either through the market or the state, is seen as central to economic growth in many of those economies (Smart and Lee, 2003). The 4 percent interest rate subsidy policy is perhaps the most overt attempt by any East Asia government to stimulate the demand for private home ownership through direct state effort. Interestingly, this stand was made clear in an article written by a senior Macao government official. Chiang (2005), as the President of the Housing Bureau, wrote:

> The Macao government has been *explicit in its intention* to use the Scheme to reinvigorate the economy and especially the declining housing market. The Scheme had a number of effects on: 1) encouraging households to become homeowners; 2) stimulating housing market activities; 3) accelerating the pace of economic growth; 4) regulating residential flat prices (Chiang, 2005: 151).

Table 11.4 provides evidence of the extent to which the scheme influenced the housing market. Property bought under the scheme took up an average of one-quarter of total property transaction values between 1996 and 2000. The government ended the scheme in 2001 when the property market began to rebound. However, after intense house price speculation resumed in the first two quarters of 2009, the government again reintroduced the policy towards the end of that year (Macao Housing Bureau, 2009; Jones Lang LaSalle, 2009).

Other than direct mortgage subsidies, there are other policies in place that directly facilitate the running of the property sector. For example, the stamp duty on property transactions was cut from 3 to 1 percent in 2009 and the property transaction tax was replaced with stamp duty (Asia Pacific Tax Notes, 2009). Another important move in simplifying property transaction procedures was the introduction of a one-stop service provided by the Legal Affairs Bureau in late 2002 that cut out the need to proceed through many different bureaux to register a purchased property. The

Table 11.4: Transaction Values of Residential Units Bought under the 4 Percent Interest Subsidy Scheme (in billions MOP)

Year	Total value of residential units bought	Residential units bought under the scheme	Percentage of the subsidised unit
1996–1997	4.8	1.1	23.6
1997–1998	5.8	1.2	20.8
1998–1999	6.1	1.3	21.5
1999–2000	4.0	1.2	29.6
2000–2001	10.2	1.2	11.7

Source: C. M. Chiang (2005) 'Government Intervention in Housing: The Case of Macao', *Housing Studies*, 20 (1), 153.

introduction of the law for investor immigrants in 1995 has also exerted a positive effect on the real estate market. The law aims to attract foreign investment in the local property market. Foreigners who purchase property valued at more than MOP1 million are entitled to apply for residency status in Macao. In sum, the last two decades have witnessed rapid neoliberal changes in urbanisation which have led to a restructuring of Macau's housing system, characterised by the creation of new institutions and measures to facilitate private home ownership as the major form of tenure, with the 4 percent mortgage interest subsidy scheme exemplifying the process. The following section will consider how public housing has been marginalised and how traditional neighbourhood housing has made way for the development of speculative real estate projects.

Transformation of the Built Environment

By Hong Kong standards, the size of the social housing sector in Macao is small (only 4.2 percent) (Table 11.6). The dominant tenure has always been home ownership in post-war low-rise buildings of four to six stories high. Social housing is largely small rental flats in high-rise buildings concentrated in the northern part of the Macao peninsula near the Chinese border and the industrial district, averaging 30–45 square metres for a tiny flat-let. Since the peninsula is small and heavily built up, the first phase of urban transformation took place in Taipa where land was more abundant. However, since 2004, the western part of old Macao, where traditional wharf facilities were located, has made way for new casinos and hotel developments. Since the opening of the Sands Macau in 2004, the property market has skyrocketed and house prices have doubled. Table 11.5 indicates that since the first quarter of 2004, property prices appreciated on average by an annual increase of 30 percent for two years before slowing down in 2006 as a result of government regulation. Investors from across Asia have scrambled for high-end properties that have seen an almost three-fold increase since 2000. From Table 11.5, it can be seen that house price inflation in 2004–2005 (recording 20–39 percent quarterly increases) far exceeded the rise in income (which was 10–15 percent on average quarterly). This has created enormous affordability problems for the middle and low-income groups who increasingly find private housing unaffordable. Figure 11.1 illustrates the sharp rise of house prices from the third quarter of 2003 to the third quarter of 2005. According to this crude index of affordability, a family with median income has to work for 12 years and save all its income before it could afford a medium-size two-bedroom flat.

Table 11.5: Annual Growth of Monthly Income, Real GDP and House Price

Year/ Quarter	Annual Change (in percent)		
	Median Monthly Employment Earnings	**Real GDP**	**Average Transaction Price***
2002			
1	1.1	7.7	...
2	-1.1	9.9	...
3	-1.3	7.2	...
4	2.7	15.2	...
2003			
1	1.8	16.2	0.5
2	4.3	-3.1	2.4
3	3.4	21.8	1.2
4	1.5	20.3	2.4
2004			
1	0.7	26.2	19.3
2	4.0	50.1	20.9
3	11.2	24.4	27.1
4	16.2	18.9	30.1
2005			
1	16.3	7.2	25.2
2	15.0	7.6	31.3
3	10.3	2.6	39.2
4	4.3	10.1	17.6
2006			
1	5.5	18.8	6.1
2	12.9	16.6	-0.6
3	16.3	10.8	1.4
4	25.3	20.1	8.0

Source: Statistics and Census Service (2008) *Macao Economic Bulletin.* Macao: Statistics and Census Service, 45.

Note: 1. *Average transaction price of residential unit per square metre of usable area.

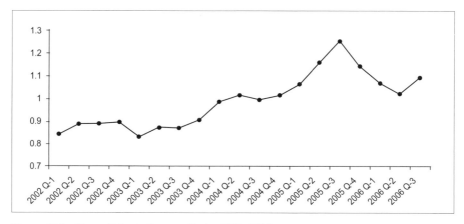

Figure 11.1: House Price to Income Ratio, 2002–2006

Source: P. S. Un (2007).

When we look at the broad housing picture, the size of social housing is small and the supply has been sporadic. Provision of social housing has been a function of overall economic performance and housing policy. It is evident from Table 11.7 that between 2000 and 2008, social housing production was below 300 units. It could be argued that this was the result of the government's concerted efforts to promote home ownership in the 1990s when people were expected to buy economic housing units. Nonetheless, looking at Table 11.8, the production of economic housing has also declined since 2000. This has resulted in mass protests in which citizens have voiced their objections to escalating house prices and the public housing shortage (Lai, 2009). In order to deal with rising social unrest, the government promised to build at least 8,000 public housing units by the end of 2009 and up to 19,000 new units by 2011 (*Macao Daily Times*, January 30, 2009*)*.

Table 11.6: The Macau Housing System, 2009

Private Housing	Public housing
• Total private housing units 125,000 (80.3 percent)	• Total public housing units 30,682 (19.7 percent)
• Owner-occupation 75 percent • Private renting 25 percent	• Home ownership scheme 15.5 percent (24,160) • Social housing 4.2 percent (6,522)

Source: Compiled from data provided by D. Lai (2009) *Macao's Social Welfare Model: A Prototype of a Regulatory Regime*. Hong Kong: Unpublished PhD thesis, Department of Social Work and Social Administration, University of Hong Kong.

Table 11.7: Social Housing Units: Year of Construction and Type by Year

Year of construction	1 room flat	2 room flat	3 room flat	4 room flat	Studio flat	Total
1970	21	223	–	–	120	**364**
1971–1980	210	60			–	**270**
1981–1990	978	1,286	136	16	774	**3,190**
1991–2000	597	1,662	66	26	79	**2,430**
2001–2005	–	53	–	4	1	**58**
2006	–	–	–	–	–	**–**
2007	90	60	60	–	–	**210**
Total	**1,896**	**3,344**	**262**	**46**	**974**	**6,522**

Source: Statistics and Census Service (2007) *Yearbook of Statistics* 2007. Macao: Statistics and Census Service, 304.

Table 11.8: Construction of Economic Housing Units, 1981–2006

Year of construction	1 room flat	2 room flat	3 room flat	4 room flat	Studio flat	Total
1981–1990	502	3,560	742	–	3,329	**8,133**
1991–2000	1,413	9,312	3,320	59	502	**14,606**
2001–2005	48	622	379	96	–	**1,145**
2006	88	121	67	–	–	**276**
Total	**2,050**	**13,615**	**4,508**	**155**	**3,831**	**24,160**

Source: Statistics and Census Service (2007) *Yearbook of Statistics* 2007. Macao: Statistics and Census Service, 305.

From a neoliberal urbanisation framework, these developments are indicative of a process of creative destruction both in the public and the private domains. While expensive condominiums in Taipa and Macao Island selling for more than $10,000 per square feet proliferate, more households are displaced from their residences and pressure for more affordable housing continues to increase. Unfortunately, within the neoliberal scheme of urbanisation, there is always inherent instability and volatility, particularly in terms of real estate values and urban transformation. State intervention can only do so much to ameliorate the situation, but it can never really get to the root of the problem. There is a fundamental contradiction between the need to attract foreign direct investment in the gambling and tourist industry and the need to provide adequate affordable housing for a population that provides the much-needed workforce for the industry.

Conclusion

This chapter has looked at the development of Macao's public and private housing system over the last two decades, with emphasis on the rapid development of the real estate sector since the change of sovereignty in 1999. Using a framework of neoliberal urbanisation in the context of China's urbanisation, I have looked at the contestation of spaces and the inevitable process of urban destruction and creation. The results of this process are an intensification of spatial scarcity and the creation of wealth for a few through displacement and redevelopment. The process of restructuring the housing system has brought about a new emphasis on home ownership and owner-occupation — the dream of many Chinese families. Home ownership is now the aspiration of many Macao people who see it as a reliable way to accumulate wealth besides income from work. More importantly, the transformation of the built environment with new gated condominiums creates social exclusion and new spatial divisions. Such divisions initiate new social processes of contestation, tensions and competition. There is increasing demand for more social and economic housing, coupled with demand for more social welfare as low-income families struggle with rising house prices and rents. Housing and social welfare are two linked sectors in contemporary social policymaking. The degree to which these sectors can be properly integrated to meet increasing social needs presents a real challenge for governance (see Chapter 12 for a discussion of the social welfare sector). The Macao government has tried to ameliorate the housing shortage and affordability problem by building more economic housing for marginalised sectors of the population facing problems of affordability. However, the remedial and residual nature of these projects is essentially self-limiting and the effects, in the context in which they have been introduced, cause instability. The neoliberalising process in Macao will continue to push the city to its limits with the continuing dangers of asset inflation and risk of the property bubble bursting with all the potential political and social consequences that are likely to arise both before and after a major slump. The scale of Macao justifies a much more prudent approach in making use of its home ownership policy to achieve its development objectives. After all, a sustainable gaming industry depends on the containment of gambling inside, rather than outside, the casinos.

Social Welfare Policy: A 'Flexible' Strategy?

Chan Kam Wah and James Lee

Introduction

The transfer of sovereignty from Portugal to China has had a significant impact on the social welfare system in Macao. Before the 1980s, there was no strong demand for the colonial government to develop a social welfare system. Since the initiation of the Sino-Portuguese talks in the 1980s on the transition, however, the polity has changed considerably and there has been rising demand for more social welfare from local people and community organisations. After the transfer of sovereignty in 1999 and the liberalisation of the gaming industry in 2002, Macao's rapid economic growth has greatly increased the government's revenue and its financial ability to develop infrastructure and deliver more public services. But this rapid development has also led to a worsening of social problems and has helped to create the underlying conditions for an increased demand for more social welfare. Macao's social welfare system has consequently changed greatly since the 1980s. In this chapter, we explore the characteristics of the present welfare regime and whether it is capable of meeting the challenges posed by the social problems resulting from rapid economic growth.

We start with a review of the historical development of social welfare in Macao from the non-interventionist period before the 1980s, to the institutionalisation of the welfare system in subsequent years, to the emergence of a new strategy after 2000. We pay special attention to how social junctures in different periods have structured the pattern of welfare development. We then introduce the welfare system in the post-colonial era in more detail, categorising the provision of services into four major components; the Social Security Fund, Social Welfare Bureau, Non-governmental Organisations (NGOs), and other government cash subsidies. We identify the characteristics of the welfare regime in Macao, using ideas from studies on East Asian welfare regimes that focus on productivist and Confucian welfare conceptions of how welfare should be delivered. This hinges on the classical debate concerning social development, namely, economic growth versus social stability. Our purpose is not to verify or falsify whether Macao exemplifies one or the other of the East Asian welfare models. Rather, we aim at highlighting an important trend in Macao's welfare system, which has been neglected in the existing literature. We call it the 'flexible welfare strategy', in which the government is increasingly reliant on *ad hoc* cash subsidies and short-term measures to deal with social problems and to maintain social stability instead of developing long-term social policy and social services. This strategy seems increasingly popular in other places in East Asia, such as Hong Kong and Taiwan. The 'flexible welfare strategy' appears to be able to resolve grievances and restore social stability in the short term but serves to widen social inequalities and divert resources from improving the welfare system in the longer run.

The Development of Social Welfare in Macao

The development of social welfare policy in Macao can be divided roughly into three stages according to the level and pattern of intervention of the state in the social welfare system: non-interventionist (before the 1980s), institutionalisation (1980s to 1990s), and the flexibility system (after 2000). The changing level and pattern of state intervention in social welfare is largely a function of social, political and economic changes in Macao over the years.

Non-interventionist

Before the 1980s, Macao was a quiet, small city that did not have a high demand for social welfare which, in any case, beyond minimal assistance, the Portuguese colonial government did not provide. The people of Macao were used to solving their problems through traditional family and community networks and there was little call on the government to intervene to provide welfare. If individuals or their families were unable to take care of their own welfare needs, charitable organisations, churches and, traditional associations would step in to provide minimal care (Shek, 2006). Traditional associations play important roles in different economic, political and social arenas in Macao (see Chapter 5) but we focus here mainly on the roles which they and other voluntary organisations, such as the Catholic Church, perform in delivering social welfare.

Church groups have long histories in the field. For example, Santa Casa da Misericorida, (仁慈堂) established in 1569, and the Caritas de Macau (澳門明愛), which can be traced to services provided by the Catholic Church in the early 1950s, are still important providers. Other major long-serving non-government social welfare organisations include the Kiang Wu Hospital Benevolent Association (鏡湖醫院慈善會), established in 1871, and the Tong Sin Tong Good Benevolent Association (同善堂), established in 1892. Besides the church and charitable non-government organisations, traditional associations such as Fellow Townsmen Associations (同鄉會) and Kai Fong Associations (街坊會) also play significant roles in social welfare provision (Tang, 2003, 2007). These organisations retain a dominant role in the social welfare system. According to the list of traditional associations in charity work provided by the government in 2002, for example, there were 522 such organisations (quoted in Tang, 2002: 77). The major categories are social welfare/social service organisations (20.9 percent), Fellow Townsmen Associations (21.5 percent), Kaifong Associations (20.5 percent), and Mutual Aid Associations (27.2 percent) (see Table 12.1).

Table 12.1: Traditional Associations in Charity Work, 2002

Category	Number	Percentage
Charitable Fund Associations (基金會)	29	5.6
Social welfare/social services (社會福利/服務)	109	20.9
Medical/Health (醫療/衛生)	8	1.5
Fellow Townsmen Associations (同鄉會)	112	21.5
Clan Associations (宗親會)	15	2.9
Kai Fong Associations (街坊會)	107	20.5
Mutual Aid Associations (互助會)	142	27.2
Total	**522**	**100**

Source: Excerpted from Tang (2003), Table 1: 77.

The major source of funding for these organisations was charity rather than government subsidies. Due to limitation of resources, their services were often fragmented and piecemeal, the level of benefit was low, and the orientation of service was mainly remedial and the relief of hardship. The range of services provided by these organisations included emergency relief, health and medical services, elderly services, services for the disabled, and education for children.

Institutionalisation of Social Welfare

During the period between the mid-1980s and the late-1990s, there was a rapid expansion of social welfare services and the institutionalisation of a system. There were several important factors leading to this change. One of the most significant factors was the Sino-Portuguese talks on the transfer of sovereignty which began in the mid-1980s. The Chinese government started to take a more active role in social affairs in Macao and this stimulated pro-China traditional associations to expand their activities, especially in the provision of social welfare. The Portuguese colonial government also became more interventionist as it began to decolonise. It invested in infrastructure, provided more support for the tourist industry, improved public services and introduced a rudimentary social welfare system. Another important factor was the rapidly growing economy in the 1980s and 1990s. The GDP per capita at current prices rose from MOP24,976 in 1982 to MOP127,211 in 1996 but the bare statistics conceal problems such as the decline in manufacturing which led to structural unemployment and a consequently greater demand for support (Statistics and Census Service, 2010; see Chapters 1, 8). After mainland China adopted an open-door economic policy in the early 1980s, the economy of Macao was gradually transformed from a reliance on manufacturing to gaming and tourism. Macao also faced other social problems such as an influx of new arrivals, including both legal and illegal migrant workers from mainland China, deteriorating family and youth problems, and rising demands for democracy (Choi, 2004). All these changes, either directly or indirectly, increased demands for improving the social welfare system.

The Macao Department of Social Welfare was formally established in 1980. Before this, social welfare service can be traced to the Public Charity Society established in 1938 which was later reorganised by the government in 1947 to form the Public Relief Society (Wong et al, 2009). In 1960, it was again reorganised as the Public Relief Branch and in 1967 it became the Social Relief Division. Before the 1980s, services were mainly focused on charity and emergency relief. With the establishment of the Department of Social Welfare, services were improved, expanded and upgraded. Since then, there has been an increasing concern with education and professional training for social welfare practitioners. In 1986, the Department of Social Welfare was further reorganised with improved organisation and clearer objectives. New sub-unit offices were set up in different parishes to make the services more accessible to the public. A new Department of Research and Planning was established in order to develop more systematic and comprehensive services and policies. In the 1990s, the department began to expand rapidly, especially in the provision of professional services such as counselling, services for the family and for adolescents, services for drug dependents, and rehabilitation. The expenditure of the department increased from about MOP20 million in 1980 to about MOP170 million in 1996 (Lam, 1998: 26). In 1999, the department was renamed the Social Welfare Bureau and organised into five departments, eight divisions, and three sections (see www.ias.gov.mo).

The 1980s and 1990s saw a consolidation of social welfare services and an increasing professionalism in their delivery. The first professional training course started at the Social Work Institute of Macao in 1987 and the Macao Polytechnic Institute offered a Higher Diploma in Social Work Training from 1991 onwards.

Besides the rapid development of services provided by the Social Welfare Department, there were also substantial increases in subsidies for NGOs to expand their work. Until 1997, 75 percent of the salaries of social workers in NGOs was subsidised by the Social Welfare Department. By 1999, about 70 percent of the NGOs were receiving subsidies from the department. Besides expanding social welfare services, the Macao government also made a substantial effort to improve the social security system. The Social Security Fund was established in 1990 with the aim of providing retirement protection for Macao citizens.

Social Welfare in the Post-colonial Era

In the post-colonial era, the substantial increases in government revenue from gaming and tourism after 2002 could have been used to improve the social welfare system. However, expenditure on social welfare in the past decade has not matched growth in revenue. In terms of developing direct social services, the Macao government continues to rely more on non-government organisations and traditional associations rather than providing services itself through the Social Welfare Bureau. Moreover, facing economic fluctuations and rising social problems, the government has tended to use an *ad hoc* and short-term approach, which has typically involved cash subsidies, instead of formulating long-term policy and institutional changes. We call this 'the flexible social welfare system'. Government does not commit itself to expensive new programmes but rather moves money in the form of cash subsidies to people who are perceived to be disadvantaged and who could consequently become a source of political unrest. The system has four major components: the Social Security Fund, Social Welfare Bureau, services provided by NGOs and traditional associations, and flexible dispensation of cash subsidies.

Social Security Fund

A contributory social security scheme was initiated by the government in 1989. An independent organisation, the Social Security Fund (SSF), was established in 1990 to manage this scheme which covers all employees in Macao (Tang, 2003, 2007; Lai, 2003; Lui, 2007; see also www.fss.gov.mo). Anyone working more than 14 days per month has to contribute MOP15 to the fund while their employers contribute MOP30 per month. Part-timers working less than 15 days per month have to contribute MOP7.5 with their employers contributing MOP15. The scheme also covers domestic helpers. Overseas workers do not have to contribute but their employers are required to pay MOP45 per month. The self-employed can join the scheme and pay into it on a voluntary basis. The government contributes 1 percent of the government budget to the SSF. In fact, since the contribution from employers and employees is relatively low, the government's contribution constitutes a significant proportion of the fund. In 2008, 90.9 percent of the revenue of the SSF came from government transfers, significantly more than the 81.4 percent and 55 percent it contributed in 2003 and 1998 respectively (Table 12.2). Since the contribution from employers and employees is too low to meet retirement and other needs, increasingly large government transfers to the fund have become inevitable. The underlying philosophy remains, however, that people, and those who employ them, should be responsible for their own welfare.

Table 12.2: Current Revenue and Expenditure of the Social Security Fund (in millions MOP)

	1998	2003	2008
Current Revenue	251,841	475,231	2,217,887
Contributions	49,388	81,897	164,526
Other receipts	63,918	6,562	36,542
Transfers	138,535	386,772[1]	2,016,819[2]
Current expenditure	**129,255**	**557,979**	**473,480**

Source: Adapted from Statistics and Census Service (2009) *Yearbook of Statistics, 2008.* Macao: MSAR
     Government, Table 7.3.10, 215.
Note: 1. Including funding of MOP200 million for aid given to the unemployed, MOP84.37 million for
     organisations providing vocational training and professional improvement courses (with 4,000
     placements) and MOP 54 million for aid given to the unemployed with severe difficulties.
     2. Including transfers of MOP1,446,883,422.00 from gaming revenue, of which MOP171,250,848.26
     were funds for insolvent wages upon bankruptcy.

The coverage of the SSF is very wide. There are 11 different payments, including the old age pension, disability pension, social security pension, special payments, unemployment benefits, sickness allowance, birth allowance, funeral subsidy, compensation for pneumoconiosis and credit advances to workers in enterprises with financial problems (Table 12.3). There are other special payments, mainly for the unemployed, which may vary from year to year. Under the regulations on incentives and training for the unemployed, these may include aid and subsidies given to the unemployed, aid given to unemployed construction workers, aid given to workers engaged in industries with severe difficulties, vocational training and professional improvement courses, and training courses for casino dealers and for unemployed construction workers. In 2008, no special aid was granted, except for the aid given to the unemployed, from which 16 recipients were granted a total amount of MOP108,000. Including this special aid, the total number of recipients of the SSF in 2008 was 43,341 and the total amount granted was MOP436,161,000 (see Table 12.3). Although the coverage of the SSF is wide — from birth to grave, unemployment to old age — it has been criticised on the grounds that the level of benefits for some types of social security payments is too low. The SSF might provide better value for money if it were reorganised to focus on more essential items so as to raise the level of payment (Tang, 2007: 22) or further developed into a more comprehensive multi-level retirement protection system (Lai, 2003).

Table 12.3: Number of Recipients and Payments and Subsidies Granted by the Social Security Fund by Type, 2008

	Level of benefit (MOP)	Number of recipients	Amount (MOP000s)
Payment granted:		43,325	436,053
Old-age pension	$1,700 per month	26,338	364,223
Disability pension	$1,700 per month	1,228	20,421
Social security pension	$950 per month	–	–
Special payments	–	31,056	26,093
Unemployment benefits	$70 per day	6,904	15,379
Sickness allowance	Out-patient: $55/day Hospitalise: $70/day	2,341	2,652
Birth allowance	$1,000	3,632	3,692
Marriage subsidy	$1,000	2,194	2,194
Funeral subsidy	$1,300	637	827
Compensation for pneumoconiosis	Individual case	–	–
Credit advances to workers in enterprises with financial problems	Individual case	51	573
Total		**43,341**	**436,161**

Source: Adapted from Statistics and Census Service (2009) *Yearbook of Statistics, 2008.* Macao: MSAR Government, Table 7.3.9, 212.

Social Welfare Bureau

After the transfer of sovereignty in 1999, the Social Welfare Department was renamed the Social Welfare Bureau. Social services continued to be more structured, institutionalised and professional-oriented compared with the *ad hoc*, emergency relief and remedial welfare of the previous era (Ip, 2006). However, the bureau has since undergone several major reorganisations to reflect a shift in its objectives, particularly a shift to a focus on supporting the family and individual and achieving the aim of 'helping people to overcome difficulties and to build a new life together' (http://www.ias.gov.mo/en/aboutus/, accessed January 8, 2010). Services provided or funded by the Social Welfare Bureau (Social Welfare Bureau, 2009) can be divided into several major categories (Table 12.4). Although these categories represent the typical areas covered in most modern welfare states, the Macao government does not put equal emphasis on each area. Instead, individual and remedial services, such as services for the elderly, family and rehabilitation services are expanding rapidly, while developmental services, such as youth and community services, are shrinking or growing slowly. The first category is children and youth services. We can see from Table 12.4 that this has not been a major focus of social welfare over the past decade. The number of service units dropped from 78 in 1998 to 44 in 2008. The Social Welfare Bureau mainly provides statutory services, such as the court auxiliary service and adoption service. Most direct services for children and youth are provided by the NGOs and traditional associations subsidised by the bureau. The bureau refers clients to these service-providers if needed. The second category is service for the elderly, which has seen substantial development. The number of service units increased from 45 in 1998 to 62 in 2008, which included various services such as a multi-service centre for the elderly, recreational centres for the elderly, home help and supporting service, homes for the elderly, and other senior citizen benefits. The third category is rehabilitation service, which has also seen substantial growth. The number of service units increased from 14 in 1998 to 26 in 2008. The fourth category is community service, which increased from nine units in 1998 to 14 in 2008. These services are mainly provided by NGOs and traditional associations. The fifth category is service for the prevention and treatment for drug dependence, which has been newly developed over the last decade. In 2008, there were 13 service units providing treatment, rehabilitation, and education services. The last category is individual and family services, which include financial assistance for low-income and vulnerable families and individuals, subsidies for senior citizens, counselling services for individuals and families, counselling services for problem gamblers, disaster relief, and a short-term food assistance programme. Family service is one of the areas that has expanded most quickly over the past ten years, from six service units in 1998 to 30 in 2008.

Table 12.4: Number of Social Services/Facilities by Type of Service

	1998	2003	2008
Children and youth service	78	57	44
Elderly service	45	61	62
Rehabilitation service	14	23	26
Community service	9	11	14
Service of prevention and treatment for drug dependence	–	10	13
Family service	6	23	30
Other services	4	–	–
Total	**156**	**185**	**189**

Source: Adapted from Statistics and Census Service (2009) *Yearbook of Statistics, 2008*. Macao: MSAR Government, Table 7.1.2, 188–190.

The total number of service units increased from 156 in 1998 to 189 in 2008 (Table 12.4). The magnitude of the increase in total social service expenditure is reflected in Table 12.5 (Social Welfare Bureau, 2009: 66). Total expenditure increased from MOP126million in 1998 to MOP747 million in 2008, nearly a six-fold increase within ten years (Table 12.5). However, if we look at Table 12.5 in greater detail, it is evident that the major increases are in the categories of 'subventions to private institutions', 'subventions to individual and families' and the newly established 'subsidy for senior citizens'. These are all cash subsidies and subventions to private institutions rather than tangible services directly provided by the Social Welfare Bureau. The expenditure on social service facilities operated by the Social Welfare Bureau actually decreased from MOP4,409,000 to MOP1,554,000 over the past ten years, a reduction of about one-third of the expenditure in 1998. This shows a clear trend of reducing direct services from the Social Welfare Bureau while increasing subsidies and subventions to private institutions and NGOs. The reduced role of the Social Welfare Bureau in the direct provision of services is an important element in the strategy of creating a 'flexible' welfare system.

Another important trend is that the expenditure on community activities and other services to the public decreased significantly from MOP1,094,000 to MOP366,000, while the training of workers in the areas of social work and subventions to individual and families increased rapidly. The provision of social services in Macao is shifting away from community activities to a more individualistic, clinical, and professional approach.

Table 12.5: Social Services Expenditure by Item (in millions MOP)

	1998	2003	2008
Subventions to private institutions	90,104	126,219	302,435
Subventions to individuals and families	27,654	84,841	299,903
Subsidy for senior citizens	–	–	141,783
Social service facilities operated by the Social Welfare Bureau	4,409	3,265	1,554
Meal allowances to students	1,778	559	–
Community activities and other services to the general public	1,094	848	366
Training of workers in the area of social work	495	582	1,216
Subscriptions and donation to international organisations	792	288	2
Total Expenditure[1]	**126,326**	**216,602**	**747,265**

Source: Adapted from Statistics and Census Service (2008) *Yearbook of Statistics, 2008*. Macao: MSAR Government, Table 7.1.1, 187.

Note: 1. Excluding 'operational expenses and investment' and 'transfers to government departments' of Social Welfare Bureau expenditure.

Non-Government Organisations and Traditional Associations

NGOs and traditional associations have played an active role in providing social welfare since the early days of the colonial era (Shek, 2006). In 2008, there were 189 service units or facilities under the regulation of the Social Welfare Bureau, of which nearly 80 percent (153 service/facilities) were funded by the bureau (Social Welfare Bureau, 2009: 47). The subvention to private institutions in 2008 was about MOP302 million, which increased by 27.6 percent compared with that of 2007 (Social Welfare Bureau, 2009: 66) and was more than three times that of 1998 (Table 12.5). Subventions to private institutions include recurrent, occasional, and capital subsidies. In 2008, the recurrent subsidy for NGOs and traditional associations was about MOP273 million (see Table 12.6). The expenditure on social services provided by NGOs and traditional associations was far more than that of social service facilities operated by the Social Welfare Bureau (see Table 12.5).

Table 12.6: Recurrent Subsidies for NGOs and Traditional Associations, 2008

	Subsidy (in MOP)
Traditional associations	30,165,197.00
Children and youth service	67,674,534.00
Elderly service	79,538,548.80
Rehabilitation service	57,318,434.40
Community service	12,107,762.00
Family service	16,528,634.20
Service of prevention and treatment for drug dependence	10,058,664.00
Total	**273,391,774.40**

Source: Adapted from Social Welfare Bureau (2009) *Social Welfare Bureau 2008 Report*. Macao: Macao Social Welfare Bureau, Table 9.4, 72.

Traditional associations and NGOs in Macao provide a wide range of social services (see Chapter 5). Some have specialised in a particular service, such as the Kiang Wu Hospital Benevolent Association, which provides medical and health services, and the Tung Sin Tong Charitable Society, which provides charity relief and runs clinics, schools, and nurseries. The Women's General Association of Macau specialises in women and children services, providing nurseries, schools, family service centres, women's health centres, as well as youth and elderly services. The Federacao das Associações dos Operarios de Macau (Macao Federation of Trade Unions) specialises in labour services but also provides a wide range of other services, including nurseries, youth service, elderly service, health service, sport facilities and recreational activites. The União Geral das Associações dos Moradores de Macau (Macao General Union of Neighbourhood Associations) is one of the most important social service providers in Macao. It runs community centres, schools and clinics in different districts and provides children and youth services, elderly services, counselling and school social work. Caritas de Macau is one of the longest established NGOs in Macao, providing a wide range of professional social work services, including children, youth, family and elderly services, rehabilitation services, and education.

Other Flexible Cash Subsidies

As Richard Titmuss (1976) has pointed out, social welfare is not only limited to direct services provided by the state, but should also include other direct and indirect social resource transfers. In his study of the social division of welfare, Titmuss observes that in addition to social welfare, fiscal welfare and occupational welfare are also part and parcel of the welfare system. Besides tangible social services, fiscal transfers in the tax system or cash subsidies, such as the Wealth Partaking Scheme in Macao (see below), are an important part of welfare transfer. Occupational welfare, such as a social security or provident fund, is an important component of welfare benefits. Moreover, other social services, such as education, health, labour, and housing services may involve significant social resource transfers. In fact, some social welfare services in Macao are provided by departments other than the Social Welfare Bureau. For example, some youth services are delivered through the education system while some medical social work is provided in the health system. Wealth transfer is a feature of many public policies in Macao and we find examples in fields such as labour, education, housing, and urban development (see Chapters 8, 10, 11).

In this section, we focus particularly on the use of cash subsidies or transfers to deal with social problems, which has become a popular strategy of the Macao government in recent years (see Table 12.7 for more details). In 2008, in the light of the global financial crisis, a deteriorating economy, and rising discontent among Macao citizens, the government launched a Wealth Partaking Scheme (see http://www.planocp.gov.mo). Under this scheme, every Macao permanent resident identity card holder received MOP5,000 from the government, while non-permanent resident identity card holders were given MOP3,000. In 2009, the government launched a second Wealth Partaking Scheme in which every holder of a Macao permanent and non-permanent resident identity card was granted MOP6,000 and MOP3,600 respectively. At the end of 2009, the government further announced a Central Saving Scheme under the administration of the SSF (see http://fss.gov.mo). All permanent residents of Macao aged 22 and above are beneficiaries of this scheme. The SSF opened an account for each qualified recipient in 2010. Account-holders are entitled to receive cash transfers from government surpluses. They can apply to withdraw the money when they reach the age of 65 or if they suffer from severe sickness or injury or receive a disability subsidy from the Social Security Fund for more than one year or for humanitarian or reasonable need circumstances at the discretion of the Chief Executive. In 2010, the government intended to transfer MOP10,000 to each qualified recipient, which would amount to MOP3300 million from public revenue (Ho, 2009: 20). These are not the only cash subsidy schemes in Macao. In recent years the government has launched different cash subsidy schemes for senior citizens, transport subsidies for students, the elderly and all Macao citizens, subsidies for electricity expenses of domestic households, subsidies for the working poor, subsidies for home purchase (see Chapter 11), and a healthcare subsidy scheme. Under the healthcare subsidy scheme in 2009, for example, permanent residents of Macao were entitled to receive a MOP500 healthcare voucher. There are other forms of tax reduction and stamp duty exemption as well. It is estimated that the government is receiving MOP900 million less in revenue in 2010 as a result of these tax reductions and exemptions (Ho, 2009: 19).

Table 12.7 Selected Cash Subsidies

Year	Items	Details
2005–2010	Subsidy for senior citizens	For permanent residents aged 65 and above. MOP1,200 per year in 2005; increased to MOP1,500 in 2006, to MOP1800 in 2007, to MOP5,000 in 2009.
2007	Monthly bus ticket for senior citizens	Elderly aged 65 and above are entitled to purchase a monthly bus ticket for MOP20 per month.
2008/09 to 2010	Tax reduction and exemption	Exemption of stamp duty (3%) for purchase of property of value MOP3,000,000 and below; exemption from all housing taxes for owner-occupiers; increased tax allowance for Complementary Tax (from MOP32,000 to MOP200,000); tax allowance for Professional Tax (income tax) increased from MOP95,000 to MOP120,000; reduced Professional Tax by 25%; exempted Tourism Tax for restaurants; exempted licence fee for advertisements posted or placed in public areas; Industrial Tax fully exempted; $3,500 reduction in Property Tax; exempted Stamp Duty for insurance policies and for banking transactions. (Reduction of more than MOP$1100 million government income from tax).
April 2008	Special subsidies for families on social benefits	Families on social benefits are entitled to receive extra subsidies equivalent to three months of their benefit. (Extra expenditure of MOP49 million). Three types of families receiving special subsidies for vulnerable families from the Social Welfare Bureau are entitled to receive extra subsidies equivalent to three months of their existing subsidies. (Extra expenditure of MOP3 million).

2008/09 to 2010	Subsidies for electricity bills	All residents are entitled to receive subsidies of MOP150 maximum per month per household, that is, a maximum of MOP1,800 per year.
2008/09 to 2010	Subsidies for low income workers	Residents aged 40 and above, working full time (average 152 hours or above per month) with average monthly income less than MOP4,000 and contributing to the Social Security Fund are entitled to receive income subsidies to top up their income to MOP4,000 per month. This is roughly equal to 50% of the median monthly income of the Macao population. (Around 16,000 people will benefit and will incur extra expenditure of MOP350 million per fiscal year).
July 2008	Wealth Partaking Scheme	All permanent residents are entitled to receive MOP5,000. Non-permanent residents receive MOP3,000.
July 2008 to 2010	Transportation subsidies for senior citizens	Modifies the 2007 scheme. Subsidises bus fares for the elderly aged 65 and above. The beneficiaries only pay MOP0.30 for each bus trip. The outstanding amount is subsidised by the government.
October 2008 to 2010	Transportation subsidies for students	Full-time students from kindergarten to secondary school are entitled to subsidies for bus fares. They only pay MOP1.50 for each bus trip and the outstanding amount is subsidised by the government.
December 2008 to 2010	Transportation subsidies for all citizens	Citizens need only pay MOP2 to MOP3 for each bus trip. The outstanding amount is subsidised by the government.
April 2009 to 2010	Subsidy for telephone bills	A maximum subsidy of MOP150 per month on telephone bills.
May 2009	Wealth Partaking Scheme	All permanent residents are entitled to a cash subsidy of MOP6,000 and non-permanent residents MOP3,600.
Jun 2009 – June 2010	Home Ownership Mortgage Guarantee Scheme; and Home Ownership Mortgage Tax Subsidies	Permanent residents aged 21 and above, purchasing a flat to the value of MOP2.6 million or less, are entitled to a subsidy of 4% each year for ten years of the value of their mortgage loan or MOP1 million, whichever is the less. The government also guarantees the mortgage loan, 20% of the house price or MOP400,000 whichever is the less.
2008/09 to 2010	Healthcare Voucher	Permanent residents are entitled to ten vouchers of MOP50 each (total MOP500 per year). These vouchers are good for any health care services not subsidised by the government.
September 2009	Education subsidy	All permanent residents receiving formal education are entitled to MOP1,500 subsidy for each academic year.

| 2010 | Central Saving Scheme | For permanent residents aged 22 and above. The government will launch a new Central Saving Account for all beneficiaries of the Social Security Fund and will inject MOP10,000 in the account of each beneficiary. The expense is estimated to amount to MOP 3,300 million. |
| 2010 | Wealth Partaking Scheme | MOP6,000 for permanent residents and MOP3,600 for non-permanent residents. |

Source: Macao SAR Government *Policy Address*, 2008, 2009, 2010; various government websites: Government Information Bureau (www.gcs.gov.mo), Macao SAR Government Portal (www.gov. mo), Wealth Partaking Scheme (www.planocp.gov.mo); Health Subsidy Scheme Website (www. vs.gov.mo); various news websites: *China News* (www.chinanews.com), *Macao Internet Community* (http://space.qocs.com), *Today Macao Daily News* (http://www.todaymacao.com/).

Analysing Macao's Welfare Regime

Classifying welfare regimes has been one of the major concerns of social welfare studies in recent years. Esping-Andersen's (1990) study of welfare capitalism sparked a heated debate on how such welfare regimes should be categorised. One of the debates centres around the East Asian Welfare Model (Goodman et al, 1998; Aspalter, 2006; Gough, 2001). There are two major schools of thought about ways to explain the emergence of the model, one of which focuses on political economy, the other on cultural factors. The political economy explanation argues that the success of many East Asian countries, especially before the Asian financial crisis in 1997, hinged on a 'productivist' strategy that enhanced economic competitiveness. The productivist welfare regime in East Asia minimised expenditure on social welfare and liberalised the market to enhance productivity (Holliday, 2000). Adopting the productivist analysis, Lai (2006) has argued that Macao's social welfare regime exhibits some key characteristics of the East Asian welfare model. Cultural explanations rely on notions of a Confucian welfare regime (Jones, 1993). East Asian states benefit from strong mutual support networks in the family and the community that significantly reduce the government's burden in welfare provision. At the same time, Confucian values emphasise diligence and hard work that enhance productivity and competitiveness in a global economy. Leung (2006) has pointed out that the Macao social welfare system is still very much affected by Confucianism and traditional Chinese culture.

To a certain extent, the discussion on productivism and Confucianism in East Asian regimes echoes the framework discussed in Chapter 1, which is based on the dimensions of social stability and economic growth. The ideal scenario is to achieve rapid economic growth with high social stability. It seems that the productivist welfare and the Confucian welfare models in the East Asian welfare regimes are possible strategies to achieve this aim. Productivism is primarily concerned with economic growth while Confucianism focuses on social stability. This also reflects a classical debate on the contradictions of capitalist welfare state, that is, on accumulation versus legitimisation (Offe, 1984). Very often, the functions of stimulating economic growth and maintaining social stability are contradictory. The success in maintaining a high level of social harmony with a rapidly growing economy in some Asian countries depends on sacrificing the interests of many disadvantaged groups (Chan, 2008).

In this chapter, we do not intend to classify Macao in terms of the East Asian welfare model. Rather, we seek to highlight some of its major characteristics in the light of the debate. The discussion of productivism/economic growth and Confucianism/social stability in the East Asian welfare regime debate sheds light on welfare development in Macao. On the one hand, the Macao government is concerned with economic growth through the liberalisation of the gaming industry and promotion of tourism. On the other hand, it needs to face the challenges of deteriorating social problems and rising social conflicts. In the past, Macao has depended to a great extent on a traditional Confucian culture to maintain social stability (Leung, 2006). Most welfare needs were taken care of by the family network and the support system developed by traditional associations. However, with rapid economic growth and economic restructuring, social problems have become much more complex and increasingly difficult, if not impossible, for these traditional supportive networks to deal with effectively. In the 1990s, the Macao government tried to institutionalise and develop a welfare system by measures such as establishing the SSF. However, in order to avoid resistance from the public, especially from the business sector, the contributions from employers and employees have been very limited. The support provided by the SSF relies heavily on government funding (see Table 12.2). This implies a long-term financial commitment that may not be sustainable in the long run. Especially after experiencing the Asian financial crisis in 1997, an economic recession resulting from the SARS epidemic in 2003, and the global financial crisis of 2008, it is apparent that an economy based on gaming and tourism is highly susceptible to global economic fluctuations (Lo, 2009). The Macao government may have to adjust its welfare strategy accordingly.

Adopting a regulatory framework to study social policymaking in Macao, Lai (2008) points out that in the twenty-first century the mode of regulation is gradually shifting from legitimisation to reproduction and a disciplined workforce. That is, the government is developing more employment retraining and workfare programmes to encourage workers to participate in the labour market. At the same time, there are measures to discipline those who do not work hard enough to get a job. This reproduction and disciplinary strategy emphasises productivity and individual responsibility in maintaining competitiveness and there is some evidence that the Macao government is beginning to adopt such an approach (see Chapter 9).

This is consistent with what we have called in this chapter a 'flexible welfare strategy'. The traditional strategy of the institutionalisation of welfare requires a long-term commitment of funding and social resources. One of the challenges that the Macao government faces is economic instability. Although it has benefited from the booming gaming and tourist industry, its revenue base is highly dependent on those sectors. Gaming and tourism are considered luxuries in a time of financial crisis and it is reasonable to assume that the Macao government's revenue would decline if an economic downturn were prolonged. To survive a period of austerity and to reduce grievances, the government needs to provide additional welfare to maintain social stability. However, the government is reluctant to commit to long-term institutionalised welfare. The strategy instead is to provide *ad hoc*, one-off, piecemeal cash subsidies rather than improving the welfare system and related social policies. In terms of the provision of some necessary social services, the Macao government tends to subsidise NGOs and traditional associations instead of providing the services directly by the Social Welfare Bureau. This maintains some flexibility for cutting back welfare expenditure if necessary.

The 'flexible welfare system' is not completely new or exclusive to Macao. It can be traced to the discussion on post-Fordism (Amin, 1994; Jessop, 1993; Lipietz, 1997), although this mainly refers to capital accumulation and the production system rather than the welfare system. It is argued that under post-Fordism the state tries to maintain a flexible production system and deregulates controls over labour and the market to enhance economic competitiveness. We argue that this strategy could be extended to the social welfare system in order to minimise long-term financial commitments in welfare expenditure. A 'flexible welfare strategy' hinges on the assumption that market mechanisms are more efficient than state provision in the distribution of resources, including social welfare services. Under this strategy, citizens are given subsidies to purchase welfare services or any goods and services that they need in the private market. In case tangible social services are needed, the government subsidises private institutions, NGOs or traditional associations instead of providing the services directly through a government department. This could be regarded as a further extension of a neoliberal ethos, rather than a totally new invention and it is consistent with the Third Way and new public management ideology which emphasise efficiency and value-for-money in public expenditure.

This strategy is not exclusive to Macao. In fact, in reaction to the global financial crisis, Hong Kong and Taiwan have adopted similar strategies to relieve hardship or to ameliorate social grievances. Some popular measures are: providing consumption vouchers, injecting money into individual provident fund accounts, waiving rates for domestic households, tax allowances for mortgage expenses, tax rebates, subsidies for electricity expenses and subsidies for transportation expenses. This may become a new characteristic of the East Asian welfare model but it is too early to draw any definite conclusion.

The 'flexible welfare strategy' benefits many people in a short time. However, subsidies are often painkillers rather than real cures for social problems. There are several difficulties with the strategy. First, most of these cash subsidies have only very short-term and limited effects in alleviating hardship or solving social problems. Very often, these subsidies are offset by inflation or rising prices of related services in the private market. The benefit to the citizens may be illusory. For example, first-time homebuyers were unable to benefit from the 4 percent mortgage subsidy introduced by the government between 1996 and 2002 because housing price rose rapidly in the same period (see Chapter 11). Second, this strategy is sometimes very costly. For example, it is estimated that the Macao government needs to spend MOP3300 million to establish the new Central Saving Scheme (Ho, 2009: 20). This is 50 percent more than the government transferred to the Social Security Fund in 2008 (see Table 12.1). However, it is very doubtful that these cash subsidies are as effective in solving social problems as direct welfare services. Third, these subsidies are not a fair redistribution of social resources. For most subsidies, all citizens are entitled to the same amount of subsidy whether they are rich or poor. In some cases, those who are relatively well off may get more subsidies. For example, people who are wealthy enough to buy a house benefit from a subsidy for home purchase. In this respect, most subsidies are a negative redistribution of social resources and may exacerbate the widening gap between the rich and the poor. Finally, this 'flexible welfare strategy' diverts attention from pressing social problems and forestalls comprehensive and long-term social policy planning. Most social problems cannot simply be solved by the market mechanism. They need state intervention and long-term policy planning. The 'flexible welfare strategy' unnecessarily postpones the problem and makes solutions more costly in the future.

Concluding Remarks

The return of sovereignty to China in 1999 and the rapid development of the gaming economy in recent years have had a tremendous impact on the social, political, and economic system in Macao. Social problems have increased and there has been a rising demand for the improvement of welfare services. Although it has received substantial increased revenue from taxes on the gaming industry, the government has been very cautious about committing to long-term change in the welfare system and has instead adopted a 'flexible welfare strategy' in which cash subsidies are used to ameliorate social discontent.

Macao is facing some fundamental changes and pressing social problems in the twenty-first century which are very different from those of the colonial era (Wong et al, 2007; Wong et al, 2009). For example, rapid urbanisation, uncontrolled urban development, and rising housing expenses have heightened the conflict between the government and the people. These issues have to be resolved with more comprehensive urban planning and a long-term housing strategy. Problems with new immigrants and the importation of foreign workers have increased the conflict between different sectors in the community and in the labour market. This needs to be dealt with by means of comprehensive immigration and population policies. The widening gap between rich and poor and rising unemployment have led to social unrest. There is a need for better regulation of the market economy and improvement of labour legislation and protection of workers. Increasing stress on the family, deteriorating juvenile delinquency and the drug abuse problem call for more professional social work services and the implementation of family-friendly employment policy. The ageing population issue needs to be tackled with a more comprehensive retirement protection system and a fundamental review of practices and procedures that discriminate against, or exclude, older people. These are just a few of the more visible examples rather than an exhaustive list of the challenges that confront Macao citizens.

The *ad hoc* and piecemeal approach of the "flexible welfare strategy' does not serve as a cure. It is neither a resource-saving strategy nor an effective way to deal with difficulties afflicting the society. It wastes valuable resources and makes social problems more costly to correct by delaying more lasting solutions. Macao needs a comprehensive social welfare system and long-term planning to resolve its many social policy issues.

Part IV

Conclusions

13

Gaming, Governance and Public Policy: Constraints and Opportunities

Ian Scott and Newman M. K. Lam

The impact of foreign investment, concentrated on a single industry over a very short period, has resulted in a range of economic, political and social problems that need to be addressed if the polity is to be steered from its present volatility to the future calmer waters of high growth and social stability. To reach that goal requires overcoming some formidable constraints. The causes of instability lie, in some cases, in hot investment money chasing too few goods, sending prices spiralling and no doubt sparking feelings of resentment and relative deprivation among those who have not benefited from the casino boom. In other cases, the causes of instability lie in unresolved problems, such as structural unemployment, that have festered for many years. Still others lie outside the scope of the Macao government in an uncertain global economy and in the policies of the Chinese government.

For a government seeking solutions to its domestic difficulties, a natural course of action would appear to be strong intervention, devising policies and using increased revenue from taxing the gaming industry to redress the imbalances that have emerged in the economy and in society. But, for two reasons, such a solution is not immediately available to the Macao government. First, it is constrained by history. The legacy of the colonial search for political order is corporatist bodies, such as the Macao Chamber of Commerce and the Federation of Trade Unions, which are committed to a status quo in which their leaders enjoy positions of authority and privilege. Changes to that political order brought about by the new-found wealth and independence of many Macao citizens and by the emergence of new political actors in the form of the gaming industry and new civil society organisations have undermined the capacity of the corporatist bodies to maintain social discipline and stability. A second reason why the government cannot be more interventionist is that it does not have the ability to resolve Macao's economic and social problems by administrative means. Its stated ideology is *laissez-faire*. It is not supposed to intervene in the economy, still less to provide the kinds of social policy outputs which citizens are presently demanding. It lacks administrative and policy capacity and, despite the government's considerable efforts to rectify that situation, still needs to deal with fundamental problems in its own internal management before it can even begin to think about comprehensive policy solutions to the wider problems afflicting society.

A further range of constraints about which the government can do very little stems from its external environment. The continuing flow of gamblers from China is clearly important for Macao's present prosperity and its leaders will surely make that point to the Chinese government. But there is also strong anti-gambling sentiment within China which may lead to sudden changes in visa regulations with knock-on effects on the gaming industry and the economy (see Chapter 8). The global environment is, of course, completely beyond the control of the Macao government and even its ability to ameliorate its effects on the local economy is minimal. The 2008/09 financial crisis showed just how rapidly economic downturns can impact on the gaming industry and the ways in which Macao's workers can suffer from the impact of recession in other parts of the world. There is also, finally, the prospect of regional competition for the gaming industry from Taiwan, Hainan island and Singapore, which lends strength to the argument that diversification is essential.

Despite these constraints, there are also very considerable opportunities for Macao in the rapid economic growth which it has experienced since 2002. We believe that for each of the constraints that we have identified, the Macao government has a strategy. In the remainder of this concluding chapter, we evaluate that strategy in terms of the three dimensions of casino capitalism — the gaming industry, governance and public policy — that we have used to organise the material in this book.

Gaming: Constraints and Opportunities

The government's present approach to the economy places emphasis on diversification. It seeks to attract investment in new casinos but is more focused on spin-offs from the existing gaming industry and new types of investment which might enable it to ride out future downturns. In November 2009, the outgoing Chief Executive was reported as saying that he thought economic diversification was more important than the implementation of a 'few policies' and expected that this would be the main task of the new administration (Hu, 2009). The Chinese government has also repeatedly stressed the need for greater diversification and has backed this with plans to enhance Macao's integration with Pearl River Delta and Guangdong, although it is not yet clear to what extent and in what ways this will help move Macao away from its dependence on the gaming industry. The Macao government can already point to some of its own successful initiatives in the direction of greater diversification. It has made progress in creating a tourist and convention venue by renovating the World Heritage site, providing new attractions and establishing a number of excellent museums, all of which might be expected to extend the appeal of Macao beyond the casino industry.

Even in this regard, however, questions have been raised about the extent to which tourist policies are sustainable and the degree to which the Macao government's MICE (Meetings, Incentives, Conventions and Exhibitions) ambitions are feasible (Li and Tsui, 2009a; Nardkarni and Leong, 2007). Although a greater influx of non-gaming tourists and more conventions would not strain administrative and policy capacity to the same extent as developing more comprehensive social policies, Macao does rely on external transport connections through Hong Kong, which might provide serious competition in this field. The other problem is that diversification of this kind does not reduce dependence on the external environment. Global economic downturns do not only adversely affect the gaming industry; they are likely to decrease demand for MICE visitors and non-gaming tourists as well.

A macro-solution to Macao's economic problems in the form of diversification would probably still not resolve the social problems that have been attributed to the gaming industry. The government needs to look at its present relationship with the industry to see in what ways it may need to be regulated and in what ways it may work in greater harmony with the community. One of the key findings of the survey reported in Chapter 3 is that while Macao people appear to recognise the benefits of foreign investment and also the social costs that it involves, they do not expect the gaming industry to solve those problems. Rather, they believe that is a task for their government. The government does require the gaming companies to make some investment in community projects, but the respondents to the survey clearly felt that this was not enough. If we extrapolate from the findings in Chapter 2, we can see that tensions are beginning to arise between the casinos and society in the fierce competition over the use of public space. This is an area where the government will need to play a more active role. The signs of a change of heart over previous practices, discussed in Chapter 2, will need concrete policies and plans if the dangers of urban blight, associated problems such as traffic congestion, and more conflict with societal groups are to be avoided.

Governance: Constraints and Opportunities

The post-liberalisation period has seen subtle changes in the nature of governance in Macao. From a system of law made by the executive by decree after consultation with the key groups in the corporatist consensus (see Chapters 4 and 5), the system has become much more fluid. The Chief Executive is now more inclined — and indeed required — to allow the legislature more power in making laws (see Chapter 4). This serves the function of ensuring that the executive is not seen to be acting arbitrarily and it also enables legislators to voice the concerns of their constituents more publicly than they did in the past. But it also means that the idea that corporatist bodies can maintain social stability and act as behind-the-scenes representatives of their constituent groups is beginning to fade (see Chapter 5). As the traditional associations lose power, so new groups emerge to fill the vacuum. Principal among these are the gaming interests but there are also signs of support for democratic groups and young professionals. What kind of political system will eventuate is difficult to envisage but the signs are that institutions such as the Legislative Assembly and the new associations will play an increasing role in the future. The government itself is indirectly assisting that process. As it moves towards a more direct relationship with the people in the provision of services, the still important role of the traditional associations as major providers of health, welfare and education may in the longer term begin to decline. At the same time, the government needs to legitimise its presence within society in this new political environment and for that it may require the support of bodies such as the legislature in ways which were not necessary in the past.

A major focus of the government's civil service reforms has been the attempt to improve its relations with the people by increasing the efficiency and convenience of the services which it presently provides. Because the civil service that was inherited at the handover lacked both the coordination to deliver services efficiently and sufficient professional skills (see Chapter 6), public sector reform has consequently become necessary. The importance attached to public sector reform is reflected in the government's *Road Map for Public Sector Reform*, which has been implemented over the period 2007 to 2009 and which emphasises internal management reforms and improving relations with citizens, and in efforts to provide one-stop public service centres at the district level (Macao SAR Government, 2007). As a first priority, the aim is to enhance administrative capacity in the interests of promoting better relations between the civil service and the public rather than attempting to introduce new policies to deal with the social problems resulting from foreign investment. The development of a more responsive civil service is important politically because there is experience from neighbouring Hong Kong that a non-democratic government can reduce a legitimacy deficit by introducing a change of culture in the way that public servants deal with citizens and their grievances (Cheung, 1996).

In Quadrant A situations, with rapid growth and social instability (see Chapter 1), the pace of change means that policies very often lag behind the needs of the economy and the impact of inflation, in particular, on the everyday lives of citizens. Macao suffers from precisely this problem. Government policies have not been designed to deal with complex situations and the government has neither the manpower nor the experience to develop solutions to its present problems without substantial reforms to increase its policy capacity. It could be argued, however, that its public sector reform programme is entirely appropriate for the stage of development in which it finds itself. If it were to try to improve policy capacity before it had improved administrative efficiency and raised the skill levels of senior and middle-level civil servants, the government might well be placing too many burdens on its administrative system. A focus on the critical issues of the internal management processes within the civil service, on ensuring that structures are rational and wage levels and position classifications are appropriate, may be more beneficial than trying to formulate and implement complex policies (see Chapters 6 and 7).

The approach is probably correct but there are very considerable difficulties in implementing reforms that will improve administrative capacity, a theme which the Chief Executive returned to in many of his policy addresses (see Chapters 6 and 7). They include: a culture of poor performance that is reflected in an inadequate appraisal system; an unwillingness on the part of government agencies to co-operate with each other beyond their traditionally defined roles; a continuing lack of responsiveness; a lack of qualified personnel in senior positions; an imbalance between the large number of positions that are security-oriented and the relatively smaller number of positions concerned with social services provision; and a system of position classification that needs review and reform. Jeannette Taylor (see Chapter 7) also raises the question of whether the wage system contributes to productivity, especially considering that Macao's public servants are paid twice as much as their private sector counterparts. Although she does not advocate reducing wages, there is clearly a need to investigate the relationship between wages and productivity and to devise means by which productivity can be increased.

Public Policy: Constraints and Opportunities

Although the focus of the reform has been on the administrative practices of the civil service, policy issues do not simply disappear and, however reluctantly, the government must put its credibility on the line and seek to impose its solutions on fractious business and societal groups. In a capitalist system, the government can hardly avoid taking some stance on the factors of production: land, labour and capital. It has specified the financial requirements that the gaming operators must meet and has benefited from burgeoning tax revenue as a consequence. Aside from this, the only other major restriction on capital has been the requirement that croupiers are local people. As Alex Choi and Eva Hung discuss in Chapter 9, this can be seen as an implicit contract between the government and the casino operators, which stresses the reservation of a significant position for locals as a political measure to pacify potential labour unrest while permitting the importation of labour in all other areas of the casino business. More broadly, labour has been an area in which the government has become necessarily, but reluctantly, involved (see Chapter 8). The 2000, 2006 and 2007 demonstrations meant that it could scarcely sit idly by while labour unrest increased. Yet it took more than five years to introduce labour legislation for workers because no agreement could be secured within a corporatist body, the Standing Committee for the Coordination of Social Affairs, which was composed of representatives of both business and labour. The Chief Executive had to intervene directly before the bill could be passed in the Legislative Assembly (see Chapter 4). Land has been equally problematic with an unregulated system leading to corruption, inadequate to non-existent urban planning, and a shrinking of public space and destruction of the visual landscape (see Chapters 2 and 4).

Government has been involved to a greater degree than previously in the provision of education but it has not entered the field at the expense of the traditional providers. Its aims are clearly to create an education system in Macao that better satisfies the needs of the economy and leads to a more unified system with common curricula and examinations. The present system is in need of reform but the government has moved very cautiously. It has used the financial carrot to attract private schools to its net but has yet to use the regulatory stick to insist that they comply with its dictates (see Chapter 10). It is constrained by another corporatist body, the Education Committee, composed of private providers and business representatives, who are committed to maintaining the status quo. In other areas, the government appears to have retreated rather than advanced. The property market has been allowed to develop in ways which James Lee in Chapter 11 describes as 'neoliberal urbanisation'. Government has declined to intervene to control soaring house prices despite public protests and evidence that the market is being inflated by speculators at the expense of local purchasers. Even where the government has taken measures designed to improve the housing market, such as the four percent subsidy scheme for new home buyers, the effect has been to inflate house prices. In social welfare, the government has adopted 'a flexible welfare system' in which it provides subsidies for groups that it perceives to be financially disadvantaged by the imbalances in income distribution and rising inflation. As Chan and Lee (Chapter 12) point out, such an approach is something of a blunt instrument since it very often captures those not in need as well as those who are, and has the additional disadvantage that it creates situations of dependence in a society where one of the core values is supposed to be self-reliance. More critically, it does not support the development of permanent policies which reflect a state response to demonstrated need; *ad hoc* handouts which have been the Macao government's principal response to date do not constitute a policy and may undermine attempts to develop one.

Social welfare policy does get to the crux of the problem. The strategy of handouts is not specifically aimed at solving social problems but rather designed to ameliorate a political situation that has arisen because of the impact of the gaming industry. The interface between gaming, governance and public policy is evident in the question of what action the government might take if it did not provide the long list of subsidies which it presently disburses (see Chapter 12). The government's revenue position, buoyed by taxes from the gaming industry, enables it to take such measures without placing much strain on the budget. Gu and Siu believe that such action is probably a more appropriate response to the problem of the unemployed and those who have been left behind during the casino boom than seeking to apply government pressure to industries to employ unqualified labour (Gu and Siu, 2009: 82). That may well be true while economic diversification is still in its infancy and when government retraining programmes have not yet taken full effect. In the longer term, however, there is a need for greater government intervention in the labour market and education if only because there does not seem to be any other way to resolve the substantial mismatch between the needs of the economy and properly qualified employees (see Chapter 8). Macao has to fill much of its middle managerial needs by imported labour. At one stage, for example, there was a shortfall of an estimated 7,000 unfilled positions in the casino industry (Gu and Siu, 2009: 30). The market is inefficient in this respect and it requires policy action by the government in the fields of education, labour and welfare to move towards greater long-term social stability and the desirable conditions of Quadrant B (see Chapter 1).

The Macao government's cautious strategies have important political advantages. They do not immediately disturb the formal corporatist system which was designed to promote stability even if that system is now being eroded by economic and societal forces. Because many government policies remain very much at the level of principle and are not likely to be fully implemented for many years, the role of the traditional associations in delivering services and their claim to be representative of the population is at present relatively undisturbed by the expansion of government provision. If the emphasis is now on delivering present government services more efficiently, traditional associations can nonetheless still claim government funding and subsidies for their activities. Within the political system itself, however, their influence does appear to be declining. Gaming interests, for example, have increased representation in the Legislative Assembly and can use many informal channels to express their views. The government itself is slowly beginning to develop a more direct relationship with the people.

Although the government strategy has considerable political advantages and makes sense in terms of its public sector reform programme, it does not resolve the short-term problem of the needs of the economy, structural unemployment or citizen dissatisfaction. For the government to become more proactive, to move beyond the level of principle and to devise more comprehensive policies that can be implemented, there are fundamental constraints that it must overcome. These include, beyond those constraints that we have already discussed, its ideological limitations. Modern capitalist states do not run successfully on *laissez-faire* principles. Even in casino economies, there is a need to protect the capitalists from themselves and to ensure that workers receive the kinds of benefits to which their labour entitles them. The belief that the market can always work things out for itself is dangerous in any capitalist system but is especially dangerous in a situation where capital has been invested in a single industry which has multinational connections. The kind of capitalism that came to Macao did not bring with it that 'invisible hand' that would so efficiently ensure outcomes for the benefit of all. Furthermore, because the market is not efficient, and because significant groups have been further marginalised by the inflationary effects of massive foreign investment, there is a strong case for greater government policy intervention in the longer term to smooth out some of the inequalities that have arisen.

 *Appendix*

Timeline: Macao 1999–2010

1999

December   Macao reunites with China. The Macao Special Administrative Region (MSAR) government is formed.

2000

March   The Chief Executive gives his first policy address.

May   Unemployed workers gather spontaneously on the streets to protest against the government for its failure to protect the interests of the working class. The demonstration continues into June and eventually turns violent. The police use tear gas to disperse the crowd.

July   The government declares that the casino monopoly held by STDM will be allowed to lapse when it expires in 2002 to be replaced by three concessionaires.

September   The government publishes a Provisional Licensing Process for Public Mobile Telecommunications on September 8, and accepts bids from investors.

October   The government initiates a labour law review after subduing the labour protest in June.

November   The Elector Registration Law is passed on November 21. It defines the registration procedures for individual and corporate voters for direct and indirect elections to the Legislative Assembly.

2001

February   The assembly passes two important laws: the Electoral System for the Legislative Assembly of the Macao SAR and the Electoral Law for the Legislative Assembly of the Macao SAR. Major amendments include the replacement of the previous District Election Committee by a Legislative Election Commission. All nomination committees entering direct elections are entitled to expand their membership from 100 to 300–500 persons. All members are required to be registered voters.

March   The government awards Global System for Mobile communications (GSM) licences to SmarTone and Hutchison Telephone for the provision of mobile telecommunication.

April   The government launches a training system in co-operation with the Civil Service College of Singapore, initiating the Executive Management Development Programme, which is intended to improve the leadership skills of mid-ranking and senior civil servants. Courses cover public administration and organisational skills.

The Chief Executive issues By-law No. 9/2001 to amend the Free Education Subsidy By-law.

May   Electoral registration ends on May 26, by which date the total number of registered voters has reached 159,813, representing an increase of 26.09 percent over 1999. Of these, 33,559 are newly registered voters.

July   The Mainland-Macao Joint Committee on Trade and Commerce is founded to set up commercial and trade channels between the central government and Macao.

The government offers courses on basic training for civil servants, which emphasise the spirit of public service and administrative values and principles. The programme also covers fundamentals of the political system, public service law and administrative procedures. The courses are intended to help civil servants establish a lawful, non-corrupt and loyal team.

An Executive Order authorises the setting up of the Monitoring Committee on the Discipline of Commission Against Corruption (CCAC) Personnel. The committee is to analyse and monitor complaints directed against any CCAC personnel involved in a non-criminal offence. Regular reports are to be submitted to the Chief Executive.

Sheldon Adelson, the Chairman and Chief Executive of the Las Vegas Sands Company, meets with Chinese Vice-Premier Qian Qichen in Beijing to discuss the question of developing the hotel business (and implicitly the casino industry) in Macao.

August   The Legislative Assembly officially passes Law No. 16/2001: Gaming Industry Regulatory Framework. The regulations define the meanings of 'casino' and 'gaming', and lay out specific regulations about the concessions system and the conditions and process for open bidding.

The Legislative Assembly passes the Telecommunications Law that covers the construction, management and operation of a telecommunications network in Macao.

September   Legislative elections for the second post-handover term are held on September 23. Electors choose 20 Legislative Assembly members.

Under the Basic Law, the Legislative Assembly of the Macao SAR for the second post-handover term consists of 27 members. The number of appointed members is maintained at seven while the numbers of seats for directly elected members and indirectly elected members increase from eight in the first term to ten in the second term. Two extra indirectly elected seats are added, one for the sector representing professionals and charity and one for culture, education and sports.

October   The Executive Council examines and discusses the by-laws for Open Bidding for Casino Concessions: the contract and the required qualifications and financial strength of bidders and concessionaires. The regulations stipulate that a bidding committee comprising no fewer than three members should be established. It also determines the nature of the premium and the payment method.

Under the Basic Law and the Legislative Assembly Electoral System, the Chief Executive appoints Ho Teng Iat, Au Chong Kit, Philip Xavier, Vong Hin Fai, Cheong Vai Kei, José Rodrigues and Tsui Wai Kwan as new Legislative Assembly members.

The second post-handover Legislative Assembly is established on October 16 at government headquarters. All members take an oath, witnessed by the Chief Executive, to become second-term Legislative Assembly members. On the same day, the members elect Susanna Chou, Lau Cheok Va, Leonel Alberto Alves and Kou Hoi In to serve for second terms as President, Vice-President, First Secretary and Second Secretary respectively.

Anticipating the expiration of the monopoly held by Sociedade de Turismo e Diversões de Macau (STDM), the government decides to issue three casino concessions. The public tender is opened in 2001; 21 bids are received. After an initial review, 18 applicants from Macao and overseas are certified as qualified bidders.

In 2000, the Health Bureau appointed a consultant to study the reform of Macao's health system and to collect public opinion. The report 'Macao in the New Millennium — A Study and Evaluation of Macao's Healthcare System' is released on October 9.

November   A study group comprised of professors from the Faculty of Education of the University of Hong Kong is entrusted by the government to study the future of tertiary education in Macao. 'Higher Education in Macao — Strategic Development for the New Era — Report of a Consultancy Study' is released on November 23 to solicit public opinion on how to improve tertiary education in Macao.

December   The government abolishes the two provisional municipal organs and establishes the Civic and Municipal Affairs Bureau.

An Executive Order is published to provide for the establishment of the Consultative Committee for Medical Reform to canvas public opinion and collect recommendations that would help in evaluating the current health system.

2002

January   By an Executive Order published on December 21, 2001 in the supplement to the Macao SAR Gazette, members of three committees: Consultative Committee, Supervisory Committee and Follow-Up Committee of the Civic and Municipal Affairs Bureau are announced. The Administration Council which consists of seven members and is chaired by Lau Si Io is appointed for a term of two years, effective as of January 1, 2002.

The Civic and Municipal Affairs Bureau is established.

The bidding for casino concessions enters the consultative stage. The Casino Concessions Committee invites the 18 qualified bidders to present their investment plans individually to members of the Legislative Assembly.

February   The Chief Executive signs an Executive Order granting provisional casino concessions to Sociedade de Jogos de Macau (SJM), Wynn Resorts (Macau), and Galaxy Casino Company. Construction of Avenida da Bairro da Ilha Verde, linking Avenida do Comendador Ho Yin and Avenida do Conselheiro Borja, is completed and officially opens to traffic.

March   President Jiang Zemin receives Chief Executive Edmund Ho Hau Wah at the Zhongnanhai compound, and stresses the central government's support for the granting of three casino concessions.

The government and STDM sign a Concession Contract for Maritime Passenger Transportation Services between Macao and Hong Kong for a period of 25 years, effective from April 1.

The government signs the Concession Contract on Operating Games of Luck and Other Games in Casinos in the Macao Special Administrative Region with SJM for a period of 18 years. The concessionaire, beginning from April 1, takes over the operation of 11 casinos, 337 gaming tables and the employees from STDM. The croupiers union under João Cheang urges members not to sign the contract offered by SJM, pending further negotiation with management for better terms.

The Chief Executive issues Decree Law No. 06/2002, legalising the practice of junket operators in the gaming industry.

April   SJM commences operation at midnight on April 1. This marks the end of the monopoly franchise era of the gaming industry. STDM shareholder Fok Ying Tung announces his withdrawal from the company. His shares will be transferred to the Fok Ying Tung Foundation established in Macao for charity purposes as well as for developing the territory. The by-law on the Qualifications and Regulations for Casino Gaming promoters comes into effect.

June   The government signs the Concession Contract on Operating Games of Luck and Other Games in Casinos in the Macao Special Administrative Region with Wynn Resorts for a period of 20 years, valid from June 27.

The government suspends the consultation process for the labour law review because of a lack of consensus between business and labour groups.

July   On July 8, the croupier union urges members to lodge formal complaints to the Labour Affairs Bureau against STDM for not paying them holiday compensation.

On July 19, the Labour and Employment Bureau and the Macao General Labour Unions Association, SJM and the Associacao da Uniao de Amizade dos Trabalhadores da STDM (STDM Workers Association) sign a memorandum of understanding regarding staff transfers.

September The Public Administration Observatory, a consultation committee chaired by the Secretary for Justice and Administration, is established for the purpose of initiating civil service reform.

October   The foundation stone of the third Macao-Taipa bridge, the largest infrastructure project since the establishment of the Macao SAR, is laid.

November The Legislative Assembly passes legislation governing the Internal Security Law of the Macao SAR.

2003

February The Secretary for Economy and Finance issues an order under the Regulations and Rules on Provision of Special Assistance for the Unemployed with Exceptional Difficulties. Under the Regulations, the Social Security Fund will use a special allocation from the

	Macao SAR budget to provide assistance and incentives to local unemployed residents.
April	After thorough analysis and consideration of various factors, the government concludes that the present situation does not merit developing a light rail system.
July	The Labour Affairs Bureau orders STDM to pay holiday compensation to its former casino workers based on their basic wages to settle the dispute.
August	The government signs a 25-year concession contract with the Hong Kong–Macao Hydrofoil Company Limited for the operation of direct ferry services between the Hong Kong International Airport and Macao.
	The Macao SAR Gazette publishes By-law No. 26/2003 to re-regulate the examination of educational qualifications.
September	The new External Trade Law officially comes into effect, and the External Trade Operator Card (White Card) System is revoked. All individual and corporate taxpayers in Macao become eligible to engage in external trade.
October	The new Personal Income Tax Regulations come into effect. Civil servants, teachers and clergymen, who were previously exempted from paying tax, now become taxpayers.
	Vice-President Zeng Qinghong arrives in Macao to preside over the signing ceremony for the Mainland and Macao Closer Economic Partnership Arrangement (CEPA). CEPA is signed by the Vice Minister of Commerce, An Min, representing the central government, and the Secretary for Economy and Finance, Francis Tam Pak Yuen, on behalf of the Macao SAR Government. Under the arrangement, 273 Macao products would enjoy zero tariffs when entering the mainland market, with effect from January 1, 2004.
December	The Secretary for Economy and Finance, Francis Tam Pak Yuen, heads an official delegation to Beijing for the first meeting of the Joint Steering Committee of the Mainland and Macao Closer Economic Partnership Arrangement (CEPA).

2004

April	The Chief Executive Election Law officially comes into effect.
	Members of the Electoral Affairs Committee for the Election of the Chief Executive (EACCE) are sworn in.
May	The Sands Macao opens. It is the first casino run by a new operator to open since the liberalisation of the gaming industry.

	The period for accepting nominations for membership of the Chief Executive Election Committee ends. A total of 256 applications are submitted. Only the professional sub-sector requires an election for members; all the other sectors and sub-sectors have equal numbers of candidates and seats.

June
: The ground-breaking ceremony for Wynn Resorts takes place. The total investment in its first-phase construction amounts to MOP 5.6 billion, and the project is scheduled for completion by the end of 2006.

July
: The Law on Regulating Credits Related to Gaming and Betting in Casinos or Other Gaming Venues officially comes into effect.

The Government Gazette publishes a list of the 300 members of the Chief Executive Election Committee.

Chief Executive Edmund Ho Hau Wah returns his nomination form to the EACCE, thereby officially declaring that he is running for a second term of office.

The EACCE verifies Edmund Ho's candidacy; 297 members of the Election Committee endorse his nomination.

August
: The Legislative Assembly approves the Bill for the Performance Appraisal Principles for Civil Servants.

Edmund Ho Hau Wah is re-elected in the second-term Chief Executive election. He secures 296 or 98.67 percent of the votes.

October
: Casa Real Casino opens.

December
: The State Council appoints Principal Officials and a Public Prosecutor-General for the second-term Macao SAR Government, in accordance with a list of nominations submitted by Chief Executive Edmund Ho.

The 13th Session of the Standing Committee of the 10th National People's Congress (NPC) approves the constituent list of the second-term Basic Law Committee of the Macao SAR. All the members of the previous term retain their positions.

2005

February
: The government publishes the Macao Light Rapid Transit System Feasibility Study on Preliminary Alignment Options. The study proposes that most of the system be constructed underground and forecasts that it would require a total investment of approximately MOP 12 billion and take eight years to complete.

March
: The Office for Infrastructure Development launches a series of briefings to collect the public's opinions about the Macao Light Rapid Transit System Feasibility Study.

	The Legislative Assembly passes the second reading of the Bill for Adjusting Salaries, Pension Funds and Condolence Money for Civil Servants and the Amendment to Law No. 1/2000. Under its provisions, which were retroactively effective from January 1, 2005, the benefits payable to civil servants of every grade will be increased by 5 percent.
April	SJM and MGM Grand Paradise Ltd sign an 18-year sub-concession contract involving a total investment of around US$900 million (MOP7.2 billion).
	The Law Reform Consultative Committee holds its first meeting and decides to conduct preliminary research on the Commercial Code, Traffic Code and the civil servants' provident fund system.
June	The official ground-breaking ceremony is held for MGM Grand Paradise's first investment project, MGM Grand Macau. Involving a total investment of MOP7.8 billion and a construction area exceeding 180,000 square metres, the project is scheduled for completion during the second half of 2007.
	The Bill on the Fundamental Rights of Trade Union Associations is voted down during its first reading at the plenary meeting of the Legislative Assembly after failing to win the votes of more than half of the members.
July	The Galaxy Casino Company publicly urges the government to allow migrant workers to work in casinos.
	Macao is accepted as an associate member of UNESCO and is included in UNESCO's world heritage sites.
August	The Survey of the Overall Quality of Life of Macao Residents 2005 is officially launched.
September	The third-term Legislative Assembly elections are held. Twelve new Legislative Assembly members are chosen by direct election, and a further ten by indirect election. The turnout rate for the direct election is 58.39 percent, while the figure for the indirect election is 61.95 percent.
October	Chief Executive Edmund Ho appoints seven legislators to the third Legislative Assembly by executive order. They are Lee Pui Lam, Sam Chan Io, Tsui Wai Kwan, Chui Sai Peng, Philip Xavier, Ieong Tou Hong and Lao Pun Lap.
	Las Vegas Sands Corporation and the Zhuhai Municipal Government sign a letter of intent in the United States. Under its terms, Las Vegas Sands Corporation will invest US$1 billion (MOP8 billion) in developing a leisure and convention resort on Hengqin Island.

The 29 members of the third-term Legislative Assembly are sworn into office. Susanna Chou is re-elected as the Assembly's President, Lau Cheok Va as its Vice-President, Leonel Alberto Alves as its First Secretary, and Kou Hoi In as its Second Secretary.

The Subsidies for Senior Citizens Scheme is launched, starting from MOP1,200 per year in 2005 and to be subsequently raised to MOP5,000 in 2009.

Macao opens the 2005 East Asian Games amid criticism of huge over-spending. The Games run from October 29 to November 6. Some of the infrastructure built for the games is later found to have involved bribery implicating the Secretary for Transport and Public Works, who is arrested in December 2006 for corruption.

November   Venetian Macau announces in the United States that the company will raise US$2.5 billion (MOP20 billion) from the market for the design, development, construction and other preliminary work on its investment projects in Macao, including the Venetian Macao Resort Hotel complex and other projects on the Cotai Strip.

December   William P. Weidner, President and Chief Operating Officer of Las Vegas Sands Corporation, says in Zhuhai that the value of his company's investment in the Hengqin Island resort development project will be increased to US$2 billion (MOP16 billion).

The Quality-of-Life Studies Centre publishes its interim report on Survey of the Overall Quality of Life of Macao Residents 2005.

The government reopens the reform debate on labour policy because of sharp increases in labour disputes.

2006

January   The Research Centre for Sustainable Development Strategies releases the 2005 Survey on the Civic Virtue of Macao SAR Residents.

March   The Legislative Assembly passes the Bill on the Prevention and Suppression of Money Laundering.

April   The Macao Federation of Trade Unions stages an assembly against unlimited importation of labour and urges the government to immediately halt the importation of labour. More than 1,000 people attend.

The Chief Executive declares that the government will not open the croupier market to imported labour.

The Chief Executive meets the Macao Federation of Labour Unions and the representatives of seven industries, collecting their

	opinions on the importation of labour and looking into workers' employment status.
May	Chief Executive Order No. 102/2006 establishes the Curriculum Reform and Development Committee to review the school curriculum reform.
	Eight organisations jointly hold a May Day demonstration, under the banner of 'expelling illegal workers and reducing imported labour'. More than 3,000 people join the demonstration.
	The Labour Affairs Bureau, the Industrial Association of Macau and the Macao Manufacturing Industry General Union hold the first tripartite meeting of workers, employers and the Government.
June	The signing of the Supplementary Protocol to the Mainland and Macao Closer Economic Partnership Arrangement and the Letter of Confirmation of the Standards Concerning the Place of Origin of Products takes place in Macao.
July	Macau Electricity Company (CEM) and China Southern Power Grid Corporation sign new contracts concerning electricity supplies, and hold an inauguration ceremony for the second power transmission cable from the grid to Macao.
	The Court of Final Appeal rules that decree laws made by the Chief Executive are equivalent to laws passed in the Legislative Assembly.
	Migrant workers are imported to work in non-croupier positions in Wynn's Casino Resorts.
August	The Social Security Fund Authority raises pensions, disability gratuities and social relief.
	The Legislative Assembly passes the Bill on the Provident Fund Scheme for Workers in the Public Services. The scheme will come into effect on January 1, 2007. This scheme is considered the first step in addressing inequality in the civil service among employees hired under different contractual arrangements.
	The 13-day 2006 Population By-census begins.
	The expansion wing of Sands Macao Casino is inaugurated, boosting the number of the casino's gaming tables to 740 and making it the world's largest casino by number of tables.
September	Wynn Resorts opens its first Asian casino hotel in Macao.
	The Chief Executive approves a gaming sub-concession contract that Wynn Resorts (Macau) has granted to Melco PBL Gaming (Macau), a subsidiary of Melco PBL Entertainment (Macau).
October	The government grants a three-year franchise for operating a sea passenger service between Macao and Shekou in Shenzhen to Shun Tak-China Travel Ship Management Limited and Yuet Tung Shipping Company.

Galaxy StarWorld Hotel and Casino opens.

The Office for Infrastructure Development releases the Light Rapid Transit (LRT) System In-depth Study and starts the first round of consultations.

December   The Executive Council concludes discussions on the Draft Bill for Adjusting Salaries, Pension and Death Benefits for Civil Servants. The adjustments will become effective from January 1, 2007, raising each point on the civil service salary scale to MOP55.

Provision of 12 years of free education is introduced. Free education is extended to kindergarten levels one and two, and will retroactively cover students who were admitted in the school year 2005–06. Tuition subsidies for students studying in schools outside the public education network are increased to MOP5,000.

The Non-Tertiary Education System of Macao (Law No. 9/2006) standardises the schooling structure in Macao: three years of pre-school/kindergarten, six years of primary education, and six years of secondary education which consist of three years of junior and three years of senior secondary education.

Ao Man Long, the Macao SAR's first Secretary for Transport and Public Works, is arrested on suspicion of graft. It is alleged that Ao and his wife have assets equal to 57 times the total earnings of their official posts over the previous six years. On the Chief Executive's recommendation, the central government dismisses Ao from his post.

2007

January   The law on the Provident Fund Scheme for Workers in Public Services comes into effect; it benefits more than 6,000 civil servants who previously lacked retirement coverage.

The Legislative Assembly approves the establishment of two provisional committees — the Provisional Committee for the Analysis of the Land and Public Concessions System, and the Provisional Committee for the Analysis of the Public Finance System.

Bidding is held for 50 taxi licences issued by the Civic and Municipal Affairs Bureau. The licences are valid for eight years and non-transferable. Successful bidders pay between MOP1.01 million and MOP1.2 million.

The Legislative Assembly passes the Bill on Adjustment of Salaries, Pension and Death Benefits for Civil Servants, which gives civil servants a pay rise of 4.76 percent.

Gambling revenue in Macao exceeds Las Vegas and becomes the world's largest casino market.

February   The Secretary for Social Affairs and Culture, Fernando Chui Sai On, says the government plans to launch 15 years of free education ahead of schedule, in the 2007–08 academic year.

After a total investment of over MOP5 billion by SJM, the Grand Lisboa is opened to the public.

The Chief Executive issues Decree Law 69/2007 to establish the Public Services Assessment Commission. This Commission, comprised mainly of external experts, is responsible for the biannual performance management assessment of public services with identifiable external clients.

March   The Secretary for Transport and Public Works, Lau Si Io, is sworn in.

After the United States' designation of Banco Delta Asia (BDA) as a primary money-laundering concern, the Ministry of Foreign Affairs of the People's Republic of China and the Macao SAR government express deep regrets. The Monetary Authority of Macao says the Macao SAR government will continue to manage BDA.

April   The Commission Against Corruption announces the results of preliminary investigations into the Ao Man Long corruption case, and notes that Ao Man Long owns more than MOP800 million worth of unaccountable assets.

The Macao SAR government promulgates the suspension of By-law No. 3/2005 Temporary Residency Scheme for Investors, Managerial Personnel, and Technical and Professional Qualification Holders, ending applications for property investment residency.

The Macao SAR Government Gazette publishes Executive Order No. 116/2007, for establishing a human resources office.

May   The May Day demonstration initiated by six organisations triggers a clash between police and participants, prompting the police to fire warning shots.

Macao's first six-star casino hotel, Crown Macau, opens.

June   The General Office of the NPC Standing Committee, Ministry of Water Resources, and the Liaison Office of the Central People's Government hold a meeting in Macao on reducing the impact of the salinity problem with the mainland's water supplies to Macao.

After ten years of discussions and amendments, the Legislative Assembly passes the first reading of the General Law on Labour Relations (Labour Law).

The Macao SAR Government Gazette publishes Executive Order No. 184/2007, on the establishment of the Outbound Tourism Crisis Management Office.

	The government announces the Road Map for Public Administration Reform 2007–2009.

The government announces the Road Map for Public Administration Reform 2007–2009.

The Public Prosecutions Office lays charges in the Ao Man Long case in the Court of Final Appeal.

July   Mainland China and Macao sign the Fourth Supplementary Protocol to the Closer Economic Partnership Arrangement (also known as CEPA V).

August   The Bill on Laws and By-laws passes its first reading in the Legislative Assembly.

With a total investment of MOP19.2 billion (US$2.4 billion), the Venetian Macao-Resort-Hotel opens.

Provision of 15 years of free education is introduced. Free education is extended to include three years of senior secondary education.

Chief Executive Order No. 230/2007 stipulates the implementation dates of the new schooling structure. Three years of preschool education are to be implemented in the school year 2007–08. The new structure for secondary education, starting from Junior 1, is to be implemented in the school year 2008–09.

September The government publishes Administrative Regulation 18/2007 to establish the Consultation Council for Public Administration Reform (Conselho Consultivo para a Reforma da Administração Pública). This council replaces the disbanded Public Administration Observatory for initiating civil service reform and is chaired by the Chief Executive instead of the Secretary for Justice and Administration.

The 45-day public consultation on the optimised plan for the Macao Light Rapid Transit System ends. The government receives more than 100 papers with suggestions and inquiries from various organisations, professionals and members of the public.

The Secretary for Transport and Public Works, Lau Si Io, reveals that the government has decided to terminate the two public franchise bus concession contracts on October 15, 2008 after the contracts expire.

October   The Secretary for Transport and Public Works, Lau Si Io, announces the implementation of the first phase optimised plan of the Macao Light Rapid Transit System.

November The Chief Executive announces plans to reduce and exempt various taxes in the 2009/09 financial year in order to alleviate hardship of Macao citizens, including: exemption from stamp duty for purchasing property, exemption of housing taxes for owner-occupiers, allowance increase for Complementary Tax and Professional Tax, and exemption of Tourism Tax and Industrial Tax. These tax concessions are continued or further expanded in subsequent years.

| December | 1,500 protesters take to the streets, demonstrating 'against corruption and for democracy' as well as over a wide range of labour issues, such as illegal and imported labour and 'taking away locals' jobs'. |

MGM Grand Macau opens.

The second phase of Wynn Resorts opens.

The Executive Council concludes discussions on the Draft Bill on Revisions to Ranks and Grades of the Public Security Authority and Public Security Forces.

2008

| January | The government plans a levy on all enterprises hiring imported labour. |

Ao Man Long, Macao's former Secretary for Transport and Public Works, is sentenced to 27 years in prison after being found guilty of corruption, money-laundering, abuse of power and unjustified wealth charges.

| February | The Legislative Assembly passes a legislation of 'adjusting salaries, pension and death benefits for civil servants'. The adjustment takes retrospective effect from January 1, 2008 and raises each point on the civil service salary scale to MOP59. |

| March | Macao and Guangdong agree on the nine-point co-operation concept. |

The government launches a proposal to solve transport problems in Macao.

| April | The Education and Youth Affairs Bureau is prepared to foot interest tab for student loans. |

The government freezes new gaming concessions, casinos, gaming tables, slot machines and junket-tour operators.

Chief Executive Edmund Ho Hau Wah hands out a one-off subsidy of MOP5,000 each for all permanent residents and MOP3,000 each for temporary residents.

May	Six gaming operators 'agree' to limit junket commissions.
June	The Collegial Bench of the Court of First Instance finds Ao Man Long's wife, Chan Meng Leng, brother, Ao Man Fu, sister-in-law, Ao Chan Wa Choi and father, Ao Veng Kong guilty of money-laundering. Three businessmen and a civil servant are also found guilty of graft.
July	The first Wealth Partaking Scheme is introduced. All permanent residents are entitled to a one-off cash subsidy of MOP5,000.

The government consults the community on the 'Outline for Macao Urban Concept Plan'.

| August | Macao becomes a signatory to the International Convention on the Rights of Persons with Disability. |

The Legislative Assembly passes a new Labour Relations Law, effective from January 1, 2009.

October   The government signs bus franchise deals offering two-year temporary contracts.

December   The government approves proposals for two bus companies to increase fares.

The government plans to participate in the building of the Hong Kong-Zhuhai-Macau Bridge in 2009.

2009

January   Labour Relations Law (Law No. 7/2008) is enforced.

March   Article 23 State Security Law takes effect.

April   Government announces 21 'planning districts' which have not previously been disclosed to the public. The authority will revise such planning districts according to social development needs.

May   Chui Sai On resigns as Secretary for Social Affairs and Culture to run for Chief Executive.

The second Wealth Partaking Scheme is launched. All permanent residents are entitled to a one-off cash subsidy of MOP6,000.

June   The Education and Youth Affairs Bureau intends to revise the 'voluntary education' system and to punish those who do not follow the regulations.

The number of civil servants increases to 21,420, a 3.71 percent rise compared with the year before.

The Home Ownership Mortgage Guarantee Scheme is revived. Residents aged 21 or above purchasing a property of MOP2.6 million or less are entitled to a 4 percent mortgage interest subsidy for ten years. The government first introduced the scheme in 1996 but suspended it in 2002 when the housing market rebounded.

July   Chui Sai On is nominated as the third-term Chief Executive on July 26.

The Legislative Assembly passes Law 13/2009, titled 'Legal Framework for Legislation', which narrows the law-making power of the Chief Executive to issuing decree law only for the management of the public services.

August   Chui Sai On is elected as the next Chief Executive of the Macao SAR.

The government drafts a by-law to cap junket commissions.

September   The Legislative Assembly is elected on September 20. There are 149,000 voters in the election and the turnout rate reaches nearly 60 percent. Members are elected through direct election, ten members come from indirect election and seven members are nominated by the Chief Executive.

October	Election Law of Chief Executive, Legislative Assembly and voters comes into effect on October 15.

October   Election Law of Chief Executive, Legislative Assembly and voters comes into effect on October 15.

The Legislative Assembly passes a new imported labour law with the purpose of tightening the application rules for migrant workers and protecting the interests of migrant workers.

November   Chief Executive Edmund Ho Hau Wah reports the government's work in the fiscal year 2009 and presents the budget for the fiscal year 2010.

In accordance with the Macao Basic Law and the nomination of Chui Sai On as the Chief Executive of the third-term MSAR government, the State Council of the People's Republic of China appoints the Principal Officials of the new government and the Public Prosecutor-General of the Public Prosecutions Office. The new appointments take effect on December 20, the same day Chui Sai On assumes office as Chief Executive.

December   In accordance with the Basic Law, the Chief Executive, Chui Sai On, completes the formation of the Executive Council of the third-term MSAR government.

The announcement of the ten Principal Officers of the third MSAR administration includes changes to the heads of the government's two watchdog agencies. Chief Executive-designate Fernando Chui Sai On replaces Fatima Choi Mei Lei as Commissioner of Audit with Ho Weng On, the head of the outgoing Chief Executive's office. Commissioner for Corruption Cheong U is replaced by Vasco Fong Man Chong, a Court of Second Instance judge. Fatima Choi is given a two-year appointment as advisor to the Secretary for Economy and Finance, while Cheong U takes on the post of Secretary for Social Affairs and Culture, which Fernando Chui held previously.

2010

March   Chui Sai On delivers his first Policy Address.

The Chief Executive announces the third Wealth Partaking Scheme. All permanent residents are entitled to a one-off cash subsidy of MOP6,000. This subsidy will be injected into a Central Saving Account for every Macao citizen under his or her Social Security Fund account. This scheme expands the social security system into a two-tier system, comprising the comprehensive Social Security Fund and the individual Central Saving Account.

May   On May 1, an estimated 1,500 protesters clash with police in a rally that leaves 40 injured.

June Macao casino revenue has risen almost 100 percent from May 2009 to more than MOP17 billion, according to the Macao Statistics and Census Service and the government-run broadcaster TDM.

Manuel Silverio, former president of the Macao Sport Development Board, faces trial for appointing a masseuse to a public job.

Source: Government Information Bureau (2009–2010)
  Macao Daily News (2000–2010)
  Macao Yearbook (2002–2008)
  South China Morning Post (2009–2010)
  Government Information Bureau (2009–2010)
  Websites of various government bureaux and agencies (2010)

Notes and References

Chapter 1   [References]

BBC News Online (1998) 'Macau hit by petrol bomb attacks', May 8.

Bruck, Connie (2008) 'The Brass Ring', *The New Yorker*, June 30.

Bruning, Harold (1999) 'Broken tooth top man in 14K triad', *The Standard*, October 28.

Chan, S. S. (2000) *The Macau Economy*. Macau: Macau Foundation.

Chief Executive (2009) *Policy Address for the Fiscal Year 2009*. Available from: www.gov.mo.

Eisner, Manuel (1992) 'Long-term Fluctuations of Economic Growth and Social Destabilization', *Historical Social Research*, 17, 70–98.

Fung, Kwan (1992) 'Income Distribution in Macau' in Bruce Taylor et al (eds) *Socioeconomic Development and Quality of Life in Macau*. Macao: Centre of Macau Studies, University of Macau, 143–155.

Fung, Kwan (2009) 'Income Distribution and Poverty' in S. L. Wong, K. Y. Wong and P. S. Wan (eds) *The New Face of Macao Society: Achievement and Challenge*. Hong Kong: Hong Kong Institute of Asia-Pacific Studies, The Chinese University of Hong Kong, 1–19 (translated from Chinese).

Gaming Inspection and Coordination Bureau (2009) 'History'. Available from: www.dcj.gov.mo.

Godinho, Jorge (2010) 'The Ao Man Long Corruption and Money Laundering Case', *Freedom from Fear Magazine*, June 20.

Gough, Neil (2009a) 'Macau casino earnings grow by record 17pc', *South China Morning Post*, September 3.

Gough, Neil (2009b) 'Galaxy plans unpaid leave for local gaming staff', *South China Morning Post*, January 22.

Gough, Neil (2009c) 'Cotai gains as building boom restarts in Macau', *South China Morning Post*, November 23.

Gough, Neil and Ivan Zhai (2009) 'Casino stocks fall after visa rules tightened', *South China Morning Post*, October 16.

Gu, Zheng and Ricardo C. S. Siu (2009) *Macao Gaming Human Resources: Issues and Solutions*. Macao: Macao Association of Economic Sciences.

Ho, W. S. (2006) *Employment Growth in Macau's Tertiary Sector*. Macao: Macao Monetary Authority.

Hu, Fox Yi (2009a) 'Macau looks on enviously at HK's relaxed travel policies', *South China Morning Post*, March 6.

Hu, Fox Yi (2009b) 'Graft has declined, says outgoing Macau leader', *South China Morning Post*, November 20.

Hu, Fox Yi (2010) '40 hurt as Macau labour rally turns ugly', *South China Morning Post*, May 2.

Huntington, Samuel P. (1968) *Political Order in Changing Societies*. New Haven: Yale University Press.

Lee, S. P. (2006) *Social Stability and Public Policy: The Role of Special Interest Groups in Macao*. Hong Kong: Unpublished MPA dissertation, The University of Hong Kong.

Lewis, J. W. and X. Litai (2004) 'Social Change and Political Reform in China: Meeting the Challenge of Success', *China Quarterly*, No. 176, 926–942.

Lewis, Tommy and Adam Lee (1996) 'Mainland forces to add weight to Macau crime crackdown', *The Standard*, December 9.

Li, Sheng and Yanming Tsui (2009a) 'A General Equilibrium Approach to Tourism and Welfare: The Case of Macau', *Habitat International*, 33 (4), 412–424.

Li, Sheng and Yanming Tsui (2009b) 'Casino Boom and Local Politics: The City of Macao', *Cities*, 26(2), 67–73.

Lo, Shiu Hing (2008) *Political Change in Macau*. Abingdon: Routledge.

Lo, Shiu Hing and Herbert S. Yee (2005) 'Legitimacy-building in the Macau Special Administrative Region: Colonial Legacies and Reform Strategies', *Asian Journal of Political Science*, 13 (1), 51–79.

Lo, Sonny (2009) 'Casino Capitalism and Its Legitimacy Impact on the Politico-administrative State in Macau', *Journal of Current Chinese Affairs*, 1/2009, 19–47.

Macao SAR Government (2007) *The Road Map for Public Sector Reform*. Available from: www.gov.mo (translated from Chinese).

Macao SAR Government (2009) 'CE: Central Government vigorously supports Macao', November 19. Available from: www.gov.mo.

Macau Closer (2008) 'Justice was not done'. Available from: www.macaucloser.com, May.

Macau News (2009) November 20.

Melco Crown Entertainment (2009) 'Melco Crown Entertainment announces third quarter earnings'. Available from: http://www.melco-crown.com.

Migdal, Joel S. (2001) *State in Society*. Cambridge: Cambridge University Press.

Nadkarni, Sanjay and Aliana Leong Man Wai (2007) 'Macao's MICE Dreams: Opportunities and Challenges', *International Journal of Event Management Research*, 3 (2), 47–57.

Ng, Jeffrey (2009) 'Wynn Macau's net profit slips', *The Wall Street Journal*, September 21.

Olsen, Mancur (1963) 'Rapid Growth as a Destabilizing Force', *Journal of Economic History*, 23 (4), 529–552.

Pincus, Jonathon and Vu Thanh Tu Anh (2008) 'Vietnam: A Tiger in Turmoil', *Far Eastern Economic Review*, May.

Ringland, Gill (2002) *Scenarios for Public Policy*. Chichester: John Wiley and Sons.

SJM (2009) 'SJM Holdings Limited announces interim results for six months ended 30 June 2009'. Available from: http://www.sjmholdings.com/mc-pressrelease12.html.

Sousa, Ines Trigo de (2009) *Regional Integration and Differentiation in a Globalizing China: The Blending of Government and Business in Post-Colonial Macau*. Amsterdam: University of Amsterdam.

South China Morning Post (2007) 'Macau must deal with the casino boom wealth gap', Editorial, May 2.

Statistics and Census Service (2008) *Direct Investment Statistics.* Available from: http://www. decs.gov.mo/Statistic/Other.asp#KeyIndicators.

Statistics and Census Service (2009a) *Principal Statistical Indicators.* Available from: http:// www.decs.gov.mo/Statistic/Other.asp#KeyIndicators.

Statistics and Census Service (2009b) *Monthly Bulletin of Statistics, October.* Available from: www.dsec.gov.mo.

Tong, Kwok Kit (2009) 'The Development of the Gambling Industry and the Quality of Life' in S. L. Wong, K. Y. Wong and P. S. Wan (eds) *The New Face of Macao Society: Achievement and Challenge.* Hong Kong: Hong Kong Institute of Asia-Pacific Studies, The Chinese University of Hong Kong, 163–181 (translated from Chinese).

Vong, L. P. (2009*) Core Inflation: Concepts and Estimates for Macao.* Macao: Macao Monetary Authority.

Yu, Zhen (2002) 'Political Culture in Post-handover Macao' in Z. L. Wu (ed) *Macau 2002.* Macao: Macao Foundation (translated from Chinese). Available from: http://macaudata. com/macauweb/book269/main.html.

Chapter 2   [References]

Amaro, A. (1998) *Das Cabanas de Palha às Torres de Betão: Assim Cresceu Macau.* Macao: Livros do Oriente.

Andreu, P. (2010) 'Casino in Macau, China'. Available from: http://www.paul-andreu.com/ pages/projets_recents_macao_gb.html [Accessed February 11, 2010].

Architects Association of Macau (1992) 'Interview with John Prescott, NAPE planner', *Arquitectura,* July/August, 30–35.

Azevedo, P. A. (2006) 'Towering Ambitions', *Macau Business,* August.

Bega District News (2008) 'Packer casinos linked to Macau bribes'. Available from: http://prd7-libwisesearch.wisers.net/ws5/index.do?srp_restore=discard&new-login=true, 2 [Accessed September 7, 2008].

Boxer, C. R. (ed) (1988) *Ásia Sínica e Japónica.* Macao: Instituto Cultural de Macao.

Choi, C. (1991) 'Settlement of Chinese Families in Macau' in R. D. Cremer (ed) *Macau City of Commerce and Culture: Continuity and Change.* 2nd edition. Hong Kong: PI Press Ltd., 61–66.

Commission for the First Public Tender to Grant Concessions to Operate Casino Games of Chance of the Macao SAR (2001) *Information Memorandum.* Macao: Printing Bureau, December.

Costa, J. (1993) *Subsídios Para a História do Município das Ilhas. Volume I, 1689–1928. Câmara Municipal das Ilhas.* Macao: Printing Bureau.

Custodio, C. and M. Teixeira (2000) *Macau e a Sua População, 1500–2000: Aspectos Demográficos Sociais e Económicos.* Macao: Printing Bureau.

Dias, A. (2004) *Portugal, Macau e a Internacionalização da Questão do Ópio (1909–1925).* Macao: Livros do Oriente.

du Cros, H. (2009) 'Emerging Issues for Cultural Tourism in Macau', *Journal of Current Chinese Affairs,* 1, 73–99.

246 Notes and References

Gaming Inspection and Coordination Bureau (2008) 'Statistics'. Available from: http://www. dicj.gov.mo/EN/Estat/DadosEstat/2008/estat.htm#n1 [Accessed December 21, 2008].

Gaming Inspection and Coordination Bureau (2009a) 'Gaming Statistical Information'. Available from: http://www.dicj.gov.mo/CH/Estat/DadosEstat/2009/estat.htm#n4 [Accessed January 3, 2009].

Gaming Inspection and Coordination Bureau (2009b) 'Gaming Statistical Information'. Available from: http://www.dicj.gov.mo/CH/Estat/DadosEstat/2009/estat.htm#n3 [Accessed January 3, 2009].

Gaming Inspection and Coordination Bureau (2010a). Available from: http://www.dicj.gov.mo/EN/index.htm [Accessed June 3, 2010].

Gaming Inspection and Coordination Bureau (2010b). Available from: http://www.dicj.gov.mo/EN/index.htm [Accessed January 9, 2010].

Gaming Inspection and Coordination Bureau (2010c). Available from: http://www.dicj.gov.mo/EN/Contratos/Wynn/2002BORAEM27S2Sup.htm [Accessed January 9, 2010].

Guia Lighthouse Protection Concern Group (2007) 'Letter to UNESCO'. Available from: http://guialighthouse.blogspot.com/search?updated-max=2007-12-03T00%3A41%3A00%2B08%3A00 [Accessed November 26, 2008].

Guimarães, A. (2000) *Uma Relação Especial. Macau e as Relações Luso Chinesas 1780–1844.* Lisboa: Edição CIES.

Hoje Macau (2010) 'São Necrotério, Saude publica em ruptura da mais trabalho aos juízes', May 28.

Hong Kong Institute of Planners (2008) 'Position paper on the outline for the Macao Urban Concept Plan'. Available from: http://www.ceeds.gov.mo [Accessed September 27, 2008].

Hong Kong SAR Government (2006) *Hong Kong 2030 Planning Vision and Strategy.* Hong Kong: Government Printing Bureau.

Jorge, C. and B. Coelho (1997) *Viagem por Macau.* Volume 1. Macao: Livros do Oriente.

Jornal Tribuna de Macau (2006) 'A prioridade é a Politica Económica de Macau', November 10.

Jornal Tribuna de Macau (2008) 'Associação de Pais da EPM sente-se "marginalizada"', June 2.

Jornal Tribuna de Macau (2010) 'Património ameaçado por prédios altos', April 20.

Kan, W. (2007) 'Early Development of the Gambling Industry in Macau', *Journal of Macau Studies*, 40, 154–162.

Lam, I. F. and S. Sam (1999) *21st Century Macau City Planning Guideline Study.* Macao: Macau Co-operation and Development Foundation.

Lamas, R. (1998) *History of Macau: A Student's Manual.* Macao: Institute of Tourism Education.

Land, Public Works and Transport Bureau (2008) *Report on Macau's Urban Planning System.* Macao: Printing Bureau.

Legislative Assembly (2008) 'Diary of the Legislative Council (2007–2008)'. Available from: www.al.gov.mo/diario/l03/ps1-3/2008-099%20(06-30).pdf [Accessed February 12, 2008].

Lima, M. (2009) 'Losing the Connections of Hills and Sea: A Review of Macao's Nape Planning', *World Architecture*, 234 (12), 35–39.

Loi, K. I. (2008) 'Gaming and Entertainment Tourist Destinations—A World of Similarities and Differences', *Tourism Recreation Research*, 33 (2), 165–183.

Macao Daily News (2008) 'New building heights in the Guia Hill', April 17.

Macao Government (1867) *Official Gazette of Macao and Timor Province* (1867). Macao: Printing Bureau.

Macao Government (1931) *Government Gazette, the BOM 39/1931.* Macao: Printing Bureau, September.

Macao Government (1937) *Macao Gazette, BOM N.17*. Macao: Printing Bureau, April.

Macao Government (1961) *Government Gazette, the BOM 26/1961*. Macao: Printing Bureau.

Macao Government (1991) *Government Gazette, BOM, 1991. N. 15*. 2st annex. Macao: Printing Bureau.

Macao SAR Government (2001) *Decree Law 16/ 2001, Government Gazette*. Macao: Printing Bureau, September 24.

Macao SAR Government (2002) *Chief Executive Decree 93/2002*. Macao: Printing Bureau, April.

Macao SAR Government (2006) *Government Gazette, the BOM 34/2006*. Macao: Printing Bureau, August.

Macao SAR Government (2007) *Policy Address for the Fiscal Year 2007*. Macao: Printing Bureau.

Macao SAR Government (2008a) *New Order of the Development Heights of the Guia Hill*. Macao: Printing Bureau.

Macao SAR Government (2008b) *Policy Address for the Fiscal Year 2008*. Macao: Printing Bureau.

Macao SAR Government (2009) *Policy Address for the Fiscal Year 2009*. Macao: Printing Bureau.

Macao Urban Planning Institute (IPUM) (2008) *Position Paper on Macao Urban Concept Plan*. Macao: Urban Planning Institute, September 7.

Macau Daily Times (2008) 'Ao sentenced to 27 years', January 31.

Macau Post Daily (2009) 'Visual impact of heritage sites under threat for high-rise development', December 2.

Moisés, F. (2006) *Macau na Politica Externa Chinesa 1949–1979*. Lisboa: ICS Publications.

Ping, J. and W. Zhiliang (2007) *Revisar os Primórdios de Macau*. Macao: IPOR and Orient Foundation.

Pons, P. (1999) *Macao*. Hong Kong: Hong Kong University Press.

Ponto Final (2007) 'Colina da Guia a Limitacão de 90 metros não é Suficiente', June 14.

Research Centre for Sustainable Development Strategies (CEED) (2008a) 'An Outline for Macau Urban Concept Plan (OMUCP)'. Available from: http://www.ceeds.gov.mo [Accessed September 7, 2008].

Research Centre for Sustainable Development Strategies (CEED) (2008b) 'About Us'. Available from: http://www.ceeds.gov.mo/en/index.html [Accessed December 7, 2008].

Silva, B. (1995) *Cronologia da História de Macau*. Macao: DSEJ Edition.

SJM holdings (2010) 'About Us'. Available from: http://www.sjmholdings.com/mc_pressreleases 16.html [Accessed January 9, 2010].

South China Morning Post (2008a) 'Government must end land giveaway', June 13.

South China Morning Post (2008b) 'Ideas flow in on fixing urban-planning flaws', September 19.

Statistics and Census Service (2008) 'Year Book of Statistics'. Available from: http://www.dsec. gov.mo/getAttachment/7a7fece9-fe72-4bac-a2d3-f1c05b96b346/ [Accessed February 12, 2009].

Statistics and Census Service (2009a) 'Visitor Arrivals'. Available from: http://www.dsec.gov. mo/getAttachment/eae9dc95-6700-4a9d-a99f-0302d0409aa6/E_MV_FR_2009_M12. aspx [Accessed February 12, 2009].

Statistics and Census Service (2009b) 'Overall Unemployment Rate'. Available from: http:// www.dsec.gov.mo/TimeSeriesDatabase.aspx?KeyIndicatorID=24 [Accessed January 2, 2009].

Statistics and Census Service (2009c) 'Total Employed Population'. Available from: http://www.dsec.gov.mo/TimeSeriesDatabase.aspx?KeyIndicatorID=26 [Accessed January 2, 2009].

Statistics and Census Service (2009d) 'Employed Population by Industry'. Available from: http://www.dsec.gov.mo/PredefinedReport.aspx?ReportID=10 [Accessed January 2, 2009].

Tso, A. (2006) 'Guia lighthouse in the dark', *Macau Business*, December.

Vale, A. (1997) *Os Portugueses em Macau (1750–1800)*. Macao: Instituto Português do Oriente.

Wan, Y. K. P. and F. V. Pinheiro (2009) 'Challenges and Future Strategies for Heritage Conservation in Macao', *South Asian Journal of Tourism and Heritage*, 2 (1), 1–12.

Wan, Y. K. P., F. V. Pinheiro and M. Korenaga (2007) 'Planning for Heritage Conservation in Macao', *Planning and Development*, 22 (1), 17–26.

Yeung, Y. M. (2008) 'Suggestions on the Outline for Macao Urban Concept Plan'. Available from: http://www.ceeds.gov.mo [Accessed September 7, 2008].

Yu, X. (2008) 'Growth and Degradation in the Orient's "Las Vegas": Issue of Environment in Macau', *International Journal of Environmental Studies*, 65 (6), 667–683.

Zhuhai Government (2006) 'The Zhuhai Urban Space Development Strategy: Zhuhai 2030'. Available from: http://www.zhuhai.gov.cn/english/Citynews/200708/t20070821_28125.htm [Accessed October 26, 2008].

Chapter 3 [Notes]

1. We follow Ball's observation that political culture is made up of the interrelated elements of attitudes, beliefs, emotions and values in a society (Ball, 1988: 53).

2. The statistical results range between 14.3 percent and 43.7 percent depending on the survey question and the age group, with higher percentages for the older age groups.

3. These observations on the liberalisation of the gaming industry are drawn from the following newspaper reports: *Jornal do Cidadao*, January 24, 2002; February 2, 2002; February 10, 2002; February 27, 2002; April 2, 2002; April 30, 2002; *Macao Daily News*, March 4, 2002.

4. *Jornal do Cidadao*, April 29, 2004; *Macao Daily News*, April 29, 2004.

5. *Jornal do Cidadao*, July 5, 2002; April 23, 2003.

6. *Jornal do Cidadao*, May 4, 2002, March 4, 2003.

7. *Macao Daily News*, September 12, 2008; October 30, 2008.

8. *Macao Daily News*, March 27, 2008; July 1, 2008; September 14, 2009; September 30, 2009.

9. *Jornal do Cidadao*, September 15, 2008; October 13, 2008; November 19, 2008; November 22, 2008; December 14, 2008; December 23, 2008.

10. *Macao Daily News*, October 16 2009; October 25, 2009; November 1, 2009.

11. A total of 74 percent of this group supported gaming liberalisation. This result does not contradict those of a survey conducted in 2004 by the *New Generation Magazine* (see note 4). The survey results here merely indicate that the support was stronger from the older age groups.

Chapter 3 [References]

Ball, A. R. (1988) *Modern Politics and Government*. 4th edition. London: Macmillan.

Cheng, T. J. (2009) *Introduction to Sociology of Gambling*. Beijing: Social Sciences Academic Press.

Ieong, W. C. and R. C. S. Siu (1997) *Macau — A Model of Mini-Economy*. Macao: University of Macau Publication Center.

Lam, M. K. (2009) 'Interaction among Legislature, Administration and the People: Rethinking Problems after 10 Years of Handover' (Original in Chinese '立法、行政與市民互動：澳門回歸十年的問題反思') in *Proceedings of Conference on 10 Years of Macao SAR: Review of Legislative Policy Implementation and Prospects* (Original in Chinese 澳門特區十年。依法施政回顧及展望研討會). Macao: Civil Service Employee Associations, 39–41.

Lam, N. (2002) 'Government Intervention in Macao's Economy', *Asian Journal of Public Administration*, 24 (2), 211–233.

Lam, N. M. K. (2009) 'Public Finance in Macao' in Y. Hao and Z. Wu (eds) *Annual Report on Economy and Society of Macao (2008–2009)*. Beijing: Social Sciences Academic Press, 132–147.

Li, S. and Y. Tsui (2009a) 'A General Equilibrium Approach to Tourism and Welfare: The Case of Macau', *Habitat International*, 33 (4), 412–424.

Li, S. and Y. Tsui (2009b) 'Casino Boom and Local Politics: The City of Macao', *Cities*, 26 (2), 67–73.

Lin, L. S. (1998) 'Social Development and Change in Macao' (Original in Chinese '澳門的社會發展與變遷') in J. Yee (ed) *A Tale of Two Cities* (Original in Chinese 雙城記). Macao: Macao Association of Social Sciences, 313–326.

Lo, S. H. (1995) *Political Development in Macao*. Hong Kong: The Chinese University Press.

Lo, S. S. (2008) *Political Change in Macao*. New York: Routledge.

Yee, Herbert S. (1998) 'Political Culture of the People in Hong Kong and Macao' (Original in Chinese '香港和澳門的大眾政治文化') in Herbert S. Yee (ed) *A Tale of Two Cities* (Original in Chinese 雙城記). Macao: Macao Association of Social Sciences, 97–107.

Yee, Herbert S. and S. H. Lo (2000) 'Political Reform from the Perspective of Macao's Political Institutional Tradition' (Original in Chinese '從澳門政治體制傳統看特區的政治改革') in Herbert S. Yee et al (eds) *Public Administration Reform in Macao: Problems and Solutions* (Original in Chinese 澳門公共行政的改革：問題與對策). Macao: Macao Association of Public Management, 143–158.

Chapter 4   [Notes]

1. A democratic government, which embarked on a policy of decolonisation, was established in Portugal after the 1974 revolution. However, the Chinese government wanted the Portuguese to continue to administer Macao until the resolution of Hong Kong's sovereignty problem. The Portuguese authorities subsequently introduced political reforms and promulgated the Organic Statute. See Lo (1996: 33–35).

2. Available from the Legislative Assembly website: http://www.al.gov.mo/interpelacao/2006/list2006.htm.

3. A view expressed to the author by some demonstrators during the May Day demonstration in 2007.

4. A proportional representation system with a closed party list method in which electorates vote for a group of candidates instead of individual candidates is used for direct elections. For a discussion, see Lo (1996: 92–94).

5. Lei was one of the leaders of the demonstration.

6. There are three standing committees scrutinising government bills, namely the 1st, 2nd, and 3rd Standing Committees.

Chapter 4   [References]

Basic Law of the Macao Special Administrative Region (1993). Macao: Government Printing Bureau.

Cheang, K. I. (2006) 'Some Thinking on the Controversial Judgment by the Court of Second Instance' (Original in Chinese '關於中級法院裁判值得商榷之處的若干思考'), *Journal of Macau Studies*, 36, 9–11.

Cheng, W. T. and S. L. Wong (2007) 'Social Expectation and Social Reality' (Original in Chinese '社會期望與社會現實') in S. L. Wong, Y. M. Yeung, P. S. Wan and W. T. Cheng (eds) *Macao Social Indicators: A Study of the Quality of Life* (Original in Chinese 澳門社會實錄：從指標研究看生活素質). Hong Kong: Hong Kong Institute of Asia-Pacific Studies, The Chinese University of Hong Kong, 63–98.

Choi, H. K. (2005) 'Singapore's Imported Labour Policy and Its Implications for Macao Policy' (Original in Chinese '新加坡外地勞工輸入計劃給澳門的啟示'), *Journal of Macau Studies*, 27, 88–94.

Choy, C. K. and S. L. Lau (1996) 'Executive-Legislative Relations in Hong Kong before 1997' (Original in Chinese '九七回歸前夕的香港行政與立法關係'), *Hong Kong Journal of Social Sciences*, 8, 237–266.

Commission of Audit (2006) *Special Report on the 4th East Asian Games Organization* (Original in Chinese 專項報告：第四屆東亞運動會). Macao: Commission of Audit, MSAR Government.

Curtis, Michael (1978) *Comparative Government and Politics: An Introductory Essay in Political Science*. 2nd edition. New York: Harper & Row.

Fok, H. Y. T. (2004) *Tales of Macao Casinos* (Original in Chinese 澳門賭場風雲). Hong Kong: Chi Pong Press.

Jornal Cheng Pou, November 23, 2007; February 21, 2008; April 24, 2008; May 31, 2008.

Jornal Va Kio, October 10, 2000; December 25, 2001; June 25, 2002; May 13, 2006; August 3, 2008; August 7, 2009.

Lo, S. H. (1996) *Political Development in Macao*. Hong Kong: The Chinese University Press.

Lo, S. H. (2007) *Political Change in Macao*. London and New York: Routledge.

Luo, W. J. (2005) 'The Power Structure, Organizational Design and Characteristics of Executive-Led Government' (Original in Chinese '論行政主導的權力設定、結構設計及其他條件'), *Administration Magazine*, 69 (3), 879–890.

Macao Daily News, January 21, 2002; July 10, 2003; November 17, 2003; October 5, 2005; November 17, 2005; December 12, 2005; March 15, 2006; December 8, 2006; December 20, 2006; April 4, 2007; July 5, 2007; July 19, 2007; November 14, 2007; December 7, 2007; April 10, 2008; June 5, 2008; July 12, 2008; August 4, 2008; November 20, 2008; April 23, 2009; April 27, 2009; August 14, 2009; August 15, 2009; September 23, 2009; September 28, 2009; October 27, 2009.

Macao Government (1964a) *Decree Law 15362*. Macao: Printing Bureau, January.

Macao Government (1964b) *Decree Law 15361*. Macao: Printing Bureau, January.

Macao Government (1982) *Decree Law 57/82/M*. Macao: Printing Bureau, October.

Macao Government (1985) *Decree Law 78/85/M*. Macao: Printing Bureau, August.

Macao Government (1998) *Law 4/98/M*. Macao: Printing Bureau, July.

Macao SAR Government (2001) *Law 16/2001*. Macao: Printing Bureau, September.

Macao SAR Government (2002) *Decree Law 6/2002*. Macao: Printing Bureau, April.

Macao SAR Government (2004a) *Decree Law 5/2004*. Macao: Printing Bureau, June.

Macao SAR Government (2004b) *Decree Law 17/2004*. Macao: Printing Bureau, June.

Macao SAR Government (2008) *Law 7/2008*. Macao: Printing Bureau, August.

Macao SAR Government (2009a) *Law 13/2009*. Macao: Printing Bureau, July.

Macao SAR Government (2009b) *Law 29/2009*. Macao: Printing Bureau, October.

Macao SAR Government (2009c) *Standing Orders of Legislative Assembly*. Macao: Printing Bureau.

Mezey, M. L. (1985) 'The Functions of Legislatures in the Third World' in G. Loewenberg, S. C. Patterson and M. E. Jewell (eds) *Handbook of Legislative Research*. Cambridge, Mass.: Harvard University Press, 733–772.

New Macao Association (2008) *New Macao* (Original in Chinese 新澳門), 36.

Olson, D. M. and M. L. Mezey (1991) 'Parliaments and Public Policy' in D. M. Olson and M. L. Mezey (eds) *Legislatures in the Policy Process: The Dilemmas of Economic Policy*. Cambridge and New York: Cambridge University Press, 1–24.

Statistics and Census Service (various years) *Yearbook of Statistics*. Macao: Statistics and Census Service.

Wang, W. Y. (2009) 'Achievement and Issues in Macao's Gaming Industry' (Original in Chinese '澳門博彩業的成就與問題'), *Journal of Macau Studies*, 55, 9–11.

Wang, Y. (2006a) 'The rights of examination and interpretation of MSAR Law' (Original in Chinese '特區法律的審查權與解釋權'), *Macao Daily News*, December 7.

Wang, Y. (2006b) 'Investigation on the Legal Status of Administrative Statutes' (Original in Chinese '論行政法規的性質和地位'), *Journal of Macau Studies*, 36, 4–8.

Yee, H. S. (1996) 'Prospects of Democratisation: An Open-ended Game?' *China Perspectives*, 26, 28–38.

Yu, W. Y. (2007) 'Formal and Informal Politics in Macao Special Administrative Region Elections 2004–2005', *Journal of Contemporary China*, 16 (52), 417–442.

Chapter 5 [Notes]

1. The union was previously referred to as the General Union of Residual Associations, a direct translation from the Portuguese. The term used in the text is the Macao government's most recent English usage.

2. This information was provided in an interview with a senior association leader who wished to remain anonymous.

Chapter 5 [References]

CEPA (2009) *General Principles of CEPA and Its Six Annexes*. Available from: http://www.ipim. gov.mo/en/cepa/index.html [Accessed May 2, 2009].

Gaming Inspection and Coordination Bureau (2009). Available from: http://www.dicj.gov.mo/ EN/Estat/estat.htm#n1 [Accessed June 2, 2009].

General Union of Neighbourhood Associations (2009). Available from: http://home.macau.ctm. net/~ugamm/ [Accessed May 12, 2009].

Langton, Stuart (1978) *Citizen Participation in America: Current Reflections on the State of the Art*. Lexington, Mass.: Lexington Books.

Lee S. P. (2006) *Social Stability and Public Policy: The Role of Special Interest Groups in Macao*. Hong Kong: Unpublished MPA dissertation, The University of Hong Kong.

Lijphart, Arend (1977) *Democracy in Plural Societies: A Comparative Exploration*. New Haven: Yale University Press.

Lo, Sonny S. H. (1995) *Political Development in Macao*. Hong Kong: The Chinese University Press.

Lo, Sonny S. H. (2008) *Political Change in Macao*. New York: Routledge.

Lo, Sonny S. H. and Herbert S. Yee (2005) 'Legitimacy-Building in the Macau Special Administrative Region, Colonial Legacies and Reform Strategies', *Asian Journal of Political Science*, 13 (1), 51–79.

Lou, S. H. (2005) 'Popular Associations, Regime Resources and Political Development in Macao', *Macao Administration Journal*, 18 (69/3), 1015–1028.

Macao Chinese Chamber of Commerce (2009). Available from: www.acm.org.mo/main9.htm [Accessed May 5, 2009].

Macao Civic Power (2009). Available from: http://www.civimc-power.org/cp/ [Accessed November 10, 2009].

Macao Daily News (1987) *A Testimony of Macao's History*. Macao: Macao Daily News.

Macao Daily News (2009). Available from: http://www.macaodaily.com/html/2010-02/03/node_2.htm [Accessed June 10, 2009].

Macao Federation of Trade Unions (2009). Available from: http://www.faom.org.mo/web/

Macao SAR Election Law. Available from: http://www.gov.mo/egi/Portal/rkw/public/view/area.jsp?id=21 [Accessed May 5, 2009].

Macao Strategic Research Center, Macao Foundation and Center for Contemporary China Research of Peking University (2005) *Macao Citizens' Quality of Life 2005* (in Chinese). Macao: Macao Strategic Research Center.

Putnam, Robert D. (2000) *Bowling Alone*. New York: Simon & Schuster.

Richardson, Jeremy J. (1993a) *Interest Group Behaviour in Britain: Continuity and Change*. New York: Oxford University Press.

Richardson, Jeremy J. (1993b) *Pressure Groups*. New York: Oxford University Press.

Schmitter, Philippe C. (1979) 'Still the Century of Corporatism?' in P. C. Schmitter and G. Lehmbruch (eds) *Trends Towards Corporatist Intermediation*. London: Sage.

Sing Tao Daily (Hong Kong, Toronto edition), January 12, 1987.

Statistics and Census Service (2009). Available from: http://www.dsec.gov.mo [Accessed May 2, 2009].

Williamson, Peter J. (1986) *Varieties of Corporatism: A Conceptual Discussion*. Cambridge: Cambridge University Press.

Williamson, Peter J. (1989) *Corporatism in Perspective: An Introductory Guide to Corporatist Theory*. London: Sage Publications.

Wilson, Graham K. (1990) *Interest Groups*. Oxford: Basil Blackwell.

Women's General Association of Macau (2009). Available from: http://www.macauwomen.org.mo/ [Accessed May 5, 2009].

Wright, John R. (c1993) *Interest Groups and Congress, Lobbying, Contributions and Influence*. Boston, Mass.: Allyn and Bacon.

Chapter 6 [References]

Asia Times Online/China Business, December 1, 2009. Available from: http://www.atimes.com/atimes/China_Business/KL01Cb01.html [Accessed December 19, 2009].

Baptista, F. (2006) 'The Recruitment and Selection of Staff in the Portuguese Administration', Seminar on Civil Service Recruitment Procedures, Vilnius, March 21–22, 2006. Available from: http://www.oecd.org/dataoecd/12/40/36753170.pdf [Accessed February 12, 2010].

Basel Institute on Governance: International Centre for Asset Recovery (ICAR), Asset Recovery Knowledge Centre (2010). *Ao Man Long*. Available from: http://www.assetrecovery.org/kc/?wicket:interface=:2 [Accessed June 10, 2010].

Chief Executive (2000–2009) *Macao Policy Addresses: 2000–2009*. Available from: www.gov.mo.

Chiu, S. F. and S. H. Kong (2006) 'The Brain-drain from Private to Public sector in Macau: How to Make Sense of It', *Global Economics and Management Review*, 11 (3), 125–147. Available from: http://www.bprmadeira.org/imagens/documentos/File/bprdigital/revistas/ecoglogestao/2006.pdf [Accessed February 6, 2010].

Commission Against Corruption of Macao SAR (CCAC) (2009) Available from: http://www.ccac.org.mo/en/plaintext.php?cat=intro&page=history [Accessed February 2, 2010].

Eisner, M (1992) 'Long-term Fluctuations of Economic Growth and Social Destabilization', *Historical Social Research*, 17, 70–98.

Hong Kong Government, Civil Service Bureau (2009) *Strength of the Civil Service (as at 31 March 2009)*. Available from: http://www.csb.gov.hk/print/english/stat/annually/548.html [Accessed January 15, 2010].

Li S. and Y. Tsui (2009) 'A General Equilibrium Approach to Tourism and Welfare: The Case of Macao', *Habitat International* 33, 419–424.

Liu, Tai Gang (2000) *Localization Policy of the Macao Civil Service*. Hong Kong: City University of Hong Kong (in Chinese).

Lo, S. S. H. (2008) *Political Change in Macao*. Abingdon: Routledge.

Macao SAR Government (Departamento de Recursos Humanos do SAFP) (2009a) *Recursos Humanos da Administracao Publica da RAEM 2008: Dados Relativos a 31 de Dezembro de 2008*. Macao: Macao Government.

Macao SAR Government (2009b) *Report and Review of the Implementation of the Public Administration Reform*. Available from: http://www.gov.mo/suggestion/public/reform/report.jsf?lang=pt [Accessed February 4, 2010].

Macao SAR Government (2010) 'Organizational Chart of the MSAR'. Available from: http://www.gov.mo/egi/Portal/s/safp/apm/RAEM_chart_en.html [Accessed February 18, 2010].

Macau Daily Times, December 4, 2009. Available from http://www.macaudailytimes.com.mo [Accossed December 18, 2009]

Macao Daily News, November 19, December 17, 2009. Available from http://macaodaily.com.mo [Accessed December 18, 2009]

Macau News, December 15, 2009. Available from: http://www.macaunews.com.mo/index.php?option=com_content&task=view&id=695&Itemid=3 [Accessed December 18, 2009].

OECD (2009) *Fostering Diversity in the Public Service*. Available from: http://www.oecd.org/dataoecd/46/57/44212841.pdf [Accessed February 4, 2010].

Quah, J. (2010) 'Anti-Corruption Strategies in Asian Countries: A Comparative Analysis'. Paper presented to a seminar at the Centre of Anti-Corruption Studies, ICAC, Hong Kong, June 9, 2010.

Transparency International (2010) 'Corruption Perception Index'. Available from: http://www. transparency.org/policy_research/surveys_indices/cpi/previous_cpi [Accessed February 9, 2010].

World Bank (2009) *Governance Matters 2009: Worldwide Governance Indicators, 1996–2000: Control of Corruption, Comparison across Selected Countries*. Available from: http://info. worldbank.org/governance/wgi/mc_chart.asp [Accessed February 3, 2010].

Chapter 7   [Notes]

1. Before the handover, large numbers of local Chinese were recruited into the Macao civil service under a localisation scheme. The result was fewer government positions available to applicants (see Chapter 6). This problem was compounded by the rise in the number of university graduates in Macao over time and the fact that the private sector does not provide sufficient professional jobs to attract university graduates. Since the 1980s, the number of people applying for and entering the civil service has increased, while the number leaving has dropped. Labour mobility between the public and private sectors has traditionally been reported to be small (Wong, 1990).

2. The argument that changes in wages affect productivity through nutrition applies to developing countries. Linking energy intake with wages, Leibenstein (1957) wrote that countries where workers receive less than the required energy intake in order to work a full eight-hour day can increase productivity by paying a wage that permits these workers to increase their energy intake to sufficient levels to increase productivity. In developed economy contexts, wage increases are assumed to raise productivity by other means, such as lowering the incentives for workers to quit, improving worker morale, or lowering incentives to shirk (Huang et al, 1998).

3. Equity theory also raises the idea of social comparability which can be applied to wages. It proposes that individuals evaluate the ratio of their inputs to outcomes for a given task in relation to a comparative referent (Adams, 1965). The optimal point exists when the individuals perceive the ratio as a balanced one. At this point, they can focus their energies on achieving the organisation's goals as this will in turn satisfy their personal ones. On the other hand, employees who perceive that they are under-compensated or treated unfairly can resort to negative actions, such as theft, reduced output quality, and turnover (Cowherd and Levine, 1992).

4. The primary reason provided by Macao workers who changed their jobs over the past three years has consistently been 'seeking better pay' (Statistics and Census Service, 2008b).

Chapter 7   [References]

Adams J. S. (1965) 'Inequity in Social Change' in L. Berkowitz (ed) *Advances in Social Psychology*. Vol. 2. New York: Academic Press, 267–299.

Akerlof, G. A. (1982) 'Labor Contracts as Partial Gift Exchange', *Quarterly Journal of Economics*, 97 (4), 543–569.

Akerlof, G. A. and J. L. Yellen (1986) *Efficiency Wage Models of the Labor Market*. New York: Cambridge University Press.

Alexopoulos, M. (2004) 'Unemployment and the Business Cycle', *Journal of Monetary Economics*, 51 (2), 277–298.

Cappelli, P. and K. Chauvin (1991) 'An Interplant Test of the Efficiency Wage Hypothesis', *Quarterly Journal of Economics*, 106, 869–884.

Chou, B. K. P. (2004) 'Public Sector Reform in Macao After the Handover', *China Perspectives*, March–April.

Cowherd, D. M. and D. Levine (1992) 'Product Quality and Pay Equity between Lower-Level Employees and Top Management: An Investigation of Distributive Justice Theory', *Administrative Science Quarterly*, 37 (2), 302–320.

Deckop, J. R. (1995) 'Pay System Effects on Altruism Motivation', *Academy of Management Journal*, 38, Best Paper Proceedings, 359–364.

Frey, B. S. (2008) *Happiness: A Revolution in Economics*. Cambridge, Mass.: MIT Press.

Goldsmith, A. H., J. R.Veum and W. Darity, Jr. (2001) 'Working Hard for the Money? Efficiency Wages and Worker Effort', *Journal of Economic Psychology*, 21 (3), 351–385.

Herzberg, F. (1966) *Work and the Nature of Man*. Cleveland, OH: World Publishing.

Ho, E. H. W. (2000) *Policy Address for the Fiscal Year 2001 of the Macao Special Administrative Region (MSAR) of the People's Republic of China*. Macao: MSAR Government.

Ho, E. H. W. (2001) *Policy Address for the Fiscal Year 2002 of the Macao Special Administrative Region (MSAR) of the People's Republic of China*. Macao: MSAR Government.

Ho, E. H. W. (2002) *Policy Address for the Fiscal Year 2003 of the Macao Special Administrative Region (MSAR) of the People's Republic of China*. Macao: MSAR Government.

Ho, E. H. W. (2006) *Policy Address for the Fiscal Year 2007 of the Macao Special Administrative Region (MSAR) of the People's Republic of China*. Macao: MSAR Government.

Ho, E. H. W. (2007) *Policy Address for the Fiscal Year 2008 of the Macao Special Administrative Region (MSAR) of the People's Republic of China*. Macao: MSAR Government.

Huang, T. L., A. Hallam, P. F. Orazem, and E. M. Paterno (1998) 'Empirical Tests of Efficiency Wage Models', *Economica*, 65 (257), 125–143.

Lam, N. (2006a) 'Overcoming Organizational Resistance in Macao's Civil Service Reform'. Paper delivered at *Second Cross-Strait Conference on Public Administration: Policy Challenges in the 21st Century*. Macao: University of Macau, May.

Lam, N. (2006b) 'Public Finance in Hong Kong and Macao'. Paper delivered at *International Conference on the Evolution of 'One Country, Two Systems' in Hong Kong and Macao: Implications for Canada*, Waterloo. Canada: University of Waterloo, March.

Lam, N. (2007) 'The Development of Performance Assessment in the Macao Civil Service since the Handover'. Paper delivered at *Conference on Governance: Theory and Practice*. Macao: University of Macao, October.

Lam, N. (2009) 'Civil Service Reform in Macao and Hong Kong'. Paper delivered at *Conference on Post-Colonial Transformation in China's Hong Kong and Macao: Implications for Cross-Taiwan Strait and Canada-PRC Links*. Canada: University of Waterloo, June 27.

Leibenstein, H. (1957) *Economic Backwardness and Economic Growth*. New York: Wiley.

Levine, D. I. (1992) 'Can Wage Increases Pay for Themselves? Tests with a Production Function', *Economic Journal*, 102, 1102–1115.

Lo, S. (2008) *Political Change in Macau*. London: Routledge.

Lo, S. (2009) 'Bureaucratic Capacity and Civil Service Reforms in Macau', *Macau Closer*, April 28.

Macao SAR (2007) *The Road Map for Public Administration Reform 2007–2009*. Macao: MSAR Government.

Macao SAR (Departamento de Recursos Humanos do SAFP) (2009) *Recursos Humanos da Administracao Publica da RAEM 2008: Dados Relativos a 31 de Dezembro de 2008.* Macao: Macao Government.

New China Career (2008) 'Grads Find Job-Hopping Is Not a Career-Stopper', June 23.

People's Daily Online (2009) 'Macao official promises "clean" government once elected as SAR Chief', May 26.

Raff, D. M. and L. H. Summers (1987) 'Did Henry Ford Pay Efficiency Wages?' *Journal of Labor Economics*, 5 (4), pt. 2, S57–S86.

Shapiro, C. and J. E. Stiglitz (1984) 'Equilibrium Unemployment as a Worker Discipline Device', *American Economic Review*, 74 (3), 433–444.

Solow, R. (1957) 'Technical Change and the Aggregate Production Function', *Review of Economics and Statistics*, 39 (3), 312–320.

Solow, R. (1979) 'Another Possible Source of Wage Stickiness', *Journal of Macroeconomics*, 1 (1), 79–82.

Statistics and Census Service (2001–2008) *Yearbook of Statistics*. Macao: Statistics and Census Service.

Statistics and Census Service (2008b) *Survey on Job Changing of the Employed*. Macao: Statistics and Census Service.

Statistics and Census Service (2010a) *Median Monthly Employment Earnings by Industry*. Macao: Statistics and Census Service.

Statistics and Census Service (2010b) *Labour Force Participation Rate, Unemployment Rate and Underemployment Rate*. Macao: Statistics and Census Service.

Statistics and Census Service (2010c) *Median Monthly Employment Earnings by Occupation*. Macao: Statistics and Census Service.

Stiglitz, J. E. (1974) 'Alternative Theories of Wage Determination and Unemployment in LDC's.: The Labor Turnover Model', *Quarterly Journal of Economics*, 88 (2), 194–227.

Stiglitz, J. E. (1976) 'The Efficiency Wage Hypothesis, Surplus Labor, and the Distribution of Income in LDC's, *Oxford Economic Papers*, 28 (2), 185–207.

Stiglitz, J. E. (1985) 'Equilibrium Wage Distributions', *Economic Journal*, 95 (379), 595–618.

Taylor, J. E. (2003) 'Did Henry Ford Mean to Pay Efficiency Wages?' *Journal of Labor Research*, 24 (4), 683–695.

Wadhwani, S. B. and M. Wall (1991) 'A Direct Test of the Efficiency Wage Model Using UK Micro-Data', *Oxford Economic Papers*, 43, 529–548.

Weiss, A. (1980) 'Job Queues and Lay-offs in Labor Markets with Flexible Wages', *Journal of Political Economy,* 88 (3), 526–538.

Wiseman, F. and S. Chatterjee (2003) 'Team Payroll and Team Performance in Major League Baseball: 1985–2002', *Economics Bulletin*, 1 (2), 1–10.

Wong, C. L. (1990) 'The Public Personnel System in Macau', *Asian Journal of Public Administration*, 12 (2), 176–195.

Wong, J. Y., P. S. Wan and W. J. Law (2007) 'Social Class, Social Mobility and Social Policy' (Original in Chinese '社會階級，社會流動與社會政策') in S. L. Wong et al (eds) *Macao Social Facts: Quality of Life from the Perspective of Index Study* (Original in Chinese 澳門社會實錄：從指標研究看生活素質). Hong Kong: The Chinese University Press, 227–245.

Chapter 8 [Notes]

1. Persons functioning in hard count spots in the casino tally the coins, enfold them in a plastic holder, and count coins for banking purposes and for transmission to the casino floor. The soft counters work with notes (http://www.cvtips.com/career-choice/employment-as-a-hard-count-clerk-in-a-casino.html).
2. The gaming supervisor, or pit boss, is a manager and arbiter. The pit boss is in charge of several dealers operating different games simultaneously (http://www.casinojobs411.com/casino-jobs-pit-boss.html).
3. The eight labour organisations that organised the May Day march in July 2006 were the Association for Promoting Livelihood in Macau, the Association for Promoting Livelihood of Workers in Macau, the Labour Union of Macau, the Mutual Help Association for Construction Workers in Macau, the Decoration Workers' Association of Macau, the Concrete Sector Workers' Association of Macau, the Cleaners' Association of Macau, and the Property Management Workers' Association of Macau (*blogmacau.info*, June 6, 2007).
4. A tripartite platform involving labour representatives, representatives from the business community, and the MSAR government was created only in 1987 to solve and mediate labour issues (Sousa, 2009).

Chapter 8 [References]

Chan, Sau San (2003) *The Nature of Unemployment in Macao and Its Policy Implications.* Available from: www.amcm.gov.mo/publication/quarterly/Oct2003/StructuralUnemployment_en.pdf

Choi, Alex H. (2006) 'Migrant Workers in Macao: Labour and Globalisation' in Kevin Hewison and Ken Young (eds) *Transnational Migration and Work in Asia.* London: Routledge, City University of Hong Kong Southeast Asian Studies, No. 6, 144–164.

Commission Against Corruption (CCAC) of Macao. Available from: http://www.ccac.org.mo/en/.

Curso do Departamento de Formacao Profissional (2007) *blogmacau.info*. Available from: http://www.blogmacau.info/blog/?p=1709, June 6.

Curso do Departamento de Formacao Profissional (2009) *blogmacau.info*. Available from: http://www.blogmacau.info/blog/?p=1709.

Employees Retraining Board, Hong Kong (2009). Available from: http://www.erb.org/Corp/home/erb/en/.

Global Issues (2009) Available from: http://www.globalissues.org/news/2009/04/17/1240.

Ho, E. H. W. (2009a) *Policy Address for the Fiscal Year 2010 of the Macao Special Administrative Region (MSAR) of the People's Republic of China.* Macao: MSAR Government.

Ho, E. H. W. (2009b) *Review of the Government's Work in the Fiscal Year 2009 and the Financial Budget for the Fiscal Year 2010 of the Macao Special Administrative Region (MSAR) of the People's Republic of China* (Summary). Macao: MSAR Government.

ITUC-CSI-IGB (2007) *Annual Survey of Violations of Labour Union Rights*. Available from: http://survey07.ituc-csi.org/getcountry.php?IDCountry=MAC&IDLang=EN.

Layard, P. R. G., S. Nickell and R. Jackman (1991) *Unemployment: Macroeconomic Performance and the Labour Market*. Oxford: Oxford University Press.

Lo, Sonny Shiu-Hing (2008) *Political Change in Macao*. London and New York: Routledge.

Macao Daily News, June 5, 2007; March 26, 2009; October 19, 2009.

Macao Government (1989, 1993) *Labour Relations in Macao* (Decree-Law No. 24/1989/M, April 3, 1989, with amendments introduced by the Decree-Law No. 32/1990/M, July 9, 1993). Available from: http://www.dsal.gov.mo/dsallawe/law2.htm.

Macao Labour Affairs Bureau. Available from: http://www.dsal.gov.mo/english/otherstat.htm.

Macao Labour Affairs Bureau, 'On-job Training and Employment Scheme'. Available from: http://www.dsal.gov.mo/english/thireplan_e.htm.

Macao SAR Government Information Bureau (2006). Available from: http://a2zmacau.com/2268/macau-government-to-overhaul-labour-law/.

Macao SAR Government Portal. Available from: http://www.gov.mo/egi/Portal/rkw/public/view/showcomp.jsp?id=InfoShowTemp&docid=c373e925976d47a48f7b963168a33cee.

Macao SAR Legislative Assembly (2006–2007*), Official Record of Proceedings 2006–07*. Series I, III-62.

Macao Special Administrative Region (2009) *Law No. 21/2009*. Macao: MSAR government.

Macau Closer, May 11, 2009.

Macau News (2009). Available from: http://www.macaunews.com.mo/index.php?option=com_sobi2&sobi2Task=sobi2Details&sobi2Id=8&Itemid=27.

Ming Pao, November 14, 2008; December 21, 2009.

O'Connell, P. J. and F. McGinnity (1997) *Working Schemes?: Active Labour Market Policy in Ireland*. Aldershot: Ashgate.

People's Daily Online, July 13, 2009.

Price Waterhouse Coopers (2009). Available from: http://www.pwchk.com/home/eng/macau_labour_law_mar2009.html.

Sit, V. F. S., R. D. Cremer and S. L. Wong (1991) *Entrepreneurs and Enterprises in Macau: A Study of Industrial Development*. Hong Kong: Hong Kong University Press.

Sousa, Ines Trigo de (2009) *Regional Integration and Differentiation in a Globalizing China: The Blending of Government and Business in Post-Colonial Macau*. Amsterdam: University of Amsterdam.

South China Morning Post, May 2, 2010.

Statistics and Census Service. Available from: http://www.dsec.gov.mo/Statistic.

Chapter 9   [Notes]

1. It was rumoured that STDM agreed to the tax increase in exchange for the colonial government's extension of the casino monopoly contract up to the end of 2001. This extension incurred the wrath of China because it was seen as an infringement of China's resumption of control over Macao in 1999 (Eadington and Siu, 2007: 13–14; Lo, 2005: 210).

2. Some claim that the VIP room strategy first appeared in 1984 when the 'Diamond VIP Room' opened for business (Leong, 2001: 150).

3. STDM argued that the games in the VIP rooms were still operated by STDM employees and hence it was not in violation of the contract (Eadington and Siu, 2007: 15; Leong, 2001: 169).

4. STDM's power can also be seen over the issue of publishing its annual financial statement. STDM resisted publishing a statement until 1997 despite a stipulation in Macao's Commercial Code requiring all companies holding government monopoly concessions to make public their annual financial statements (Leong, 2001: 163; Liu, 2002: 323).

5. The tip pools therefore become a significant source of tax-exempted revenue for the casino. It was estimated that tips equalled around 25 percent of casino revenue in the 1980s. Apparently, the colonial state never saw tips as a tax issue (*Jornal San Wa Ou*, August 10, 2000; see also Liu, 2002: 352–353).

6. Interview with a female veteran croupier who had been in the business for 14 years, March 15, 2008.

7. It was claimed that this group was supported by Stanley Ho's sister, Winnie Ho, who fell out with her brother in a bitter dispute over her shares in STDM (*Jornal Va Kio*, September 10, 2002).

8. The Labour Affairs Bureau's ruling did not, however, prevent workers from taking their cases to the court, and there were cases where the court accepted tips as salary. SJM therefore boosted the package by topping up the compensation from MOP15 to MOP45 a day for those willing to sign the settlement (*Jornal Do Cidadao*, July 8, 2003). It was reported that, by September 2003, 97 percent of the workers had accepted the offer (*Jornal Va Kio*, September 5, 2003).

9. Venetian split with Galaxy Casino. SJM sold its sub-licence to MGM. Australia's PBL bought a licence from Wynn Resorts to operate the Crown Casino.

10. See Lo (2008: 33–38) for a succinct description of the social problems during this phase of rapid growth.

11. The demonstration did go ahead and led to a violent clash with police (*Apple Daily*, May 2, 2006) and subsequently sparked a series of anti-government protests over the next two to three years.

12. Cheang was fired from STDM. In 2002, he established the Macao Gaming Industry Labourers' Association. Its most important function is to run a government-funded training centre for croupiers (Macao Gaming Industry Labourers' Association, 2010).

13. Interview with João Bosco Cheang, September 6, 2007.

14. In September 2007, casinos hired 21,161 migrant workers, representing 26.5 percent of the total of 79,753 migrant workers in Macao. If those working under sub-contracting arrangements were counted, the figure would be much higher (see *Jornal Va Kio*, December 17, 2007).

15. For instance, the firing of 200 croupiers by Sands in November 2006 was seen as a tactic to pressurise the government to lift the ban (*Macao Daily News*, November 6, 2006).

Chapter 9   [References]

Apple Daily, May 2, 2006.

Austrin, T. and J. West (2004) 'New Deals in Gambling: Global Markets and Local Regimes of Regulation' in L. Beukema and J. Carrillo (eds) *Globalism/Localism at Work*. Boston: Elsevier, 143–158.

Azar, O. H. (2007) 'Why Pay Extra? Tipping and the Importance of Social Norms and Feelings in Economic Theory', *Journal of Socio-Economics*, 36, 250–265.

Burawoy, M. (1983) 'Between the Labor Process and the State: The Changing Face of Factory Regimes under Advanced Capitalism', *American Sociological Review*, 48, 587–605.

Burawoy, M. (1985) *The Politics of Production*. London and New York: Verso.

Choi, A. H. (2006) 'Migrant Workers in Macao: Labour and Globalization' in K. Hewison and K. Young (eds) *Transnational Migration and Work in Asia*. London and New York: Routledge, 144–164.

Choi, A. H. (2008) 'Labour Rights and the Political Economy of Growth: Migrant Workers and Labour Informalization in Macau' in D. Lee, A. Leung, R. Ofreneo and A. Sukumaran (eds) *Rights for Two-Thirds of Asia: Asian Labour Law Review*. Hong Kong: Asia Monitor Resources Centre, 57–76.

Chou, K. P. (2005) 'Interest Group Politics in Macau after the Handover', *Journal of Contemporary China*, 14 (43), 191–206.

Dicks, A. R. (1984) 'Macao: Legal Fiction and Gunboat Diplomacy' in G. Aijmer (ed) *Leadership on the China Coast*. London: Curzon Press, 129–165.

Eadington, W. R. and R. C. S. Siu (2007) 'Between Law and Custom — Examining the Interaction between Legislative Change and the Evolution of Macao's Casino Industry', *International Gambling Studies*, 7 (1), 1–28.

Fernandes, M. S. (1997) 'Portuguese Behavior towards the Political Transition and the Regional Integration of Macau in the Pearl River Region' in R. Ramos, J. R. Dinis, R. Wilson and D. Y. Yuan (eds) *Macau and Its Neighbors in Transition*. Macao: Faculty of Social Sciences and Humanities, University of Macau; Macau Foundation, 45–56.

Frey, J. H. and D. E. Carns (1987) 'The Work Environment of Gambling Casinos', *Anthropology and Work Review*, 8 (4), 38–42.

Gaming Inspection and Coordination Bureau, Macao SAR Government (2007) 'Gaming Statistics'. Available from: http://www.dicj.gov.mo/EN/Estat/DadosEstat/2007/estat.htm#n2 [Accessed February 2, 2010].

Jornal Cheng Pou, various dates.

Jornal Do Cidadao, various dates.

Jornal San Wa Ou, various dates.

Jornal Va Kio, various dates.

Lai, W. L. (2008) 'The Regulatory Role of Social Policy: Macao's Social Security Development', *Journal of Contemporary Asia*, 38 (3), 373–394.

Leonard, J. (2006) 'The Two Gaming Markets of Macao: A Product of Regulatory Difference' in Institute for the Study of Commercial Gaming, University of Macau (ed) *Law, Regulation, and Control Issues of the Asian Gaming Industry*. Macao: Institute for the Study of Commercial Gaming, University of Macau, 156–172.

Leong, V. M. (2001) *Macau: Crime and the Casino State*. Hong Kong: Unpublished M.Phil. thesis, The University of Hong Kong.

Liu, P. L. (2002) *Gaming Industry in Macao* (Original in Chinese 澳門博彩業縱橫). Hong Kong: Joint Publishing Limited.

Liu, S. D. (2008) 'Casino Colony', *New Left Review*, 50, 109–124.

Liu, S. H. (2004). *A Study of the Social Groups in Macao during the Transition Period* (Original in Chinese 轉型時期澳門社團研究). Guangdong: Guangdong renmin chubanshe.

Lo, S. S. H. (1995) *Political Development in Macau*. Hong Kong: The Chinese University Press.

Lo, S. S. H. (2005) 'Casino Politics, Organized Crime and the Post-Colonial State in Macau', *Journal of Contemporary China*, 14, 207–224.

Lo, S. S. H. (2008) *Political Change in Macao*. New York: Routledge.

Lynn, M. and G. Withiam (2008) 'Tipping and Its Alternatives: Business Considerations and Directions for Research', *Journal of Services Marketing*, 22 (4), 328–336.

Macao Daily News, various dates.

Macau Gaming Industry Labourers' Association (2010). Available from: http://www.mgila.org.mo/introduction.php. [Accessed February 13, 2010].

Pina-Cabral, J. de. (2002) *Between China and Europe: Person, Culture and Emotion in Macao.* London and New York: Continuum.

Pina-Cabral, J. de. (2005) 'New Age Warriors, Negotiating the Handover on the Streets of Macao', *Journal of Romance Studies*, 5 (1), 9–22.

Sallaz, J. (2002) 'The House Rules: Autonomy and Interests among Service Workers in the Contemporary Casino Industry', *Work and Occupations*, 29 (4), 394–427.

Sallaz, J. (2009) *The Labor of Luck: Casino Capitalism in the United States and South Africa.* Berkeley and Los Angeles: University of California Press.

Smith, R., F. Preston and H. L. Humphries (1976) 'Alienation from Work: A Study of Casino Card Dealers' in W. R. Eadington (ed) *Gambling and Society: Interdisciplinary Studies on the Subject of Gambling.* Springfield: Illinois University Press, 229–246.

Statistics and Census Service (2009) 'Survey on Manpower Needs and Wages — Gaming Sector, 2nd Quarter 2009'. Available from: http://www.dsec.gov.mo/getAttachment/32a26367-f692-4df5-9e11-0e7ba6f2c995/E_NECJ_FR_2009_Q2.aspx [Accessed November 11, 2009].

Yee, H. S. (2001) *Macau in Transition: From Colony to Autonomous Region.* Hampshire: Palgrave.

Yu, E. W. Y. (2007) 'Formal and Informal Politics in Macao Special Administrative Region Elections 2004–2005', *Journal of Contemporary China*, 16 (52), 417–44.

Chapter 10 [Notes]

1. The phrase 'Bringing the State back in' is borrowed from Skocpol, T. (1985) 'Bringing the State Back In: Current Research' in P. B. Evans, D. Reuschemeyer and T. Skocpol (eds) *Bringing the State Back In*, Cambridge: Cambridge University Press, 3–37.

2. The Luso-Chinese schools use Chinese as the main medium of instruction but teach Portuguese as a compulsory subject. They were established by the Portuguese administration to provide bilingual people with primary education for low-ranking positions in the civil service. In the 1970s and 1980s, the Luso-Chinese education system was expanded and upgraded as the official track of Chinese schooling in parallel with the Portuguese education system.

3. Ms. S. P. Lau, the Vice-President of the Chinese Educators' Association and a teaching professional for more than 40 years, strongly supported the existence of diverse education systems in Macao which she thought had the advantage of pluralism in that the school actors enjoyed a high degree of autonomy and flexibility. She disagreed with scholars who have pointed out the weaknesses in terms of provision and standards of the different education systems in Macao (Interview with the author, December 5, 2009).

4. Interview with Mr. Tong Chi Kin, Macao SAR Executive Councillor and Supervisor of the Workers' Children High School (November 26, 2009).

5. The provision of free education by the government is for 15 years but, statutorily, it is ten years of free and compulsory education (see Law No. 34/97M).

6. Information provided by Mr. Zheng Jie Zhao, Vice-Principal of the Workers' Children High School (November 26, 2009).

7. Interview with Ms. Ho Sio Kam, Chairman of Administrative Board, Chinese Educators' Association of Macau (November 26, 2009).

8. Information provided by Ms. Ho Sio Kam, Chairman of Administrative Board, Chinese Educators' Association of Macau (November 26, 2009). Available also in Lau Sin Peng (2009) 'A History of Education in Macao', translated by Sylvia S. L. Ieong and Victoria L. C. Lei. Macao: Faculty of Education, University of Macau, 28.
9. Information provided by Ms. Ho Sio Kam, Chairman of Administrative Board, Chinese Educators' Association of Macau (November 26, 2009), available also from 澳門中華 教育會 Association of Macau website: http://home.macau.ctm.net/~edum/content.htm [Accessed November 4, 2009].
10. Information collected by the author based on interviews with teachers and administrators in the school sector.

Chapter 10 [References]

Adamson, B. and S. T. Li (2005) 'Primary and Secondary Schooling' in M. Bray and R. Koo (eds) *Education and Society in Hong Kong and Macao: Comparative Perspectives on Continuity and Change.* Dordrecht, The Netherlands: Comparative Education Research Centre, The University of Hong Kong and Springer, 35–59.

Barkey, K. and S. Parikh (1991) 'Comparative Perspectives on the State', *Annual Review of Sociology*, 17, 523–549.

Boli, J., F. O. Ramirez and J. W. Meyer (1985) 'Explaining the Origins and Expansion of Mass Education', *Comparative Education Review*, 29 (2), 145–170.

Chandhoke, N. (1995) *State and Civil Society: Explorations in Political Theory.* New Delhi: Sage Publications.

Chui, S. O. (2009) *Political Platform for the Campaign of Macao Chief Executive.* Available from: http://www.chuisaion.org.mo, June [Accessed July 20, 2009].

Dale, R. (1997) 'The State and the Governance of Education: An Analysis of the Restructuring of the State-Education Relationship' in A. H. Halsey, H. Lauder, P. Brown and A. S. Wells (eds) *Education: Culture, Economy and Society.* Oxford: Oxford University Press, 273–282.

Evans, P. B. (1995) *Embedded Autonomy: States and Industrial Transformation.* Princeton, N.J.: Princeton University Press.

Hao, Z. D. (2006) 'Social Problems in Macau'. Available from: http://chinaperspectives.revues. org/document552.html [Accessed August 13, 2009].

Hong Kong SAR, Census and Statistics Department (2009) *Hong Kong Annual Digest of Statistics 2008.* Available from: http://www.censtatd.gov.hk/products_and_services/ products/publications/statistical_report/general_statistical_digest/index_cd_B1010003_ dt_detail.jsp [Accessed October 30, 2009].

Lall, M. C. and E. Vickers (eds.) (2009) *Education as a Political Tool in Asia.* London and New York: Routledge.

Lau, S. P. (2007) *A History of Education in Macao* (Original in Chinese 澳門教育史). Macao: Macau Publications Association.

Macao SAR: Education and Youth Affairs Bureau (2009) *Education Statistics 2008–9 and Education Indicators 2007–8.* Macao: Education and Youth Bureau (in Chinese).

Macao SAR Government (2007) 'Policy Address for the Fiscal Year 2007'. Available from: http://www.gov.mo/egi/PMC/ContentMgmtService/resources?id=c373e91090eb91898f7 bb28a6f14be4b [Accessed November 3, 2009].

Macao SAR Government (2008) 'Policy Address for the Fiscal Year 2008'. Available from: http://www.gov.mo/egi/PMC/ContentMgmtService/resources?id=c373e9182fa5084b8f7b 29b1d05fc547 [Accessed November 3, 2009].

Macao SAR Government (2009) 'Policy Address for the Fiscal Year 2009'. Available from: http://www.gov.mo/egi/PMC/ContentMgmtService/resources?id=c373e91e875c3d6d8f7a fb3778a5ed73 [Accessed October 30, 2009].

Macao SAR: Statistics and Census Service (2009) *Yearbook of Statistics 2008*. Macao: Statistics and Census Service. Available from: http://www.dsec.gov.mo/Statistic/General. aspx?lang=en-US [Accessed November 7, 2009].

Morrison, K. and W. P. H. Gu (2008) 'Does Macau Need a Territory-wide Public Examination System?', *Journal of Macau Studies*, 44, 97–113.

Ramirez, F. O. and R. Rubinson (1979) 'Creating Members: The Political Incorporation and Expansion of Public Education' in J. W. Meyer and M. T. Hannan (eds) *National Development and the World System*. Chicago: University of Chicago Press, 72–82.

Rosa, A. (1990) 'Macau Education in the Period of Transition: An Overview and Prospects'. Paper delivered at the *UNESCO International Congress of Planning and Management of Educational Development*, Mexico City, March 26–30.

Shan, P. W. J. and S. S. L. Ieong (2008) 'Post-Colonial Reflections on Education Development in Macau', *Comparative Education Bulletin*, 11, 37–68.

Skocpol, T. (1985) 'Bringing the State Back In: Current Research' in P. B. Evans, D. Reuschemeyer and T. Skocpol (eds) *Bringing the State Back In*. Cambridge: Cambridge University Press, 3–37.

Sou, C. F. (1998) 'Reforming Basic Education in Macau' in R. Ramos, J. R. Dinis, R. Wilson and D. Y. Yuan (eds) *Macau and Its Neighbors Toward the 21st Century*. Macau: Publications Center, University of Macau; Macao Foundation, 239–244.

Tang, K. C. (1998) 'The Development of Education in Macau' in R. Ramos, J. R. Dinis, R. Wilson and D. Y. Yuan (eds) *Macau and Its Neighbors Toward the 21st Century*. Macau: Publications Center, University of Macau, 221–238.

Tang, K. C. (2003) 'The Social Origins and Development of Macau's Decentralized Education System' in K. H. Mok (ed) *Centralization and Decentralization: Educational Reforms and Changing Governance in Chinese Societies*. Hong Kong: Comparative Education Research Centre, The University of Hong Kong; Kluwer Academic Publishers, 81–98.

Tang, K. C. and M. Bray (2000) 'Colonial Models and the Evolution of Education Systems — Centralization and Decentralization in Hong Kong and Macau', *Journal of Educational Administration*, 38 (5), 468–485.

Vong, S. K. (2006) 'An Excursion into the Time Tunnel of Curriculum Development in Macau: A Story of Discourses and Practices', *US-China Education Review*, 3 (5), 11–19.

Vong, S. K. (2009) 'Govern-mentality and Education Policy in Post-1999 Era in Macao'. Paper delivered at the *2009 Asian-Pacific Forum on Sociology of Education*. Taiwan: National University of Taiwan, May 5–8.

Yee, A. H. (1990) 'A Comparative Study of Macau's Education System', *Comparative Education*, 26 (1), 61–71.

Chapter 11 [References]

Asia Pacific Tax Notes (2009) 'Recent Major Tax Developments in Macau'. Available from: http://www.pwccn.com/webmedia/doc/633784181984955749_aptn22_may2009_macau.pdf [Accessed February 20, 2010].

Brenner, N. and N. Theodore (2002) *Spaces of Neoliberalism: Urban Restructuring in North America and Western Europe*. Oxford: Blackwell.

Centaline (2009) 'Transaction Records of December 2009'. Available from: http://www.centaline-macau.com/icms/attachmentDownload.aspx?download/62-23351-19220/Transaction%201-15%20on%20Jan%202010.pdf.

Chiang, C. M. (2005) 'Government Intervention in Housing: The Case of Macau', *Housing Studies*, 20 (1), 149–155.

Commission Against Corruption (CCAC) (2008) *2008 Annual Report of the Commission Against Corruption of Macao*. Available from: http://202.175.15.161/en/subpage.php?cat=intro&page=report.

Forrest, R., A. Murie, and P. Williams (1990) *Home Ownership: Differentiation and Fragmentation*. London: Unwin.

Haila, A. (1999) 'The Singapore and Hong Kong Property Market: Lessons for the West from Successful Global Cities', *European Planning Studies*, 7 (2), 175–187.

Harvey, D. (1989) *The Urban Experience*. Oxford: Oxford University Press.

Jones Lang LaSalle (2009) 'A Strong Rebound in Macau's Residential Market in 2009 amidst Lower Interest Rate and Improved Economy'. Available from: http://www.joneslanglasalle.com.mo/Macau/EN-GB/Pages/NewsItem.aspx?ItemID=18323 [Accessed February 20, 2010]

Lai, D. (2008) *Macao's Social Welfare Model: A Prototype of a Regulatory Regime*. Hong Kong: Unpublished Doctoral dissertation, The University of Hong Kong.

Lam, N. (2002) 'Government Intervention in Macao's Economy', *Asian Journal of Public Administration*, 24 (2), 211–233.

Lam, N. M. K. (2009) 'Public Finance in Macao' in Y. Hao and Z. Wu (eds) *Annual Report on Economy and Society of Macao (2008–2009)*. Beijing: Social Sciences Academic Press, 132–147.

Lo, S. H. (2005) 'Casino Politics, Organised Crime and the Post-Colonial State in Macau', *Journal of Contemporary China*, 14 (43), 207–224.

Macao Housing Bureau (2009) '4% Bank Interest Subsidy'. Available from: http://www.ihm.gov.mo/en/info/interest_allowance.php.

Massey, D. B. (1995). *Spatial Divisions of Labour: Social Structures and the Geography of Production*. New York: Routledge.

People's Daily (2009) 'China's urbanization rate expected to reach 48% in 2010', December 22.

Smart, A. and J. Lee (2003) 'Financialization and the Role of Real Estate in Hong Kong's Regime of Accumulation', *Economic Geography*, 79 (2), 153–171.

Statistics and Census Service (2008) *Direct Investment Statistics 2008*. Available from: http://www.dsec.gov.mo/getAttachment/75088955-0c42-4ef5-8042-ef6475e7db02/E_EID_PUB_2008_Y.aspx.

Statistics and Census Service (2009) 'Private Sector Construction and Real Estate Transaction, 3rd Quarter/2009 No.3'. Available from: http://www.dsec.gov.mo/getAttachment/6240d58f-5709-40c9-a726-ce11e7301f52/E_CPTI_FR_2009_Q3.aspx.

Un, P. S. (2007) *House Price Developments in Macao*. Working Paper of the Research and Statistics Department, Macao Monetary Authority. Available from: http://www.amcm.gov. mo/publication/quarterly/Apr2007/HousePrice_en.pdf.

Yiu, C. Y. (2007) 'Housing Price Gradient Changes between Macau and Hong Kong.' Conference Paper for AsRES 2007 Conference in Macau, June 15.

Chapter 12 [References]

Amin, A. (ed) (1994) *Post-Fordism: A Reader*. Oxford and Cambridge, Mass.: Blackwell.

Aspalter, C. (2006) 'The East Asian Welfare Model', *International Journal of Social Welfare*, 15 (4), 290–301.

Chan, K. W. (2008) 'Deconstructing the Asian Welfare Model: Social Equality Matters,' *Journal of Asian Public Policy*, 1 (3), 302–312.

Choi, A. H. (2004) *Migrant Workers in Macao: Labour and Globalisation*. Hong Kong: The Southeast Asia Research Centre of the City University of Hong Kong, Working Paper Series, no. 66, 144–164.

Esping-Andersen, G. (1990) *The Three Worlds of Welfare Capitalism*. Princeton: Princeton University Press.

Goodman, R., G. White and H. J. Kwon (eds) (1998) *The East Asian Welfare Model: Welfare Orientalism and the State*. London and New York: Routledge.

Gough, I. (2001) 'Globalization and Regional Welfare Regimes: The East Asian Case', *Global Social Policy*, 1 (2), 163–189.

Ho, E. H. W. (2009) *Macao SAR Government 2009 Government Report and 2010 Budget* (Original in Chinese 中華人民共和國澳門特別行政區政府二零零九年財政年度政府工作總結及二零一零年財政年度預算安排). Macao: MSAR Government.

Holliday, I. (2000) 'Productivist Welfare Capitalism: Social Policy in East Asia', *Political Studies*, 48, 706–723.

Ip, P. K. (2006) 'Building Service Quality, Improving Service Institution: Improving Efficiency of Welfare Service', in W. C. Yang (ed) *Development of Macau Social Welfare System: Characteristics and Tendency* (Original in Chinese '構建服務質素持續改進機制，提升社會福利服務表現成效'，楊允中（編），澳門社會福利發展：特點與趨勢). Macao: University of Macau, Macau Research Centre, 112–120.

Jessop, B. (1993) 'Towards a Schumperterian Workfare State? Preliminary Remarks on Post-Fordist Political Economy', *Studies in Political Economy*, 40, 7–39.

Jones, C. (1993) 'The Pacific Challenge: Confucian Welfare States' in C. Jones (ed) *New Perspectives on the Welfare State in Europe*. London: Routledge, 198–217.

Lai, W. L. (2003) 'Reform of the Social Security System in Macao' in P. M. Chang, S. Wang and K. Y. Wong (eds) *Administrative Reform in Asia: Proceedings of the International Conference on Reform in Public Administration and Social Services in Asia* (Original in Chinese '澳門社會保障制度之改革'，張保民、汪碩、王建陽（編），亞洲地區的行政改革：「亞洲地區公共行政及社會服務之改革」國際會議論文集). Macao: Macao Polytechnic Institute, 438–449.

Lai, W. L. (2006) 'The Macao Social Welfare Model: A Productivist Welfare Model' (Original in Chinese '澳門社會福利模式：一個生產主導福利模式'), *The Hong Kong Journal of Social Work*, 40 (1/2), 47–59.

Lai, W. L. (2008) 'The Regulatory Role of Social Policy: Macao's Social Security Development', *Journal of Contemporary Asia*, 38 (3), 373–394.

Lam, A. O. I. (1998) *Social Welfare Policy of Macau during the Transitional Period*. Hong Kong: Unpublished MA thesis, Department of Social Work and Social Administration, the University of Hong Kong.

Leung, K. Y. (2006) 'Macao: A Confucian Welfare State? — A Reflection on Welfare Regime and Citizen Rights' in W. C. Yang (ed) *Development of Macau Social Welfare System: Characteristics and Tendency* (Original in Chinese 梁啓賢，'澳門：儒家的福利國——福利體制、公民權利的反思'，楊允中（編），澳門社會福利發展：特點與趨勢). Macao: University of Macau, Macau Research Centre, 153–165.

Lipietz, A. (1997) 'The Post-Fordist World: Labour Relations, International Hierarchy and Global Ecology', *Review of International Political Economy*, 4 (1), 1–41.

Lo, S. (2009) 'The Decline of Macao's Casino Economy and the Challenges Ahead', *Hong Kong Journal*, 14, April. Available from: www.hkjournal.org/archive/2009_summer/5.htm [Accessed February 3, 2010].

Lui, H. N. (2007) 'A Study of the Trend of Social Security Reform' (Original in Chinese 呂開顏 '社會保障制度改革趨勢探析'), *Macao Studies*, 39, April, 98–103.

Offe, C. (1984) *Contradictions of the Welfare State*. London: Hutchinson.

Shek, C. K. (2006) 'Analysing the Relations between Traditional Associations and Social Welfare in Macao' in W. C. Yang (ed) *Development of Macau Social Welfare System: Characteristics and Tendency* (Original in Chinese 石滄金，'簡析澳門社團與社會福利活動的關係'，楊允中（編），澳門社會福利發展：特點與趨勢). Macao: University of Macau, Macau Research Centre, 148–152.

Social Welfare Bureau (SWB) (2009) *Social Welfare Bureau 2008 Report* (Original in Chinese, 社會工作局工作報告2008). Macao: Macao Social Welfare Bureau.

Statistics and Census Service (2009) *Yearbook of Statistics, 2008*. Macau: MSAR Government.

Statistics and Census Service (2010) 'GDP per capita at current price over the years'. Available from: www.dsec.gov.mo/TimeSeriesDatabase.aspx [Accessed February 12, 2010].

Tang, Y. W. (2003) *Social Welfare and Social Security in Macao* (Original in Chinese, 鄧玉華, 澳門社會福利與社會保障). Macao: Macao Social Security Association.

Tang, Y. W. (2007) *Social Welfare and Social Security in Macao II* (Original in Chinese, 鄧玉華, 澳門社會福利與社會保障 II). Macao: Wah Fai Publishing Co. Ltd.

Titmuss, R. (1976) 'Social Division of Welfare: Some Reflections on the Search for Equity' in *Essays on the Welfare State*. 3rd edition. London: Allen and Unwin, 34–55.

Wong, K. Y., S. L. Wong, P. S. Wan and W. T. Cheng (eds) (2009) *The New Face of Macau: Achievements and Challenges*. Hong Kong: The Chinese University Press.

Wong, S. L., Y. M. Yeung, P. S. Wan and W. T. Cheng (eds) (2007) *Documentation of Macao Society: A Glimpse of Quality of Life from Social Indicator Study* (Original in Chinese, 黃紹倫、楊汝萬、尹寶珊、鄭宏泰（編）澳門社會實錄：從指標研究看生活素質). Hong Kong: Hong Kong Asian Pacific Research Centre, the Chinese University of Hong Kong.

Chapter 13 [References]

Cheung, A. B. L. (1996) 'Public Sector Reform and the Re-legitimation of Public Bureaucratic Power: The Case of Hong Kong', *International Journal of Public Sector Management*, 9 (5/6), 37–50.

Gu, Zheng and Ricardo C. S. Siu (2009) *Macao Gaming Human Resources: Issues and Solutions*. Macao: Macao Association of Economic Sciences.

Hu, Fox Yi (2009) 'Graft has declined, says outgoing Macau leader', *South China Morning Post*, November 20.

Li, Sheng and Yanming Tsui (2009) 'A General Equilibrium Approach to Tourism and Welfare: The Case of Macau', *Habitat International*, 33 (4), 412–424.

Lo, Sonny (2009) 'Casino Capitalism and Its Legitimacy Impact on the Politico-administrative State in Macau', *Journal of Current Chinese Affairs*, 1/2009, 19–47.

Macao SAR Government (2007) *The Road Map for Public Sector Reform*. Available from: www.gov.mo (translated from Chinese).

Nadkarni, Sanjay and Aliana Leong Man Wai (2007) 'Macao's MICE Dreams: Opportunities and Challenges', *International Journal of Event Management Research*, 3 (2), 47–57.

Selected Bibliography

Primary Sources

Commission for the First Public Tender to Grant Concessions to Operate Casino Games of Chance of the Macao SAR (2001) *Information Memorandum*. Macao: Printing Bureau.

Guia Lighthouse Protection Concern Group (2007) 'Letter to UNESCO'. Available from: http://guialighthouse.blogspot.com/search?updated-max=2007-12-03T00%3A41%3A00%2B08%3A00

Ho, E. H. W. (2009) *Review of the Government's Work in the Fiscal Year 2009 and the Financial Budget for the Fiscal Year 2010 of the Macao Special Administrative Region (MSAR) of the People's Republic of China*. Macao: Macau SAR Government.

Hong Kong Institute of Planners (2008) *Position Paper on the Outline for Macao Urban Concept Plan*. Hong Kong: Hong Kong Institute of Planners. Available from: http://www.ceeds.gov.mo

Hong Kong SAR Government (2006) *Hong Kong 2030 Planning Vision and Strategy*. Hong Kong: Government Printing Bureau.

Hong Kong SAR Census and Statistics Department (2009) *Quarterly Report on General Household Survey*. Hong Kong: Census and Statistics Department. Available from: http://www.censtatd.gov.hk/products_and_services/products/publications/statistical_report/labour/index_cd_B1050001_dt_latest.jsp

ITUC-CSI-IGB (2007) *Annual Survey of Violations of Labour Union Rights*. Belgium: ITUC-CSI-IGB. Available from: http://survey07.ituc-csi.org/getcountry.php?IDCountry=MAC&IDLang=EN

Macao SAR Commission of Audit (2006) *Special Report on the 4th East Asian Games Organization* (Original in Chinese 專項報告：第四屆東亞運動會). Macao: Commission of Audit.

Macao SAR Economic Services (2009) *The General Principles of CEPA and Its Six Annexes*. Macau: Macao Special Administrative Region Economic Services, Available from: http://www.ipim.gov.mo/en/cepa/index.html

Macao SAR Education and Youth Affairs Bureau (2009) *Education Statistics 2008–09 and Education Indicators 2007–08*. Macao: Education and Youth Affairs Bureau (in Chinese).

Macao SAR Government (1990) *Decree-Law No. 24/1989/M, April*. Macao: Printing Bureau.

Macao SAR Government (2000–2009) *Policy Address for the Fiscal Years 2000–2009*. Available from: http://www.gov.mo/egi/PMC/ContentMgmtService/resources?id=c373e90089911e 438f6a59b9766fb195

Macao SAR Government (2001) *Government Gazette, BOM 39/2001, Decree Law 16/2001, September 24*. Macao: Printing Bureau.

Macao SAR Government (2002) *Chief Executive Decree 93/2002*. Macao: Printing Bureau.

Macao SAR Government (2006) *Government Gazette, BOM 34/2006*. Macao: Printing Bureau.

Macao SAR Government (2007) *The Road Map for Public Sector Reform*. Available from: www. gov.mo.

Macao SAR Government (2008) *New Order of the Development Heights of the Guia Hill*. Macao: Printing Bureau.

Macao SAR Government (Departamento de Recursos Humanos do SAFP) (2009) *Recursos Humanos da Administracao Publica da RAEM 2008: Dados Relativos a 31 de Dezembro de 2008*. Macao: Macao Government.

Macao SAR Government (2009) *CE: Central Government Vigorously Supports Macao*. Available from: www.gov.mo

Macao SAR Government (2009) *Macau Labour Relations Law (Decree-Law No. 7/2008)*. Macao: Price Waterhouse Coopers, March.

Macao SAR Government (2009) *Macao Special Administrative Region Law No. 21/2009*. Macao: Printing Bureau.

Macao SAR Land, Public Works and Transport Bureau (2008) *Report on Macau's Urban Planning System*. Macao: Printing Bureau.

Macao SAR Legislative Assembly (2007) *Official Record of Proceedings 2006–07, Series I, III-62*. Macao: Printing Bureau.

Macao SAR Social Welfare Bureau (2009) *Social Welfare Bureau 2008 Report*. Macao: Macao Social Welfare Bureau.

Macao SAR Statistics and Census Service (2000–2008) *Yearbook of Statistics 2000– 2009*. Macao: Statistics and Census Service. Available from: http://www.dsec.gov.mo/Statistic/ General.aspx#Release

Macao SAR Statistics and Census Service (2006) *Estimates of Population, Birth and Death, Marriage and Divorce*. Macao: Statistics and Census Service. Available from: http://www. dsec.gov.mo/index.asp?src=/english/indicator/e_demindicator.html

Macao SAR Statistics and Census Service (2008) *Direct Investment Statistics*. Macao: Statistics and Census Service. Available from: http://www.decs.gov.mo/Statistic/Other. asp#KeyIndicators

Macao SAR Statistics and Census Service (2008) *Survey on Job Changing of the Employed*. Macao: Statistics and Census Service. Available from: http://www.dsec.gov.mo

Macao SAR Statistics and Census Service (2008) *Visitor Arrivals*. Macao: Statistics and Census Service. Available from: http://www.dsec.gov.mo/TimeSeriesDatabase.aspx?lang=en-US&KeyIndicatorID=27

Macao SAR Statistics and Census Service (2009) *Employed Population by Industry*. Macao: Statistics and Census Service. Available from: http://www.dsec.gov.mo/PredefinedReport. aspx?ReportID=10

Macao SAR Statistics and Census Service (2009) *Monthly Bulletin of Statistics*. Macao: Statistics and Census Service. Available from: www.dsec.gov.mo

Macao SAR Statistics and Census Service (2009) *Overall Unemployment Rate.* Macao: Statistics and Census Service. Available from: http://www.dsec.gov.mo/TimeSeriesDatabase.aspx? KeyIndicatorID=24

Macao SAR Statistics and Census Service (2009) *Principal Statistical Indicators.* Macao: Statistics and Census Service. Available from: http://www.decs.gov.mo/Statistic/Other. asp#KeyIndicators

Macao SAR Statistics and Census Service (2009) *Total Employed Population.* Macao: Statistics and Census Service. Available from: http://www.dsec.gov.mo/TimeSeriesDatabase. aspx?KeyIndicatorID=26

Macao Urban Plan Institute (2008) *Position Paper on Macao Urban Concept Plan.* Macao: Macao Urban Planning Institute, September 7.

SJM (2009) *SJM Holdings Limited Announces Interim Results for Six Months Ended 30 June 2009.* Available from: http://www.sjmholdings.com/mc-pressrelease12.html

SJM Holdings (2010) *SJM to Open Casino Oceanus at Jai Alai the 'First' Casino in Macau.* Available from: http://www.sjmholdings.com/mc-pressrelease16.html

Strategy Study Center for the Sustainable Development of Macao SAR (2008) *An Outline for Macau Urban Concept Plan.* Macau: Research Centre for Sustainable Development Strategies of the Government of the Macao SAR. Available from: http://www.ceeds.gov.mo

Zhuhai Government (2006) *The Zhuhai Urban Space Development Strategy: Zhuhai 2030.* Zhuhai: Zhuhai Government.

Secondary Sources

Adamson, B. and S. T. Li (2005) 'Primary and Secondary Schooling' in M. Bray and R. Koo (eds) *Education and Society in Hong Kong and Macao: Comparative Perspectives on Continuity and Change.* Dordrecht, The Netherlands: Comparative Education Research Centre, The University of Hong Kong and Springer, 35–59.

Akerlof, G. A. (1982) 'Labor Contracts as Partial Gift Exchange', *Quarterly Journal of Economics,* 97 (4), 543–569.

Akerlof, G. A. and J. L. Yellen (1986) *Efficiency Wage Models of the Labor Market.* Cambridge; New York: Cambridge University Press.

Alexopoulos, M. (2004) 'Unemployment and the Business Cycle', *Journal of Monetary Economics,* 51 (2), 277–298.

Amaro, A. (1998) *Das Cabanas de Palha as Torres de Betão. Assim Cresceu Macau.* Macao: Livros do Oriente.

Amin, A. (1994) *Post-Fordism: A Reader.* Oxford: Blackwell.

Aspalter, C. (2006) 'The East Asian Welfare Model', *International Journal of Social Welfare,* 15 (4), 290–301.

Austrin, T. and J. West (2004) 'New Deals in Gambling: Global Markets and Local Regimes of Regulation' in L. Beukema and J. Carrillo (eds) *Globalism/Localism at Work.* Boston: Elsevier, 143–158.

Austrin, T. and J. West (2005) 'Skills and Surveillance in Casino Gaming: Work, Consumption and Regulation', *Work, Employment and Society,* 19 (2), 305–326.

Azevedo, P. A. (2006) 'Towering Ambitions', *Macau Business,* August. Macao: De Ficção Multimedia Projects.

Barkey, K. and S. Parikh (1991) 'Comparative Perspectives on the State', *Annual Review of Sociology*, 17, 523–549.

Bastos, B. (1995) *Cronologia da Historia de Macau, Seculo XIX*. Macao: DSEJ Education Services.

Bentley, A. F. (1967) *The Process of Government*. Cambridge, Mass.: The Belknap Press of Harvard University Press.

Benz, D. (2004) 'Labor's Ace in the Hole: Casino Organizing in Las Vegas', *New Political Science*, 26 (4), 525–550.

Berry, J. M. (1997a) *Lobbying for the People*. Princeton, N.J.: Princeton University Press.

Berry, J. M. (1997b) *The Interest Group Society*. New York: Longman.

Bezlova, A. (2009) 'China: Macau Gaming Boom at a Cost', *Global Issues*, April 17.

Birch, A. H. (1971) *Representation*. London: Pall Mall Press.

Boli, J., F. O. Ramirez and J. W. Meyer (1985) 'Explaining the Origins and Expansion of Mass Education', *Comparative Education Review*, 29 (2), 145–170.

Boxer, C. (1988) *Ásia Sínica e Japónica*. Macao: Instituto Cultural de Macao.

Brenner, N. and N. Theodore (2002) *Spaces of Neoliberalism: Urban Restructuring in North America and Western Europe*. Malden, Mass.; Oxford: Blackwell.

Browne, W. P. (1998) *Groups, Interests, and US Public Policy*. Washington, D.C.: Georgetown University Press.

Bruck, C. (2008) 'The Brass Ring', *The New Yorker*, June 30.

Burawoy, M. (1983) 'Between the Labor Process and the State: The Changing Face of Factory Regimes under Advanced Capitalism', *American Sociological Review*, 48, 587–605.

Cappelli, P. and K. Chauvin (1991) 'An Interplant Test of the Efficiency Wage Hypothesis', *Quarterly Journal of Economics*, 106, 869–884.

Chan, K. W. (2008) 'Deconstructing the Asian Welfare Model: Social Equality Matters', *Journal of Asian Public Policy*, 1 (3), 302–312.

Chan, S. S. (2000) *The Macau Economy*. Macau: Publications Centre, University of Macau.

Chan, S. S. (2003) *The Nature of Unemployment in Macao and Its Policy Implications*. Macau: Monetary Authority of Macau. Available at: www.amcm.gov.mo/publication/quarterly/Oct2003/StructuralUnemployment_en.pdf

Chandhoke, N. (1995) *State and Civil Society: Explorations in Political Theory*. New Delhi: Sage Publications.

Cheung, A. B. L. (2002) 'The Changing Political System: Executive-led Government or "Disabled" Governance?' in S. K. Lau (ed) *The First Tung Chee-hwa Administration: The First Five Years of the Hong Kong Special Administrative Region*. Hong Kong: The Chinese University Press, 41–68.

Chiang, C. M. (2005) 'Government Intervention in Housing: The Case of Macau', *Housing Studies*, 20 (1), 149–155.

Choi, Alex H. (2006) 'Migrant Workers in Macao: Labour and Globalisation' in Kevin Hewison and Ken Young (eds) *Transnational Migration and Work in Asia*. London: Routledge, 144–164.

Choi, C. (1991) 'Settlement of Chinese Families in Macau' in R. D. Cremer (ed) *Macau City of Commerce and Culture: Continuity and Change*. Hong Kong: PI Press Ltd, 61–66.

Chou, B. K. P. (2004) 'Public Sector Reform in Macao after the Handover', *China Perspectives*, March–April, 52, 56–63.

Chou, B. K. P. (2005) 'Interest Group Politics in Macau after the Handover', *Journal of Contemporary China*, 14 (43), 191–206.

Chubb, J. E. (1983) *Interest Groups and the Bureaucracy: The Politics of Energy.* Stanford: Stanford University Press.

Cobb, R. W., J. K. Ross, and M. H. Ross (1976) 'Agenda Building as a Comparative Political Process', *American Political Science Review*, 70 (1), 126–138.

Costa, J. (1993) *Subsídios Para a Historia do Município das Ilhas.* Volume I, 1689–1928. Câmara Municipal das Ilhas. Macao: Printing Bureau.

Coxall, W. N. (1981) *Parties and Pressure Groups.* Harlow: Longman Group Limited.

Custodio, C. and M. Teixeira (2000) *Macau e a Sua População 1500–2000: Aspectos Demográficos Sociais e Económicos.* Macao: Printing Bureau.

Dahl, R. A. (1982) *Dilemmas of Pluralist Democracy: Autonomy vs. Control.* New Haven, Conn.: Yale University Press.

Dale, R. (1997) 'The State and the Governance of Education: An Analysis of the Restructuring of the State-Education Relationship' in A. H. Halsey, H. Lauder, P. Brown and A. S. Wells (eds) *Education: Culture, Economy and Society.* Oxford: Oxford University Press, 273–282.

Deckop, J. R. (1995) 'Pay System Effects on Altruism Motivation', *Academy of Management Journal*, 38, 359–364.

du Cos, H. (2009) 'Emerging Issues for Cultural Tourism in Macau', *Journal of Current Chinese Affairs*, 1 (Special Issue), 73–99.

Dye, T. R. (2005) *Understand Public Policy.* N.J.: Prentice Hall.

Eadington, W. R. and R. C. S. Siu (2007) 'Between Law and Custom — Examining the Interaction between Legislative Change and the Evolution of Macao's Casino Industry', *International Gambling Studies*, 7 (1), 1–28.

Eisner, M. (1992) 'Long Term Fluctuations of Economic Growth and Social Destabilization', *Historical Social Research*, 17, 70–98.

Enarson, E. (1993) 'Emotion Workers on the Production Line: The Feminising of Casino Card Dealing', *NWSA Journal*, 5 (2), 218–232.

Esping-Andersen, G. (1990) *The Three Worlds of Welfare Capitalism.* Cambridge: Polity Press.

Evans, P. B. (1995) *Embedded Autonomy: States and Industrial Transformation.* Princeton, N.J.: Princeton University Press.

Fok, H. Y. T. (2004) *Tales of Macao Casinos* (Original in Chinese 澳門賭場風雲). Hong Kong: Chi Pong Press.

Frey, J. H. and D. E. Carns (1987) 'The Work Environment of Gambling Casinos', *Anthropology and Work Review*, 8 (4), 38–42.

Frey, J. H. and D. E Carns (1988) 'Job Satisfaction of Casino Card Dealers', *Sociology and Social Research*, 72 (3), 159–164.

Fung, K. (1992) 'Income Distribution in Macau' in Bruce Taylor et al (ed) *Socioeconomic Development and Quality of Life in Macau.* Macau: Centre of Macau Studies, University of Macau, 143–155.

Fung, K. (2009) 'Income Distribution and Poverty' in S. L. Wong, K. Y. Wong and P. S. Wan (eds) *The New Face of Macau Society: Achievement and Challenge.* Hong Kong: Hong Kong Institute of Asia-Pacific Studies, The Chinese University of Hong Kong, 1–19.

Godinho, Jorge (2010) 'The Ao Man Long Corruption and Money Laundering Case', *Freedom from Fear Magazine*, June 20.

Goldsmith, A. H., J. R. Veum, and W. J. Darity (2001) 'Working Hard for the Money? Efficiency Wages and Worker Effort', *Journal of Economic Psychology*, 21 (3), 351–385.

Goodman, R. (1995) *The Luck Business: The Devastating Consequences and Broken Promises of America's Gambling Explosion.* New York: Free Press.

Goodman, R., H. Kwon, and G. White (1998) *The East Asian Welfare Model: Welfare Orientalism and the State*. London; New York: Routledge.

Gough, I. (2001) 'Globalization and Regional Welfare Regimes: The East Asian Case', *Global Social Policy*, 1 (2), 163–189.

Gough, N. and I. Zhai (2009) 'Casino stocks fall after visa rules tightened', *South China Morning Post*, October 16.

Grover, Chris and John Stewart (1999) 'Market Workfare: Social Security, Social Regulation and Competitiveness in the 1990s', *Journal of Social Policy*, 28 (1), 73–96.

Gu, Z. and R. C. S. Siu (2009) *Macao Gaming Human Resources: Issues and Solutions*. Macao: Macao Association of Economic Sciences.

Guimarães, A. (2000) *Uma Relação Especial. Macau e as Relações Luso Chinesas 1780–1844.* Lisboa: Edição CIES.

Gunn, G. C. (2005) *Encountering Macau: A Portuguese City-state on the Periphery of China, 1557–1999*. Macao: Tipografia Macau Hung Heng Ltd.

Haila, A. (1999) 'The Singapore and Hong Kong Property Market: Lessons for the West from Successful Global Cities', *European Planning Studies,* 7 (2), 175–187.

Hao, Z. D. (2006) 'Social Problems in Macau', *China Perspectives*, 62. Available from: http://chinaperspectives.revues.org/document552.html

Harvey, D. (1989) *The Urban Experience*. Baltimore: Johns Hopkins University Press.

Ho, W. S. (2006) *Employment Growth in Macau's Tertiary Sector*. Macau: Monetary Authority of Macau.

Holliday, I. (2000) 'Productivist Welfare Capitalism: Social Policy in East Asia', *Political Studies*, 48, 706–723.

Hsueh, F., R. D. Cremer, and S. Wong (1991) *Entrepreneurs and Enterprises in Macau: A Study of Industrial Development*. Hong Kong: Hong Kong University Press.

Huang, T. L., A. Hallam, P. F. Orazem, and E. M. Paterno (1998) 'Empirical Tests of Efficiency Wage Models', *Economica*, 65 (257), 125–143.

Hunter, K. G. (1999) *Interest Groups and State Economic Development Policies*. Westport, Conn. and London: Praeger.

Huntington, S. P. (1968) *Political Order in Changing Societies*. New Haven: Yale University Press.

Jonas, A. E. G. (1996) 'Local Labour Control Regimes: Uneven Development and the Social Regulation of Production', *Regional Studies*, 30 (4), 323–338.

Jones, C. (1993) 'The Pacific Challenge: Confucian Welfare States' in C. Jones (ed) *New Perspectives on the Welfare State in Europe*. London: Routledge, 198–217.

Jones, J. B. and S. Chandler (2001) 'Connecting Personal Biography and Social History: Women Casino Workers and the Global Economy', *Journal of Sociology and Social Welfare*, 28 (4), 173–193.

Jordan, G. (1981) 'Iron Triangles, Woolly Corporatism and Elastic Nets: Images of the Policy Process', *Journal of Public Policy*, 1, 95–123.

Kan, W. (2007) 'Earlier Development of Gambling Industry in Macau', *Journal of Macau Studies*, 40, 154–162.

Kelly, P. F. (2001) 'The Political Economy of Local Labor Control in the Philippines', *Economic Geography*, 77 (1), 1–22.

Kingdon, J. W. (1997) *Agenda, Alternatives, and Public Policies*. Chicago: University of Chicago Press.

Lafferty, G. and J. McMillen (1989) 'Labouring For Leisure: Work and Industrial Relations in the Tourism Industry. Case Studies of Casinos', *Labour and Industry*, 2 (2), 32–59.

Lai, W. L. (2003) 'Reform of Social Security System in Macao' in P. Chang, S. S. Wang and A. K. Y. Wong (eds) *Administrative Reform in Asia: Proceedings of the International Conference on Reform in Public Administration and Social Services in Asia, Macao*. Macao: Macao Polytechnic Institute, 438–449.

Lai, W. L. (2006) 'The Macao Social Welfare Model: A Productivist Welfare Model', *The Hong Kong Journal of Social Work*, 10 (1/2), 47–59.

Lai, W. L. (2008) 'The Regulatory Role of Social Policy: Macao's Social Security Development', *Journal of Contemporary Asia*, 38 (3), 373–394.

Lall, M. C. and E. Vickers (eds) (2009) *Education as a Political Tool in Asia*. London and New York: Routledge.

Lam, A. O. I. (1998) *Social Welfare Policy of Macau During the Transitional Period*. Hong Kong: Unpublished PhD thesis, Department of Social Work and Social Administration, The University of Hong Kong.

Lam, I. F. and S. Sam (1999) *21st Century Macau City Planning Guideline Study*. Macao: Macau Cooperation and Development Foundation.

Lam, N. (2006) 'Public Finance in Hong Kong and Macao'. Paper delivered at an *International Conference on 'The Evolution of "One Country, Two Systems' in Hong Kong and Macao: Implications for Canada'*, University of Waterloo, Canada, March 2006.

Lam, T. and I. Iam (1979) *Ou Mun Kei Leok: A Monografia de Macau*. Macao: Tipografia Mandarim.

Lamas, R. (1998) *History of Macau: A Student's Manual*. Macao: Institute of Tourism Education.

Langton, S. (1978) *Citizen Participation in America: Current Reflections on the State of the Art*. Lexington, Mass.: Lexington Books.

Lau, S. P. (2007) *A History of Education in Macao* (Original in Chinese 澳門教育史). Macao: Macau Publications Association.

Lee, S. P. (2006) *Social Stability and Public Policy: The Role of Special Interest Groups in Macao*. Hong Kong: Unpublished MPA dissertation, The University of Hong Kong.

Leibenstein, H. (1957) *Economic Backwardness and Economic Growth*. New York: Wiley.

Leonard, J. (2006) 'The Two Gaming Markets of Macao: A Product of Regulatory Difference' in Institute for the Study of Commercial Gaming, University of Macau (ed) *Law, Regulation, and Control Issues of the Asian Gaming Industry*. Macau: Institute for the Study of Commercial Gaming, 156–172.

Levine, D. I. (1992) 'Can Wage Increases Pay for Themselves? Tests With a Production Function', *Economic Journal*, 102, 1101–1115.

Lewis, J. W. and X. Litai (2004) 'Social Change and Political Reform in China: Meeting the Challenge of Success', *China Quarterly*, 176, 926–942.

Li, S. and Y. Tsui (2009a) 'A General Equilibrium Approach to Tourism and Welfare: The Case of Macau', *Habitat International*, 33 (4), 412–424.

Li, S. and Y. Tsui (2009b) 'Casino Boom and Local Politics: The City of Macao', *Cities*, 26 (2), 67–73.

Lijphart, A. (1977) *Democracy in Plural Societies: A Comparative Exploration*. New Haven: Yale University Press.

Lipietz, A. (1997) 'The Post-Fordist World: Labour Relations, International Hierarchy and Global Ecology', *Review of International Political Economy*, 4 (1), 1–41.

Lo, S. H., Sonny and Herbert S. Yee (2005) 'Legitimacy-building in the Macau Special Administrative Region: Colonial Legacies and Reform Strategies', *Asian Journal of Political Science*, 13 (1), 51–79.

Lo, S. S. H. (1989) 'Aspects of Political Development in Macao', *The China Quarterly*, 120, 837–851.

Lo, S. S. H. (1996) *Political Development in Macao*. Hong Kong: The Chinese University Press.

Lo, S. S. H. (2007) *Political Change in Macao*. London and New York: Routledge.

Lo, S. S. H (2009a) 'Bureaucratic Capacity and Civil Service Reforms in Macau', *Macau Closer,* April 2.

Lo, S. S. H. (2009b) 'Casino Capitalism and Its Legitimacy Impact on the Politico-administrative State in Macau', *Journal of Current Chinese Affairs*, 1/2009, 19–47.

Loi, K. I. (2008) 'Gaming and Entertainment Tourist Destinations — A World of Similarities and Differences', *Tourism Recreation Research*, 33 (2), 165–183

Loi, K. I. and G. K. Woo (2010) 'Macao's Casino Industry: Reinventing Las Vegas in Asia', *Cornell Hospitality Quarterly*, May, 51, 268–283

Lou, S. H. (2005) 'Popular Associations Regime Resources and Political Development in Macao', *Macao Administration Journal*, 18, No. 69 (3), 1015–1028.

Luo, W. J. (2005) 'The Power Structure, Organizational Design and Characteristics of Executive-Led Government (Original in Chinese 論行政主導的權力設定、結構設計及其他條件)', *Administration Magazine*, 69, 879–890.

Macao Development Strategic Research Center (2000) *The Present and Future of Social Organizations in Macao* (Original in Chinese 澳門社團現狀與前瞻．澳門：澳門發展策略研究中心．) Macao: Macao Strategic Research Center.

Macao Strategic Research Center, Macao Foundation and Center for Contemporary China Research of the Peking University (2005) *Survey on 'Macao Citizen's Quality 2005'* (in Chinese). Macao: Macao Strategic Research Center.

Mahood, H. R. (2000) *Interest Groups in American National Politics: An Overview*. Upper Saddle River, N.J.: Prentice Hall.

Massey, D. B. (1995) *Spatial Divisions of Labour: Social Structures and the Geography of Production*. Basingstoke, Hampshire: Macmillan Press.

McCartney, G. (2006) 'Casino Gambling in Macao: Through Legalization to Liberalization' in Cathy H. C. Hsu (ed) *Casino Industry in Asia Pacific: Development, Operation and Impact*. New York: Haworth Hospitality Press, 37–54.

Migdal, J. S. (2001) *State in Society: Studying How States and Societies Transform and Constitute One Another*. Cambridge: Cambridge University Press.

Moisés, F. (2006) *Macau na Politica Externa Chinesa 1949–1979*. Lisboa: ICS Publications.

Morrison, K. and W. P. H. Gu (2008) 'Does Macau Need a Territory-wide Public Examination System?', *Journal of Macau Studies*, 44, 97–113.

Morse, E. A. and E. P. Goss (2007) *Governing Fortune: Casino Gambling in America*. Ann Arbor: University of Michigan Press.

Nadkarni, S. and Aliana M. Leong (2007) 'Macao's MICE Dreams: Opportunities and Challenges', *International Journal of Event Management Research*, 3 (2), 47–57.

Nakamura, Robert T. and Frank Smallwood (1980) *The Politics of Policy Implementation*. New York: St. Martin's Press.

Nelson, J. M. (1987) 'Political Participation' in G. A. Almond, S. P. Huntington and M. Weiner (eds) *Understanding Political Development: An Analytic Study*. Boston: Little, Brown and Company, 103–159.

Offe, C. and J. Keane (1984) *Contradictions of the Welfare State*. Cambridge, Mass.: MIT Press.

Olson, M. (1963) 'Rapid Growth as a Destabilizing Force', *Journal of Economic History*, 23 (4), 529–552.

Olson, M. (1982) *The Rise and Decline of Nations: Economic Growth, Stagflation, and Social Rigidities*. New Haven: Yale University Press.

Peck, J. (1996) *Work-place: The Social Regulation of Labor Markets*. New York: Guilford Press.

Pina-Cabral, J. D. (2005) 'New Age Warriors, Negotiating the Handover on the Streets of Macao', *Journal of Romance Studies*, 5 (1), 9–22.

Pincus, J. and Vu Thanh Tu Anh (2008) 'Vietnam: A Tiger in Turmoil', *Far Eastern Economic Review*, May.

Pinho, A. (1991) 'Gambling in Macau' in R. D. Cremer (ed) *Macau City of Commerce and Culture: Continuity and Change*. Hong Kong: API Press Ltd, 247–257.

Polsby, N. W. (1980) *Community Power and Political Theory: A Further Look at Problems of Evidence and Inference*. New Haven: Yale University Press.

Pons, P. (1999) *Macao*. Hong Kong: Hong Kong University Press.

Powell, M. (2000) 'New Labour and the Third Way in the British Welfare State: A New and Distinctive Approach', *Critical Social Policy*, 20 (1), 39–60.

Putnam, R. D. (2000) *Bowling Alone: The Collapse and Revival of American Community*. New York: Simon & Schuster.

Raff, D. M. and L.H. Summers (1987) 'Did Henry Ford Pay Efficiency Wages?', *Journal of Labor Economics*, 5 (4, pt. 2), S57–S86.

Ramirez, F. O. and R. Rubinson (1979) 'Creating Members: The Political Incorporation and Expansion of Public Education' in J. W. Meyer and M. T. Hannan (eds) *National Development and the World System*. Chicago: University of Chicago Press, 72–82.

Richardson, J. J. (1993a) *Interest Group Behaviour in Britain: Continuity and Change*. New York: Oxford University Press.

Richardson, J. J. (1993b) *Pressure Groups*. Oxford: Oxford University Press.

Ringland, G. (2002) *Scenarios for Public Policy*. Chichester: John Wiley and Sons.

Rosa, A. (1990) 'Macau Education in the Period of Transition: An Overview and Prospects'. Paper delivered at the *UNESCO International Congress of Planning and Management of Educational Development, Mexico City*, March 26–30, 1990.

Salisbury, R. H. (1984) 'Interest Representation: The Dominance of Institutions', *American Political Science Review*, 78, 64–68.

Salisbury, R. H., J. P. Heinz, E. O. Laumann, and R. L. Nelson (1987) 'Who Works with Whom? Group Alliances and Opposition', *American Political Science Review*, 81, 1217–1234.

Sallaz, J. (2002) 'The House Rules: Autonomy and Interests among Service Workers in the Contemporary Casino Industry', *Work and Occupations*, 29 (4), 394–427.

Schmitter, P. C. and L. Gerhard (1982) *Trends Towards Corporatist Intermediation*. London: Sage.

Scholten, I. (1987) *Political Stability and Neo-corporatism: Corporatist Integration and Societal Cleavages in Western Europe*. London: Sage.

Scott, I. (2005) *Public Administration in Hong Kong: Regime Change and Its Impact on the Public Sector*. Singapore: Marshall Cavendish Academic.

Scott, R. (1990) *Interest Groups and Public Policy: Case Studies from the Australian States*. Melbourne: Macmillan.

Shan, P. W. J. and S. S. L. Ieong (2008) 'Post-Colonial Reflections on Education Development in Macau', *Comparative Education Bulletin*, 11, 37–68.

Shapiro, C. and J. E. Stiglitz (1984) 'Equilibrium Unemployment as a Worker Discipline Device', *American Economic Review*, 74 (3), 312–320.

Sharp, E. B. and Y. M. Alex-Assensoh (2005) *Morality Politics in American Cities*. Lawrence, Kan.: University Press of Kansas.

Silva, B. (1992–1995) *Cronologia da Historia de Macau*. Macao: The Education and Youth Affairs Bureau.

Siu, R. (2006) 'Evolution of Macao's Casino Industry from Monopoly to Oligopoly: Social and Economic Reconsideration', *Journal of Economic Issues*, 40 (4), 967–989.

Siu, R. S. (2007) 'Formal Rules, Informal Constraints, and Industrial Evolution — The Case of the Junket Operator Regulation and the Transition of Macao's Casino Business', *UNLV Gaming Research & Review Journal*, 11 (2), 49–62.

Skocpol, T. (1985) 'Bringing the State Back in: Current Research' in P. B. Evans, D. Reuschemeyer and T. Skocpol (eds) *Bringing the State Back In*. Cambridge: Cambridge University Press, 3–37.

Smart, A. and J. Lee (2003) 'Financialization and the Role of Real Estate in Hong Kong's Regime of Accumulation', *Economic Geography*, 79 (2), 153–171.

Smith, R., F. Preston and H. L. Humphries (1976) 'Alienation from Work: A Study of Casino Card Dealers' in W. R. Eadington (ed) *Gambling and Society: Interdisciplinary Studies on the Subject of Gambling*. Springfield: Illinois University Press, 229–246.

Solow, R. (1957) 'Technical Change and the Aggregate Production Function', *Review of Economics and Statistics*, 39 (3), 312–320.

Solow, R. (1979) 'Another Possible Source of Wage Stickiness', *Journal of Macroeconomics*, 1 (1), 79–82.

Sou, C. F. (1999) '10-Year Review of Education Reform' in Z. L. Wu, Y. Z. Yang and S. R. Feng (eds) *Macao 1999* (Original in Chinese '教育教革的十年回顧澳門', 澳門1999). Macao: Macau Foundation, 196–223.

Sousa, I. T. d. (2009) *Regional Integration and Differentiation in a Globalizing China: The Blending of Government and Business in Post-Colonial Macau*. Amsterdam: University of Amsterdam.

Stiglitz, J. E. (1974) 'Alternative Theories of Wage Determination and Unemployment in LDC.'s: The Labor Turnover Model', *Quarterly Journal of Economics*, 88 (2), 194–227.

Stiglitz, J. E. (1985) 'Equilibrium Wage Distributions', *Economic Journal*, 95 (379), 595–618.

Tang, K. C. (1998) 'The Development of Education in Macau' in R. Ramos, J. R. Dinis, R. Wilson and D. Y. Yuan (eds) *Macau and Its Neighbors Toward the 21st Century*. Macau: Publications Center, University of Macau, 221–238.

Tang, K. C. (2003) 'The Social Origins and Development of Macau's Decentralized Education System' in K. H. Mok (ed) *Centralization and Decentralization: Educational Reforms and Changing Governance in Chinese Societies*. Hong Kong: Comparative Education Research Centre, The University of Hong Kong; Kluwer Academic Publishers, 81–98.

Tang, K. C. and M. Bray (2000) 'Colonial Models and the Evolution of Education Systems — Centralization and Decentralization in Hong Kong and Macau', *Journal of Educational Administration*, 38 (5), 468–485.

Tang, Y. W. (2007) *Social Welfare and Social Security in Macao II*. Macao: Wah Fai Publishing Co. Ltd.

Taylor, J. E. (2003) 'Did Henry Ford Mean to Pay Efficiency Wages?', *Journal of Labor Research*, 24 (4), 683–695.

Titmuss, R. (1976) 'Social Division of Welfare: Some Reflections on the Search for Equity' in R. Titmuss (ed) *Essays on the Welfare State*. London: Allen & Unwin, 34–55.

Tong, K. K. (2009) 'The Development of the Gambling Industry and the Quality of Life' in S. L. Wong, K. Y. Wong and P. S. Wan (eds) *The New Face of Macao Society: Achievement and Challenge*. Hong Kong: Hong Kong Institute of Asia-Pacific Studies, The Chinese University of Hong Kong, 163–181.

Tosun, C. (2001) 'Challenges of Sustainable Tourism Development in the Developing World: The Case of Turkey', *Tourism Management*, 21 (6), 613–633.

Truman, D. B. (1981) *The Governmental Process: Political Interests and Public Opinion*. Westport, Conn.: Greenwood Press.

Tso, A. (2006) 'Guia Lighthouse in the Dark', *Macau Business*, December.

Vale, A. (1997) *Os Portugueses em Macau (1750–1800)*. Macao: Instituto Português do Oriente.

Vitalis, A. and R. A. Zepp (1989) *Business Research and Statistics*. Hong Kong: API Press Ltd.

Vong, L. P. (2009) *Core Inflation: Concepts and Estimates for Macao*. Macao: Macao Monetary Authority.

Vong, S. K. (2006) 'An Excursion into the Time Tunnel of Curriculum Development in Macau: A Story of Discourses and Practices', *US-China Education Review*, 3 (5), 11–19.

Vong, S. K. (2009) 'Govern-mentality and Education Policy in Post-1999 Era in Macao'. Paper delivered at the *2009 Asian-Pacific Forum on Sociology of Education*. Taiwan: National University of Taiwan, May 5–8, 2009.

Wadhwani, S. B. and M. Wall (1991) 'A Direct Test of the Efficiency Wage Model Using UK Micro-Data', *Oxford Economic Papers*, 43, 529–548.

Wan, Y. K. P. and F. V. Pinheiro (2009) 'Challenges and Future Strategies for Heritage Conservation in Macao', *South Asian Journal of Tourism & Heritage*, 2 (1), 1–12.

Wan, Y. K. P., F. V. Pinheiro, and M. Korenaga (2007) 'Planning for Heritage Conservation in Macao', *Planning and Development*, 22 (1), 17–26.

Wang, Y. (2006) 'The rights of examination and interpretation of MSAR Law' (Original in Chinese '特區法律的審查權與解釋權'). *Macao Daily News*, December 7.

Weiss, A. (1980) 'Job Queues and Layoffs in Labor Markets with Flexible Wages', *Journal of Political Economy*, 88 (3), 526–538.

Williamson, P. J. (1985) *Varieties of Corporatism: A Conceptual Discussion*. Cambridge: Cambridge University Press.

Williamson, P. J. (1989) *Corporatism in Perspective: An Introductory Guide to Corporatist Theory*. London: Sage.

Wilson, G. K. (1990) *Interest Groups*. Oxford: Blackwell.

Wiseman, F. and S. Chatterjee (2003) 'Team Payroll and Team Performance in Major League Baseball: 1985–2002', *Economics Bulletin*, 1 (2), 1–10.

Wittmann, D. C. (2002) *All That Glitters Is Sure to Fade: A Gendered Analysis of Casino Work and Culture in the Dockside Gaming Industry*. Boston: Unpublished PhD thesis, Northeastern University.

Wong, C. L. (1990) 'The Public Personnel System in Macau', *Asian Journal of Public Administration*, 12 (2), 176–195.

Wright, J. R. (1996) *Interest Groups and Congress: Lobbying, Contributions, and Influence*. Boston: Allyn and Bacon.

Yee, A. H. (1990) 'A Comparative Study of Macau's Education System', *Comparative Education*, 26 (1), 61–71.

Yee, A. H. (1996) 'Prospects of Democratization: An Open-ended Game?', *China Perspectives*, 26, 28–38.

Yee, H. S. (2001) *Macau in Transition: From Colony to Autonomous Region*. Basingstoke, Hampshire; New York: Palgrave.

Yeung, Y. M. (2008) 'Suggestions to the Outline for Macao Urban Concept Plan'. Available from: http://www.ceeds.gov.mo

Yiu, C. Y. (2007) 'Housing Price Gradient Changes between Macau and Hong Kong'. Conference Paper for *Asian Real Estate Society 2007 Conference* Macau, Macau: June 15, 2007.

Yu, X. (2008) 'Growth and Degradation in the Orient's "Las Vegas": Issue of Environment in Macau', *International Journal of Environmental Studies*, 65 (6), 667–683.

Yu, Z. (2002) 'Political Culture in Post-handover Macao' in Z. L. Wu (ed) *Macau 2002*. Macau: Macau Foundation (in Chinese). Available from: http://www.macaudata.com/macauweb/book269/main.html

Zhuhai Government (2006) 'The Zhuhai Urban Space Development Strategy: Zhuhai 2030'. Available at: http://www.zhuhai.gov.cn/english/Citynews/200708/t20070821_28125.htm

Websites

Commission Against Corruption of Macao, http://www.ccac.org.mo/en/

Employees Retraining Board, http://www.erb.org/Corp/home/erb/en/

Gaming Inspection and Coordination Bureau, http://www.dicj.gov.mo/

General Union of Neighbourhood Associations of Macao, http://home.macau.ctm.net/~ugamm/

Macao Chamber of Commerce, www.acm.org.mo/main9.htm

Macao Civic Power, http://www.civic-power.org/cp

Macao Federation of Trade Unions, http://www.faom.org.mo/web/

Macao Labour Affairs Bureau, http://www.dsal.gov.mo/english/thireplan_e.htm

Macao SAR Government, http://www.gov.mo

Statistics and Census Service of the Macao SAR Government, http://www.dsec.gov.mo

Women's General Association of Macau, http://www.macauwomen.org.mo/

Newspapers and Magazines

Bega District News, http://www.begadistrictnews.com.au/

Curso do Departamento de Formacao Profissional 'blogmacau.info', http://www.blogmacau. info/blog/?p=1709

Hong Kong Economic Journal, http://www.hkej.com/

Jornal Cheng Pou (正報), http://www.chengpou.com.mo/#frames(contentIL=../NEWS/Default_ IL_List.html,contentIW=../NEWS/Default_IW_List.html)

Jornal Do Cidadao (市民日報), http://www.shimindaily.net/dev/

Jornal San Wa Ou (新華澳報), http://www.waou.com.mo/

Jornal Tribuna de Macau (澳門論壇週報), http://www.jtm.com.mo/

Jornal Va Kio (華僑報), http://www.vakiodaily.com/index.php?tn=viewer&ncid=3

Macao Business, http://www.macaubusiness.com/

Macao Daily News, http://www.macaodaily.com/html/2010-02/23/node_2.htm

Macao Daily Times, http://www.macaudailytimesnews.com/

Macao News, http://macaotoday.com/

Macau Closer, http://www.macaucloser.com/

Ming Pao, http://www.mingpao.com/

People's Daily Online, http://english.peopledaily.com.cn/
Ponto Final, http://pontofinalmacau.wordpress.com/
South China Morning Post, http://www.scmp.com/portal/site/SCMP/
The Standard, http://www.thestandard.com.hk/

Index